An Introduction to Six Sigma & Process Improvement

James R. Evans

University of Cincinnati

William M. Lindsay

Northern Kentucky University

THOMSON
™
SOUTH-WESTERN

Australia · Canada · Mexico · Singapore · Spain · United Kingdom · United States

THOMSON
SOUTH-WESTERN

An Introduction to Six Sigma & Process Improvement

James R. Evans and William M. Lindsay

VP/Editorial Director:
Jack W. Calhoun

Sr. Acquisitions Editor:
Charles McCormick

Developmental Editor:
Taney Wilkins

Marketing Manager:
Larry Qualls

Sr. Production Editor:
Deanna Quinn

Technology Project Editor:
Chris Wittmer

Web Coordinator:
Kelly Reid

Manufacturing Coordinator:
Diane Lohman

Production House:
Pre-Press Company, Inc.

Printer:
Banta
Harrisonburg, VA

Sr. Art Director:
Anne Marie Rekow

Internal Designer:
Christy Carr

Cover Designer:
Christy Carr

Cover Image:
© Creatas.com

BRIEF CONTENTS

CONTENTS

_____

PREFACE

Six Sigma[1] has taken the corporate world by storm and represents the thrust of numerous efforts in manufacturing and service organizations to improve products, services, and processes. Although Six Sigma brings a new direction to quality and productivity improvement, its underlying tools and philosophy are grounded in the fundamental principles of total quality and continuous improvement that have been used for many decades. Nevertheless, Six Sigma has brought a renewed interest in quality and improvement that few can argue with, and has kept alive the principles of total quality developed in the latter part of the twentieth century.

Numerous professional references and trade books have been published, promoting Six Sigma tools and various customized spins on the philosophy and implementation process. We wrote this book to provide a succinct and basic introduction to Six Sigma and process improvement concepts in a style and format suitable for use in both undergraduate and graduate courses in operations management, industrial engineering, and related disciplines, as well as professional development and continuing education short courses. The ten chapters of the book are divided logically into four parts: principles of Six Sigma, Six Sigma DMAIC methodology, design for Six Sigma, and Six Sigma implementation. Because of the close relationship of the Six Sigma DMAIC process to projects and project management, curriculum developers or trainers may wish to combine the content areas of Six Sigma with introductory or advanced concepts of project management in the same course.

PART I: PRINCIPLES OF SIX SIGMA

Chapter 1, Foundations of Six Sigma: Principles of Quality Management, introduces the concept of Six Sigma and traces its evolution from earlier approaches to quality management. It also lays the foundation for Six Sigma by reviewing basic definitions of quality and the fundamental principles on which quality management philosophies are based. Finally, Chapter 1 also discusses the link between Six Sigma, business results, and competitive advantage.

---

[1] Six Sigma is a federally registered trademark and service mark of Motorola, Inc.

Chapter 2, Principles of Six Sigma, begins with a discussion of process concepts and systems thinking. We introduce the Six Sigma Body of Knowledge promoted by the American Society for Quality (ASQ), discuss the importance of metrics and measurement in Six Sigma, describe the DMAIC problem-solving methodology that forms the framework for subsequent chapters, and also discuss the growing importance of Six Sigma in service organizations.

PART II: SIX SIGMA DMAIC METHODOLOGY

Chapter 3, Project Organization, Selection, and Definition, focuses on organizational issues in developing Six Sigma projects and teams, including the role of project management in coordinating projects, skills needed by team members, and team dynamics. Techniques and approaches for selecting appropriate Six Sigma projects are discussed. This chapter also describes the Define phase of DMAIC, focusing on developing high-level process maps and identifying critical-to-quality characteristics of customers.

Chapter 4, Process Measurement, deals with a variety of basic topics associated with the Measure phase of DMAIC, namely, metric selection, data collection, and statistical data summarization. This chapter also discusses metrology and measurement system evaluation, process capability evaluation, and benchmarking.

Chapter 5, Process Analysis, emphasizes statistical tools and other valuable methods for analyzing data and identifying root causes in the Analyze phase of DMAIC. This discussion includes a review of probability distributions and basic statistical methods, and the application of process maps, value stream maps, statistical thinking, root cause analysis, and cause-and-effect diagrams.

Chapter 6, Process Improvement, focuses on the Improvement phase of DMAIC. Principles of process improvement, including flexibility and cycle time reduction, as well as continuous versus breakthrough improvement are discussed. Useful tools for process improvement, such as process map analysis, kaizen blitz, mistake-proofing, and creative thinking are described. Also included are the synergistic role of lean production in Six Sigma, and the use of the Deming cycle and the seven management and planning tools for implementation planning.

Chapter 7, Process Control, deals with the final phase of DMAIC—Control—and describes the role of control systems in maintaining performance improvements. Techniques of statistical process control and developing and using control charts are the major focus of this chapter.

PART III: DESIGN FOR SIX SIGMA

Chapters 8 and 9 focus on tools and methods associated with DFSS—Design for Six Sigma. In Chapter 8, Design for Six Sigma—Concept and Design Development, we introduce the concepts of DFSS. This chapter focuses on developing design concepts and applying various tools for establishing functional designs that have high quality and reliability. Quality function deployment is introduced along with such tools as design for manufacturability and failure mode and effects analysis.

This chapter also introduces basic concepts of reliability and how those concepts are used in design activities to predict product and system reliability performance.

Chapter 9, Design for Six Sigma—Optimization and Verification, continues with additional topics in DFSS and describes the application of design of experiments and Taguchi methods for robust design. In addition, design for reliability, reliability evaluation, the role of simulation in DFSS, and design verification are discussed.

PART IV: SIX SIGMA IMPLEMENTATION

In the concluding chapter, Chapter 10, Implementing Six Sigma, we discuss a variety of issues that affect an organization's ability to successfully implement and sustain Six Sigma, including effective project management, organizational culture and change management, enterprise leadership, and knowledge management.

CHAPTER FEATURES

Each chapter has a unique case study using real organizations that illustrates the application of one or more key principles or techniques studied in the chapter; a set of review and discussion questions designed to help students check their understanding of key concepts and think originally about critical issues; "Things to Do," which provide interesting experiential or field investigation activities for students; and, as relevant, problems to apply various tools and techniques.

STUDENT CD-ROM

The CD-ROM that comes with new copies of the textbook contains Microsoft Excel templates for various tools used in the book, and data sets for problems and exercises. The CD-ROM also contains a student version of Crystal Ball, an Excel add-in designed for simulation and risk analysis, and used in Chapter 9 to illustrate an application of simulation in Six Sigma. Students and instructors are encouraged to visit the Web site, www.crystalball.com, for additional examples, articles, and case studies that address similar applications.

SUPPORT MATERIALS FOR INSTRUCTORS

The following support materials are available from http://evans.swlearning. com or the Thomson Learning Academic Resource Center at 800-423-0563.

- The Instructor's Manual—Prepared by author William Lindsay, contains teaching suggestions and answers to all end-of-chapter questions, exercises, problems, and cases.
- PowerPoint® presentation slides—Prepared by author Jim Evans for use in lectures.

ACKNOWLEDGMENTS

We are grateful to the following reviewers who have provided valuable comments on early drafts of this book:

Mohamad R. Nayebpour, University of St. Thomas
Aubrey L. Mendelow, Kent State University
Matthew Stephens, Purdue University
Kailash C. Kapur, University of Washington
William Figg, Dakota State University
Diane Byrne, Johnson Controls Inc.
Kenneth Paetsch, Cleveland State University

Our thanks also go to senior acquisitions editor Charles McCormick, Jr., developmental editor Taney Wilkins, senior production editor Deanna Quinn, art director Anne Marie Rekow, and designer Christy Carr at Thomson Business and Professional Publishing for their outstanding work.

James R. Evans (james.evans@uc.edu)
William M. Lindsay (lindsay@nku.edu)

P A R T

Principles of Six Sigma

Chapter 1
The Foundations of Six Sigma:
Principles of Quality Management

Chapter 2
Principles of Six Sigma

1

The Foundations of Six Sigma: Principles of Quality Management

BUSINESS PERFORMANCE IMPROVEMENT AND SIX SIGMA

To compete in today's world, every business needs to improve. Improvement can include better design of goods and services, reduction of manufacturing defects and service errors, more streamlined and efficient operations, faster customer response, better employee skills—clearly the list can go on and on. One good illustration is Hyundai Motor Co. Although Hyundai dominated the Korean car market, it had a poor reputation for quality overseas, with doors that didn't fit properly, frames that rattled, and engines that delivered puny acceleration. And the company was losing money. When Chung Mong Koo became CEO in 1999, he visited Hyundai's plant at Ulsan. To the shock of his employees, who had rarely set eyes on a CEO, Chung strode onto the factory floor and demanded a peek under the hood of a Sonata sedan. He didn't like what he saw: loose wires, tangled hoses, bolts painted four different colors—the kind of sloppiness you'd never see in a Japanese car. On the spot, he instructed the plant chief to paint all bolts and screws black and ordered workers not to release a car unless all was orderly under the hood. "You've got to get back to basics. The only way we can survive is to raise our quality to Toyota's level," he fumed. The next year, U.S. sales rose by 42 percent, and in a few short years, Hyundai's performance in the J.D. Power Initial Quality Study has jumped remarkably.[1]

Improving business performance requires a structured approach, disciplined thinking, and the engagement of everyone in the organization. These elements have been the foundation for many approaches to productivity and quality improvement over the years. Six Sigma has emerged as a popular approach to improvement that focuses on outputs that are critical to customers and justifies improvements by demonstrating a clear financial return for the organization. As such, Six Sigma can be an important strategic initiative from both a market and financial perspective.

Six Sigma can be best described as a business process improvement approach that seeks to find and eliminate causes of defects and errors, reduce cycle times and cost of operations, improve productivity, better meet customer expectations, and achieve higher asset utilization and returns on investment in manufacturing and service processes. It is based on a simple problem solving methodology—**DMAIC**, which stands for Define, Measure, Analyze, Improve, and Control—that incorporates a wide variety of statistical and other types of process improvement tools.

The business case for Six Sigma was eloquently stated over a century ago. In October 1887, William Cooper Procter, grandson of the founder of Procter & Gamble, told his employees, "The first job we have is to turn out quality merchandise that consumers will buy and keep on buying. If we produce it efficiently and economically, we will earn a profit, in which you will share." Procter's statement addresses four key issues: *quality, productivity, cost,* and *profitability.* The quality of the goods and services that create customer satisfaction, productivity (the measure of efficiency defined as the amount of output achieved per unit of input), and the cost of operations, and all contribute to profitability. Six Sigma is focused on improving each of these four basic metrics. Figure 1.1, below, provides a model that suggests how Six Sigma, through the DMAIC process, can provide a bridge for improvement of existing business processes that will help to realize the performance goals of improved quality, productivity, cost, and profitability.

FIGURE 1.1   SIX SIGMA AND PROCESS IMPROVEMENT

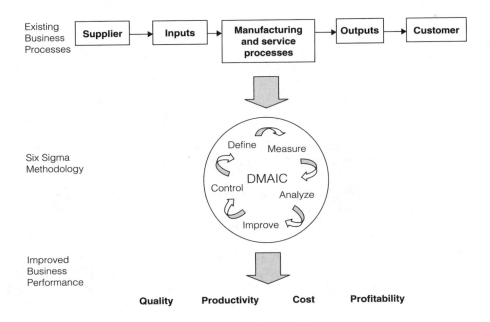

Motorola pioneered the concept of Six Sigma as an approach to measuring product and service quality, and it has garnered significant credibility over the last decade because of its acceptance at such major firms as Allied Signal (now part of Honeywell) and General Electric. The term *six sigma* is actually based on a statistical measure that equates to 3.4 or fewer errors or defects per million opportunities. An ultimate "stretch" goal of all organizations that adopt a Six Sigma philosophy is to have all critical processes, regardless of functional area, at a six-sigma level of capability.

The late Bill Smith, a reliability engineer at Motorola, is credited with originating the concept during the mid-1980s and selling it to Motorola's CEO, Robert Galvin. Smith noted that system failure rates were substantially higher than predicted by final product test, and suggested several causes, including higher system complexity that resulted in more opportunities for failure, and a fundamental flaw in traditional quality thinking. He concluded that a much higher level of internal quality was required and convinced Galvin of its importance.[2] As a result, Motorola set the following goal in 1987:

> Improve product and service quality ten times by 1989, and at least one hundred fold by 1991. Achieve six-sigma capability by 1992. With a deep sense of urgency, spread dedication to quality to every facet of the corporation, and achieve a culture of continual improvement to assure total customer satisfaction. There is only one ultimate goal: zero defects—in everything we do.

The core philosophy of Six Sigma is based on some key concepts:[3]

1. Think in terms of key business processes and customer requirements with a clear focus on overall strategic objectives.
2. Focus on corporate sponsors responsible for championing projects, support team activities, help to overcome resistance to change, and obtain resources.
3. Emphasize such quantifiable measures as *defects per million opportunities (dpmo)* that can be applied to all parts of an organization: manufacturing, engineering, administrative, software, and so on.
4. Ensure that appropriate metrics are identified early in the process and that they focus on business results, thereby providing incentives and accountability.
5. Provide extensive training followed by project team deployment to improve profitability, reduce non-value-added activities, and achieve cycle time reductions.
6. Create highly qualified process improvement experts who can apply improvement tools and lead teams.
7. Set stretch objectives for improvement.

These concepts provide a logical and disciplined approach to improving business performance, engaging the workforce, and meeting the goals and objectives of top management. Thus, Six Sigma, unlike many other improvement approaches such as reengineering, fits well within existing organizational structures.

THE EVOLUTION OF SIX SIGMA

Although Six Sigma has emerged as a unique discipline only quite recently, the tools and approaches it uses were created throughout the long history of quality management, which itself has drawn on other disciplines such as industrial engineering, statistics, human resource management, and organization theory. In this section we briefly review the history of quality management leading to Six Sigma.

From Craftsmanship to the Industrial Revolution

Quality management dates back thousands of years. Egyptian wall paintings circa 1450 B.C. show evidence of measurement and inspection.[4] Stones for the pyramids were cut so precisely that even today it is impossible to put a knife blade between the blocks. The Egyptians' success was due to the consistent use of well-developed methods and procedures and precise measuring devices for assuring quality.

During the Middle Ages in Europe, the skilled craftsperson served both as manufacturer and inspector. "Manufacturers" who dealt directly with the customer took considerable pride in workmanship. Craft guilds, consisting of masters, journeymen, and apprentices, emerged to ensure that craftspeople were adequately trained. Quality assurance was informal; every effort was made to ensure that quality was built into the final product by the people who produced it. These themes, which were lost with the advent of the Industrial Revolution, are important foundations of modern quality assurance efforts.

During the middle of the eighteenth century, a French gunsmith, Honoré Le Blanc, developed a system for manufacturing muskets to a standard pattern using interchangeable parts. Thomas Jefferson brought the idea to America, and in 1798 the new U.S. government awarded Eli Whitney a two-year contract to supply 10,000 muskets to its armed forces. The use of interchangeable parts necessitated careful control of quality. Whereas a customized product built by a craftsperson can be tweaked and hammered to fit and work correctly, random matching of mating parts provides no such assurance. The parts must be produced according to a carefully designed standard. Whitney designed special machine tools and trained unskilled workers to make parts following a fixed design, which were then measured and compared to a model. He underestimated the effect of variation in production processes, however (an obstacle that continues to plague companies to this day). Because of the resulting problems, Whitney needed more than 10 years to complete the project. Nonetheless, the value of the concept of interchangeable parts was recognized, and it eventually led to the Industrial Revolution, making quality assurance a critical component of the production process.

The Early Twentieth Century

In the early 1900s the work of Frederick W. Taylor, often called the "father of scientific management," led to a new philosophy of production. Taylor's philosophy was to separate the planning function from the execution function. Managers and engineers were given the task of planning; supervisors and workers took on the task of execution. This approach worked well at the turn of the century, when workers lacked the education needed for doing planning. By segmenting a job into specific work tasks and focusing on increasing efficiency, quality assurance fell into the hands of inspectors. Manufacturers were able to ship good-quality products, but at great costs. Defects were present, but were removed by inspection. Plants employed hundreds, even thousands, of inspectors. Inspection was thus the primary means of quality control during the first half of the twentieth century.

Eventually, production organizations created separate quality departments. This artificial separation of production workers from responsibility for quality assurance led to indifference to quality among both workers and their managers. Concluding that quality was the responsibility of the quality department, many upper managers turned their attention to output quantity and efficiency. Because they had delegated so much responsibility for quality to others, upper managers gained little knowledge about quality, and when the quality crisis hit, they were ill-prepared to deal with it.

The Bell System was the leader in the early modern history of industrial quality assurance.[5] It created an inspection department in its Western Electric Company in the early 1900s to support the Bell operating companies. Although the Bell System achieved its noteworthy quality through massive inspection efforts, the importance of quality in providing telephone service across the nation led it to research and develop new approaches. In the 1920s, employees of Western Electric's inspection department were transferred to Bell Telephone Laboratories. The duties of this group included the development of new theories and methods of inspection for improving and maintaining quality. The early pioneers of quality assurance—Walter Shewhart, Harold Dodge, George Edwards, and others, including W. Edwards Deming—were members of this group. These pioneers not only coined the term *quality assurance*, they also developed many useful techniques for improving quality and solving quality problems. Thus, quality became a technical discipline of its own.

The Western Electric group, led by Walter Shewhart, ushered in the era of statistical quality control (SQC), the application of statistical methods for controlling quality. SQC goes beyond inspection to focus on identifying and eliminating the problems that cause defects. Shewhart is credited with developing control charts, which became a popular means of identifying quality problems in production processes and ensuring consistency of output. Others in the group developed many other useful statistical techniques and approaches.

During World War II the United States military began using statistical sampling procedures and imposing stringent standards on suppliers. The War Production Board offered free training courses in the statistical methods developed within the Bell System. The impact on wartime production was minimal, but the effort developed quality specialists, who began to use and extend these tools within their organizations. Thus, statistical quality control became widely known and gradually adopted throughout manufacturing industries. Professional societies—notably the American Society for Quality

Control (now called the American Society for Quality, http://www.asq.org)— were founded to develop, promote, and apply quality concepts.

Post–World War II

After the war, during the late 1940s and early 1950s, the shortage of civilian goods in the United States made production a top priority. In most companies, quality remained the province of the specialist. Quality was not a priority of top managers, who delegated this responsibility to quality managers. Top management showed little interest in quality improvement or the prevention of defects and errors, relying instead on mass inspection.

During this time, two U.S. consultants, Dr. Joseph Juran and Dr. W. Edwards Deming, introduced statistical quality control techniques to the Japanese to aid them in their rebuilding efforts. A significant part of their educational activity was focused on upper management, rather than quality specialists alone. With the support of top managers, the Japanese integrated quality throughout their organizations and developed a culture of continuous improvement (sometimes referred to by the Japanese term *kaizen*, pronounced kī–zen).

Improvements in Japanese quality were slow and steady; some 20 years passed before the quality of Japanese products exceeded that of Western manufacturers. By the 1970s, primarily due to the higher quality levels, Japanese companies penetrated many Western markets, such as computer memory chips, consumer electronics, and automobiles. For example, the June 8, 1987, *Business Week* special report on quality noted that the number of problems reported per 100 domestic models in the first 60 to 90 days of ownership averaged between 162 and 180. Comparable figures for Japanese and German automobiles were 129 and 152, respectively. Consumers began to notice these quality differences and consequently began to expect and demand high quality and reliability in goods and services at a fair price. U.S. business recognized the crisis.

The U.S. "Quality Revolution"

The decade of the 1980s was a period of remarkable change in business perceptions of quality and how it should be managed. Quality became vital to organizational survival. Xerox, for instance, discovered that its Japanese competitors were selling small copiers for what it cost Xerox to make them at the time, and as a consequence, initiated a corporate-wide quality improvement focus to meet the challenge. Xerox, and its former CEO David Kearns who led its "Leadership Through Quality" initiative, was a major influence in the promotion of quality among U.S. corporations. In the five years of continuous improvement culminating in the firm's winning the Malcolm Baldrige National Quality Award in 1989, defects per 100 machines were decreased by 78 percent, unscheduled maintenance was decreased by 40 percent, manufacturing costs dropped 20 percent, product development time decreased by 60 percent, overall product quality improved 93 percent, service response time was improved by 27 percent, and the company recaptured much of the market it had lost. The company experienced strong growth during the 1990s. However, Xerox had lost focus on quality as a key business driver, much of it due to shortsightedness on the part of former top management. Fortunately, new corporate leadership recognized the crisis and renewed its focus and commitment to quality (see the case study at the end of this chapter).

A Westinghouse (now CBS) vice president of corporate productivity and quality summed up the situation by quoting Dr. Samuel Johnson's remark: "Nothing concentrates a man's mind so wonderfully as the prospect of being hanged in the morning." Quality excellence became recognized as a key to worldwide competitiveness and was heavily promoted throughout industry.[6] Most major U.S. companies instituted extensive quality improvement campaigns, directed not only at improving internal operations, but also toward satisfying external customers.

One of the most influential individuals in the quality revolution was W. Edwards Deming. In 1980 NBC televised a special program entitled "If Japan Can . . . Why Can't We?" The widely viewed program revealed Deming's key role in the development of Japanese quality, and his name was soon a household word among corporate executives. Although Deming had helped to transform Japanese industry three decades earlier, it was only after the television program that U.S. companies asked for his help. From 1980 until his death in 1993, his leadership and expertise helped many U.S. companies to revolutionize their approach to quality.

Early Successes in Quality Management

As business and industry began to focus on quality, the government recognized how critical quality is to the nation's economic health. In 1987 the Malcolm Baldrige National Quality Award, a statement of national intent to provide quality leadership, was established by an act of Congress. The Baldrige Award became the most influential instrument for creating quality awareness among U.S. businesses.

From the late 1980s and through the 1990s, interest in quality grew at an unprecedented rate. Companies made significant strides in improving quality. Many gaps between Japanese and U.S. quality began to narrow, and U.S. firms regained much of the ground they had lost. In 1989 Florida Power and Light was the first non-Japanese company to be awarded Japan's coveted Deming Prize for quality, followed by AT&T Power Systems five years later. Quality practices expanded into the service sector and into such nonprofit organizations as schools and hospitals. By the mid-1990s thousands of professional books had been written, and quality-related consulting and training had blossomed into an industry. Companies began to share their knowledge and experience through formal and informal networking. The majority of states in the United States developed award programs for recognizing quality achievements in business, education, not-for-profits, and government. In 1999, Congress added nonprofit education and health care sectors to the Baldrige Award.

The Rise and Fall of TQM

Although quality initiatives focused initially on reducing defects and errors in products and services, organizations began to recognize that lasting improvement could not be accomplished without significant attention to listening to customers and engaging the participation of all employees. This led to the notion of **total quality management**, or **TQM**, which was based on three key principles:

- focusing on customers
- continuous improvement
- employee participation and empowerment.

Although the TQM philosophy provided a comprehensive approach to building excellence in organizations, many top managers had difficulty implementing it. Top management often did not fully understand it, nor did they see measurable returns. Quite often, TQM was simply viewed as a collection of tools applied at low levels of the organization. TQM was not viewed strategically, and as a result, it lost favor among many business executives. We should point out, however, that although the term *TQM* is not used much anymore, the principles are still alive in many organizations and underlie the Six Sigma philosophy. For example, in Dell's 2003 annual report, the company stated that "[we] regularly assess ourselves against a broad range of customer focused measures, including the timeliness with which we deliver built-to-order systems, the reliability with which they perform, and the speed and quality of service and support . . . More than $800 million in savings last year came from employee initiated process improvement teams."

Enter Six Sigma

The recognized benchmark for Six Sigma implementation is General Electric. The efforts by General Electric in particular, driven by former CEO Jack Welch, brought significant media attention to the concept and made Six Sigma a popular approach to quality improvement. In the mid-1990s, quality emerged as a concern of many employees at GE. Jack Welch invited Larry Bossidy, then CEO of Allied Signal, who had phenomenal success with Six Sigma, to talk about it at a Corporate Executive Council meeting. The meeting caught the attention of GE managers and as Welch stated, "I went nuts about Six Sigma and launched it," calling it the most ambitious task the company had ever taken on.[7] To ensure success, GE changed its incentive compensation plan so that 60 percent of the bonus was based on financials and 40 percent on Six Sigma, and provided stock option grants to employees in Six Sigma training. After many years of implementation, Six Sigma has become a vital part of GE's company culture. In fact, as GE continues to acquire new companies, integrating Six Sigma into different business cultures is a significant challenge. Six Sigma is a priority in acquisitions and is addressed early in the acquisition process.

Six Sigma is appealing to top executives because of its focus on measurable bottom-line results, a disciplined fact-based approach to problem solving, and rapid project completion. Consequently, it has received the support from CEOs that TQM was generally unable to receive.

Six Sigma has many different characteristics as compared with TQM.[8]

- TQM is based largely on worker empowerment and teams; Six Sigma is owned by business leader champions.

- TQM activities generally occur within a department, process, or individual workplace; Six Sigma projects are often cross-functional and more strategic in nature.
- TQM training is generally limited to simple improvement tools and concepts; Six Sigma focuses on a more rigorous and advanced set of statistical methods and a structured problem-solving methodology DMAIC—define, measure, analyze, improve, and control—which will be discussed in detail in Chapter 2.
- TQM is focused on improvement with little financial accountability; Six Sigma requires a verifiable return on investment and focus on the bottom line.

In addition, Six Sigma has elevated the importance of statistics and statistical thinking in business improvement.

Like TQM however, Six Sigma requires strong management leadership, focus on customers, team processes, training in tools and problem solving approaches, and a change in organizational culture. These factors make it difficult for many organizations to successfully introduce it. In addition, we feel strongly that Six Sigma alone is not sufficient for organizational performance excellence, and should be integrated with more comprehensive performance excellence approaches such as the Baldrige perspective (see www.baldrige.org for more information). Thus, we are not advocating (as opposed to many consultants) that Six Sigma is a magic cure.

QUALITY AS A BUSINESS PERFORMANCE METRIC

The quest for improved quality of products, processes, and indeed, all aspects of business performance, is the driving force behind Six Sigma. Quality can be a confusing concept, partly because people view quality in relation to differing criteria based on their individual roles in the production-marketing value chain. In addition, the meaning of quality continues to evolve as the quality profession grows and matures. Neither consultants nor business professionals agree on a universal definition. A study that asked managers of 86 firms in the eastern United States to define quality produced several dozen different responses, including the following:

1. Perfection
2. Consistency
3. Eliminating waste
4. Speed of delivery
5. Compliance with policies and procedures
6. Providing a good, usable product
7. Doing it right the first time
8. Delighting or pleasing customers
9. Total customer service and satisfaction[9]

These "definitions" relate to product design (#6), customer satisfaction (#8 and 9), and operations performance (#1, 2, 3, 4, 5, and 7). Thus, understanding the various perspectives from which quality is viewed helps to fully appreciate the role it plays in the many parts of a business organization.[10]

Quality from the Design Perspective

One way of defining quality is a function of a specific, measurable variable and that differences in quality reflect differences in quantity of some product attribute, such as in the number of stitches per inch on a shirt or in the number of cylinders in an engine. This assessment implies that higher levels or amounts of product characteristics are equivalent to higher quality. As a result, quality is often mistakenly assumed to be related to price: the higher the price, the higher the quality, although most consumers know that this is not always true. However, a product—a term used in this book to refer to either a manufactured good or a service—need not be expensive to be considered a quality product by consumers.

Quality from the Customer Perspective

Another definition of quality is based on the presumption that what a customer wants determines quality. Individuals have different wants and needs and, hence, different quality standards, which leads to a user-based definition: quality is defined as *fitness for intended use*, or how well the product performs its intended function. Both a Cadillac sedan and a Jeep are fit for use, for example, but they serve different needs and different groups of customers. If you want a highway-touring vehicle with luxury amenities, then a Cadillac may better satisfy your needs. If you want a vehicle for camping, fishing, or skiing trips, a Jeep might be viewed as being better fit for use. An interesting example comes from many years ago when a U.S. appliance company's stoves and refrigerators were admired by Japanese buyers. Unfortunately, the small living quarters of the typical Japanese home lack enough space to accommodate the U.S. models. Some could not even pass through the narrow doors of Japanese kitchens. Although the products' performance characteristics were high, the products were simply not fit for use in Japan.

Customers often assess quality in relation to price; this is referred to as *value*. From this perspective, a quality product is one that is as useful as competing products and is sold at a lower price, or one that offers greater usefulness or satisfaction at a comparable price. Thus, one might purchase a generic product, rather than a brand name one, if it performs as well as the brand-name product at a lower price. An example of this perspective in practice is evident in a comparison of the U.S. and Japanese automobile markets. A Chrysler marketing executive noted "One of the main reasons that the leading Japanese brands—Toyota and Honda—don't offer the huge incentives of the Big Three (General Motors, Ford, and Chrysler) is that they have a much better reputation for long-term durability." In essence, incentives and rebates are payments to customers to compensate for lower quality.[11] From this perspective, it is clear why productivity and cost are as significant as quality from the perspective of the business.

Quality from the Operations Perspective

A third view of quality is manufacturing-based and defines quality as the desirable outcome of operations practice, or *conformance to specifications*. **Specifications** are targets and tolerances determined by designers of products and services. Targets are the ideal values for which production is to strive; tolerances are specified because designers recognize that it is impossible to meet targets all of the time in manufacturing. For example, a part dimension might be specified as "0.236 ± 0.003 cm." These measurements would mean that the target, or ideal value, is 0.236 centimeters, and that the allowable variation is 0.003 centimeters from the target (a tolerance of 0.006 cm). Thus, any dimension in the range 0.233 to 0.239 centimeters is deemed acceptable and is said to conform to specifications. Likewise, in services, "on-time arrival" for an airplane might be specified as within 15 minutes of the scheduled arrival time. The target is the scheduled time, and the tolerance is specified to be 15 minutes.

Conformance to specifications is a key definition of quality, because it provides a means of measuring quality. Specifications are meaningless, however, if they do not reflect attributes that are deemed important to the consumer.

Customer-Driven Quality

By the end of the 1980s, many companies had begun using a simpler, yet powerful, customer-driven definition of quality that remains popular today: *Quality is meeting or exceeding customer expectations.*

To better understand this definition, one must first understand the meanings of "customer." Most people think of a customer as the ultimate purchaser or end user of a product or service; for instance, the person who buys an automobile for personal use or the guest who registers at a hotel is considered an ultimate purchaser. These customers are more precisely referred to as **consumers.** Clearly, meeting the expectations of consumers is the ultimate goal of any business. Before a product reaches consumers, however, it may flow through a chain of many firms or departments, each of which adds some value to the product. For example, an automobile engine plant may purchase steel from a steel company, produce engines, and then transport the engines to an assembly plant. The steel company is a supplier to the engine plant; the engine plant is a supplier to the assembly plant. The engine plant is thus a customer of the steel company, and the assembly plant is a customer of the engine plant. These customers are called **external customers.**

Every employee in a company also has **internal customers** who receive goods or services from suppliers within the company. An assembly department, for example, is an internal customer of the machining department, and managers are internal customers of the secretarial pool. Most businesses consist of many such "chains of customers." Thus, the job of an employee is not simply to please his or her supervisor; it is to satisfy the needs of particular internal and external customers. Failure to meet the needs and expectations of internal customers can result in a poor-quality product. For example, a poor design for a computerized hotel reservation system makes it difficult for reservation clerks to do their job, and consequently affects consumers' satisfaction. Identifying who one's customers are and understanding their expectations are fundamental to achieving customer satisfaction. This focus is a radical departure from traditional ways of thinking in a functionally oriented organization. It allows workers to understand their place in the larger system and their contribution to the final product.

Customer-driven quality is fundamental to Six Sigma. The president and CEO of Fujitsu Network Transmission Systems, a U.S. subsidiary of Fujitsu, Ltd., stated, "Our customers are intelligent; they expect us to continuously evolve to meet their ever-changing needs. They can't afford to have a thousand mediocre suppliers in today's competitive environment. They want a few exceptional ones."

QUALITY PRINCIPLES AND SIX SIGMA

Modern quality management is based on three fundamental principles (introduced earlier in this chapter):

1. A focus on customers
2. Participation and teamwork by everyone in the organization
3. A process focus supported by continuous improvement and learning

These principles underlie the Six Sigma philosophy, and despite their obvious simplicity, they are quite different from traditional management practices. Historically, companies did little to understand external customer requirements, much less those of internal customers. Managers and specialists controlled and directed production systems; workers were told what to do and how to do it, and rarely were asked for their input. Teamwork and employee participation in business improvement was virtually nonexistent. A certain amount of waste and error was tolerable and was controlled by postproduction inspection. Improvements in quality generally resulted from technological breakthroughs instead of a relentless mind-set of continuous improvement. With a true focus on quality, an organization actively seeks to identify customer needs and expectations, to build quality into work processes by tapping the knowledge and experience of its workforce, and to continually improve every facet of the organization. Understanding and implementing these principles is vital to Six Sigma.

Customer Focus

The customer is the principal judge of quality. Perceptions of value and satisfaction are influenced by many factors throughout the customer's overall purchase, ownership, and service experiences. To accomplish this task, a company's efforts need to extend well beyond merely meeting specifications, reducing defects and errors, or resolving complaints. They must include both designing new products that truly delight the customer and responding rapidly to changing consumer and market demands. A company close to its customer knows what the customer wants, how the customer uses its products, and anticipates needs that the customer may not even be able to express. It also continually develops new ways of enhancing customer relationships. To meet or exceed customer expectations, organizations must fully understand all product and service attributes that contribute to customer value and lead to satisfaction and loyalty. A firm also must recognize that internal customers are as important in assuring quality as are external customers who purchase the product. Employees who view themselves as both customers of and suppliers to other employees understand how their work links to the final product. After all, the responsibility of any supplier is to understand and meet customer requirements in the most efficient and effective way possible.

Customers are sometimes a "hidden" part of Six Sigma efforts, because the focus tends to be on the improvement projects and measurement issues. However, a focus on the customer is vital at every stage of Six Sigma projects. For instance, product design (and design of associated manufacturing or service delivery processes) will be far more successful if the "voice of the customer," is included. A fundamental aspect of Six Sigma methodology is identification of *critical to quality (CTQ)* characteristics that are vital to customer satisfaction.

During the process of producing a product or service, it is important to gather information needed by internal customers for process control activities to ensure that the product is meeting the CTQs. If the CTQs are not being met, then the organization needs to develop a better measurement and control system.[12] Often, internal data that can improve control processes—such as whether materials arrived on time, how often an accounting report had incorrect data, or how many employees were absent from work—are kept in departmental records, where they are difficult to access. The solution may require a Six Sigma study to determine the types of data and information that are needed to provide necessary monitoring and control, and how the information gap (if one exists) can be closed.

Finally, at the delivery stage, customer satisfaction measures can provide clear information about the success of Six Sigma efforts. An interesting result of the impact of service recovery on customer satisfaction was reported in a *Fortune* magazine article:

> A global hotel chain was stunned to discover a perverse consequence of its customer-centric Six Sigma quality initiative. Apparently guests were mildly pleased by the chain's sincere efforts to provide a hassle-free stay. But what really moved the customer-satisfaction needle was how well the hotel responded when something went wrong. Guests who had experienced a problem that was quickly and politely resolved rated the hotel service higher than guests who had had no problems at all. What's more, more guests with happy resolution of their hassle said they were likely to recommend the hotel than did the trouble-free guests.[13]

In fact, many common Six Sigma projects revolve around developing appropriate customer satisfaction measurement processes, as well as trying to improve the design and delivery of CTQs identified through voice of the customer processes.

Participation and Teamwork

Joseph Juran credited Japanese managers' full use of the knowledge and creativity of the entire workforce as one of the reasons for Japan's rapid quality achievements. In any organization, the person who best understands his or her job and how to improve both the product and the process is the one performing it. When managers give employees the tools to make good decisions and the freedom and encouragement to make contributions, they virtually guarantee that better quality products and production processes will result. Employees who are allowed to participate—both individually and in teams—in decisions that affect their jobs and the customer can make substantial contributions to quality and business performance.

This attitude represents a profound shift in the typical philosophy of senior management; the traditional view was that the workforce should be "managed"—or to put it less formally, the workforce should leave their brains at the door. Good intentions alone are not enough to encourage employee involvement. Management's task includes formulating the systems and procedures and then putting them in place to ensure that participation becomes a part of the culture. Teamwork focuses attention on customer-supplier relationships and encourages the involvement of the total workforce in attacking systemic problems, particularly those that cross functional boundaries. Ironically, although problem-solving teams were introduced in the United States in the 1940s to help solve problems on the factory floor, they failed, primarily because of management resistance to workers' suggestions. The Japanese, however, began widespread implementation of similar teams, called quality circles, in 1962 with dramatic results. Eventually, the concept returned to the United States. Today, the use of self-managed teams that combine teamwork and empowerment is a powerful method of employee involvement.

Six Sigma relies on the participation and teamwork of employees at all levels—from the front lines to top management—to understand business problems, uncover their sources, generate solutions for improvement, and implement them. One of the unique characteristics of Six Sigma is the development of a hierarchy of process improvement experts using a martial arts analogy—green belts, black belts, and master black belts—equipped with the tools and knowledge to make significant improvements in business performance.

Process Focus and Improvement

A **process** is a sequence of activities that is intended to achieve some result. Processes are fundamental to Six Sigma, because, according to AT&T, a process is how work creates value for customers.[14] We typically think of processes in the context of production: the collection of activities and operations involved in transforming *inputs* (physical facilities, materials, capital, equipment, people, and energy) into *outputs* (products and services).

Common types of production processes include machining, mixing, assembly, filling orders, or approving loans. However, nearly every major activity within an organization involves a process that crosses traditional organizational boundaries. For example, an order fulfillment process might involve a salesperson placing the order; a marketing representative entering it on the company's computer system; a credit check by finance; picking, packaging, and shipping by distribution and logistics personnel; invoicing by finance; and installation by field service engineers. This is illustrated in Figure 1.2. A process perspective links together all necessary activities and increases one's understanding of the entire system, rather than focusing on only a small part. Many of the greatest opportunities for improving organizational performance lie in the organizational interfaces—those spaces between the boxes on an organization chart.

FIGURE 1.2 PROCESS VS. FUNCTION

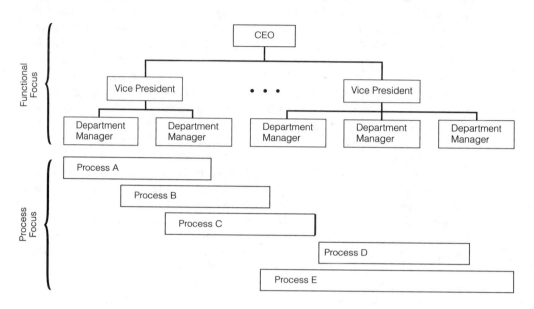

A former executive at a Texas Instruments division had a sign that said "Unless you change the process, why would you expect the results to change?" Improving processes is the principal activity of Six Sigma. **Improvement** refers to both incremental changes, which are small and gradual, and breakthrough, or large and rapid, improvements. These improvements may take any one of several forms:

1. Enhancing value to the customer through new and improved products and services
2. Reducing errors, defects, waste, and their related costs
3. Increasing productivity and effectiveness in the use of all resources
4. Improving responsiveness and cycle time performance for such processes as resolving customer complaints or new product introduction

Thus, response time, quality, and productivity objectives should be considered together. A process focus supports continuous improvement efforts by helping to understand these synergies and to recognize the true sources of problems. Major improvements in response time may require significant simplification of work processes and often drive simultaneous improvements in quality and productivity.

SIX SIGMA AND COMPETITIVE ADVANTAGE

As we noted earlier in this chapter, quality is a key source of competitive advantage; that is, a firm's ability to achieve market superiority. In the long run, a sustainable competitive advantage provides above-average performance. The

FIGURE 1.3 QUALITY AND PROFITABILITY

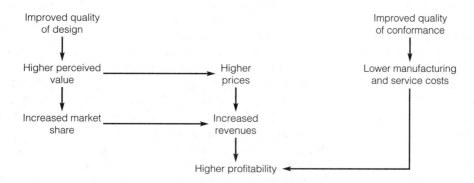

importance of quality in achieving competitive advantage was demonstrated by several research studies during the 1980s. PIMS Associates, Inc., a subsidiary of the Strategic Planning Institute, maintains a database of 1,200 companies and studies the impact of product quality on corporate performance.[15] PIMS researchers found the following:

1. Product quality is an important determinant of business profitability.
2. Businesses that offer premium-quality products and services usually have large market shares and were early entrants into their markets.
3. Quality is positively and significantly related to a higher return on investment for almost all kinds of products and market situations. (PIMS studies showed that firms whose products were perceived as having superior quality earned more than three times the return on sales of firms whose products were perceived as having inferior quality.)
4. Instituting a strategy of quality improvement usually leads to increased market share, but at the cost of reduced short-run profitability.
5. High-quality producers can usually charge premium prices.

These findings are summarized in Figure 1.3. A product's value in the marketplace is influenced by the quality of its design. Improvements in design will differentiate the product from its competitors, improve a firm's quality reputation, and improve the perceived value of the product. These factors allow the company to command higher prices as well as to achieve a greater market share, which in turn leads to increased revenues that offset the costs of improving the design. Six Sigma initiatives address both the quality of design and quality of conformance. As such, it can help organizations build a competitive advantage centered on quality.

Six Sigma and Business Results

As an old saying goes, "The proof is in the pudding." Considerable evidence exists that Six Sigma initiatives positively impact bottom-line results. Companies that invest in such efforts experience outstanding returns and improvements in performance. Various research studies show that quality-focused companies achieved better employee participation and relations, improved product and service quality, experienced higher productivity and greater customer satisfaction, increased market share, and improved profitability.[16]

In the first year of Six Sigma implementation at GE, they trained 30,000 employees at a cost of $200 million and got back about $150 million in savings. From 1996 to 1997, GE increased the number of Six Sigma projects from 3,000 to 6,000 and achieved $320 million in productivity gains and profits. By 1998, the company had generated $750 million in Six Sigma savings over and above their investment, and would receive $1.5 billion in savings the next year.

GE had many early success stories. GE Capital, for example, fielded about 300,000 calls each year from mortgage customers who had to use voicemail or call back 24 percent of the time because employees were busy or unavailable. A Six Sigma team analyzed one branch that had a near perfect percentage of answered calls and applied their best practices to the other 41 branches, resulting in a 99.9 percent chance of customers' getting a representative on the first try. A team at GE Plastics improved the quality of a product used in CD-ROMs and audio CDs from a 3.8 sigma level to 5.7 level and captured a significant amount of new business from Sony.[17] GE credits Six Sigma with a tenfold increase in the life of CT scanner X-ray tubes, a 400 percent improvement in return on investment in its industrial diamond business, a 62 percent reduction in turnaround time at railcar repair shops, and $400 million in savings in its plastics business.[18]

One of the key learnings GE discovered was that Six Sigma is not only for engineers. Welch observed the following:[19]

- Plant managers can use Six Sigma to reduce waste, improve product consistency, solve equipment problems, or create capacity.
- Human resource managers need it to reduce the cycle time for hiring employees.
- Regional sales managers can use it to improve forecast reliability, pricing strategies, or pricing variation.
- For that matter, plumbers, car mechanics, and gardeners can use it to better understand their customers' needs and tailor their service offerings to meet customers' wants.

Many other organizations such as Texas Instruments, Allied Signal (which merged with Honeywell), Boeing, 3M, Home Depot, Caterpillar, IBM, Xerox, Citibank, Raytheon, and the U.S. Air Force Air Combat Command have developed business performance improvement approaches designed around the Six Sigma concept and also report significant results. Between 1995 and the first quarter of 1997, Allied Signal reported cost savings exceeding $800 million from its Six Sigma initiative. Citibank groups reduced internal callbacks by 80 percent, credit processing time by 50 percent, and cycle times of processing statements from 28 days to 15 days.[20] More recently, Six Sigma has infiltrated health care, financial services, and other service industries.

We conclude this chapter with a case study of the evolution of quality management at Xerox, leading up to the company's current Six Sigma initiatives.

 Case Study

The Evolution of Quality at Xerox: From Leadership Through Quality to Lean Six Sigma[21]

The Xerox 914, the first plain-paper copier, was introduced in 1959. Regarded by many people as the most successful business product ever introduced, it created a new industry. During the 1960s Xerox grew rapidly, selling all it could produce, and reached $1 billion in revenue in record-setting time. By the mid-1970s its return on assets was in the low 20 percent range. Its competitive advantage was due to strong patents, a growing market, and little competition. In such an environment management was not pressed to focus on customers.

Facing a Competitive Crisis

During the 1970s, however, IBM and Kodak entered the high-volume copier business—Xerox's principal market. Several Japanese companies introduced high-quality low-volume copiers, a market that Xerox had virtually ignored, and established a foundation for moving into the high-volume market. In addition, the Federal Trade Commission accused Xerox of illegally monopolizing the copier business. After negotiations, Xerox agreed to open approximately 1,700 patents to competitors. Xerox was soon losing market share to Japanese competitors, and by the early 1980s it faced a serious competitive threat from copy machine manufacturers in Japan; Xerox's market share had fallen to less than 50 percent. Some people even predicted that the company would not survive. Rework, scrap, excessive inspection, lost business, and other problems were estimated to be costing Xerox more than 20 percent of revenue, which in 1983 amounted to nearly $2 billion. Both the company and its primary union, the Amalgamated Clothing and Textile Workers, were concerned. In comparing itself with its competition, Xerox discovered that it had nine times as many suppliers, twice as many employees, cycle times that were twice as long, 10 times as many rejects, and seven times as many manufacturing defects in finished products. It was clear that radical changes were required.

Leadership Through Quality

In 1983 company president David T. Kearns became convinced that Xerox needed a long-range, comprehensive quality strategy as well as a change in its traditional management culture (see Figure 1.4). Kearns was aware of Japanese subsidiary Fuji Xerox's success in implementing quality management practices and was approached by several Xerox employees about instituting total quality management. He commissioned a team to outline a quality strategy for Xerox. The team's report stated that instituting it would require changes in behaviors and attitudes throughout the company as well as operational changes in the company's business practices. Kearns determined that Xerox would initiate a total quality management approach, that they would take the time to "design it right

FIGURE 1.4 ORIGIN OF THE 1983 XEROX QUALITY IMPERATIVE

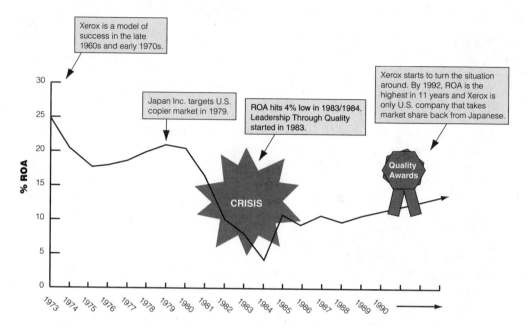

the first time," and that the effort would involve all employees. Kearns and the company's top 25 managers wrote the Xerox Quality Policy, which states:

> Xerox is a quality company. Quality is the basic business principle for Xerox. Quality means providing our external and internal customers with innovative products and services that fully satisfy their requirements. Quality improvement is the job of every Xerox employee.

This policy led to a process called Leadership Through Quality, which had three objectives:

1. To instill quality as the basic business principle in Xerox, and to ensure that quality improvement becomes the job of every Xerox person.
2. To ensure that Xerox people, individually and collectively, provide our external and internal customers with innovative products and services that fully satisfy their existing and latent requirements.
3. To establish, as a way of life, management and work processes that enable all Xerox people to continuously pursue quality improvement in meeting customer requirements.

In addition, Leadership through Quality was directed at achieving four goals in all Xerox activities:

- *Customer Goal:* To become an organization with whom customers are eager to do business.
- *Employee Goal:* To create an environment where everyone can take pride in the organization and feel responsible for its success.

- *Business Goal:* To increase profits and presence at a rate faster than the markets in which Xerox competes.
- *Process Goal:* To use Leadership Through Quality principles in all Xerox does.

Leadership Through Quality radically changed the way Xerox did business. All activities, such as product planning, distribution, and establishing unit objectives, began with a focus on customer requirements. Benchmarking—identifying and studying the companies and organizations that best perform critical business functions and then incorporating those organizations' ideas into the firm's operations—became an important component of Xerox's quality efforts. Xerox benchmarked more than 200 processes with those of noncompetitive companies. For instance, ideas for improving production scheduling came from Cummins Engine Company, ideas for improving the distribution system came from L.L. Bean, and ideas for improving billing processes came from American Express.

Measuring customer satisfaction and training were important components of the program. Every month, 40,000 surveys were mailed to customers, seeking feedback on equipment performance, sales, service, and administrative support. Any reported dissatisfaction was dealt with immediately and was usually resolved in a matter of days. When the program was instituted, every Xerox employee worldwide, and at all levels of the company, received the same training in quality principles. This training began with top management and filtered down through each level of the firm. Five years, 4 million labor-hours, and more than $125 million later, all employees had received quality-related training. In 1988 about 79 percent of Xerox employees were involved in quality improvement teams.

Several other steps were taken. Xerox worked with suppliers to improve their processes, implement statistical methods and a total quality process, and to support a just-in-time inventory concept. Suppliers that joined in these efforts were involved in the earliest phases of new product designs and rewarded with long-term contracts.

Employee involvement and participation was also an important effort. Xerox had always had good relationships with its unions. In 1980 the company signed a contract with its principal union, the Amalgamated Clothing and Textile Workers, encouraging union members' participation in quality improvement processes. It was the first program in the company that linked managers with employees in a mutual problem-solving approach and served as a model for other corporations. A subsequent contract included the provision that "every employee shall support the concept of continuous quality improvement while reducing quality costs through teamwork."

Most important, management became the role model for the new way of doing business. Managers were required to practice quality in their daily activities and to promote Leadership Through Quality among their peers and subordinates. Reward and recognition systems were modified to focus on teamwork and quality results. Managers became coaches, involving their employees in the act of running the business on a routine basis.

From the initiation of Leadership Through Quality until the point at which Xerox's Business Products and Systems organization won the Malcolm Baldrige

National Quality Award in 1989, some of the most obvious impacts of the Leadership Through Quality program included the following:

1. Reject rates on the assembly line fell from 10,000 parts per million to 300 parts per million.
2. Ninety-five percent of supplied parts no longer needed inspection; in 1989, 30 U.S. suppliers went the entire year defect-free.
3. The number of suppliers was cut from 5,000 to fewer than 500.
4. The cost of purchased parts was reduced by 45 percent.
5. Despite inflation, manufacturing costs dropped 20 percent.
6. Product development time decreased by 60 percent.
7. Overall product quality improved 93 percent.

Xerox learned that customer satisfaction plus employee motivation and satisfaction resulted in increased market share and improved return on assets. In 1989 president David Kearns observed that quality is "a race without a finish line."

Crisis and Quality Renewal

Throughout the 1990s, Xerox grew at a steady rate. However, at the turn of the century, the technology downturn, coupled with a decreased focus on quality by top corporate management, resulted in a significant stock price drop and a new crisis (see Figure 1.5). A top management shake-up, resulting in new corporate leadership, renewed the company's focus on quality, beginning with "New Quality" in 2001, which was built on the quality legacy established in the 1983 Leadership Through Quality process.

Soon after, Xerox embarked on a Six Sigma initiative after experiencing the power of Six Sigma firsthand from GE.[22] After Xerox consolidated 36 administrative centers into 3 in 1999 along with reorganizing its sales division, it found its

FIGURE 1.5 RESTRENGTHENING QUALITY TO ADDRESS A NEW CRISIS

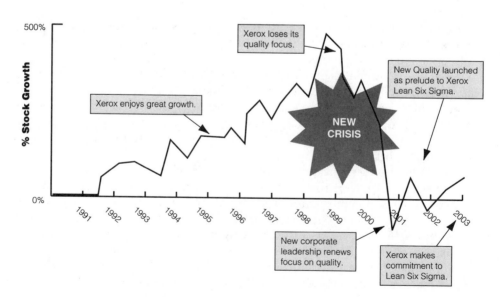

billing system in chaos. Customers received invoices quoting prices they had never agreed to or detailing equipment they had never ordered. Worse, the mistakes took months to sort out, prompting some longtime customers to defect. After struggling to fix the problem itself, it hired General Electric Capital to handle its billing. GE applied Six Sigma and lean manufacturing concepts, showing Xerox how it could omit steps from its design, manufacturing, and servicing processes, fine-tune those that remained, and deliver better printers and copiers to customers far faster and at lower cost.

After this experience, Xerox began a new thrust called "Lean Six Sigma" (see Chapter 10 for a detailed discussion), which includes a dedicated infrastructure and resource commitment to focus on key business issues: critical customer opportunities, significant training of employees and "black belt" improvement specialists, a value-driven project selection process, and an increased customer focus with a clear link to business strategy and objectives. It began with training for top executives including CEO Anne M. Mulcahy, who has spearheaded the effort. The company has since launched about 250 projects, both for itself and its customers. In one project, teams from supply, manufacturing, and research and development resolved a problem with a new $500,000 printing press. Customers quickly found that the fuser roll (which uses heat and pressure to bond toner to paper) was wearing out sooner than expected. The Xerox team used Lean Six Sigma tools to identify the cause—the oil on the roller—and worked with the oilmaker to change the chemistry and save Xerox $2 million while keeping its customers happy.

The basic principles of Lean Six Sigma support the core value "We Deliver Quality and Excellence in All We Do" and are stated as:

- Customer-focused employees, accountable for business results, are fundamental to our success.
- Our work environment enables participation, speed, and teamwork based on trust, learning, and recognition.
- Everyone at Xerox has business objectives aligned to the Xerox direction. A disciplined process is used to assess progress towards delivery of results.
- Customer-focused work processes, supported by disciplined use of quality tools, enable rapid changes and yield predictable business results.
- Everyone takes responsibility to communicate and act on benchmarks and knowledge that enable rapid change in the best interests of customers and shareholders.

The key components of Xerox's Lean Six Sigma approach are as follows:

1. Performance excellence process
   - Supports clearer, simpler alignment of corporate direction to individual objectives
   - Emphasizes ongoing inspection/assessment of business priorities
   - Clear links to market trends, benchmarking, and Lean Six Sigma
   - Supports a simplified "Baldrige-type" business assessment model
2. DMAIC (define, measure, analyze, improve, control) process
   - Based on industry-proven Six Sigma approach with speed and focus
   - Four steps support improvement projects, set goals

- Used to proactively capture opportunities or solve problems
- Full set of lean and Six Sigma tools
3. Market trends and benchmarking
   - Reinforces market focus and encourages external view
   - Disciplined approach to benchmarking
   - Establishes a common four-step approach to benchmarking
   - Encourages all employees to be aware of changing markets
   - Strong link to performance excellence process and DMAIC
4. Behaviors and leadership
   - Reinforces customer focus
   - Expands interactive skills to include more team effectiveness
   - Promotes faster decision making and introduces new meeting tool
   - Supports leadership skills required for transition and change

The heart of Xerox's Lean Six Sigma is the performance excellence process, illustrated in Figure 1.6. It consists of three phases: setting direction, deploying direction, and delivering and inspecting results. It starts at the top of the organization—even the chair and CEO, Anne Mulcahy, has an individual performance excellence plan with objectives that are aligned with organization goals and measures and targets for assessment. This approach provides clear communication of direction and accountability for objectives. A structured approach is used to prioritize and select projects that have high benefits relative to the effort involved in accomplishing them. Statistical methods, lean work flow methods, and other process management skills are used to drive improvement from a factual, objective basis, driven by the DMAIC methodology.

Market trends and benchmarking help provide an external perspective required to lead the market with innovative products, services, and solutions and add value to the customer experience. This component encourages all people to share information and knowledge that enables changes in the best interest of customers and shareholders. Finally, behaviors and leadership reinforce customer-focused behaviors, based on the principle that "Quality is the responsibility of every Xerox employee."

FIGURE 1.6   XEROX PERFORMANCE EXCELLENCE PROCESS

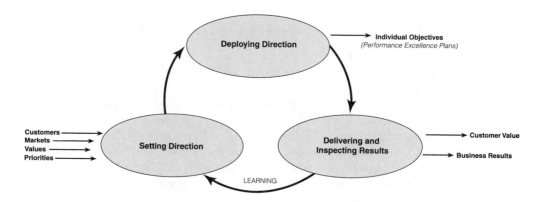

In 2003, Xerox trained more than 1,000 senior leaders across the company and communicated this business approach, the key differences from their quality legacy, and current expectations to every employee, and is rapidly moving Lean Six Sigma concepts from manufacturing and supply chain into all business areas. They recognize that full leadership commitment is the key ingredient. As Anne Mulcahy noted, "What I worry most about is how to return Xerox to greatness. . . . Lean Six Sigma is not the only answer, but it's a significant part of the equation."

REVIEW QUESTIONS

1. Define "Six Sigma." From where did the term originate?
2. What are the core concepts of the Six Sigma philosophy?
3. What are the key determinants of profitability that underlie Six Sigma? How does Six Sigma address these?
4. Describe the evolution of Six Sigma. What impact has it had on General Electric?
5. Briefly summarize the history of quality. What caused the most significant changes?
6. What are the fundamental differences between Six Sigma and TQM?
7. Explain the various definitions of quality. Can a single definition suffice? Why?
8. Distinguish among consumers, external customers, and internal customers. Illustrate how these concepts apply to a McDonald's restaurant, a Pizza Hut, or a similar franchise.
9. Describe the three fundamental principles of quality.
10. Why is it important to identify critical to quality (CTQ) characteristics in the design stage of a new product?
11. What is a process? How does a process focus differ from a traditional organization?
12. Explain the role of quality in improving a firm's profitability.

DISCUSSION QUESTIONS

1. Discuss how either good or poor quality affects you personally as a consumer. For instance, describe experiences in which your expectations were met, exceeded, or not met when you purchased goods or services. Did your experience change your regard for the company and/or its product? How?
2. Discuss the importance of quality to the national interest of any country in the world.
3. How might the definitions of quality apply to your college or university? Provide examples of its customers and ways in which their expectations can be met or exceeded.
4. Think of a product or a service that you are considering purchasing. Develop a list of fitness-for-use criteria that are meaningful to you.

5. Select a service activity with which you are familiar. If you were the manager of this activity, what "conformance to specifications" criteria would you use to monitor it?

6. Choose a product or service to illustrate how several definitions of quality can apply simultaneously.

7. What definition of quality (design, customer, technical) is implied by the following consumer advertisements?

   a. A Tiffany & Co. ad for timepieces entitled "The Business Gift." In describing the gift, the ad suggests that "It must honor the recipient. It must express your gratitude. It must reflect well upon you and your firm. It is packaged neatly, securely, elegantly. It arrives on time every time. It is an honest design. Original and timeless."

   b. An ad for certified pre-owned Ford vehicles that describes how it has been quality checked by a rigorous 115-point bumper-to-bumper inspection.

   c. A Land Rover ad that states, "Polished walnut and select leather combined with Electronic Air Suspension and a 460-watt, 12-speaker audio system make the best of even the worst conditions. As do permanent four-wheel drive and four-wheel Electronic Traction Control."

   d. A Xerox ad that explains that its printer is three times faster than one produced by Hewlett-Packard, with the caption "Xerox color printers exceed all speed limits."

   e. A Lands' End ad that states, "The $68 down jacket that turns winter inside out," and explains how it is packed with goose down—the warmest insulation on earth.

8. Choose some organization that you have read about or with which you have personal experience and describe their sources of competitive advantage. For each, state whether you believe that quality supports their strategy or does not support it.

9. How might the principles of Six Sigma be used to improve a quality process in a school or university? What elements of the Six Sigma philosophy might be difficult to obtain support for in the educational environment? Why?

10. Contrast Leadership for Quality and Lean Six Sigma as quality initiatives for Xerox. How did their motivations differ? What differences or similarities are evident in the principles behind these initiatives and the way in which they were implemented?

11. What lessons might Xerox's experiences—particularly in responding to the new crisis—have for other organizations?

12. Discuss the meaning of "Quality is a race without a finish line." What is its significance to Xerox, or to any organization?

THINGS TO DO

1. Develop a portfolio of advertisements from newspapers and magazines and illustrate how quality is used in promoting these products. Do the ads suggest any of the different definitions of quality?

2. Visit the Malcolm Baldrige National Quality Award Web site at http://www.baldrige.org and summarize the key results of winners for the past two years. In addition, investigate the latest report on stock performance of Baldrige-winning companies.

3. Prepare a case study similar to the one about Xerox using sources such as business periodicals, personal interviews, and so on. Focus your discussion on how their approach to total quality and Six Sigma supports their competitive strategy.

4. Examine the annual reports of one company over a period of years. Summarize how quality is discussed or implied in the company's statements and philosophy. Are any changes in the perspectives of quality evident over time? For example, have they instituted a Six Sigma process?

5. Find a company that has implemented a Six Sigma process. What changes have they made in the organization in order to develop their Six Sigma approach?

ENDNOTES

1. "Hyundai Gets Hot," *Business Week*, December 17, 2001, 84–85.

2. "Origin of Six Sigma: Designing for Performance Excellence," *Quality Digest* (May 2000), 30; and Mikel Harry and Richard Schroeder, *Six Sigma* (New York: Currency, 2000), 9–11.

3. A composite of ideas suggested by Stanley A. Marash, "Six Sigma: Business Results Through Innovation," *ASQ's 54th Annual Quality Congress Proceedings*, 2000, 627–630; and Dick Smith and Jerry Blakeslee, *Strategic Six Sigma: Best Practices from the Executive Suite* (New York: Wiley, 2002).

4. Early history is reported in Delmer C. Dague, "Quality—Historical Perspective," *Quality Control in Manufacturing* (Warrendale, PA: Society of Automotive Engineers, 1981); and L. P. Provost and C. L. Norman, "Variation through the Ages," *Quality Progress* 23, no. 12 (December 1990), 39–44. Modern events are discussed in Nancy Karabatsos, "Quality in Transition, Part One: Account of the '80s," *Quality Progress* 22, no. 12 (December 1989), 22–26; and Joseph M. Juran, "The Upcoming Century of Quality," address to the ASQC Annual Quality Congress, Las Vegas, May 24, 1994. A comprehensive historical account may be found in J. M. Juran, *A History of Managing for Quality* (Milwaukee, WI: ASQC Quality Press, 1995).

5. M. D. Fagan (ed.), *A History of Engineering and Science in the Bell System: The Early Years, 1875–1925* (New York: Bell Telephone Laboratories, 1974).

6. "Manufacturing Tops List of Concerns Among Executives," *Industrial Engineering* 22, no. 6 (June 1990), 8.

7. Jack Welch, *Jack: Straight from the Gut* (New York: Warner Books, 2001), 329–330.

8. Ronald D. Snee, "Guest Editorial: Impact of Six Sigma on Quality Engineering," *Quality Engineering* 12, no. 3 (2000), ix–xiv.

9. Nabil Tamimi and Rose Sebastianelli, "How Firms Define and Measure Quality," *Production and Inventory Management Journal* 37, no. 3 (Third Quarter, 1996), 34–39.

10. Four comprehensive reviews of the concept and definition of quality are David A. Garvin, "What Does Product Quality Really Mean?" *Sloan Management Review*, 26, no. 1 (1984), 25–43; Gerald F. Smith, "The Meaning of Quality," *Total Quality Management* 4, no. 3 (1993), 235–244; Carol A. Reeves and David A. Bednar, "Defining Quality: Alternatives and Implications," *Academy of Management Review* 19, no. 3 (1994), 419–445; and Kristie W. Seawright and Scott T. Young, "A Quality Definition Continuum," *Interfaces* 26, 3 (May–June 1996), 107–113.

11. Alex Taylor III, "Detroit's Used-Car Blues," *Fortune*, September 16, 2002, 147–150.

12. Mike Carnell, "Gathering Customer Feedback," *Quality Progress*, 36, no. 1 (January 2003), 60.

13. Michael Schrage, "Make No Mistake?" *Fortune*, December 11, 2001.

14. *AT&T's Total Quality Approach*, AT&T Corporate Quality Office (1992), 6.

15. *The PIMS Letter on Business Strategy*, no. 4 (Cambridge, MA: Strategic Planning Institute, 1986).

16. U.S. General Accounting Office, "Management Practices: U.S. Companies Improve Performance Through Quality Efforts," GA/NSIAD-91-190 (May 1991); "Progress on the Quality Road," *Incentive*, April 1995, 7.

17. Jack Welch, ibid., 333–334.

18. "GE Reports Record Earnings with Six Sigma," *Quality Digest*, December 1999, 14.

19. See note 3.

20. Rochelle Rucker, "Six Sigma at Citibank," *Quality Digest*, December 1999, 28–32.

21. Courtesy of Xerox Corporation. Information for this case was obtained from "Xerox Quest for Quality and the Malcolm Baldrige National Quality Award" presentation script; Norman E. Rickard, Jr., "The Quest for Quality: A Race without a Finish Line," *Industrial Engineering*, January 1991, 25–27; Howard S. Gitlow and Elvira N. Loredo, "Total Quality Management at Xerox: A Case Study," *Quality Engineering* 5, no. 3 (1993), 403–432; *Xerox Quality Solutions, A World of Quality* (Milwaukee, WI: ASQC Quality Press, 1993); and "Restrengthening Xerox: Our Lean Six Sigma Journey," presentation slides, May 2003. Courtesy of Xerox Corporation. Our thanks go to George Maszle of Xerox Corporation for providing the information on current Six Sigma initiatives.

22. "How Xerox Got Up to Speed," *Business Week*, May 3, 2004, Special Report: Quality Manufacturing.

CHAPTER

2

Principles of Six Sigma

PROCESS CONCEPTS AND SYSTEMS THINKING

In Chapter 1 we introduced the notion of a process as a fundamental way of viewing work in an organization. Common business processes include acquiring customer and market knowledge, strategic planning, research and development, purchasing, developing new products or services, manufacturing and assembly, fulfilling customer orders, managing information, measuring and analyzing performance, and training employees, to name just a few. Understanding processes is vital to effectively applying Six Sigma, as many Six Sigma projects focus on improving them.

In general, we can define two general types of processes in any organization.

1. **Value-creation processes** (sometimes called *core processes*), which are most important to "running the business" and maintaining or achieving a sustainable competitive advantage
2. **Support processes,** which are those that contribute to the successful performance of an organization's value-creation processes, employees, and daily operations

Value-creation processes drive the creation of products and services, are critical to customer satisfaction, and have a major impact on the strategic goals of an organization. They typically include design, production/delivery, and other critical business processes. **Design processes** involve all activities that are performed to incorporate customer requirements, new technology, and past learning into the functional specifications of a product (that is, a manufactured good or service), and thus define its fitness for use. **Production/delivery processes** create or deliver the actual product; examples are manufacturing, assembly, dispensing medications, teaching a class, and so on. These processes must be designed to ensure that the product will conform to specifications (the manufacturing definition of quality) and also be produced economically and efficiently. Product design greatly influences the efficiency of manufacturing as well as the flexibility of service strategies, and therefore must be coordinated with production/delivery processes. The ultimate value of the product, and hence the perceived quality to the consumer, depend on both these types of processes.

Support processes provide infrastructure for value-creation processes but generally do not add value directly to the product or service. A process such as order entry that might be thought of as a value-creation process for one company (for example, a direct mail distributor) might be considered as a support process for another (for example, a custom manufacturer). In general, value-creation processes are driven by external customer needs while support processes are driven by internal customer needs. Because value-creation processes do add value to products and services, they require a higher level of attention than do support processes.

Table 2.1 shows the value-creation processes and their requirements defined by Pal's Sudden Service, a privately owned, quick-service restaurant chain in the southeast United States that serves hamburgers, hot dogs, chipped ham, chicken, French fries, beverages, and other food items primarily to drive-through customers. (Pal's was a recipient of the Malcolm Baldrige National Quality Award; visit www.baldrige.org for further information). Their support processes include accounting/finance, human resources, maintenance, management information systems, ordering, and stocking. Other critical support processes that lead to business success and growth might be research and development, technology acquisition, supply chain management and supplier partnering, mergers and acquisitions, project management, or sales and marketing. These processes will differ greatly among organizations, depending on the nature of products and services, customer and market requirements, global focus, and other factors. By measuring the performance of process requirements, organizations can identify how well they meet (or fail to meet) customer expectations, and use Six Sigma approaches to improve process performance.

TABLE 2.1   VALUE-CREATION PROCESSES FOR PAL'S SUDDEN SERVICE

Process	Principal Requirements
Order Taking	Accurate, fast, friendly
Cooking	Proper temperature
Product Assembly	Proper sequence, sanitary, correct ingredients and amounts, speed, proper temperature, neat
Cash Collection	Accurate, fast, friendly
Slicing	Cut/size, freshness/color
Chili preparation	Proper temperature, quantity, freshness
Ham/chicken preparation	Proper temperature, quantity, freshness
Supply chain management	Price/cost, order accuracy
Property acquisition	Sales potential, adherence to budget
Construction	On time, within budget
Marketing & advertising	Clear message, brand recognition

Source: Courtesy of Pal's Sudden Service.

Systems Thinking

Taken together, a set of processes forms a **system**—an integrated set of activities within an organization that work together for the aim of the organization. For example, the system at Pal's Sudden Service includes the order-taker/cashier, grill and food preparation, drive-through, purchasing, and training processes. These processes are linked together as internal customers and suppliers. In many organizations, individual processes are often seen as separate units on an organization chart. However, managers need to view the organization as a whole and concentrate on the important organizational links among them, because changing any of them might have positive or negative impacts on the system as a whole. This is an important perspective for the successful application of Six Sigma.

Russell Ackoff, a noted authority in **systems thinking,** explained the importance of systems thinking in the following way:

> A combination of the best practices by each part of a system taken separately does not yield the best system. We may not even get a good one. A company that has 12 facilities, each producing the same variations of the same type of beverage, had broken the production process down into 15 steps. It produced a table showing each factory (a column) and each of the 15 steps (rows). The company then carried out a study to determine the cost of each step at each factory (a costly study), which identified for each step the factory with the lowest cost. At each factory, the company tried to replace each of its steps that was not the lowest cost with the one used in the factory that had the lowest cost. Had this succeeded, each factory would be producing with steps that had each attained the lowest cost in any factory. It did not work! The lowest-cost steps did not fit together. The result was only a few insignificant cosmetic changes that did not justify the cost of the exercise.[1]

Ackoff concluded that management should focus on the interactions of parts and of the system with other systems, rather than the actions of parts taken separately.

THE SIX SIGMA BODY OF KNOWLEDGE

Systems thinking can also be applied to the Six Sigma philosophy and its associated organization structure. A good way to understand what Six Sigma is all about is to examine the Six Sigma Body of Knowledge shown in Table 2.2. This body of knowledge forms the basis for the Six Sigma Black Belt (see Chapter 3) Certification examination from the American Society for Quality. As you can see from this list, Six Sigma encompasses a vast collection of concepts, tools, and techniques that are drawn from many areas of business, statistics, engineering, and practical experience. Many of these subjects are technical; others deal with management and organizational issues. Practitioners need a balanced set of both the "hard" and the "soft" disciplines in order to apply and implement Six Sigma effectively.

TABLE 2.2 SIX SIGMA BODY OF KNOWLEDGE[2]
(NUMBERS IN PARENTHESES CORRESPOND TO PAGE NUMBERS FOR CHAPTER SECTIONS IN THIS BOOK THAT ADDRESS THE TOPICS.)

I.   Enterprise-Wide Deployment
   A.   Enterprise view
      1.   Value of Six Sigma (2, 16)
      2.   Business systems and processes (13)
      3.   Process inputs, outputs, and feedback (13)
   B.   Leadership
      1.   Enterprise leadership (309)
      2.   Six Sigma roles and responsibilities (52)
   C.   Organizational goals and objectives
      1.   Linking projects to organizational goals (66)
      2.   Risk analysis (66)
      3.   Closed-loop assessment/knowledge management (312)
   D.   History of organizational improvement/foundations of Six Sigma (2, 5)
II. Business Process Management
   A.   Process vs. functional view
      1.   Process elements (13, 29)
      2.   Owners and stakeholders (13)
      3.   Project management and benefits (52)
      4.   Project measures (52)
   B.   Voice of the customer
      1.   Identify customer (76)
      2.   Collect customer data (76)
      3.   Analyze customer data (76)
      4.   Determine critical customer requirements (76)
   C.   Business results
      1.   Process performance metrics (92)
      2.   Benchmarking (122)
      3.   Financial benefits (16)
III. Project Management
   A.   Project charter and plan
      1.   Charter/plan elements (76)
      2.   Planning tools (76, 180)
      3.   Project documentation (76)
      4.   Charter negotiation (76)
   B.   Team leadership
      1.   Initiating teams (52)
      2.   Selecting team members (62)
      3.   Team stages (62)
   C.   Team dynamics and performance
      1.   Team-building techniques (62)
      2.   Team facilitation techniques (62)
      3.   Team performance evaluation (62)
      4.   Team tools (168)
   D.   Change agent
      1.   Managing change (304)
      2.   Organizational roadblocks (304)
      3.   Negotiation and conflict resolution techniques (307)
      4.   Motivation techniques (307)
      5.   Communication (300)
   E.   Management and Planning Tools

(continued)

TABLE 2.2   (*continued*)

IV. Six Sigma Improvement Methodology and Tools—*Define*
    A.   Project scope (52)
    B.   Metrics (35, 92)
    C.   Problem statement (52)
V. Six Sigma Improvement Methodology and Tools—*Measure*
    A.   Process analysis and documentation
        1. Tools (168)
        2. Process inputs and outputs (13)
    B.   Probability and statistics
        1. Drawing valid statistical conclusions (138)
        2. Central limit theorem and sampling distribution of the mean (138)
        3. Basic probability concepts (134)
    C.   Collecting and summarizing data
        1. Types of data (92)
        2. Measurement scales
        3. Methods for collecting data (97)
        4. Techniques for assuring data accuracy and integrity (109)
        5. Descriptive statistics (103)
        6. Graphical methods (103)
    D.   Properties and applications of probability distributions
        1. Distributions commonly used by black belts (134)
        2. Other distributions (134)
    E.   Measurement systems
        1. Measurement methods (109)
        2. Measurement system analysis (109)
        3. Metrology (109)
    F.   Analyzing process capability
        1. Designing and conducting process capability studies (116)
        2. Calculating process performance vs. specification (116)
        3. Process capability indices (116)
        4. Process performance indices
        5. Short-term vs. long-term capability
        6. Non-normal data transformations (process capability for non-normal data)
        7. Process capability for attributes data
VI. Six Sigma Improvement Methodology and Tools—*Analyze*
    A.   Exploratory data analysis
        1. Multi-vari studies
        2. Measuring and modeling relationships between variables (138)
            a. Simple and multiple least-squares linear regression (138)
            b. Simple linear correlation (138)
            c. Diagnostics
    B.   Hypothesis testing
        1. Fundamental concepts of hypothesis testing (138)
            a. Statistical vs. practical significance
            b. Significance level, power, type I and type II errors
            c. Sample size
        2. Point and interval estimation (138)
        3. Tests for means, variances, and proportions
        4. Paired-comparison tests
        5. Goodness-of-fit tests
        6. Analysis of variance (ANOVA) (138)
        7. Contingency tables
        8. Non-parametric tests

(*continued*)

TABLE 2.2   *(continued)*

To use this body of knowledge as a framework for an introductory book is a logical but challenging task. Our goal is to provide a broad overview so that readers will be able to understand the value of Six Sigma, while also providing sufficient details to allow readers to begin implementing the tools and techniques on real projects. However, we do not intend this book to fully cover all of this knowledge. Many of these topics, such as statistical methods, project management, team dynamics, and lean concepts are covered in more depth in other courses and texts. Others topics, such as design of experiments, response surface methodology, and robust design, require more advanced treatment than is possible here. Mastering this vast array of information requires much time and study, and we encourage you to continue to research and enhance your skills beyond this book.

Many of the tools and techniques used in Six Sigma have been around for a long time and have been used extensively in quality improvement. For example, Deming long advocated using statistics to understand and reduce variation, and Juran promoted the use of many simple tools for quality problem solving and improvement. Thomas Pyzdek, a noted quality consultant, states that more than 400 tools are now available in the "TQM Toolbox."[3] However, most organizations rarely go beyond the basic improvement tools and fail to recognize the benefits from more sophisticated statistical tools such as design of experiments. Six Sigma exploits the power of advanced statistical methods, takes them beyond the realm of engineering, and integrates them into management systems across the organization using a rational problem-solving framework that we introduce in this chapter.

METRICS AND MEASUREMENT

A **metric** is a verifiable measurement of some particular characteristic, stated either numerically (for example, percentage of defects) or in qualitative terms (for example, level of satisfaction—"poor" or "excellent").[4] Metrics provide information on performance and allow managers to evaluate performance and make decisions, communicate with one another, identify opportunities for improvement, and frame expectations for employees, customers, suppliers, and other stakeholders. Metrics are vital in Six Sigma applications because they facilitate fact-based decisions.

Six Sigma began by stressing a common measure for quality. In Six Sigma terminology, a **defect,** or **nonconformance,** is any mistake or error that is passed on to the customer. A **unit of work** is the output of a process or an individual process step. A measure of output quality is **defects per unit (DPU):**

Defects per unit = Number of defects discovered/Number of units produced

However, this type of output measure tends to focus on the final product, not the process that produces the product. In addition, it is difficult to use for processes of varying complexity, particularly service activities. Two different processes might have significantly different numbers of opportunities for error, making appropriate comparisons difficult. The Six Sigma concept redefines quality performance as **defects per million opportunities (dpmo):**

dpmo = (Number of defects discovered/opportunities for error) × 1,000,000

For example, suppose that an airline wishes to measure the effectiveness of its baggage handling system. A DPU measure might be lost bags per customer.

TABLE 2.3   OPPORTUNITIES FOR HOSPITAL MEDICATION ERRORS

Type of Error	Opportunity
Prescription	Miscalculation of dosage Wrong drug Oral or written communication error
Dispensing	Misinterpretation of Rx Name confusion Poor labeling
Administration	Wrong time Wrong dosage Incorrect drug Wrong patient

Source: Adapted from Lee Revere and Ken Black, "Integrating Six Sigma With Total Quality Management: A Case Example for Measuring Medication Errors," *Journal of Healthcare Management*, Vol. 48, issue 6, Nov.–Dec. 2003, 377–393.

However, customers may have different numbers of bags; thus, the total number of opportunities for error is the average number of bags per customer times the number of customers. If the average number of bags per customer is 1.6, and the airline recorded 3 lost bags for 8,000 passengers in one month, then there are (8,000)(1.6) opportunities for error, and

$$\text{dpmo} = 3/[(8,000)(1.6)] \times 1,000,000 = 234.375$$

The use of dpmo allows us to define quality broadly. In the airline case, an "opportunity" could be defined as every potential for failure to meet customer expectations from initial ticketing until bags are retrieved. Thus, a failure to meet customer expectations might include excessive waiting time at check-in, an incorrect reservation, a rude gate agent, or a delay in departure. This method provides a more comprehensive measure of potential failures that affect customer satisfaction. Table 2.3 provides an example of opportunities for error in providing medications in a hospital (studies have shown that on average, a hospital has about 225 medication errors each year that result in patient harm).

Metrics such as dpmo, while useful to teams addressing specific Six Sigma projects, need to be translated into the "language of management"—money. This translation provides the justification for selecting a Six Sigma project as well as appealing to top managers.

The Statistical Basis of Six Sigma

From a measurement perspective, "six sigma" represents a quality level of at most 3.4 defects per million opportunities. From where did this concept arise? It stems from the notion of design specifications in manufacturing and the ability of a process to achieve the specifications. *A six sigma quality level corresponds to a process variation equal to half of the design tolerance while allowing the mean to shift as much as 1.5 standard deviations from the target.* Figure 2.1 explains the theoretical basis for

FIGURE 2.1 THEORETICAL BASIS FOR SIX SIGMA

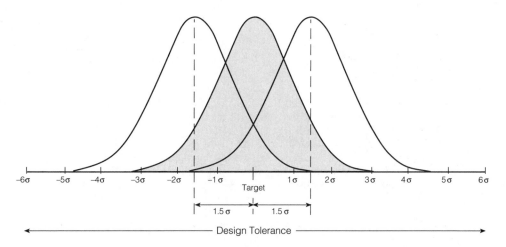

six sigma in the context of manufacturing specifications. Motorola chose this figure because field failure data suggested that Motorola's processes drifted by this amount on average. The allowance of a shift in the distribution is important, because no process can be maintained in perfect control. As will be discussed in Chapter 7, many common statistical process control (SPC) plans are based on sample sizes that only allow detection of shifts of about two standard deviations. Thus, it would not be unusual for a process to drift this much and not be noticed.

In Figure 2.1, the area under the tail of one of the shifted curves *beyond* the six sigma range (that is, *either* above or below the tolerance limit) is only 0.0000034, or 3.4 parts per million. Thus, if the process mean can be controlled to allow a one-way shift of at most 1.5 standard deviations of the target, then a maximum of 3.4 defects per million can be expected. If it is held exactly on target (the shaded distribution in Figure 2.1), only one defect per billion would be expected beyond the six sigma range in either tail. If shifts can occur in *both* directions, then the defect rate at a six sigma level would be at most 6.8 per million; and if held exactly on target, only two per billion.

In a similar fashion we could define 3-sigma quality, 5-sigma quality, and so on. The easiest way to understand it is to think of the distance from the target to the upper or lower specification (half the tolerance), measured in terms of standard deviations of the inherent variation, at the sigma level. A k-sigma quality level satisfies the equation:

$$k * \text{Process standard deviation} = \text{Tolerance}/2$$

Note that in Figure 2.1, if the design specification limits were only four standard deviations away from the target, the tails of the shifted distributions begin to exceed the specification limits by a significant amount.

Table 2.4 shows the number of defects per million in one tail of the normal distribution for different sigma quality levels and different amounts of off-centering.

TABLE 2.4 NUMBER OF DEFECTIVES (PARTS PER MILLION) FOR SPECIFIED OFF-CENTERING OF THE PROCESS AND QUALITY LEVELS (ONE TAIL ONLY)

Off-Centering	Quality Level						
	3-sigma	3.5-sigma	4-sigma	4.5-sigma	5-sigma	5.5-sigma	6-sigma
0	1350	233	32	3.4	0.29	0.017	0.001
0.25-sigma	3,577	666	99	12.8	1.02	0.1056	0.0063
0.5-sigma	6,440	1,382	236	32	**3.4**	0.71	0.019
0.75-sigma	12,288	3,011	665	88.5	11	1.02	0.1
1-sigma	22,832	6,433	1,350	233	32	**3.4**	0.39
1.25-sigma	40,111	12,201	3,000	577	88.5	10.7	1
1.5-sigma	66,803	22,800	6,200	1,350	233	32	**3.4**
1.75-sigma	105,601	40,100	12,200	3,000	577	88.4	11
2-sigma	158,700	66,800	22,800	6,200	1,300	233	32

Source: Pandu R. Tadikamalla, "The Confusion over Six-Sigma Quality. "*Quality progress* 27, no. 11 (November 1994). © 1994 American Society for Quality. Reprinted with permission.

(*Note:* The original published table values for off-centering of zero were incorrect and are corrected here.)

Note that a quality level of 3.4 defects per million can be achieved in several ways, for instance:

- with 0.5-sigma off-centering and 5-sigma quality
- with 1.0-sigma off-centering and 5.5-sigma quality
- with 1.5-sigma off-centering and 6-sigma quality

In many cases, controlling the process to the target is less expensive than reducing the process variability. This table can help assess these trade-offs.

The sigma level can be easily calculated on an Excel spreadsheet using the formula

$$=\text{NORMSINV}(1 - \text{Number of Defects}/\text{Number of Opportunities}) + \text{SHIFT}$$

or equivalently,

$$=\text{NORMSINV}(1 - \text{dpmo}/1{,}000{,}000) + \text{SHIFT}$$

SHIFT refers to the off-centering as used in Table 2.4. Using the airline example discussed earlier, if we had 3 lost bags for 8,000(1.6) = 12,800 opportunities, we would find =NORMSINV(1 − 3/12,800) + 1.5 = 4.99828 or about a 5-sigma level. The truth is less impressive. It was reported that 3.67 mishandled baggage reports per 1,000 passengers were filed in May 2003, which was up from 3.31 per 1,000 a year earlier.[5] This result yields a sigma level of only 4.33, assuming 1.6 bags per passenger.

Although originally developed for manufacturing in the context of tolerance-based specifications, the Six Sigma concept has been operationalized to any process and has come to signify a generic quality level of at most 3.4 defects per million opportunities. Six Sigma has been applied in product development, new business acquisition, customer service, accounting, and many other business functions. For example, suppose that a bank tracks the number of errors reported in customers' checking account statements. If they find 12 errors in 1,000 statements, it is equivalent to an error rate of 12,000 per million, somewhere between 3.5 and 4 sigma levels. The difference between a 4- and 6-sigma quality level can be surprising. Put in practical terms, if your cellular phone system operated at a 4-sigma level, you would be without service for more than 4 hours each month, whereas at 6-sigma, it would only be about 9 seconds a month; a 4-sigma process for a package delivery service would result in one nonconforming package for every three truckloads while a 6-sigma process would have only one nonconforming package in more than 5,000 truckloads. And, if you play 100 rounds of golf each year, you would only miss one putt every 163 years at a 6-sigma level! What may be more surprising to realize is that a change from 3 to 4 sigma represents a 10-fold improvement; from 4 to 5 sigma, a 30-fold improvement; and from 5 to 6 sigma, a 70-fold improvement—difficult challenges for any organization.

However, not all processes should operate at a Six-Sigma level.[6] The appropriate level should depend on the strategic importance of the process and the cost of improvement relative to the benefit. It is generally easy to move from a 2- or 3-sigma level to a 4-sigma level, but moving beyond that requires much more effort and sophisticated technology. In addition to a focus on defects, Six Sigma seeks to improve all aspects of operations. Thus, other key metrics include cycle time, process variation, yield, and throughput. Selecting the appropriate metric depends on the scope and objectives of the project, making Six Sigma a universal approach for improvement in all aspects of a business.

SIX SIGMA PROBLEM SOLVING

Problem solving is the activity associated with changing the state of what is actually happening to what should be happening. Many years ago, Juran defined **breakthrough** as the accomplishment of any improvement that takes an organization to unprecedented levels of performance. A breakthrough approach attacks chronic losses or, in Deming's terminology, common causes of variation. The objectives of Six Sigma projects often focus on breakthrough improvements that add value to the organization and its customers through systematic approaches to problem solving.

Successful quality and business performance improvement depends on the ability to identify and solve problems; this ability is fundamental to the Six Sigma philosophy. Many nonquantitatively inclined managers (which may include 75 or 80 percent of the population) have difficulty in grasping the concept of a systematic fact-based, often statistical, problem-solving approach. Yet, using such an approach is vital to effectively identifying sources of problems, understanding their causes, and developing improvement solutions. "Speaking the same language" builds confidence and assures that solutions are developed objectively, rather than by guesswork. Leaders in the quality revolution—W. Edwards Deming, Joseph Juran, and Philip Crosby—proposed specific methodologies for improvement in the early days of the quality revolution. Although each methodology is distinctive in its own right, they share many common themes:[7]

1. *Redefining and analyzing the problem:* Collect and organize information, analyze the data and underlying assumptions, and reexamine the problem for new perspectives, with the goal of achieving a workable problem definition.

2. *Generating ideas:* "Brainstorm" to develop potential solutions.
3. *Evaluating and selecting ideas:* Determine whether the ideas have merit and will achieve the problem solver's goal.
4. *Implementing ideas:* Sell the solution and gain acceptance by those who must use them.

These themes are reflected in the principal problem solving methodology used by Six Sigma, DMAIC—define, measure, analyze, improve, and control—which we discuss next. A structured problem-solving process provides all employees with a common language and a set of tools to communicate with each other, particularly as members of cross-functional teams.

The DMAIC Methodology

One of the first things that a Six Sigma quality analyst who is being trained for a green belt learns are the five steps in the DMAIC methodology.

1. Define   After a Six Sigma project is selected, the first step is to clearly define the problem. This activity is significantly different from project selection. *Project selection* generally responds to symptoms of a problem and results in a project charter granting authority and responsibility to the Six Sigma team. The general nature of the problem is usually described in the project charter, but is often rather vague. One must describe the problem in very specific operational terms that facilitate further analysis. For example, a firm might have a history of poor reliability in the electric motors it manufactures, resulting in a Six Sigma project to improve motor reliability. A preliminary investigation of warranty and field service repair data suggest that the source of most problems was brush wear, and more specifically, a problem with brush hardness variability. Thus, the problem might be defined as "reduce the variability of brush hardness." This process of drilling down to a more specific problem statement is sometimes called **project scoping.**

A good problem statement should also identify customers and the CTQs that have the most impact on product or service performance, describe the current level of performance or the nature of errors or customer complaints, identify the relevant performance metrics, benchmark best performance standards, calculate the cost/revenue implications of the project, and quantify the expected level of performance from a successful Six Sigma effort. The Define phase should also address such project management issues as what will need to be done, by whom, and when. Chapter 3 focuses on these issues.

2. Measure   This phase of the DMAIC process focuses on how to measure the internal processes that impact CTQs. It requires understanding the causal relationship between process performance and customer value. Six Sigma methodology uses the notion of a function in mathematics to portray this relationship:

$$Y = f(X)$$

where Y represents the set of critical response variables, or CTQs, and X represents the set of critical input variables that influence Y. For example, Y might represent the time to deliver bags from an airplane to baggage handling and the number of lost bags. X might include the number of baggage handlers, number of trucks, time they are dispatched, bar code scanning accuracy, and so on. This approach helps to communicate the most important factors that can be controlled or changed to improve the CTQs. It helps define the experiments that need to be conducted to confirm how input variables affect response variables. It also sets the stage for the Control phase by defining those factors that require monitoring and control.

Once these causal relationships are characterized, procedures for gathering facts—collecting good data, observation, and careful listening—must be defined and implemented. Data from existing production processes and practices often provide important information, as does feedback from supervisors, workers, customers, and field service employees.

Data collection should not be performed blindly. One must first ask some basic questions:

- What questions are we trying to answer?
- What type of data will we need to answer the questions?
- Where can we find the data?
- Who can provide the data?
- How can we collect the data with minimum effort and with minimum chance of error?

Many of the issues relating to measurement that must be considered in a Six Sigma project are discussed in Chapter 4.

3. Analyze   A major flaw in many problem-solving approaches is a lack of emphasis on rigorous analysis. Too often, we want to jump to a solution without fully understanding the nature of the problem and identifying the source, or "root cause," of the problem. The Analyze phase of DMAIC focuses on *why* defects, errors, or excessive variation occur.

After potential variables are identified and measured, experiments are conducted to verify the hypothesized relationships. That is, do the Xs truly influence the Ys? This is often done by formulating some hypothesis to investigate, analyzing the data collected or conducting additional experiments, and reaching reasonable and statistically supportable conclusions as to the root cause of the problem. Statistical thinking and analysis plays a critical role in this phase. It is one of the reasons why statistics are an important part of Six Sigma training (and one that engineering and many business curricula often ignore). Other experiments might employ computer simulation techniques. We discuss this further in Chapter 5.

4. Improve   Once the root cause of a problem is understood, the analyst or team needs to generate ideas for removing or resolving the problem and improve the performance measures of the X variables and thereby improve the CTQs. This idea-gathering phase is a highly creative activity, because many solutions are not obvious. One of the difficulties in this task is the natural instinct to prejudge ideas before thoroughly evaluating them. Most people have a natural fear of proposing a "silly" idea or looking foolish. However, such ideas may actually form the basis for a creative and useful solution. Effective problem solvers must learn to defer judgment and develop the ability to generate a large number of ideas at this stage of the process, whether practical or not.

After a set of ideas have been proposed, it is necessary to evaluate them and select the most promising. This process includes confirming that the proposed solution will positively impact the key process variables and the CTQs, and identifying the maximum acceptable ranges of these variables.

Problem solutions often entail technical or organizational changes. Often some sort of decision or scoring model is used to assess possible solutions against important criteria such as cost, time, quality improvement potential, resources required, effects on supervisors and workers, and barriers to implementation such as resistance to change or organizational culture. To implement a solution effectively, responsibility must be assigned to a person or a group who will follow through on what must be done, where it will be done, when it will be done, and how it will be done. Project management techniques are helpful in implementation planning. Approaches to improvement are discussed in Chapter 6.

5. Control The Control phase focuses on how to maintain the improvements, and includes putting tools in place to ensure that the key variables remain within the maximum acceptable ranges under the modified process. These improvements might include establishing the new standards and procedures, training the workforce, and instituting controls to make sure that improvements do not die over time. Controls might be as simple as using checklists or periodic status reviews to ensure that proper procedures are followed, or employing statistical process control charts to monitor the performance of key measures. These topics are discussed in Chapter 7.

The following simple example describes how DMAIC was used at American Express to improve the number of customers who received renewal cards.[8] (In this example, data have been masked to protect confidentiality.)

Define and Measure: On average in 1999, American Express (Amex) received 1,000 returned renewal cards each month. Of these renewals, 65 percent were due to the fact that the card members changed their addresses and did not tell the company. The U.S. Post Office calls these forwardable addresses. Amex does not currently notify a card member when they receive a returned plastic card.

Analyze: Analysis of the data noted significant differences in the causes of returned plastics between product types. The American Express Optima card had the highest incidence of defects, but was not significantly different from other card types in the percentage of defects. Renewals had by far the highest defect rate among the three areas of replacement, renewal, and new accounts. After additional testing, returns with forwardable addresses were overwhelmingly the largest percentage and quantity of returns.

Improve: An experimental pilot study was run on all renewal files issued, comparing records against the National Change of Address database. As a result, they were able to reduce the dpmo rate by 44.5 percent, from 13,500 to 6,036 defects per million opportunities. This action enabled many card members who would not have automatically received their credit cards to receive them, increasing revenue and customer satisfaction.

Control: Amex began tracking the proportion of returns over time as a means of monitoring the new process to ensure that it remains in control.

SIX SIGMA IN SERVICE ORGANIZATIONS

Because Six Sigma was developed in the manufacturing sector, and most publicity has revolved around such companies as Motorola and GE, many people in the service sector think that Six Sigma does not apply to their organizations. Nothing can be further from the truth. All Six Sigma projects have three key characteristics:

1. A problem to be solved
2. A process in which the problem exists
3. One or more measures that quantify the gap to be closed and can be used to monitor progress

These characteristics are present in all business processes; thus, Six Sigma can easily be applied to a wide variety of transactional, administrative, and service areas. In fact, it is generally agreed that 50 percent or more of the total savings opportunity in an organization lies outside of manufacturing. Within the service sector, Six Sigma is beginning to be called **transactional Six Sigma**. One retail service organization that is applying Six Sigma is Albertson's Inc., which owns Osco and Save-on drug chains (not coincidentally, Albertson's CEO is a former GE executive). Albertson's is the first food and drug retailer to launch a company-wide Six Sigma effort. Other service organizations using Six Sigma include Carlson Wagonlit Travel, Starwood Hotels and Resorts, and many hospitals and health care organizations.

However, while Six Sigma applies equally well in service areas, it is true that services have some unique characteristics relative to manufacturing processes. First, the culture is usually less scientific and service employees typically do not think in terms of processes, measurements, and data. The processes are often invisible, complex, and not well defined or well documented. Also, the work typically requires considerable human intervention, such as customer interaction, underwriting or approval decisions, or manual report generation. These differences make opportunities difficult to identify, and projects difficult to define. Finally, similar service activities are often done in different ways. If you have three people doing the same job, perhaps in three different locations, it is unlikely that they will do the job in the same way.

Because service processes are largely people-driven, measurements are often nonexistent or ill defined, as many believe that defects cannot be measured. Therefore, one must create measurement systems before collecting any data. Applying Six Sigma to services requires examination of four key measures of the performance:

*   *Accuracy,* as measured by correct financial figures, completeness of information, or freedom from data errors
*   *Cycle time,* which is a measure of how long it takes to do something, such as pay an invoice

- *Cost*, that is, the internal cost of process activities (in many cases, cost is largely determined by the accuracy and/or cycle time of the process; the longer it takes, and the more mistakes that have to be fixed, the higher the cost)
- *Customer satisfaction*, which is typically the primary measure of success

Fortunately, important similarities can be shown between manufacturing and non-manufacturing processes. First, both types of processes have "hidden factories," those places where the defective "product" is sent to be reworked or scrapped (revised, corrected, or discarded in non-manufacturing terms). Find the hidden factory and you also find opportunities to improve the process. Performing manual account reconciliation in accounting, revising budgets repeatedly until management will accept them, and making repeat sales calls to customers because all the information requested by the customer was not available are all examples of the hidden factory.

Consider how a janitorial service company might use DMAIC. In the Define stage, a key question would be to define what a defect represents. One might first create a flowchart of the cleaning process, specifying what activities are performed. One example of a defect might be leaving streaks on windows as a source of customer dissatisfaction, a CTQ. In the Measure stage, not only would the firm want to collect data on the frequency of defects, but also information about what products and tools employees use. The Analyze stage might include evaluating differences among employees to determine why some appear better at cleaning than others. Developing a standard operating procedure might be the focus of the Improve stage. Finally, Control might entail teaching employees the correct technique and measuring improvement over time.

In one application at CNH Capital, Six Sigma tools were applied to decrease asset management cycle time in posting repossessions to a bid list and remarketing Web site.[9] Cycle time was reduced 75 percent, from 40 days to 10 days, resulting in significant ongoing dollar savings. A facility management company had a high level of "days sales outstanding." Initially, they tried to fix this issue by reducing the term of days in its billing cycle, which upset customers. Using Six Sigma, they found that a large percentage of accounts with high days sales outstanding received invoices having numerous errors. After understanding the source of the errors and making process changes, the invoice process improved and days sales outstanding were reduced. At DuPont, a Six Sigma project was applied to improve cycle time for an employee's application for long-term disability benefits.[10] Some examples of financial applications of Six Sigma include the following:[11]

- Reduce the average and variation of days outstanding of accounts receivable.
- Close the books faster.
- Improve the accuracy and speed of the audit process.
- Reduce variation in cash flow.
- Improve the accuracy of journal entries (most businesses have a 3–4 percent error rate).
- Improve accuracy and cycle time of standard financial reports.

Other applications of Six Sigma in service organizations include a large insurance company that reduced its defect rate by more than 70 percent, increasing customer satisfaction dramatically, and saving over $250,000 in the first five months of the project; a financial services company that reconfigured its Web site to better reflect the questions asked at its call center, reducing costs and improving the quality of customer service as customers could more easily access account information on the Web; and a facility management company that discovered a large percentage of accounts with high days sales outstanding received error-ridden invoices from the company—by preventing these errors, days sales outstanding were reduced.[12]

CASE STUDY

Ford's Drive to Six Sigma Quality[13]

Ford Motor Company began developing its Six Sigma quality approach, called Consumer-Driven Six Sigma, in 1999. However, the company didn't really get serious about reclaiming their motto of the 1980s, "Quality is Job 1," until 2001—when J.D. Power and Associates' Initial Quality Study ranked Ford last among the big seven automakers. By 2003, the same survey ranked Ford number four and found that they were the most improved automaker of the group.

The company now has more than 200 master black belts, 2,200 black belts, nearly 40,000 green belts, and 3,000 project champions. Ford's training of green, black, and master black belts and project champions generally follows the conventional Six Sigma training process. Black belt training is "hands-on" and "just in time." Each trainee gets one week of full-time training per month for four months. The other three weeks of the month require that the trainees apply their training to a live project. Their Six Sigma teams typically have a member of management, a master black belt (MBB), a black belt (BB), and several green belts (GB) assigned to take on various roles in a project.

BBs are expected to handle two to three projects at a time. They can choose their own projects, but are asked to choose them carefully to ensure that they contribute to waste elimination or customer portion of the reduction of "Things Gone Wrong" (in "Ford-speak") will be improved through successful Six Sigma projects. Ford has implemented a unique project tracking system that has helped to promote organizational learning. The system allows members of project teams to observe what other teams are working on via an internal database.

Leaders are also expected to have hands-on involvement as project champions. Senior leaders are required to partner with MBBs to run performance cells. These cells are managed similarly to a manufacturing operation and benefit from the technical expertise of the MBB and the administrative experience of the manager. The process keeps new projects coming in and ensures that projects that are under way stay on track.

An example of a typical project was the one led by master black belt Pauline Burke. The problem was recognized after customers complained that body side moldings on the Ford Focus were lifting at the edges. It became evident to Burke that this issue was a "mega project" when the number of CTQ (critical to quality) issues began to multiply. In total, the project required nine months to complete, compared to the average of four months for a typical Six Sigma project at Ford.

Burke and her team followed the DMAIC problem-solving process rigorously. The Define stage uncovered four critical issues:

1. The tape that was designed to secure the molding was not contacting the car body enough.
2. Holes located on the body and used to line up the molding were too high, hitting an indent on the body sides.
3. Pressure used to apply the tape was too low.
4. The body was not clean enough, so the tape was not sticking well.

In the Measure stage, measurements were taken on the location of the holes, flatness of the molding, pressure being applied, and percent of area being cleaned. Analysis required that team experts, stakeholders such as maintenance personnel and tier 1 and tier 2 suppliers, as well as management, use the data. They were all seeking to understand the process and to discover ways in which it could be improved. In Stage 4 of DMAIC, improvements were proposed, including moving holes on the body side down by 2 millimeters; changing molds for the body side molding to ensure flatness and 100 percent contact between the molding, tape, and body side; using optimum pressure to apply the molding (as determined by a design of experiment process); and replacing the head on the cleaning fixture to ensure optimum cleaning of the body side.

One element of the Control stage was to monitor the hole locations using routine quality checks. It was also necessary to ensure that the supplier implemented a new procedure for checking the moldings for flatness. Other quality checks were performed to meet specifications for optimum pressure used to apply the moldings to the body, and to maintain cleaning equipment. The project resulted in savings of $100,000 and no customer complaints since the improvements were implemented.

Overall, Ford's Six Sigma approach contributed impressively to the bottom line. More than 6,000 projects have been completed in just three years, and Six Sigma has saved more than $1 billion since its inception. Louise Goeser, Ford's vice president of quality, cited a number of benefits of the company's Six Sigma effort, including improved quality of products, better measurement of results and success, and improved decision making. However, she also noted some challenges, such as selecting projects that are linked to strategic objectives and the company's revitalization plan. Ford's goal is corporate-wide adoption of Six Sigma tools and methodology, so that everyone from the CEO down will possess data-driven decision-making skills.

The slogan, "Quality is Job 1," has been given a new emphasis with the development of three components: operating systems to define standards and processes, quality leadership to engage all employees, and Consumer-Driven Six Sigma to be the primary data-driven decision process. These elements have helped to integrate Six Sigma into the overall quality program. Finally, the company plans to continue its emphasis on value creation and waste prevention, while widening and deepening deployment. This focus will involve increasing use of Design for Six Sigma, strengthening ties with suppliers, and continued integration of Six Sigma tools, methods, and mind-set as a mechanism for delivering results based on corporate objectives.

 ## REVIEW QUESTIONS

1. Define the principal categories of processes and provide examples of each.
2. Explain how design processes and production/delivery processes contribute to value creation.
3. Explain the concept of a system. Why is systems thinking important to Six Sigma?
4. Briefly summarize the Six Sigma Body of Knowledge.
5. What is a metric? Why are metrics vital to Six Sigma applications?
6. Define the term *defect*. Explain how to compute defects per million opportunities (dpmo).
7. Explain the theoretical basis for Six Sigma quality.
8. Describe the Six Sigma problem-solving approach (DMAIC).
9. What does the term *root cause* mean?
10. What are the key themes common to all problem-solving methodologies?
11. Explain the unique characteristics of services that must be considered in designing a Six Sigma program for a service company.
12. What are the four key measures of performance that must be examined when applying Six Sigma to services?

DISCUSSION QUESTIONS

1. Identify some of the key processes associated with the following business activities for a typical company: sales and marketing, supply chain management, managing information technology, and managing human resources.
2. List some of the common processes that a student performs. How can these processes be improved using a Six Sigma approach?
3. Outline how the DMAIC process might be used to improve a process in a school or university. What data or information might be difficult to obtain? Why?
4. In a true story related by our colleague Professor James W. Dean, Jr., the general manager of an elevator company was frustrated with the lack of cooperation between the mechanical engineers who designed new elevators and the manufacturing engineers who determined how to produce them. The mechanical engineers would often completely design a new elevator without consulting with the manufacturing engineers, and then expect the factory to somehow figure out how to build it. Often the new products were difficult or nearly impossible to build, and their quality and cost suffered as a result. The designs were sent back to the mechanical engineers (often more than once) for engineering changes to improve their manufacturability, and customers sometimes waited for months for deliveries. The general manager believed that if the two groups of engineers would communicate early in the

design process, many of the problems would be solved. At his wits' end, he found a large empty room in the plant and had both groups moved into it. The manager relaxed a bit, but a few weeks later he returned to a surprise. The two groups of engineers had finally learned to cooperate—by building a wall of bookcases and file cabinets right down the middle of the room, separating them from each other! What would you do in this situation? Relate this to Six Sigma and systems thinking.

5. Review the Six Sigma Body of Knowledge and identify where topics are covered in other course in your curriculum.

6. The Six Sigma philosophy seeks to develop technical leadership through extensive training, then use it in team-based projects designed to improve processes. To what extent are these two concepts (technical experts vs. team experts) at odds? What must be done to prevent them from blocking success in improvement projects?

7. Discuss the following questions related to the case study on Ford:
   a. Why do you think that the 2001 J.D. Power and Associates results were so poor even though the company had started its Six Sigma process in 1999?
   b. Why did it take almost twice the average project time in order to complete the Ford Focus body-molding project? What were some possible technical difficulties encountered in analyzing and correcting the CTQ issues that were uncovered in the design stage of that project?
   c. A major roadblock in Ford's Six Sigma effort was employee skepticism. How do you think they overcame it?

THINGS TO DO

1. Write down *your* process for preparing for an exam. How could this process be improved to make it shorter and/or more effective? Compare your process to those of your classmates. How might you collectively develop an improved process?

2. Interview a manager at a local organization to identify the value-creation and support processes used. What techniques does the company use to improve them?

3. Three popular Web sites for Six Sigma are http://www.ge.com/sixsigma, http://www.isixsigma.com, and http://www.sixsigmaforum.com. Explore these sites and classify information you can find there into the topical areas of the Six Sigma Body of Knowledge.

4. Interview managers or employees at an organization and develop a list of opportunities for error for processes they perform.

PROBLEMS

1. An insurance firm has set a standard that policy applications be processed within three days of receipt. If, out of a sample of 1,000 applications, 50 fail to meet this requirement, at what sigma level is this process operating?

2. During one month, 35 preflight inspections were performed on a military aircraft. Eighteen nonconformances were noted. Each inspection checks 60 items. What sigma level does this correspond to?

3. Over the last year 1,054 injections were administered at a clinic. Quality is measured by the proper amount of dosage as well as the correct drug. In two instances, the incorrect amount was given, and in one case, the wrong drug was given. At what sigma level is this process?

4. The *Wall Street Journal* reported on February 15, 2000, that about 750,000 airplane components are manufactured, machined, or assembled for Boeing Co. by workers from the Seattle Lighthouse for the Blind. A Boeing spokeswoman noted that the parts have an "exceptionally low" rejection rate of one per thousand. At what sigma level is this process operating?

5. An electronics firm manufactures 500,000 circuit boards per month. A random sample of 5,000 boards is inspected every week for five characteristics. During a recent week, two defects were found for one characteristic, and one defect, each, was found for the other four characteristics. If these inspections produced defect counts that were representative of the population, what is the overall sigma level for the process? What is the sigma level for the characteristic that showed two defects?

6. As noted in the text, a typical hospital has 225 medication errors per year. Approximately 35 percent of these are a result of the prescription, 30 percent from dispensing, and the remaining from administration. Suppose that a hospital has 9,000 annual admissions, and that the average patient receives five prescriptions during a hospital stay. Patients stay an average of 5.3 days, and each ordered medication is dispensed daily. The average patient receives 12 medications per day. Compute the average dpmo for each of the three categories of medication errors. To what sigma levels do these values correspond? Use Table 2.4 to find additional information for your analysis.

ENDNOTES

1. Russell L Ackoff, Recreating the Corporation: A Design of Organizations for the 21st Century, (Oxford, U.K.: Oxford University Press, 1999).

2. "Six Sigma Body of Knowledge" *ASQ website*: http://www.asq.org/cert/types/sixsigma/bok.html © 2004 American Society for Quality. Reprinted with permission.

3. Thomas Pyzdek, *The Six Sigma Handbook* Tuscon, AZ: McGraw-Hill/Quality Publishing, 2001), 301.

4. Steven A. Melnyk, "Metrics—The Missing Piece in Operations Management Research," *Decision Line*, March 1999, 8–9.

5. "Up, Up, and Away?" *Fortune*, July 21, 2003, 149.

6. Kevin Linderman, Roger G. Schroeder, Srilata Zaheer, and Adrian S. Choo, "Six Sigma: A Goal-Theoretic Perspective," *Journal of Operations Management* 21, 2003, 193–203.

7. A. VanGundy, "Comparing 'Little Known' Creative Problem-Solving Techniques," in *Creativity Week III, 1980 Proceedings* (Greensboro, NC: Center for Creative Leadership, 1981). The reader is also referred to James R. Evans, *Creative Thinking in the Decision and Management Sciences* Cincinnati, OH: South-Western, 1991), for a thorough treatment of creative problem solving.

8. Chris Bott, Elizabeth Keim, Sai Kim, and Lisa Palser, "Service Quality Six Sigma Case Studies," *ASQ's 54th Annual Congress Proceedings*, 2000, 225–231. © 2000 American Society for Quality. Reprinted with permission.

9. Adapted from Elizabeth Keim, LouAnn Fox, and Julie S. Mazza, "Service Quality Six Sigma Case Studies," *ASQ's 54th Annual Congress Proceedings*, 2000 (CD-ROM).

10. Lisa Palser, "Cycle Time Improvement for a Human Resources Process," *ASQ's 54th Annual Quality Congress Proceedings*, 2000 (CD-ROM).

11. Roger Hoerl, "An Inside Look at Six Sigma at GE," *Six Sigma Forum* 1, no. 3, May 2002, 35–44.

12. Kennedy Smith, "Six Sigma for the Service Sector," *Quality Digest*, May 2003, 23–27.

13. Kennedy Smith. "Six Sigma at Ford Revisited," *Quality Digest* 23, no. 6, June 2003, 28–32.

P A R T

II

─────────

Six Sigma DMAIC Methodology

Chapter 3
Project Organization, Selection,
and Definition

Chapter 4
Process Measurement

Chapter 5
Process Analysis

Chapter 6
Process Improvement

Chapter 7
Process Control

3

Project Organization, Selection, and Definition

T he first step in the DMAIC process is Define, which entails selecting the problem to address, clearly defining the improvement opportunity, building commitment among all stakeholders, and understanding the process and customer requirements from a high-level perspective. However, before starting the Define step, an organization must create an effective structure to carry out the effort.

ORGANIZING FOR SIX SIGMA PROJECTS

Six Sigma improvements are generally carried out by projects. A **project** is a temporary work structure that starts, produces an output or outcome, and then shuts down.[1] Projects are implemented by teams. A team-based project approach provides for broad participation and ensures including the right mix of skills. Participation by process owners and decision makers also increases the likelihood that those involved will act on the results.

Six Sigma Project Management

Project management involves all activities associated with planning, scheduling, and controlling projects. Good project management ensures that an organization's resources are used efficiently and effectively. Such management is particularly important for Six Sigma, because projects generally cut across organizational boundaries and require the coordination of many different departments and functions.

Projects fail for a variety of reasons, including not adhering to schedules, poor planning, and "scope creep" when the nature of the project gradually loses its focus and becomes unwieldy, mismatching of skills, and insufficient knowledge transfer.[2] Being able to manage a large portfolio of projects, as is typically found in Six Sigma environments, is vital to organizational success. The project management body of knowledge defines 69 tools that a project manager must master, but few have done so. Achieving professional certification in project management can significantly assist Six Sigma efforts.

The key leadership role belongs to the project manager. Project managers are often generalists who have diverse backgrounds. They lead the project activities, plan and track progress of the work, and provide direction to the project team. In addition, they must manage the relationships and communication among the members of the project team. Thus, the project manager's ability to facilitate is usually more important than his or her ability to supervise. The project manager must also have sufficient technical expertise to resolve disputes among functional specialists. Successful project managers have four key skills: a bias toward task completion, technical and administrative credibility, interpersonal and political sensitivity, and leadership ability.

Traditional project management methodologies were developed before the advent of the quality revolution; hence, principles of total quality were not often incorporated. Approaches such as identifying customer requirements, using a customer-supplier model, teamwork principles, cycle time reduction, and in-process measurements can improve the quality of the result. For example, although each project is unique, projects have similar underlying processes, and attention to these processes can improve the overall quality of the project effort.

A project typically unfolds in stages, which can be called a **life cycle.** This closely parallels the stages in the DMAIC process, which can also be thought of as a life cycle. The stages of a typical project follow:[3]

1. *Project Initiation:* Define directions, priorities, limitations, and constraints.
2. *Project Planning:* Create a blueprint for the scope of the project and resources needed to accomplish it.
3. *Project Assurance:* Use appropriate, qualified processes to meet technical project design specifications.
4. *Project Control:* Use appropriate communication and management tools to ensure that managerial performance, process improvements, and customer satisfaction are tracked.
5. *Project Closure:* Evaluate customer satisfaction with project deliverables and assess success and failures that provide learning for future projects and referrals from satisfied customers.

These basic components are applicable to any project management endeavor, but are directly relatable to Six Sigma design and improvement projects.

Project Initiation

Projects are implemented to satisfy a need of a customer or process owner; thus, the first step in managing a project is to clearly define the goals of the project, and when and how they must be accomplished. Initiation also includes identifying a project champion, project manager, and other team members. The customer must be a vital participant in all stages of the process, not just at the beginning and the end.

Project Planning

All project management decisions involve four factors: *time, resources, costs*, and *performance*. Project managers need to know how much time a project should take and when specific activities should be started and completed so that deadlines can be established and progress of the project monitored. They must also determine the resources, such as people and equipment available for the project, and how they should be allocated among the various activities. Projects usually have limited budgets and costs generally depend on the resources expended; thus, they must be monitored and controlled. Project managers seek ways to minimize costs without jeopardizing deadlines. Finally, performance, which can be defined as how well the results of the project meet customer requirements, should be a measurable entity. Software packages, such as Microsoft Project®, incorporate various quantitative analysis tools for scheduling, budgetary analysis, and tracking factors of time, resources, and costs, and should be selected at this stage.

The project-planning process involves determining the set of activities that must be performed, who will do them, how long each is estimated to take, and when they should be completed to meet the organization's goals. The project-planning process consists of the following steps:

1. *Project definition.* Define the project, its objectives, and deliverables. Determine the activities that must be completed and the sequence required to perform them.
2. *Resource planning.* For each activity, determine the resource needs: personnel, time, money, equipment, materials, and so on.
3. *Project scheduling.* Specify a time schedule for each activity.
4. *Project tracking and control.* Establish the proper control methods to be used for tracking progress. Develop alternative plans in anticipation of problems in meeting the planned schedule.

When projects are late, it is often because of failure to perform these four tasks adequately.

Project Assurance

Project assurance can be thought of as "customer relationship management" while the project is in process. It requires communication, interpersonal, and diplomacy skills on the part of the project manager. He or she must manage upward to the project champion and out to the client, while keeping a firm, but participative, hand on the pulse of team members and those who are actually doing the "hands-on" project work. Project assurance allows the project manager to estimate how successfully the final "deliverable" will perform, not just whether it will be on time and below budgeted cost. Software packages such as Microsoft Project are not designed to track "deliverable" performance measures, although some of the project tracking data for estimated final costs and estimated completion dates may be of interest to customers. Performance tracking is often subjective, but can be quantified using communication processes and customer surveys, tracking and controlling changes in the project plan, and performing regular project reviews or audits.

Project Control

Project control involves systematically reviewing the time, resources, cost, and performance measures as the project is being carried out. Because of the uncertainty of task times, unavoidable delays, or other problems, projects rarely, if ever, progress on schedule. Managers must therefore monitor performance of the project and take corrective action when needed. A typical project control system includes the following:

- A project plan covering expected scope, schedule, cost, and performance goals or requirements
- A continuous monitoring system that measures the current results or status against the project plan through the use of monitoring tools
- A reporting system that identifies deviations from the project plan by means of trends and forecasts
- Timely actions to take advantage of beneficial trends or to correct deviations

Project Closure

Project closeout is one of those mundane but vitally important processes that facilitate future improvement in project management performance. It consists of such steps as the following:

- Ensuring that the project has been signed off by those who must do so
- Ensuring that all bills have been paid and all financial records have been completed
- Ensuring that team members have not only been thanked, but provided for, which may involve following up with recommendations for reassignment to new projects or departments
- Ensuring that "lessons learned" are examined and documented, often by performing a final project audit
- Ensuring that project successes and best practices are communicated and disseminated to other parts of the organization

Project Reviews

Project reviews are status checks that serve to evaluate progress toward achieving the project plan. Team leaders should ensure that regular project reviews are scheduled. They will help to keep the project visible and moving forward. Project reviews include consideration of timelines, proper use of Six Sigma tools, and key deliverables. They may be conducted informally with the team leader or mentor (but ideally with other knowledgeable reviewers present), or formally with the team champion or sponsor. Some of the benefits of good project reviews are:

- *Monitor Project Progress*—Ensure that everyone on the team is focused on the goal and are working in concert.
- *Provide Guidance*—Assist teams in setting the right direction and obtaining resources as needed.
- *Check Focus and Alignment*—Ensure that project activities are all focused to achieving the goal.

- *Display Support*—Offer visible support in order to motivate and energize the team.
- *Knock Down Barriers*—Use project reviews to identify roadblocks and barriers for sponsors and champions to remove.
- *Share Best Practices*—Bring in subject matter experts or team leaders of other projects to avoid time wasted in "reinventing the wheel" as needs arise during project execution.
- *Recognize and Reward*—Letting team members know they are doing a good job is important for continued motivation.

Each project should be reviewed after each phase has been completed. For the DMAIC Six Sigma improvement process, a review should take place after every phase: Define, Measure, Analyze, Improve, Control. A typical review agenda would include:

1. *Introduction by Project Champion or Sponsor* This allows the champion or sponsor to set the stage for the review and reiterate the importance of the project.
2. *Project Team Presentation* A brief summary of previous reviews should be presented, but the bulk of the time should be spent on the recently completed project phase.
3. *Evaluation* The team should identify the work that has been completed on the current phase, discuss issues or problems that may have arisen during execution, and capture "lessons learned" for the remaining phases and future projects. If any serious issues are uncovered that might require the team to go back and conduct further analyses, formal sign-off of the phase might be delayed.
4. *Closing by Project Champion or Sponsor* The champion—who is ultimately accountable for the project success—should provide continued encouragement.

Six Sigma Project Teams

A **team** is a small number of people with complementary skills who are committed to a common purpose, set of performance goals, and an approach for which they hold themselves mutually accountable.[4] Six Sigma projects require a diversity of skills that range from technical analysis and creative solution development to implementation. Thus, teams are natural vehicles to implement Six Sigma projects.

Six Sigma project teams are chartered with a specific mission to develop something new or to accomplish a complex task. One key characteristic of these teams is that they are **cross-functional**—they cut across boundaries of different departments or functions regardless of their organizational home. Such teams include several types of individuals:

Champions
Senior-level managers who promote and lead the deployment of Six Sigma in a significant area of the business. Champions understand the philosophy and tools of Six Sigma, select projects, set objectives, allocate resources, and mentor teams. Champions own Six Sigma projects and are responsible for their completion and results; typically they also own the process that the project is focused on

improving. They select teams, set strategic direction, create measurable objectives, provide resources, monitor performance, make key implementation decisions, report results to top management, and help teams celebrate success. More importantly, champions work toward removing barriers—organizational, financial, personal—that might inhibit the successful implementation of a Six Sigma project.

Master Black Belts

Full-time Six Sigma experts who are responsible for Six Sigma strategy, training, mentoring, deployment, and results. Master black belts are highly trained in how to use Six Sigma tools and methods and provide advanced technical expertise. They work across the organization to develop and coach teams, conduct training, and lead change, but are typically not members of Six Sigma project teams. Their principal role is to coach and advise teams on technical directions and assist when problems arise.

Black Belts

Fully trained Six Sigma experts with up to 160 hours of training who perform much of the technical analyses required of Six Sigma projects, usually on a full-time basis. They have advanced knowledge of tools and DMAIC methods, and can apply them either individually or as team leaders. Black belts need to translate technical issues into a language that champions can understand. They may help select team members, conduct training, and usually lead the team to ensure that the project stays on schedule. After project completion, they often work with functional managers and process owners to implement and monitor solutions. They also mentor and develop green belts. Black belts need good leadership and communication skills in addition to technical skills and process knowledge. They should be highly motivated, eager to gain new knowledge, and well respected among their peers. As such, organizations often target black belts as future business leaders.

Green Belts

Functional employees who are trained in introductory Six Sigma tools and methodology and work on projects on a part-time basis, assisting black belts while developing their own knowledge and expertise. They conduct basic analyses of data and provide ideas for improvement. Typically, one of the requirements for receiving a green belt designation is to successfully complete a Six Sigma project. Successful green belts are often promoted to black belts.

Team Members

Individuals from various functional areas who support specific projects. They often gather data or conduct experiments because of their functional knowledge of process details. The roles of the Six Sigma champion and the master black belt leader are similar to those of the champion and sponsor. The role of a black belt is similar to a staff quality expert, while green belts are typically given the team leadership role.

Table 3.1 summarizes the roles of different individuals in Six Sigma project teams. The inter-relationships between the stages of the project life cycle and the critical roles of team members are shown in Table 3.2.

TABLE 3.1 TEAM MEMBER ROLES, RESPONSIBILITIES, AND PERFORMANCE ATTRIBUTES

Role Name	Responsibility	Definition	Attributes of Good Role Performance
Champion	Advocate	The person initiating a concept or idea for change/improvement	• Is dedicated to seeing it implemented • Holds absolute belief it is the right thing to do • Has perseverance and stamina
Sponsor	Backer; risk taker	The person who supports a team's plans, activities, and outcomes	• Believes in the concept/idea • Has sound business acumen • Is willing to take risk and responsibility for outcomes • Has authority to approve needed resources • Will be listened to by upper management
Team leader	Change agent; chair; head	A person who: • Staffs the team or provides input for staffing requirements • Strives to bring about change/improvement through the team's outcomes • Is trusted by followers to lead them • Has the authority for, and directs the efforts of, the team • Participates as a team member • Coaches team members in developing or enhancing necessary competencies • Communicates with management about the team's progress and needs • Handles the logistics of team meetings • Takes responsibility for team records	• Is committed to the team's mission and objectives • Has experience in planning, organizing, staffing, controlling, and directing • Is capable of making and maintaining channels that enable members to do their work • Is capable of gaining the respect of team members; serves as a role model • Is firm, fair, and factual in dealing with a team of diverse individuals • Facilitates discussion without dominating • Actively listens • Empowers team members to the extent possible within the organization's culture • Supports all team members equally • Respects each team member's individuality
Facilitator	Helper; trainer; adviser; coach	A person who: • Observes the team's processes and team members' interactions and suggests changes to facilitate positive movement toward the team's goals and objectives • Intervenes if discussion develops into multiple conversations	• Is trained in facilitating skills • Is respected by team members • Is tactful • Knows when and when not to intervene • Deals with the team's process, not content • Respects the team leader and does not override his or her responsibility • Respects confidential information shared by individuals or within the team

TABLE 3.1 (CONTINUED)

Role	Description	Characteristics
(Facilitator, continued) Gatekeeper; monitor	• Intervenes to skillfully prevent an individual from dominating the discussion or to engage an overlooked individual in the discussion of the team as a whole • Assists the team leader in bringing discussions to a close • May provide training in team building, conflict management, and so forth	• Will not accept facilitator role if expected to report to management information that is proprietary to the team • Will abide by the ASQ Code of Ethics
Timekeeper	• A person designated by the team to watch the use of allocated time and remind the team members when their time objective may be in jeopardy	• Is capable of assisting the team leader in keeping the team meeting within the predetermined time limitations • Is sufficiently assertive to intervene in discussions when the time allocation is in jeopardy • Is capable of participating as a member while still serving as a timekeeper
Scribe Recorder; note taker	• A person designated by the team to record critical data from team meetings (Formal "minutes" of the meetings may be published and distributed to interested parties).	• Is capable of capturing on paper, or electronically, the main points and decisions made in a team meeting and providing a complete, accurate, and legible document (or formal minutes) for the team's records • Is sufficiently assertive to intervene in discussions to clarify a point or decision in order to record it accurately • Is capable of participating as a member while still serving as a scribe
Team members Participants: subject matter experts	• The persons selected to work together to bring about a change/improvement, achieving this goal in a seated environment of mutual respect, sharing of expertise, cooperation, and support	• Are willing to commit to the purpose of the team • Are able to express ideas, opinions, and suggestions in a nonthreatening manner • Are capable of listening attentively to other team members • Are receptive to new ideas and suggestions. • Are even-tempered and able to handle stress and cope with problems openly • Are competent in one or more fields of expertise needed by the team • Have favorable performance records • Are willing to function as team members and forfeit "star" status

Source: Bauer, John E. Grace L. Duffy, and Russell T. Westcott (eds.), *The Quality Improvement Handbook* (Milwaukee, WI: ASQ Quality Press, 2002), 43–44. © 2002 American Society for Quality. Reprinted with permission.

TABLE 3.2 PROJECT LIFE CYCLE ACCOUNTABILITY MATRIX

Stage/ Role	Project Initiation	Project Planning	Project Assurance
Champion	Select project manager, promote Six Sigma use, align and select project, commit to charter	Determine decisionmaking authority, commit to plan, allocate resources needed for project success	Conduct external customer communications, mentor project manager, clear obstacles as needed
External Customer (or Process Owner)	Identify and prioritize expectations, commit to charter	Contribute process knowledge, identify customer satisfaction standards and trade-off values, commit to plan	Participate in ongoing communications, assist in obtaining approvals for changes in processes
Master Black Belt (Technical Consultant)	Assist in strategic project selection, promote Six Sigma vision, tools, and process	Assist in identifyingdata collection and analysis needs, provide training resources, ensure that processes are statistically sound	Participate in ongoing communications, mentor project manager, facilitate cross-project sharing and learning
Project Manager (SSBB and/or SSGB)	Select core team, identify risks, empower performance, commit to charter	Identify customer satisfaction standards and trade-off values, plan for short-term training if needed, develop quality and communications plans, commit to plan	Conduct customer/ management communications, select tools, confirm qualified processes used, oversee data gathering and analysis, manage quality audits and planning
Core Team	Determine team operating principles, flowchart project, identify lessons learned, commit to charter	Plan project, contribute special expertise, identify suppliers, qualify the process, identify data to collect, commit to plan	Use qualified processes, gather data, find root causes, conduct quality audits, plan future work

TABLE 3.2 (CONTINUED)

Stage/ Role	Project Control	Project Closure
Champion	Conduct external customer communications, mentor project manager, approve or reject process improvements, clear obstacles as needed	Sign off on completed project, recognize and reward participants, assess project to improve system
External Customer (or Process Owner)	Confirm ongoing satisfaction level, accept deliverables	Verify when usage training and support are completed, assess project to improve system, ensure that new processes are implemented, signoff
Master Black Belt (Technical Consultant)	Provide expertise in design of process improvements, support project manager (SSBB and/or SSGB)	Assist in development of management presentations, do project signoffs, ensure that project results are publicized, disseminate best practices and lessons learned
Project Manager (SSBB and/or SSGB)	Track progress, critical success factors, and costs versus plan; implement mid-course corrections; measure customer satisfaction; manage process improvements	Notify champion of project completion, recognize and reward participants, assess project to improve system
Core Team	Measure customer satisfaction, test deliverables, correct defects, endorse deliverables	Provide customer support and training, assess project to improve system

Source: Adapted from Timothy J. Kloppenborg and Joseph A. Petrick, *Managing Project Quality* (Vienna, VA: Management Concepts, 2003), 11. © 2002, Management Concepts, Inc. All rights reserved. Used with permission.

Cooper and Noonan have begun compiling a national database on Six Sigma and teams.[5] Preliminary information from this database indicated that the most important lesson learned by the teams that were surveyed was "determine who the stakeholders are for the project and ask them for their input on how to improve the process." Other aspects considered important for team success included management support and participation, communication during projects about Six Sigma as well as project progress, alignment of team members with organizational vision, mission and values, and definition and use of sound metrics.

PEOPLE SKILLS

People are key to process improvement and Six Sigma efforts. Good people discover opportunities, develop innovative solutions, and find ways to make them work. Technical skills, for sure, are vital for a successful Six Sigma project. However, it is not as much a question of what things people need to know as it is a question of what things do they need to know *how* to do. Clearly, Six Sigma team members need to have the technical skills to conduct the analyses required for the DMAIC process. However, compared to the technical tools, the "soft skills"—those that involve people—such as project management and team facilitation, are more difficult to teach and learn. One team or one team member can make or break an improvement project or a Six Sigma initiative. People skills can be learned, but often take more time than is available for a single project; thus, they should be a routine part of every employee's educational program.

Some of the essential elements for effective process improvement from a people perspective are a *shared vision* and *behavioral skills*. A shared vision can unify a team and provide the motivation for successfully implementing the project. Developing one generally requires team discussions early on; unfortunately, inexperienced project leaders frequently bypass these discussions in an effort to get the project under way.

People who are technically oriented may neglect behavioral skills, thinking that such skills are unnecessary in order to solve technical problems. Behavioral skills require both knowledge and practice.

Skills for Team Leaders

Team members often assume the role of project leaders and project managers and yet must defer to superior knowledge of other team members and take on roles as followers. In an insightful book on team-based project management, James Lewis characterized the most important people skills needed by project managers.[6] These skills include the following:

- Conflict management and resolution
- Team management
- Leadership skills
- Decision making
- Communication

- Negotiation
- Cross-cultural training

Conflict management involves dealing proactively with disagreements that may occur when two or more technical experts get together. Team management involves ensuring that project members remain focused on the goals, time frame, and costs of their part of the project. Leadership skills require that the project leader guide the work of the team, including team development, while managing upward to the project champion and outward to other project teams and team leaders. Decision making requires that good decisions be made in a timely fashion. Communication channels must be established and maintained throughout the course of the project. Negotiation is needed in order to secure the resources required for successful project completion. Cross-cultural training may involve team members of other nationalities, or it may simply involve people from different functional areas with divergent points of view. In either case, it is extremely important for team members to be able to listen and learn about different perspectives on shared project goals from team and non-team people who may have widely differing thoughts about issues under consideration. In addition, being able to lead and facilitate project reviews is an important skill for the team leader.

Skills for Team Members

Six Sigma team members are, in a sense, leaders and role models for people throughout the organization. They should demonstrate enthusiasm for the process and keep themselves and others motivated, especially as roadblocks and setbacks may appear. They also need good communication skills for gathering data and information from others and sharing their findings among the team.

Perhaps the two areas of greatest importance in team functioning for process improvement project team members are meetings and shared decision making. Meetings are important because they consume considerable valuable time of team members. Peter Scholtes, a leading authority on teams for quality improvement, provides some rules for effective meetings:[7]

- Use agendas.
- Have a facilitator.
- Take minutes.
- Draft the next agenda.
- Evaluate the meeting.
- Adhere to the "100-mile" rule.

Scholtes suggests the use of detailed agendas that include topics, a sentence about the importance of each, who will present them, the estimated time for each topic, and the type of item, such as discussion, decision, or information topics. A facilitator can keep the discussion on time and on target, prevent anyone from dominating or being overlooked, and help bring the discussion to a close. A scribe who takes minutes can record subjects, decisions, and who will be responsible for actions taken. Drafting the next agenda at the end of the meeting serves to set a plan of action for going forward.

Evaluating the meeting incorporates a continuous improvement step. Adhering to the "100-mile" rule requires a commitment to focus on the meeting so clearly that "no one should be called from the meeting unless it is so important that the disruption would occur even if the meeting was 100 miles away from the workplace."[8]

Shared decision making is important because most individuals in organizations have more practice in receiving direction from a supervisor, or making an individual decision in their own workplace. Shared decisions are new territory for many individuals. Decision-making techniques abound in quality improvement literature. One of the most powerful is called the nominal group technique (NGT), developed to provide a way to prioritize and focus on important project objectives in the project definition stage.[9] One of the major advantages of the technique is that it balances the power of each individual involved in the decision process. Key steps in the process include the following:

1. Request that all participants (usually 5–10 persons) write or say which problem or issue they feel is most important.
2. Record all problems or issues.
3. Develop a master list of problems or issues.
4. Generate and distribute to each participant a form that numbers the problems or issues in no particular order.
5. Request that each participant rank the top five problems or issues by assigning five points to their most important perceived problem and one point to the least important of their top five.
6. Tally the results by adding the points for each problem or issue.
7. The problem or issue with the highest number is the most important one for the team as a whole.
8. Discuss the results and generate a final ranked list for process improvement action planning.[10]

This approach provides a more democratic way of making decisions and helps individuals to feel that they have contributed to the process.

Team Dynamics

Introducing Six Sigma teams into an organization cannot be done haphazardly. Robbins and Finley list 14 reasons why teams fail, although they are quick to point out that no one reason, and often multiple reasons, explain why it happens.[11] Their list includes organizational problems (bad policies, stupid procedures, bleary vision, ill-conceived reward system, confused goals, unresolved roles, anti-team culture), leadership problems (bad leadership, insufficient feedback and information, the wrong tools), and individual/team barriers (mismatched needs, hidden agendas, personality conflicts, lack of team trust, unwillingness to change). Thus, managers need to carefully evaluate how teams are introduced in their organizations and address team building as a critical work process. Any organizational change, especially one as significant as Six Sigma, is often met with resistance. Keys to overcoming resistance are early involvement by all parties, open and honest dialogue, and good planning. Management holds the key, however. As the organizational leaders, they must believe in workers and their ability to contribute. As leaders, managers must also show commitment and support by providing the right training, rewards, and recognition.

The key stages of a team's life cycle are called *forming, storming, norming, performing,* and *adjourning*.[12] Teams go through a fairly predictable cycle of formation and growth, regardless of their charge and goals. Teams are generally formed in organizational settings by direction from a manager, leader, or governing body. They are typically given a broad objective (operate this process according to certain guidelines, put a man on the moon in this decade, design a process to make cookies using elves as workers, etc.). The team may also be given a time frame and resource limits, if it is a project team. *Forming* takes place when the team is introduced, meets together, and explores issues of their new assignment. *Storming* occurs when team members disagree on team roles and challenge the way that the team will function. The third stage, *norming,* takes place when the issues of the previous stage have been worked out, and team members agree on roles, ground rules, and acceptable behavior when doing the work of the team. Stage four, *performing,* characterizes the productive phase of the life cycle when team members cooperate to solve problems and complete the goals of their assigned work. In the *adjourning* phase, the team wraps up the project, satisfactorily completes its goals, and prepares to disband or move on to another project.

More than any other type of organizational structure, the team structure depends on cooperation, communication, and clarity. Eckes estimates that 60 percent of failures of Six Sigma teams are due to failures in the "mechanics" of team operations, as opposed to poor project selection or improper use of tools.[13] He cites contributing factors such as lack of application of meeting skills, improper use of agendas, failure to determine meeting roles and responsibilities, lack of setting and keeping ground rules, and lack of appropriate facilitative behaviors.

Peter Scholtes suggested 10 ingredients for a successful team. These items provide some guidance during the forming stage and can mitigate issues that might lead to "storming":

1. *Clarity in team goals.* As a sound basis, a team agrees on a mission, purpose, and goals.
2. *An improvement plan.* A plan guides the team in determining schedules and mileposts by helping the team decide what advice, assistance, training, materials, and other resources it may need.
3. *Clearly defined roles.* All members must understand their duties and know who is responsible for what issues and tasks.
4. *Clear communication.* Team members should speak with clarity, listen actively, and share information.
5. *Beneficial team behaviors.* Teams should encourage members to use effective skills and practices to facilitate discussions and meetings.
6. *Well-defined decision procedures.* Teams should use data as the basis for decisions and learn to reach consensus on important issues.
7. *Balanced participation.* Everyone should participate, contribute their talents, and share commitment to the team's success.
8. *Established ground rules.* The group outlines acceptable and unacceptable behaviors.

9. *Awareness of group process.* Team members exhibit sensitivity to nonverbal communication, understand group dynamics, and work on group process issues.
10. *Use of the scientific approach.* With structured problem-solving processes, teams can more easily find root causes of problems.[14]

Team-related topics, including organizational effectiveness, team assessment, facilitation tools, and team development, are part of standard Six Sigma training. Teams also require various leadership and maintenance activities, especially if the team is large and the project or work assignment is complex. Six Sigma efforts often result in significant change recommendations to the organization; work processes change and employees need to do things differently. Understanding how changes affect people is a necessary issue that organizations must address after Six Sigma projects are completed. In addition, managers must pay attention to selecting the right people to serve on teams, training and skill development, and reward and recognition approaches to drive behavior.

SIX SIGMA PROJECT SELECTION

One of the more difficult challenges in Six Sigma is the identification of the most appropriate problems to attack. Six Sigma projects can range from small problems confined to one work area to broad issues that cut across the entire organization. One of the requirements for achieving green belt status is to successfully complete a basic Six Sigma project by solving a meaningful business problem that positively impacts customers or business performance. Often green belt projects address small problems within a department or work function. As employees develop their skills, become black belts, and start applying Six Sigma on a routine basis, they begin to address larger and more complex issues, such as problems associated with key value-creation or cross-functional processes, such as supply chains.

Problems and opportunities are typically ill defined at the outset. In the words of Russell Ackoff, managers must learn "mess management." Ackoff, a noted authority on problem solving, defines a **mess** as a "system of external conditions that produces dissatisfaction."[15] High costs, excessive defects, a rash of customer complaints, or low customer satisfaction often characterize quality- and performance-related messes.

These symptoms can arise from several sources:

- A lack of knowledge about how a process works, which is particularly critical if the process is performed by different people. Such lack of knowledge results in inconsistency and increased variation in outputs.
- A lack of knowledge about how a process *should* work, including understanding customer expectations and the goal of the process.
- A lack of control of materials and equipment used in a process.
- Inadvertent errors in performing work.
- Waste and complexity, which manifest themselves in many ways, such as unnecessary steps in a process and excess inventories.
- Hasty design and production of parts and assemblies; poor design specifications; inadequate testing of incoming materials and prototypes.

- Failure to understand the capability of a process to meet specifications.
- Lack of training.
- Poor instrument calibration and testing.
- Inadequate environmental characteristics such as light, temperature, and noise.

The goal of the DMAIC process is to progress from identifying symptoms of problems, to identifying their causes, and ultimately finding a solution or improvement.

A useful way of classifying problems that can help more clearly identify a Six Sigma project is by problem type.[16] According to Kepner and Tregoe, a **problem** is a deviation between what should be happening and what actually is happening that is important enough to make someone think the deviation ought to be corrected.[17] Research using more than 1,000 published cases describing quality problem-solving activities suggests that virtually every instance of quality problem solving falls into one of five categories:

1. *Conformance problems* are defined by unsatisfactory performance by a well-specified system. Users are not happy with system outputs, such as quality or customer service levels. The system has worked before, but for some reason it is not performing acceptably. The causes of deviations must be identified, and the system restored to its intended mode of functioning.

2. *Unstructured performance problems* result from unsatisfactory performance by a poorly specified system. That is, the task is nonstandardized and not fully specified by procedures and requirements. An example would be poor sales. Poor sales might result from many reasons; one cannot simply find a policy change or standard operating procedure that will eliminate this problem. Unstructured problems require more creative approaches to solving them.

3. *Efficiency problems* result from unsatisfactory performance from the standpoint of stakeholders other than customers. Typical examples are cost and productivity issues. Even though the quality of the outputs may be acceptable, the system's performance does not achieve internal organizational goals. Identification of solutions often involves streamlining processes.

4. *Product design problems* involve designing new products that better satisfy user needs—the expectations of customers that matter most to them. In Six Sigma, those vital characteristics are called critical-to-quality (CTQ) issues.

5. *Process design problems* involve designing new processes or substantially revising existing processes. The challenge here is determining process requirements, generating new process alternatives, and linking these processes to customer needs. Techniques such as benchmarking and reengineering, which we discuss in later chapters, are useful tools for process design.

Understanding these problem categories creates greater awareness of potential project opportunities.

Lynch and colleagues point out two ways to generate projects: top-down and bottom-up.[18] Each has advantages and disadvantages. Top-down projects generally are tied to business strategy and are aligned with customer needs. Their major weakness is that they are often too broad in scope to be completed in a timely manner. In addition, top managers may underestimate the cost and overestimate the capabilities of the team or teams to which the project is assigned. In a bottom-up approach, black belts (or master black belts) choose the projects that are well suited to the capabilities of teams. However, a major drawback of this approach is that the projects may not be tied closely to strategic concerns of top management, thus receiving little support and low recognition from the top. Perhaps the best way to ensure success is for executive champions, who understand the impact of projects from a strategic perspective, to work closely with the technical experts in choosing the most relevant projects that fit within the capabilities of Six Sigma teams.

Factors in Project Selection

Factors that should be considered when selecting Six Sigma projects include the following:

• Impact on customers and organizational effectiveness
• Probability of success
• Impact on employees
• Fit to strategy and competitive advantage
• Financial return, as measured by costs associated with quality and process performance, and impacts on revenues and market share

These must clearly be articulated in a "business case" that states the rationale for conducting the project.

Six Sigma projects should seek to improve either external performance that directly affects customers, such as improvements in product design, faster response or delivery, or other attributes of customer satisfaction; or internal measures of organizational effectiveness, such as reductions in defects and errors or improvements in productivity. Project ideas often result from analysis of customer complaints or satisfaction studies, or recognition of high costs or defect rates of internal processes.

Projects chosen should have a high likelihood of success. Considerable risk comes in choosing problems that can best be compared with "solving world hunger." At the outset of a Six Sigma initiative, it is beneficial to pick the "low-hanging fruit"—projects that are easy to accomplish, or even can be completed by a single individual in order to show early successes. This visible success helps to build momentum and support for future projects. Studies show that many projects are significantly over budget, behind schedule, or do not result in desired outcomes.[19] Thus, good project management, as we have discussed, is essential.

Six Sigma projects should fit within the capabilities of the people and teams that work on them. Many indirect benefits accrue. The training received as green or black belts improves employee and organizational knowledge, and participating in Six Sigma projects improves team and leadership skills. Six Sigma can motivate employees to innovate and improve their work environment, and ultimately their satisfaction on the job and personal self-esteem. Many projects offer opportunities to reduce frustration with inadequate work processes or to provide increased value to customers; these types of projects are certainly important candidates for selection.

Six Sigma projects should support the organization's vision and competitive strategy. Earlier, we stressed the importance of creating action plans that help an organization achieve its chosen strategies. At GE, for example, business goals work their way down the organization, helping employees to distinguish between projects that will not have a significant effect on business performance and those that do.[20]

Top managers, who provide the resources to implement Six Sigma projects, need to be convinced that the efforts are worthwhile. Measurements are vital in "selling" Six Sigma projects to top management. Some of the key benefits of Six Sigma as seen from the eyes of process owners are reductions in defects and errors, lower cycle times, improved customer satisfaction, or improved productivity. Unfortunately, quality problems expressed as the number of defects typically have little impact on Six Sigma champions who are held accountable for the financial returns of the projects. Thus, the benefits of Six Sigma need to be translated into the "language" of upper management—the language of money. The principal justification of Six Sigma projects should be made from a financial perspective using measures such as cost savings or increased revenues. However, non-financial benefits are also important because they often drive the financial measures of a firm. Thus, project selection should be based on measuring and understanding both the financial and non-financial benefits to the organization. Six Sigma methodology requires measuring and reporting performance goals, and using performance indicators to control and sustain improvements. A **cost of quality (COQ)** process often facilitates identifying opportunities and measuring results.

Cost of Quality

The concept of the cost of quality emerged in the 1950s. Traditionally, the reporting of quality-related costs had been limited to inspection and testing; other costs were accumulated in overhead accounts. As managers began to define and isolate the full range of quality-related costs, a number of surprising facts emerged.[21] First, quality-related costs were much larger than previously reported, generally in the range of 20 to 40 percent of sales. Second, quality-related costs were not only related to manufacturing operations, but to ancillary services such as purchasing and customer service departments as well. Third, most of the costs resulted from poor quality and were avoidable. Finally, while the costs of poor quality were avoidable, no clear responsibility for action to reduce them was assigned, nor was any structured approach formulated to do so. As a result, many companies began to develop cost of quality programs. The "costs of quality"—or more specifically, the costs of *poor* quality—are those costs associated with avoiding poor quality or those incurred as a result of poor quality.

Quality Cost Classification
Quality costs can be organized into four major categories: prevention costs, appraisal costs, internal failure costs, and external failure costs.

Prevention costs are investments made to keep nonconforming products from occurring and reaching the customer, including the following specific costs:

- *Quality planning costs*, such as salaries of individuals associated with quality planning and problem-solving teams, the development of new procedures, new equipment design, and reliability studies
- *Process control costs*, which include costs spent on analyzing production processes and implementing process control plans
- *Information systems costs* expended to develop data requirements and measurements
- *Training and general management costs*, including internal and external training programs, clerical staff expenses, and miscellaneous supplies

Appraisal costs are those associated with efforts to ensure conformance to requirements, generally through measurement and analysis of data to detect nonconformances. Categories of appraisal costs include the following:

- *Test and inspection costs* associated with incoming materials, work-in-process, and finished goods, including equipment costs and salaries
- *Instrument maintenance costs* due to calibration and repair of measuring instruments
- *Process measurement and control costs*, which involve the time spent by workers to gather and analyze quality measurements

Internal failure costs are incurred as a result of unsatisfactory quality found before the delivery of a product to the customer; some examples include the following:

- *Scrap and rework costs*, including material, labor, and overhead
- *Costs of corrective action*, arising from time spent determining the causes of failure and correcting production problems
- *Downgrading costs*, such as revenue lost when selling a product at a lower price because it does not meet specifications
- *Process failures*, such as unplanned machine downtime or unplanned equipment repair

External failure costs occur after poor-quality products reach the customer, specifically:

- *Costs due to customer complaints and returns*, including rework on returned items, cancelled orders, and freight premiums
- *Product recall costs* and *warranty claims*, including the cost of repair or replacement as well as associated administrative costs
- *Product liability costs*, resulting from legal actions and settlements

Experts estimate that 60 to 90 percent of total quality costs are the result of internal and external failure and are the responsibility of, but not easily controllable by, management. In the past, managers reacted to high failure costs by increasing inspection. Such actions, however, only increase appraisal costs. The overall result is little, if any, improvement in quality or profitability. In practice, an increase in prevention usually generates larger savings in all other cost

FIGURE 3.1 COST OF QUALITY MATRIX

	Design Engineering	Purchasing	Production	...	Finance	...	Accounting	Totals
Prevention costs Quality planning Training . . .								
Appraisal costs Test and inspection Instruments . . .								
Internal failure costs Scrap Rework . . .								
External failure costs Returns Recall costs . . .								
Totals								

categories. In a typical scenario, the cost of replacing a poor-quality component in the field might be $500; the cost of replacement after assembly might be $50; the cost of testing and replacement during assembly might be $5; but the cost of changing a component at the design phase to avoid the problem might be only 50 cents.

A convenient way of reporting quality costs to assist Six Sigma project selection is through a breakdown by organizational function as shown in Figure 3.1. This matrix helps to pinpoint areas of high quality cost and turns attention toward improvement efforts. Such a report can be implemented easily on a spreadsheet.

The nature of quality costs differs between service and manufacturing organizations. In manufacturing, quality costs are primarily product-oriented; for services, however, they are generally labor-dependent, with labor often accounting for up to 75 percent of total costs. Traditional external failure costs such as warranty and field support are less relevant to services than to manufacturing. Process-related costs, such as customer-service and complaint-handling staff and lost customers, are more critical. Internal failure costs might not be as evident in services as in manufacturing. For example, a small distributor focused a great deal of attention on minimizing inventories while trying to improve service. The company knew that back orders existed, but believed that they were simply the nature of the business. Further analysis revealed nearly one back order for every five orders. After examining the process, the cost of back orders was determined to be $30 per transaction, for an annual cost of $200,000. The reasons included suppliers not meeting delivery dates, errors in sales orders, and other non-value-added operations.[22] Internal failure costs tend to be much lower for service organizations with high customer contact, which have little opportunity to correct an error before it reaches the customer. By that time, the error becomes an external failure.

Work measurement and sampling techniques are often used to gather quality costs in service organizations. For example, work measurement can be used to determine how much time an employee spends on various quality-related activities. The proportion of time spent multiplied by the individual's salary represents an estimate of the quality cost for that activity. Consumer surveys and other means of customer feedback are also used to determine quality costs for services. In general, however, the intangible nature of the output makes quality cost accounting for services difficult.

Six Sigma can have a significant impact on the cost of quality because of its focus on financial return; in fact, one survey observed that the top three measures used to quantify Six Sigma success are cost reductions, productivity, and revenue generation.[23] Many Six Sigma projects focus on reducing the costs of poor quality that result from low sigma levels of performance, and improved designs that will increase customer satisfaction and, hence, revenue. The different categories of the cost of quality described earlier in this chapter provide many opportunities for Six Sigma projects. For example, a company might identify all costs that would vanish if sigma performance levels were increased. The list might include costs associated with credits given to customers because of late delivery, billing errors, scrap and rework, unplanned downtime, extra inventory to buffer against defects, errors in specifications and drawings, and accounts payable mistakes. Quantifying these costs establishes the justification for Six Sigma projects.

Pareto Analysis

Joseph Juran observed that a high proportion of quality issues resulted from only a few causes. He named this technique **Pareto analysis** after Vilfredo Pareto (1848–1923), an Italian economist who determined that 85 percent of the wealth in Milan was owned by only 15 percent of the people. For instance, in an analysis of 200 types of field failures of automotive engines, only five accounted for one-third of all failures; the top 25 accounted for two-thirds of the failures. Pareto analysis helps to identify the "vital few" from the "trivial many" and provides direction for selecting projects for improvement.

A **Pareto distribution** is one in which the characteristics observed are ordered from largest frequency to smallest. A **Pareto diagram** is a histogram of the data from the largest frequency to the smallest. Pareto analysis is often used to analyze data collected in check sheets. One may also draw a cumulative frequency curve on the histogram, as shown in Figure 3.2. Such a visual aid clearly shows the relative magnitude of defects and can be used to identify opportunities for improvement. The most costly or significant problems stand out. Pareto diagrams can also show the results of improvement programs over time. They are less intimidating to employees who are fearful of statistics. A good example of Pareto analysis is found at Rotor Clip Company, Inc., of Somerset, New Jersey, a major manufacturer of retaining rings and self-tightening hose clamps, and a believer in the use of simple quality improvement tools.[24] One application involved the use of a Pareto diagram to study rising premium freight charges for shipping retaining rings. The study covered three months in order to collect

FIGURE 3.2 PARETO DIAGRAM

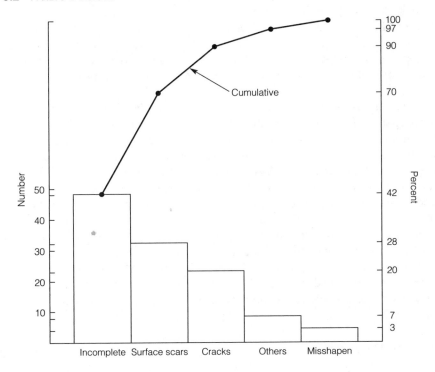

FIGURE 3.3 PARETO DIAGRAM OF CUSTOMER CALLS

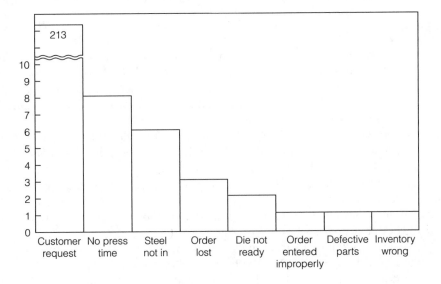

enough data to draw conclusions. The Pareto diagram is shown in Figure 3.3. The results were startling. The most frequent cause of higher freight charges was customer requests. The decision was made to continue the study to identify which customers consistently expedited their shipments and to work closely with them to find ways of reducing costs. The second largest contributor was the lack of available machine time. Once a die was installed in a stamping press, it ran until it produced the maximum number of parts (usually a million) before it was removed for routine maintenance. Although this policy resulted in efficient utilization of tooling, it tied up the press and ultimately accounted for rush shipments. The policy was revised to limit die runs to fill orders more efficiently.

Pareto analysis can easily be applied to cost of quality data. If we rank internal failure costs from largest to smallest, for example, chances are that 70 or 80 percent of all internal failure costs are due to only one or two manufacturing problems. Identifying these "vital few," as they are called, pinpoints Six Sigma project opportunities with high returns for low investments. In this fashion, quality costs can be used to identify trends or areas that require significant attention. For example, a steady rise in internal failure costs and decline in appraisal costs might indicate a problem in assembly, testing equipment maintenance, or a lack of proper control of purchased parts. Of course, such information can only signal areas for improvement; it cannot tell managers what the specific problems are.

Pareto diagrams help analysts to progressively focus in on specific problems. Figure 3.4 shows one example. At each step, the Pareto diagram stratifies the data to more detailed levels (or it may require additional data collection), eventually isolating the most significant issues.

Process Definition

Poor performance is often a symptom of a design or operations flaw in a process. One approach for identifying good Six Sigma projects is to find work processes having poor performance and analyze them. Such an approach can be described as follows:[25]

1. Define the process: its start, end, and what it does. This is often accomplished by a high-level process map using a "SIPOC" diagram. This is simply a flowchart showing the suppliers, inputs, processes, outputs, and customers that define the boundaries of the process. Note that suppliers and customers might be internal to the organization.
2. Describe the process: list the key tasks performed and sequence of steps, people involved, equipment used, environmental conditions, work methods, and materials used.
3. Describe the players: external and internal customers and suppliers, and process operators.
4. Define customer expectations: what the customer wants, when, and where, for both external and internal customers.
5. Determine what historical data are available on process performance, or what data need to be collected to better understand the process.
6. Describe the perceived problems associated with the process; for instance, failure to meet customer expectations, excessive variation, long cycle times, and so on.

We will discuss more about process analysis in Chapter 5, as it is a significant part of the Analyze phase of DMAIC.

FIGURE 3.4 USE OF PARETO DIAGRAMS FOR PROGRESSIVE ANALYSIS

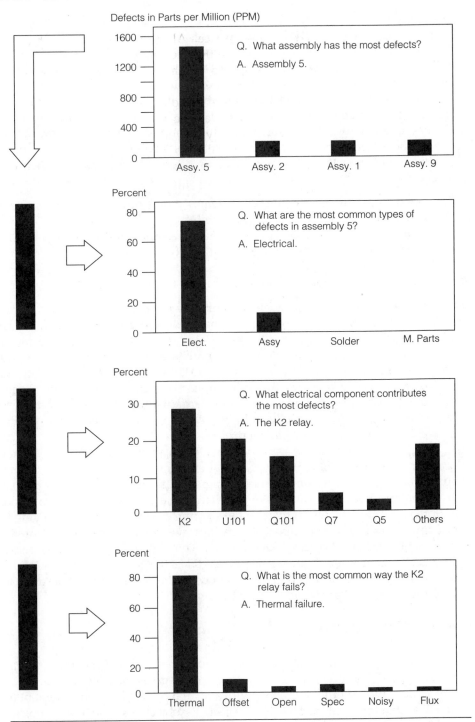

Source: Small Business Guidebook to Quality Management, Office of the Secretary of Defense, Quality Management Office, Washington, D.C.

Models for Project Selection

Most organizations probably have more opportunities for Six Sigma projects than available resources to do them. In many cases, project selection is often political in nature. Senior executives who champion Six Sigma projects might exercise political influence to get their pet projects recognized and accepted. However, taking a more objective viewpoint is more effective. Prioritizing and selecting projects using some rational criteria can contribute to greater effectiveness. Project steering committees that include at least a portion of the organization's senior leadership often guide these decisions. This group can act as a filter for the voices of both the external and internal customers in evaluating and prioritizing projects.

Six Sigma projects can be categorized in different levels, based on their impact on results:[26]

1. Level 1 projects directly affect an organization's profit margin (projects have a clear, hard dollar impact on profitability).
2. Level 2 projects result in redeployment of resources inside an organization to increase operating efficiency or productivity.
3. Level 3 projects directly affect operations by avoiding expenditures or increasing the chances of obtaining higher future revenues.

One of the pitfalls experienced in organizations new to Six Sigma is a lack of ability of senior managers to estimate what the resources they allocate (or fail to allocate) to Six Sigma projects will "buy" in the way of bottom-line returns. Thus, it becomes important to be able to differentiate between, and to estimate fairly accurately, the differences in resources required to bring a $250,000 project versus a $50,000 project to a successful conclusion. Six Sigma projects should lead to improved customer satisfaction and organizational performance. Such improvements can lead directly to higher sales or market share, thus providing financial justification for selecting a project.

Simple scoring models may be used to evaluate and prioritize potential projects. An example of a project selection matrix is shown in Figure 3.5. The top box shows the customer importance ratings on a set of key CTQs using the scale at the bottom left. The numbers in the main table are based on the scale on the bottom right, and are determined by the steering committee. By multiplying these rankings by the customer importance ratings, we can arrive at a total score in the right-hand column (Project ranking metric). The higher the number, the more the project affects customer issues. This process takes the guesswork and opinions out of the project selection process and focuses on the important issues to the customer and the organization.

PROJECT DEFINITION

A Six Sigma project can be defined as "a problem scheduled for solution that has a set of metrics that can be used to set project goals and monitor progress."[27] Project definition should culminate with a formal project mission statement (often called a **charter**) that defines the project, its objectives, and deliverables. The charter represents a contract between the project team and the sponsor. Six Sigma project charters should clearly define the problem to be addressed, the (internal or

FIGURE 3.5 EXAMPLE OF A PROJECT SELECTION MATRIX

Customer Issues	Missing parts ordered	Late delivery	Damaged orders	Wrong orders	More parts than ordered	On hold too long
Customer importance	8	5	7	10	3	3

Project	Project ranking based on correlation to customer issues						Project ranking metric
Order fill process flow optimization	5	8	3	3	5	0	146
Replenishment cycle time reduction project	5	8	5	0	0	0	115
Customer service feedback reporting	5	3	3	8	0	5	171
Delivery vendor certification	0	10	8	0	0	0	106
IT upgrade process integration	7	5	0	8	8	3	194

Customer importance	Relationship to customer importance
0	Not important
3	Slightly important
5	Important
8	Very important
10	Critical

Project rank	Relationship to customer issue
0	No correlation
3	Very little correlation
5	Some correlation
8	High correlation
10	Complete correlation

Source: William Michael Kelly, "Three Steps to Project Selection," Six Sigma Forum Magazine 2, no. 1 (November 2002), 29–32. © 2002. American Society for Quality. Reprinted with permission.

external) customer requirements on which the project focuses, existing measures and performance benchmarks, the expected benefits of the project in terms of performance measures and financial justification, a project timeline, and the resources and data needed to carry out the project.

Two important parts of a project definition are a high level map of the process and a clear identification and validation of customer requirements.

High Level Process Maps: SIPOC

A high-level process map defines the boundaries of the Six Sigma project by identifying the process being investigated, its inputs, and outputs, and its suppliers and customers. An example of a SIPOC process map—a block diagram or flowchart—deriving from "Suppliers, Inputs, Process, Outputs, and Customers," is shown in Figure 3.6. SIPOC maps provide a broad overview of the key elements in the process and help to explain who is the process owner, how inputs are acquired, who the process serves, and how it adds value. Inputs are goods and services required by a process to generate its outputs. Outputs may be physical items, documentation, electronic information, and so on. Inputs are provided by suppliers, who may be external or internal to the organization (suppliers may also be customers, for example, in a product design process). Customers are the people, departments, or organizations that receive outputs, and which also can be external or internal to the organizations. Different outputs may have different customers. Customer requirements (see next section) are often added to the diagram (and then called SIPOCR).

FIGURE 3.6 GENERAL STRUCTURE OF A SIPOC PROCESS MAP

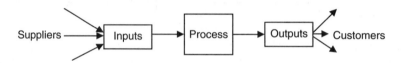

It is usually best to start with the process and identify the major activities that occur in the process working backward toward suppliers and forward toward the customers (more detailed process maps will be developed in subsequent steps of the DMAIC process). Some experts suggest that SIPOC maps have no more than six or seven major activities. A simple example is shown in Figure 3.7 for a typical automobile manufacturing process.

FIGURE 3.7 SIMPLE SIPOC PROCESS MAP

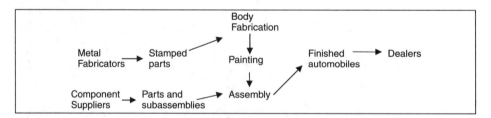

Identifying Customer CTQs

Many characteristics of products and services are "critical to quality" (CTQ) from customers' perspectives. As one example, credit card users might have the following expectations for four key business activities associated with the card:

1. *Applying for an account:* Accessible, responsive, accurate, and professional
2. *Using the card:* Easy to use and hassle-free, features, credit limit
3. *Billing:* Accurate, timely, easy to understand
4. *Customer service:* Accessible, responsive, and professional

Product characteristics can generally be classified as:[28]

1. *Performance:* A product's primary operating characteristics. Using an automobile as an example, characteristics would include such things as acceleration, braking distance, steering, and handling.
2. *Features:* The "bells and whistles" of a product. A car may have power options, a tape or CD deck, antilock brakes, and power seats.
3. *Reliability:* The probability of a product's surviving over a specified period of time under stated conditions of use. A car's ability to start on cold days and frequency of failures are reliability factors.
4. *Conformance:* The degree to which physical and performance characteristics of a product match pre-established standards. A car's fit and finish and freedom from noises and squeaks can reflect this dimension.
5. *Durability:* The amount of use one gets from a product before it physically deteriorates or until replacement is preferable. For a car it might include corrosion resistance and the long wear of upholstery fabric.
6. *Serviceability:* The speed, courtesy, and competence of repair work. An automobile owner might be concerned with access to spare parts, the number of miles between major maintenance services, and the expense of service.
7. *Aesthetics:* How a product looks, feels, sounds, tastes, or smells. A car's color, instrument panel design, control placement, and "feel of the road," for example, may make it aesthetically pleasing.

For services, research shows that five key dimensions of service quality contribute to customer perceptions:

1. *Reliability:* The ability to provide what was promised, dependably and accurately. Examples include customer service representatives responding in the promised time, following customer instructions, providing error-free invoices and statements, and making repairs correctly the first time.
2. *Assurance:* The knowledge and courtesy of employees, and their ability to convey trust and confidence. Examples include the ability to answer questions, having the capabilities to do the necessary work, monitoring credit card transactions to avoid possible fraud, and being polite and pleasant during customer transactions.
3. *Tangibles:* The physical facilities and equipment, and the appearance of personnel. Tangibles include attractive facilities, appropriately dressed employees, and well-designed forms that are easy to read and interpret.
4. *Empathy:* The degree of caring and individual attention provided to customers. Some examples might be the willingness to schedule deliveries at the customer's convenience, explaining technical jargon in a layperson's language, and recognizing regular customers by name.
5. *Responsiveness:* The willingness to help customers and provide prompt service. Examples include acting quickly to resolve problems, promptly crediting returned merchandise, and rapidly replacing defective products.

CTQs may be classified into three categories, as suggested by a Japanese professor, Noriaki Kano:

1. *Dissatisfiers:* Requirements that are expected in a product or service. In an automobile, a radio, heater, and required safety features are examples, which are generally not stated by customers but assumed as given. If these features are not present, the customer is dissatisfied.
2. *Satisfiers:* Requirements that customers say they want. Many car buyers want a sunroof, power windows, or antilock brakes. Although these requirements are generally not expected, fulfilling them creates satisfaction.
3. *Exciters/delighters:* New or innovative features that customers do not expect. The presence of unexpected features, such as a weather channel button on the radio or separate rear-seat audio controls that allow children to listen to different music than their parents, leads to high perceptions of quality.

Meeting customer expectations (that is, providing satisfiers) is often considered the minimum required to stay in business. To be truly competitive, companies must surprise and delight customers by going beyond the expected. In the Kano classification system, dissatisfiers and satisfiers are relatively easy to determine through routine marketing research. However, traditional market research efforts may not be effective in understanding exciters/delighters, and may even backfire. For example, Ford listened to a sample of customers and asked whether they wanted a fourth door on the Windstar minivan. Only about one-third thought it was a great idea, so Ford scrapped the idea.

Chrysler, on the other hand, spent a lot more time living with owners of vans and observing their behavior, watching them wrestle to get things in and out, noting all the occasions where a fourth door would really be convenient, and was very successful after introducing a fourth door.[29] Thus, a company must make special effort to identify exciters/delighters.

Understanding customer CTQs helps to select meaningful Six Sigma projects. Identifying CTQs requires understanding the **voice of the customer**, which are customer requirements as expressed in the customer's own terms. Some of the key approaches to gathering customer information include the following:

-   Comment cards and formal surveys
-   Focus groups
-   Direct customer contact
-   Field intelligence
-   Complaint analysis
-   Internet monitoring

Formal customer satisfaction surveys and measurements allow a business to discover customer perceptions of how well the business is doing in meeting customer needs, and identify causes of dissatisfaction and failed expectations as well as drivers of delight; discover areas for improvement in the design and delivery of products and services; and track trends to determine whether changes actually result in improvements, thus validating Six Sigma initiatives.

Customer satisfaction measures may include product attributes such as product quality, product performance, usability, and maintainability; service attributes such as attitude, service time, on-time delivery, exception handling, accountability, and technical support; image attributes such as reliability and price; and overall satisfaction measures.

FIGURE 3.8   PERFORMANCE-IMPORTANCE COMPARISON

	Performance	
Importance	Low	High
Low	Who cares?	Overkill
High	Vulnerable	Strengths

One way to ensure that measurement is appropriate is to collect information on both the importance and the performance of key CTQ characteristics. For example, a hotel might ask how important check-in speed, check-out speed, staff attitude, and so on, are, as well as how the customer rates the hotel on these attributes. Evaluation of such data can be accomplished using a grid similar to the one shown in Figure 3.8, on which mean performance and importance scores for individual attributes are plotted.[30]

Results in the diagonal quadrants (the shaded areas) are good. A firm ideally wants high performance on important characteristics and not to waste resources on characteristics of low importance. Results off the diagonal indicate that the firm either is wasting resources to achieve high performance on unimportant customer attributes (overkill), or is not performing acceptably on important customer attributes, leaving the firm vulnerable to competition. The results of such an analysis can help target areas for improvement and cost savings, as well as provide useful input for strategic planning. Often, competitor data are also plotted, providing a comparison against the competition.

PROJECT REVIEW—DEFINE PHASE

A project review of the Define phase should ensure that

- The team has reached agreement on and has clearly defined the problem or opportunity to address.
- The project charter is developed and agreed on.
- The team understands the strategic and financial impact of the project.
- The team agrees that the project can be completed successfully.
- A project plan and timeline have been developed to guide the entire Six Sigma project.
- The right mix of people are on the team.
- Key stakeholders outside of the team have been identified.
- All team members have consistent expectations.
- Team members have received any necessary "just-in-time" training.
- Appropriate resources—financial and human—have been committed to conduct the project.
- The voice of the customer and CTQs are fully understood and documented
- The team has developed a high-level process map to define the boundaries of the project and identify relationships between suppliers, inputs, processes, outputs, and customers.
- Key performance measures have been identified for measuring success of the project.

CASE STUDY

Defining the "Not Found" Project at Fidelity Investments[31]

Fidelity Investments is an international provider of financial services and investment resources that strives to help individuals and institutions meet their financial objectives.[32] Fidelity employs over 29,000 people in its Boston head-quarters and eight regional operations centers and manages over $1 trillion in assets. It is the largest mutual fund company in the United States, and the largest provider of 401(k) retirement savings plans.

The Fidelity Wide Process (FWP) Image Capture Services department in Covington, Kentucky, provides document scanning, data capture, and data transmission to business partner information systems, inside and outside the company. Employee Services group is an internal customer of the Image Capture group and handles all transactions with Fidelity's external customers—companies that provide pension and other financial services for their employees through Fidelity.

Within the Image Capture process, exceptions, or rejects, sometimes occur. When images are captured by an optical scanning process, certain codes or fields on a page that were expected to be "found" by the scanner software may be missing or incorrect for a variety of reasons. These could be codes that were not filled in, filled in incorrectly, or don't match with other data in the system. These are termed *Not Found (NF)* rejects. Rejected forms must then be corrected and reprocessed through the scanners, which is inefficient. From January to September 2003, NF rejects were 0.319 percent of all Employee Services' business volume. A Six Sigma project was approved to study two measures—volume of NFs and the cycle time required to find and correct rejects, with a goal of reducing NF quantities by 50 percent.

Defining the project required some effort to familiarize the team members with all of the aspects of the system and why NF error transactions occur. Members of the NF development team explained that an NF is created when the combination of indices that include client code, product code, plan number, and social security number (SSN), fails to be validated. Data used for validation can be collected by two methods—manual or auto index sheets. Manual index sheets hold all the validation data while auto index sheets have a "4CC barcode" that signals the scanner to look up the validation data already in the computer for the transaction. On some forms, a 4CC barcode is printed on the form to reduce space and allow for updates in the central computer system. Adding 4CC barcodes is not centralized, so many people within Employee Services add these barcodes to forms. Although several quality checks, procedures, and checklists are used, significant growth and more advanced features of the image technology have created the need to enhance current procedures, checklists, etc.

The data entry process involves moving documents through three departments within the organization: Employees Services Prep group, Image Capture group, and Transaction Process group (TPG). The Employee Services Prep group prepares the material for scanning by sorting the material into segments and categorizing them into transaction types (New Account, Beneficiary, Return from Post Office, etc.).

FIGURE 3.9 INITIAL PROCESS

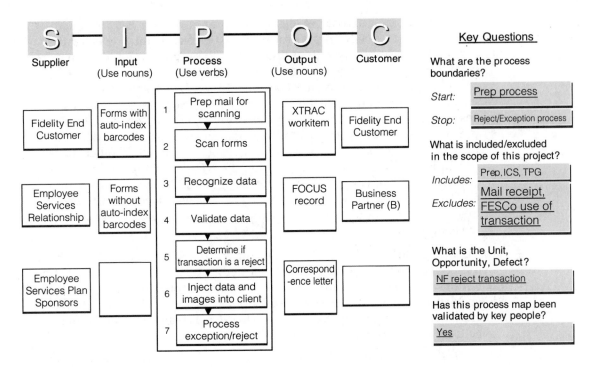

Image Capture then scans them and the TPG must find and correct any rejects for all business partners. Employee Services has at least five major customer segments that experience some NF rejects.

The subprocess in the TPG requires creating a reject worksheet and identifying the proper group to rework and reenter the material in the process. TPG then transmits the transactions back to Employee Services Prep. The total current process was mapped using a standard SIPOC (Supplier-Input-Process-Output-Customer) diagram, shown in Figure 3.9.

The project team was organized and included eight representatives from several groups including Employee Services Prep (one of several subject matter experts, or SMEs), TPG, Quality Control (Quality), Systems Development, and a Technical lead/project manager/Six Sigma analyst.

The project team members and the roles they played in the project were:

- Image Capture and TPG director (*Champion*)
- Quality director/Six Sigma black belt (*Sponsor*)
- The manager who oversaw several Employee Services Prep groups and Employee Services scanning/ICS (*SME: Input process owner*)
- A mid-level manager of an Employee Services Prep group (*SME*)
- Reject process owner and manager of the reject process that includes NF rejects (*SME*); forms development manager (*SME*)
- Quality manager (*Six Sigma green belt*)
- A project manager in training as green belt (*Technical lead*).

The project team identified its mission and scope of the project (paraphrased) as:

Our specific goal is to reduce the volume of Employee Services documents that are routed to the NF reject process by 50 percent, thereby reducing the cost and processing cycle time. Internal process failure metrics include labor costs and missing service delivery customer targets. NF rejects required rework amounting to 2,000 hours for 2002. In-scope activities will include examination of all NF data for all 5 major Employee Services customer segments, reviewing labor performed, and reviewing activities previously taken to reduce NF volumes. Out-of-scope areas include: Non-FWP NF transactions (created in other divisions) in NF totals; other types of Employee Services rejects (not within the NF definition); and business partner (BP) reviewing cycle time. The budget was 288 man-hours across 6 FTE (full-time equivalent) resources over 12 calendar weeks. On average, this equates to 4 hours/wk per resource. The time needed peaks during the analysis phase.

Using the SIPOC, Voice of the Customer (VOC) surveys, and a critical-to-quality (CTQ) tree, two CTQs were identified. A CTQ tree is simply a listing of quality factors that are important to the customer, from the highest level to the lowest level of detail. High-level CTQ factors at the top of the tree determine the overall performance of the process, where low-level factors, further down the tree, affect only a small part of the process. The CTQs were:

1. *NF Rejects Percentage.* Rejects are identified when a combination of indices fails to result in a valid product code. The indices are used to direct the transaction to the correct destination and must all be correctly entered.
2. *Reject process cycle time.* Cycle time is defined as minutes from when a transaction enters the NF queue to when the reworked transaction with the correct indices is directed to the correct destination.

During the CTQ discussions, the team first focused on eliminating the NF rejects. However, they were unsure if this objective was feasible. Because of the low level of rejects, the team hypothesized that cost-benefit analysis might show that permitting the current reject level to continue could be cheaper than the activity needed to eliminate it. This led to discussion and adoption of the reject process cycle time CTQ. If the team cannot eliminate NF volumes, they should then focus on timely resolution. The CTQ tree helped the project team focus from requirement generalities to specific measurable requirements.

Once the project was clearly defined, the team focused on the remaining steps of the DMAIC process. The year-to-date NF rejects and Employee Services' total document-processed volumes were measured to allow the project team to understand the relationship between them. The data showed that NF rejects were a small percentage of total volume (< 0.4 percent). However, the analysis revealed that although the NF percentages were declining, there was not a direct relationship between Employee Services total and NF volume.

The project team, along with members from the original NF development team, brainstormed ideas to understand the possible causes of NF rejects, using a cause-effect (fishbone) diagram, shown in Figure 3.10 (see Chapter 5 for more details). The team believed that the most likely reasons for the NF rejects were

FIGURE 3.10 POSSIBLE CAUSES FOR NF REJECTS

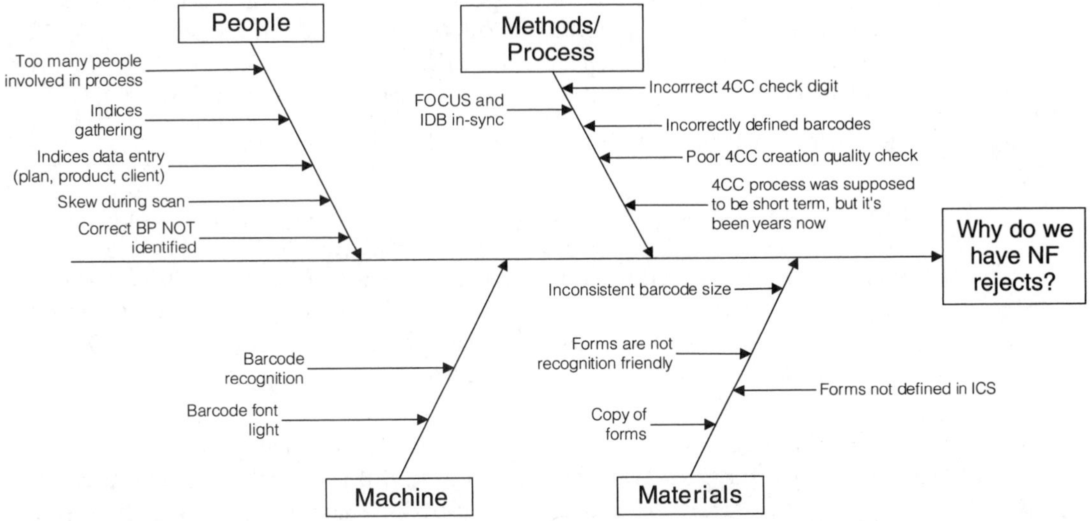

Materials (forms not defined or recognition-friendly) and Methods (defining and checking barcodes) are thought to be the root issues. Additional sampling and data analysis are needed.

1. Forms not defined or recognition friendly
2. Incorrect definition and poor quality check of barcodes

These hypotheses were analyzed using data from production samples:

Cause	Supporting Data
Forms that are not easily recognized by the scanner failed to correctly look up Employee Services data in the system more often than easily recognized forms.	Sample—100 percent failed when an auto index sheet was used and the 4CC barcode was not recognized.
If the 4CC barcode was not installed during the preproduction phase in Prep, an NF was created.	Sample—100 percent failed when an auto index sheet was used and the 4CC barcode was not set up in production.

It was found that a NF failure was certain to occur when an auto index sheet was used and the 4CC barcode was not recognized, because it had not been set up in preproduction. Most of the failures occurred from one scanner and most occurred on the Beneficiary forms (Bene's). None of the returned by post office forms (RPO) were NF defects.

The team developed a list of proposed improvements based on their analysis. The team recommended reducing the volume of NFs by taking the following steps.

1. Make Bene forms easier for the scanner to recognize. Replace Bene forms with the new Integrated Bene that use "landmarks" and "field recognition" instead of the older 4CC barcodes.

2. Perform scanner maintenance at the beginning of each shift.
3. Request that the originating departments verify and install correct 4CC barcodes during the pre-production phase in the Employee Services Prep, update the new/revised form checklist (so that the proper form is used), and add control steps to ensure that the checklist is being followed.

To reduce the resolution cycle time the team also recommended:

Move the resolution process before client identification. This could be accomplished by enhancing use of the Process from Image (PFI) process, which allows a scanned image to be prepared and corrected, allowing the FWP (human) operators to resolve problems without having to re-prepare, rescan, and reprocess physical documents. Enhancing the PFI process to easily resolve NFs would require:

a. Expansion beyond the currently supported customer segments
b. Ability to change a 4CC barcode, so that, if it is not read, the operator could type it, or perform a "manual" look-up of a correct index in the computer system.
c. Permit the operator to manually change the client code, because some plans can have more than one client.

As of the time of this case, these measures were being tested for full implementation.

REVIEW QUESTIONS

1. Explain the importance of projects and project management in Six Sigma. What stages does a typical project go through during its life cycle?
2. What are the four factors involved in all project management decisions?
3. Explain the steps of the project-planning process.
4. What are the elements of a typical project control system?
5. What is a *team*? What are the characteristics of the different types of individuals that make up Six Sigma teams?
6. What are the essential people skills needed by project managers and team members?
7. Discuss the five key stages that teams typically go through during their life cycle.
8. What are Peter Scholtes's ten ingredients for a successful team?
9. Why do messes arise in organizations? How can the DMAIC process help to untangle messes?
10. What is Kepner and Tregoe's definition of a problem? How does this definition apply to quality issues? Provide some examples.
11. List and explain the five categories into which all quality problem solving can be classified.
12. What factors should be considered when selecting Six Sigma projects?
13. Why are cost of quality programs valuable to managers?

14. List and explain the four major categories of quality costs. Give examples of each.
15. How do quality costs differ between service and manufacturing organizations?
16. Explain the difference between a histogram and a Pareto diagram. Do they apply to the same types of data?
17. What are the levels into which Six Sigma projects can be categorized?
18. How does a Six Sigma project differ from a traditional project? What should be included in the Six Sigma project charter?
19. What is a SIPOC diagram? How is it used in the Six Sigma Define phase?
20. What are the categories of critical-to-quality characteristics?
21. Define the "voice of the customer." What are some of the key approaches to gathering customer information?

DISCUSSION QUESTIONS

1. What can an organization do about individuals who "aren't good with numbers" if they have a policy that they become green belts, and later, black belts, as a prerequisite for promotion to higher levels of management?
2. Discuss what the different categories of quality costs might mean to your college and university? How can they be measured?
3. Many quality experts like Joseph Juran and Philip Crosby advocate cost-of-quality evaluations. Deming, however, states that "the most important figures are unknown and unknowable." How can these conflicting opinions be resolved?
4. How does the adoption of a Six Sigma approach within an organization change the amount and types of data that may be gathered routinely, as well as for specific projects?
5. For services, how do the eight quality dimensions defined by David Garvin relate to the five dimensions of reliability, assurance, tangibles, empathy, and responsiveness identified by other researchers? Do they all fit into one of these categories?
6. Which of the five key dimensions of service quality—reliability, assurance, tangibles, empathy, or responsiveness—would the following items from a retail banking customer survey address?
   a. Following through on promises
   b. Offering convenient banking hours
   c. Providing prompt customer service
   d. Properly handling any problems that arise
   e. Maintaining clean and pleasant branch office facilities
   f. Demonstrating knowledge of bank products and services
   g. Giving undivided attention to the customer
   h. Never being too busy to respond to customer requests
   i. Charging reasonable service fees
   j. Maintaining a professional appearance
   k. Providing error-free bank statements
   l. Keeping customer transactions confidential

7. Give several examples of dissatisfiers, satisfiers, and exciters/delighters in products or services that you have recently purchased. Why did you classify them into these categories?

8. Consider the following customer expectations for a fast-food (quick-service) restaurant. Would you classify them as dissatisfiers, satisfiers, and exciters/delighters?
    a. Special prices on certain days
    b. Food is safe to eat
    c. Hot food is served hot
    d. Service is friendly
    e. Background music
    f. Playland for children
    g. Restaurant is clean inside
    h. Food is fresh
    i. A "one-bite" money-back guarantee
    j. Orders can be phoned in for pickup at a separate window

9. For the Fidelity Investments case study, discuss the following questions:
    a. At what Sigma level was the NF process before the project began?
    b. Why was this not adequate for this type of process?
    c. What conclusions can you reach on the importance of team member selection to the Define stage, and eventual success of Six Sigma projects, such as the Fidelity project?
    d. How do the roles of the Fidelity team members, described in the case, match or not match the roles in Table 3.2 (the Project Lifecycle Accountability Matrix) in the chapter? Why do you think that they differ?
    e. How easy or difficult might it be to implement the suggestions for improvement?

THINGS TO DO

1. Investigate the extent of team participation at some local companies. What kinds of teams do you find? Do managers believe these teams are effective?

2. Find a small- to medium-size company that is using Six Sigma teams. Where have they changed the GE/Motorola model in the way that they train and use team leaders and resource people (green, black, and master black belts). Are they using those roles for management development purposes?

3. Identify an important problem around your school or in some related function, such as a student organization, and define a suitable Six Sigma project. Write a project charter and identify the important CTQs.

4. Develop a SIPOC for some process around your college, for example, admissions, registration, instruction, and so on. Use these to describe possible project charters for Six Sigma projects.

PROBLEMS

1. Compute a sales dollar base index for Midwest Sales, Inc. to analyze the quality cost data in worksheet *Prob.3-1* in the Excel workbook *Ch3Dataset* on the student CD-ROM and prepare a memo to management.

2. Analyze the cost data in the worksheet *Prob.3-2* in the Excel workbook *Ch3Dataset* on the student CD-ROM. What are the implications of these data for management?

3. Compute a labor cost base index for Miami Valley Steel Co. from data in the worksheet *Prob.3-3* in the Excel workbook *Ch3Dataset* on the student CD-ROM, and prepare a memo to management.

4. Jeans Are Us, Inc. has a distribution center in Cincinnati where it receives and breaks down bulk orders from suppliers' factories, and ships out products to retail customers. Prepare a graph or chart showing the different quality cost categories and percentages for the company's quality costs that were incurred over the past year (use data in the worksheet *Prob.3-4* in the Excel workbook *Ch3Dataset* on the student CD-ROM).

5. Use Pareto analysis to investigate the quality losses at Oakton Paper Mill, using data in the worksheet *Prob.3-5* in the Excel workbook *Ch3Dataset* on the student CD-ROM. What conclusions do you reach?

6. Use Pareto analysis to investigate the quality losses at Beecom Software Corp. using data in the worksheet *Prob.3-6* in the Excel workbook *Ch3Dataset* on the student CD-ROM. What conclusions do you reach?

7. National Computer Repairs, Inc. has a thriving business repairing and upgrading computers. The data in the worksheet *Prob.3-7* in the Excel workbook *Ch3Dataset* on the student CD-ROM represent costs of quality that they have collected over the past year. Use Pareto analysis to investigate their quality losses and to suggest which areas they should address first in an effort to improve their quality.

8. Legal Sea Foods operates several restaurants and fish markets in the Boston area and other East Coast locations. The company's standards of excellence mandate that it serves only the freshest, highest-quality seafood. It guarantees the quality by buying only the "top of the catch" fish daily. Although Legal Sea Foods tries to make available the widest variety every day, certain species of fish are subject to migratory patterns and are not always present in New England waters. Weather conditions may also prevent local fishermen from fishing in certain areas. Freshly caught fish are rushed to the company's quality control center where they are cut and filleted in an environmentally controlled state-of-the-art facility. All shellfish come from government-certified beds and are tested in an in-house microbiology laboratory for wholesomeness and purity. There are even special lobster storage tanks so that all lobsters are held under optimum conditions, in clean, pollution-free water. Every seafood item is inspected for quality eight separate times before it reaches the table. At Legal Sea Foods' restaurants, each meal is cooked to order. Even though servers make every effort to deliver all meals within

minutes of each other, they will not jeopardize the quality of an item by holding it beneath a heat lamp until the entire order is ready. The service staff is trained to work as a team for better service. More than one service person frequently delivers food to a table. When any item is ready, the closest available person serves it. Customer questions can be directed to any employee, not just the person who took the initial order.

a. Draw a high-level SIPOC map of this process.

b. Suggest a set of CTQ's for Legal Sea Food customers.

ENDNOTES

1. Paula K. Martin and Karen Tate, "Projects That Get Quality Treatment," *The Journal for Quality and Participation*, November/December 1998, 58–61.
2. H. James Harrington, "Creating Organizational Excellence—Part Two," *Quality Digest*, February 2003, 14.
3. Timothy J. Kloppenborg and Joseph A. Petrick, *Managing Project Quality* (Vienna, VA: Management Concepts, 2003), 9, 11.
4. Jon R. Katzenback and Douglas K. Smith, "The Discipline of Teams," *Harvard Business Review* March/April 1993, 111–120.
5. Nancy Page Cooper and Pat Noonan. "Do Teams and Six Sigma Go Together?" *Quality Progress* 36, no. 6, June 2003, 26–27.
6. James P. Lewis, *Team-Based Project Management* (New York: Amacom, 1998).
7. Peter R. Scholtes, *The Team Handbook*, 3rd ed. (Madison, WI: Oriel, 2003), 4-2–4-5. Used with permission.
8. Scholtes) 4–5. Used with permission.
9. Andre L. Delbecq, Andre H. Van de Ven, and David H. Gustafson, *Group Techniques for Program Planning* (Glenview, IL: Scott Foresman, 1975).
10. John E. Bauer, Grace L. Duffy, and Russell T. Westcott (eds.), *The Quality Improvement Handbook* (Milwaukee, WI: ASQ Quality Press, 2002), 108–109. © 2002 American Society for Quality. Reprinted with permission.
11. Harvey A. Robbins and Michael Finley, *Why Teams Don't Work: What Went Wrong and How to Make It Right* (Princeton, NJ: Peterson's/Pacesetter Books, 1995), 14–15.
12. Samuel C. Certo, *Modern Management*, 9th ed. (Upper Saddle River, NJ: Prentice Hall, 2003), 389.
13. George Eckes, *The Six Sigma Revolution* (New York: John Wiley & Sons, 2001), 251–254.
14. Peter R. Scholtes et al., *The Team Handbook: How to Use Teams to Improve Quality* (Madison, WI: Joiner Associates, 1988) 6-10–6-22. Used with permission.
15. Russell Ackoff, "Beyond Problem Solving," presented at the Fifth Annual Meeting of the American Institute for Decision Sciences (now the Decision Sciences Institute), Boston, November 16, 1973.
16. Gerald F. Smith, "Too Many Types of Quality Problems," *Quality Progress*, April 2000, 43–49.
17. Charles H. Kepner and Benjamin B. Tregoe, *The Rational Manager* (New York: McGraw-Hill, 1965).
18. Donald P. Lynch, Suzanne Bertolino, and Elaine Cloutier, "How to Scope DMAIC Projects," *Quality Progress* 36, no. 1, January, 2003, 37–44.
19. Jeffrey K. Pinto, "The Power of Project Management," *Industry Week*, August 18, 1997, 138–140.
20. "Six Sigma at GE-Lunar, Manufacturing and Technology Matters," Erdman Center for Manufacturing and Technology Management, University of Wisconsin-Madison School of Business, Fall/Winter 2002, 1–3.
21. Frank M. Gryna, "Quality Costs," in *Juran's Quality Control Handbook*, 4th ed. (New York: McGraw-Hill, 1988).
22. ASQ Quality Costs Committee, "Profiting from Quality in the Service Arena," *Quality Progress*, May 1999, 81–84.
23. Brian Swayne and Brent Harder, "Where Has All the Magic Gone?" *Six Sigma Forum Magazine* 2, no. 3, May 2003, 22–32.

24. Adapted from Bruce Rudin, "Simple Tools Solve Complex Problems." Reprinted with permission from *Quality magazine*, April 1990, 50–51.

25. Adapted from *Small Business Guidebook to Quality Management*, Office of the Secretary of Defense, Quality Management Office, Washington, DC, 1998.

26. George Byrne and Bob Norris, "Drive Baldrige Level Performance," *Six Sigma Forum Magazine* 2, no. 3, May 2003, 13–21.

27. R. D. Snee, "Frontiers of Quality: Dealing with the Achilles' Heel of Six Sigma Initiatives, *Quality Progress*, 34, no. 3, 66–72.

28. David A. Garvin, "What Does Product Quality Really Mean?" *Sloan Management Review* 26, no. 1, 1984, 25–43.

29. "Getting an Edge," *Across the Board*, February 2000, 43–48.

30. Importance-performance analysis was first introduced by J. A. Martilla and J. C. James, "Importance-Performance Analysis," *Journal of Marketing*, 41, 1977, 77–79.

31. Appreciation is expressed to one of the author's students, Troy Bitter, a Fidelity project manager, who wrote the paper on which this case is based, as part of the requirements for MGT 650, Advanced Project Management, 2003, at Northern Kentucky University. Our thanks also go to Doug Suttton, president of FWP and Linda Nourse, quality director at FWP, who provided access and support for student Six Sigma projects at Fidelity's Covington, Kentucky, mail processing facility.

32. Adapted from http://personal.fidelity.com/myfidelity/InsideFidelity/index.html.

CHAPTER

Process Measurement

The second step in the DMAIC process is *Measure*, which focuses on understanding the current performance of the process selected for improvement, and collecting any necessary data needed for analysis. It also includes assessment of the measurement system to ensure validity of measurements and evaluating the capability of the process being studied.

Measurement should be addressed early in planning a Six Sigma project, as suggested in the Project Life Cycle Accountability Matrix in Table 3.2. Identifying the right metrics early and planning how data will be collected will help to avoid costly and time-consuming errors once the actual data collection begins. Note that the role of a master black belt is to "assist in identifying data collection and analysis needs, provide training resources, and assure that processes are technically sound" in support of the project manager. Data gathering should only begin after CTQ characteristics have been clearly identified and selected, performance standards have been defined, measurement systems and associated tools have been agreed on, and people are committed to the plan.

PROCESS METRICS

A **metric** is a unit of measurement that provides a way to objectively quantify a process.[1] For example, the presence or absence of surface defects for a brass sink fixture might be assessed by visual inspection. A useful metric to monitor the quality of operations might be the percentage of fixtures that have surface defects. As another example, the diameters of machined ball bearings might be measured with a micrometer. Statistics such as the mean diameter and standard deviation provide information to evaluate the ability of the production process to meet specifications. For services, examples of metrics would be the percentage of orders filled accurately and the time taken to fill a customer's order. Metrics provide a scorecard for assessing performance of Six Sigma projects and are necessary to ensure that decisions are made on the basis of facts.

Measurement is the act of quantifying the performance dimensions of products, services, processes, and other business activities. **Measures** and **indicators** refer to the numerical information that results from measurement; that is, measures and indicators are numerical values associated with a metric. The term *indicator* is often used for measurements that are not a direct or exclusive measure of performance. For instance, you cannot directly measure dissatisfaction, but you can use the number of complaints or lost customers as indicators of dissatisfaction. Measurements and indicators provide critical information about business performance and are fundamental to Six Sigma.

Metrics can be either discrete or continuous. A **discrete metric** is countable. For example, a dimension is either within tolerance or out of tolerance, an order is complete or incomplete, or an invoice can have one, two, three, or any number of errors. Some examples are whether the correct zip code was used in shipping an order; or by comparing a dimension to specifications, such as whether the diameter of a shaft falls within specification limits of 1.60 ± 0.01 inch. They are typically expressed as numerical counts or as proportions. **Continuous metrics**, such as length, time, or weight, are concerned with the degree of conformance to specifications. Thus, rather than determining whether the diameter of a shaft simply meets a specification of 1.60 ± 0.01 inch, a measure of the actual value of the diameter is taken. Thus, a key performance dimension might be measured using either a continuous or a discrete metric. The differences are that discrete metrics are usually easier to capture, for example, by visual inspection, while continuous metrics usually require some type of measurement instrument such as a gauge or stopwatch. However, one must collect a larger amount of discrete data to draw appropriate statistical conclusions as compared to continuous data.

At the Six Sigma project level, product and service quality indicators focus on the outcomes of manufacturing and service processes. A common indicator of manufacturing quality is the number of **nonconformities per unit,** or **defects per unit.** Because of the negative connotation of "defect" and its potential implications in liability suits, many organizations use the term *nonconformance;* however, quite a few still use the term *defect.* In this book, both terms are used interchangeably to be consistent with current literature and practice. In services, a measure of quality analogous to defects per unit is **errors per opportunity.** Each customer transaction provides an opportunity for many different types of errors. Regardless of the terminology, defects, nonconformities, or errors must be clearly defined in terms of failure to meet customer requirements or internal specifications.

Nonconformities per unit or errors per opportunity are often reported as rates per thousand or million. A common measure used in Six Sigma is **dpmo—defects per million opportunities.** Thus, a defect rate of 2 per 1,000 is equivalent to 2,000 dpmo. At some Motorola factories, quality is so good that they measure defects per billion!

Many companies classify defects into three categories:

1. *Critical defect:* A critical defect is one that judgment and experience indicate will surely result in hazardous or unsafe conditions for individuals using, maintaining, or depending on the product and will prevent proper performance of the product.

2. *Major defect:* A major defect is one not critical but likely to result in failure or to materially reduce the usability of the unit for its intended purpose.
3. *Minor defect:* A minor defect is one not likely to materially reduce the usability of the item for its intended purpose, or to have any bearing on the effective use or operation of the unit.[2]

Critical defects may lead to serious consequences or product liability suits; thus, they should be monitored and controlled for carefully. On the other hand, minor defects might not be monitored as closely, because they do not affect fitness for use. For many products, however, even minor defects can lead to customer dissatisfaction. To account for each category, many companies create a composite index in which major and critical defects are weighted more heavily than minor defects. For example, FedEx has an extensive quality measurement system that includes a composite measure, called the service quality indicator (SQI), which is a weighted sum of 10 factors that reflect customers' expectations of company performance. Different weights reflect the importance of each failure; losing a package, for instance, is more serious than delivering it a few minutes late. The index is reported weekly and summarized on a monthly basis.

Identifying and Selecting Process Metrics

Metrics used in Six Sigma projects should be simple and meaningful, easy to apply, and be related to key customer and business requirements. Many organizations use the acronym *SMART* to characterize good measures and indicators: *simple*, *measurable*, *actionable* (they provide a basis for decision-making), *related* (to customer requirements and to each other), and *timely*.

To generate useful process performance measures a systematic process is required.[3]

1. *Identify all customers of the system and determine their requirements and expectations.* Organizations need answers to key questions: Who are my customers? and What do they expect? What are the CTQs—the critical-to-quality characteristics that are vital to customer satisfaction? Many of the "customer listening" approaches introduced in Chapter 3 can be used in this step. Customer expectations change over time; thus, regular feedback must be obtained.
2. *Define the work process that provides the product or service.* Key questions include: What do I do that affects customer needs? What is my process? The use of flowcharts for process mapping can stimulate the definition of work processes and internal customer–supplier relationships.
3. *Define the value-adding activities and outputs that compose the process.* This step—identifying each part in the system in which value is added and an intermediate output is produced—weeds out activities that do not add value to the process and contribute to waste and inefficiency. Analysis performed in this step identifies the internal customers within the process along with their needs and expectations.
4. *Develop specific performance measures or indicators.* Each key activity identified in step 3 represents a critical point where value is added to the output for the next (internal) customer until the final output is produced. At these checkpoints, performance can be measured. Key questions include: What factors determine

how well the process is producing according to customer requirements? What deviations can occur? What sources of variability can occur?

5. *Evaluate the performance measures to ensure their usefulness.* Questions to consider: Are measurements taken at critical points where value-adding activities occur? Are measurements controllable? Is it feasible to obtain the data needed for each measure? Have operational definitions for each measurement been established? Operational definitions are precise definitions of measurements that have no ambiguities. For example, when measuring "invoice errors," a precise definition of what is an error and what is not is needed. Does an error include an omission of information, wrong information, or misspelling? Operational definitions provide a common understanding and enhance communication throughout the organization.

To illustrate this approach, consider the process of placing and filling a pizza order. Customer expectations include a quick response and a fair price. The process that provides this service is shown in Figure 4.1. To begin, the order taker is an (internal) customer of the caller (who provides the pizza order). Later, the caller is a customer of the deliverer (either at the pickup window or the caller's home). Also, the cook is a customer of the order taker (who prepares the documentation for the ordered pizza).

FIGURE 4.1 EXAMPLE OF A PIZZA ORDERING AND FILLING PROCESS FOR HOME DELIVERY

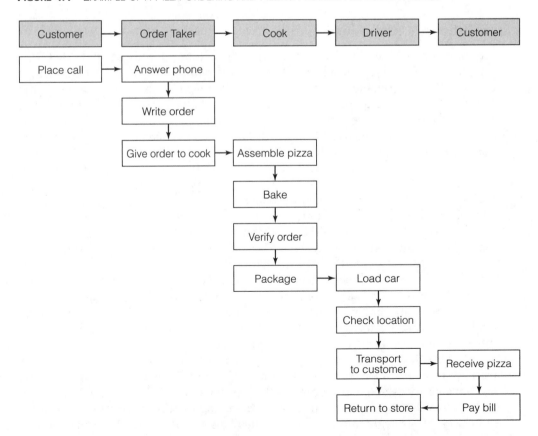

Some possible metrics include:

- Number of pizzas, by type per hour. If this number is high relative to the kitchen's capacity, then perhaps cooking time and/or preparation is being cut short or delivery times are stretched out.
- Order accuracy (as transmitted to the kitchen). This measure can indicate a lack of attention or knowledge on the part of the order taker.
- Number of pizzas rejected per number prepared. A high number for this measure can indicate a lack of proper training of cooks, resulting in poor products and customer complaints.
- Time to delivery. This measure might indicate a problem within the restaurant or inadequate training of the driver. (Of course, as happened with Domino's, measuring delivery time could encourage drivers to drive too fast and lead to safety problems.)
- Number of errors in collections. Errors here can result in lost profits and higher prices.
- Raw materials (dough, etc.) or finished pizzas inventory. A high number might result in spoilage and excess costs. Low inventory might result in lost orders or excessive customer waiting time.

Notice that these metrics—only a few among many possible metrics—are related to customer expectations and business performance.

Dashboards and Scorecards

Measurements should be clearly aligned with customer requirements—the CTQs established in the Define step of DMAIC. This helps to clarify the relationships between the controllable inputs (the Xs) and the response variables (the Ys) in the $Y = f(X)$ concept we discussed in Chapter 2 and helps employees to understand how their work processes affect customer requirements.

Many organizations use "dashboards" to track key measurements at the operational level, which are linked to a "balanced scorecard" at the strategic level of the organization. The dashboard concept stems from the analogy to an automobile's dashboard—a collection of indicators (speed, RPM, oil pressure, temperature, etc.) that summarize performance. Dashboards often use graphs, charts, and other visual aids to communicate key measures and alert managers when performance is not where it should be. Dashboards provide the information for daily management and control of processes. Dashboard information can be aggregated to give a picture of overall organizational performance, leading to the concept of a balanced scorecard. The concept of a balanced scorecard was pioneered by Analog Devices in 1987, and is a summary of broad performance measures across the organization. Balanced scorecards typically include financial measures, quality and time performance, customer satisfaction, employee satisfaction, and other measures of market and work performance.

Dashboards and scorecards provide a consistent source of information for tracking progress, a clear means of communication with managers and sponsors, and a means for establishing control in the last step of DMAIC. Linking dashboards and scorecards forces an organization to tie operational measures to higher-level indicators of strategic success. This is often done quantitatively, using various statistical methods such as correlation and regression to establish empirical relationships among the data.

DATA COLLECTION

Six Sigma relies on good data for understanding process performance and tracking improvements that result from design changes. Thus, considerable effort must be made to collect accurate data. Data collection should not be performed blindly. One must first ask some basic questions:

- What questions are we trying to answer?
- What type of data will we need to answer the question?
- Where can we find the data?
- Who can provide the data?
- How can we collect the data with minimum effort and with minimum chance of error?

The first step in any data collection effort is to develop **operational definitions** for all measures that will be used. For example, what does it mean to have "on-time delivery"? Does it mean within one day of the promised time? One week? One hour? What is an error? Is it wrong information on an invoice, a typographical mistake, or either? Clearly, any data are meaningless unless they are well defined and understood without ambiguity.

The Juran Institute suggests ten important considerations for data collection:

1. Formulate good questions that relate to the specific information needs of the project.
2. Use appropriate data analysis tools and be certain the necessary data are being collected.
3. Define comprehensive data collection points so that job flows suffer minimum interruption.
4. Select an unbiased collector who has the easiest and most immediate access to the relevant facts.
5. Understand the environment and make sure that data collectors have the proper experience.
6. Design simple data collection forms.
7. Prepare instructions for collecting the data.
8. Test the data collection forms and the instructions and make sure they are filled out properly.
9. Train the data collectors as to the purpose of the study, what the data will be used for, how to fill out the forms, and the importance of remaining unbiased.
10. Audit the data collection process and validate the results.[4]

These guidelines can greatly improve the process of uncovering relevant facts necessary to identify and solve problems.

Data required for Six Sigma projects may be collected in a variety of ways. Nearly any kind of form may be used to collect data. **Data sheets** use simple columnar or tabular forms to record data. Many types of automated systems are now available to improve both the accuracy and speed of data collection. However, much data collection is done manually. Check sheets provide a convenient means of recording data that facilitates analysis.

Check Sheets

Check sheets integrate data analysis with the data collection effort. **Check sheets** are special types of data collection forms in which the results may be interpreted on the form directly without additional processing. In manufacturing, check sheets similar to Figure 4.2 are simple to use and easily interpreted by shop personnel. Including information such as specification limits makes the number of noncon-

FIGURE 4.2   CHECK SHEET FOR DATA COLLECTION

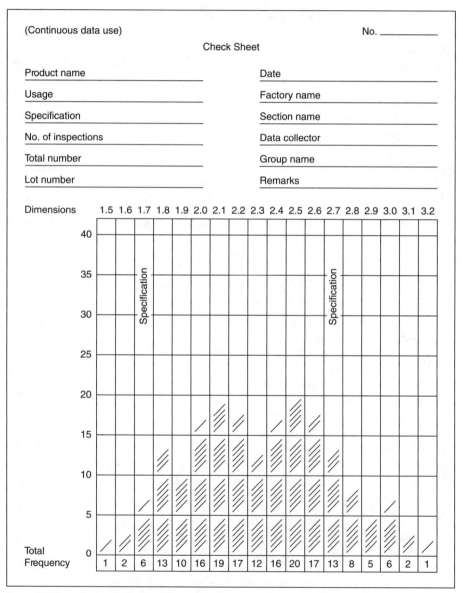

Source: K. Ishikawa, Guide to Quality Control (Tokyo: Asian Productivity Organization, 1982), 31. Used with permission.

FIGURE 4.3   DEFECTIVE ITEM CHECK SHEET

Check Sheet

Product: _____   Date: _____

                                      Factory: _____

Manufacturing stage: final insp. ___   Section: _____

                                      Inspector's
                                      name: _____

Type of defect: scar, incomplete,   Lot no. _____
misshapen _____
                                      Order no. _____

Total no. inspected: 2530 _____

Remarks: all items inspected _____

Type	Check	Subtotal
Surface scars	//// //// //// //// //// //// //	32
Cracks	//// //// //// //// ///	23
Incomplete	//// //// //// //// //// //// //// //// //// ///	48
Misshapen	////	4
Others	//// ///	8
	Grand total	115
Total rejects	//// //// //// //// //// //// //// //// //// //// //// //// //// //// //// //// //// /	86

Source: K. Ishikawa, Guide to Quality Control (Tokyo: Asian Productivity Organization, 1982), 33. Used with permission.

forming items easily observable and provides an immediate indication of the quality of the process. For example, in Figure 4.2 a significant proportion of dimensions are clearly out of specification, with a larger number on the high side than the low side.

A second type of check sheet for defective items is illustrated in Figure 4.3, which shows the type of defect and a tally in a resin production plant. Such a check sheet can be extended to include a time dimension so that data can be monitored and analyzed over time, and trends and patterns, if any, can be detected.

Figure 4.4 shows an example of a defect location check sheet. Kaoru Ishikawa relates how this check sheet was used to eliminate bubbles in laminated automobile windshield glass.[5] The location and form of bubbles were indicated on the check sheet; most of the bubbles occurred on the right side. On investigation, workers discovered that the pressure applied in laminating was off balance—the right side was receiving less pressure. The machine was adjusted, and the formation of bubbles was eliminated almost completely.

Sampling and Sampling Error

Sampling forms the basis for most data collection efforts. Suppose that you worked in a 1,000-bed hospital and needed to collect data about the quality of care

FIGURE 4.4   DEFECT LOCATION CHECK SHEET

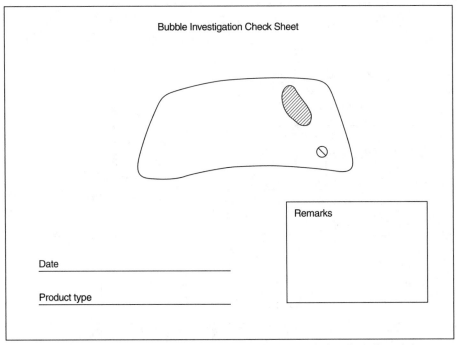

Source: K. Ishikawa, *Guide to Quality Control* (Tokyo: Asian Productivity Organization, 1982), 34. Used with permission.

a group of patients received while in the hospital for a Six Sigma study. Several factors should be considered before making this study:

1. What is the objective of the study?
2. What type of sample should be used?
3. What possible error might result from sampling?
4. What will the study cost?

One approach to tackling this problem would be to take a complete census—a survey of every person in the entire population. However, the objective of the study will dictate which method should be used to perform the study in the most effective and efficient manner. This decision requires sensitivity to the needs of the user and an understanding of the strengths and weaknesses of the specific techniques being used. Would sampling work just as well? If the user needs the results next week to make a decision involving the expenditure of $1,000, the study will require a different design from one in which the results influence a decision that will be made in six months and has a $1 million expenditure. Sampling provides a distinct advantage over a complete census in that much less time and cost are required to gather the data. In many cases, such as inspection, sampling may be more accurate than 100 percent inspection because of reduction of inspection errors. However, sampling is frequently subject to a higher degree of error.

Several approaches to sampling can be used. The following are some of the most common:

1. *Simple random sampling:* Every item in the population has an equal probability of being selected.
2. *Stratified sampling:* The population is partitioned into groups, or strata, and a sample is selected from each stratum.
3. *Systematic sampling:* Every *n*th (4th, 5th, etc.) item is selected.
4. *Cluster sampling:* A typical group (division of the company, for example) is selected, and a random sample is taken from within the group.
5. *Judgment sampling:* Expert opinion is used to determine the location and characteristics of a definable sample group.

In choosing the appropriate type of sampling method, an analyst must consider what the sample is designed to do. Suppose that your objective is to provide a report to top management of the hospital to help them decide whether to expand the use of quality control measures within the hospital. Some issues that would have to be considered before choosing a sample would be the time frame for completing the study, the size and cost limitations of the sample, the accessibility of the population of patients, and the desired accuracy. Assume that you have six weeks to complete the study, a limited operating budget of $1,500, and a population of 1,600 maternity patients (the category in which you are interested) who could be involved in the quality study. Further assume that the accuracy of your study requires a sample of at least 400 patients and that the cost of each response would vary from $2 to $4, depending on how the survey is administered. Obviously, you would have to select a sample, because a complete census of all patients would not be feasible because of the budget limitation. Time limitations would make travel to conduct face-to-face interviews virtually impossible. Thus, the only feasible alternatives would be mailed questionnaires, telephone interviews, or a combination of the two.

Given this information, what type of sample should be chosen? A good sampling plan should select a sample at the lowest cost that will provide the best possible representation of the population, consistent with the objectives of precision and reliability that have been determined for the study. Each type has advantages and disadvantages. A simple random sample would be easy to select but might not include sufficient representation by floor or ward. If a list of the patients, perhaps in alphabetical order, was available, a systematic sample of every fourth name could easily be selected. It would have the same disadvantages as the random sample, however. On the other hand, a cluster sample or judgment sample could be selected to include more representatives from floors or wards. However, cluster and judgment samples frequently take more time to identify and select appropriate sampling units. Also, because more subjective judgment is involved, a biased, nonrepresentative sampling plan is more likely to be developed.

Errors in sampling generally stem from two causes: **sampling error** and **systematic error** (often called non-sampling error). Sampling error occurs naturally and results from the fact that a sample may not always be representative of the population, no matter how carefully it is selected. The only way to reduce sampling error is to take a larger sample from the population. Systematic errors, however, can be reduced or eliminated by design.

Sources of systematic error include the following:

1. *Bias:* The tendency to systematically over- or underestimate true values.
2. *Non-comparable data:* Data that come from two populations but are erroneously considered to have come from one.
3. *Uncritical projection of trends:* The assumption that what has happened in the past will continue into the future.
4. *Causation:* The assumption that because two variables are related, one must be the cause of changes in the other.
5. *Improper sampling:* The use of an erroneous method for gathering data, thus biasing results (for example, using electronic mail surveys to get opinions from a population having few individuals with electronic mail services).

These sources of error can be overcome through careful planning of the sampling study. Bias can be reduced by frequent interaction with end users of the study as well as crosschecking of research designs with knowledgeable analysts. Non-comparable data can be avoided by a sensitivity to conditions that could contribute to development of dissimilar population segments. In the hospital example, data gathered from different floors, wards, or shifts could prove to be non-comparable. In production firms, different shifts, machines, or products may define different populations, even though the characteristics being measured are the same for each. Uncritical projection of trends can be avoided by analysis of the underlying causes of trends and a constant questioning of the assumption that tomorrow's population will be the same as yesterdays. Reasons for causation must be investigated. Relationships between variables alone are not sufficient to conclude that causality exists. Causation can often be tested by holding one variable constant while changing the other to determine effects of the change. Finally, improper sampling can be avoided by a thorough understanding of sampling techniques and a determination of whether the method being used is capable of reaching any unit in the population in an unbiased fashion.

Sampling error is determined by the sample size and can be easily quantified. First, consider the sample size when using $\bar{x}$ to provide a point estimate of the population mean for variables data. A $100(1 - \alpha)$ percent confidence interval on $\bar{x}$ is given by

$$\bar{x} \pm z_{\alpha/2}\sigma/\sqrt{n}$$

Thus, a $1 - \alpha$ probability exists that the value of the sample mean will provide a sampling error of $z_{\alpha/2}\sigma/\sqrt{n}$ or less. E denotes this sampling error. Solving the equation

$$E = z_{\alpha/2}\sigma/\sqrt{n}$$

for *n*, we find

$$n = (z_{\alpha/2})^2\sigma^2/E^2$$

This sample size will provide a point estimate having a sampling error of E or less at a confidence level of $100(1 - \alpha)$ percent.

To use this formula, specify the confidence level (from which $z_{\alpha/2}$ is obtained); the maximum sampling error E; and the standard deviation σ. If σ is unknown, at least a preliminary value is needed in order to compute n. A preliminary sample or a good guess based on prior data or similar studies can be used to estimate σ.

A similar task is to determine the sample size for estimating a population proportion for attributes data. A point estimate of the population proportion, p, is given by the sample proportion $\bar{p}$. The standard error of the proportion is

$$\sigma_{\bar{p}} = \sqrt{\bar{p}(1 - \bar{p})/n}$$

Thus, a 100 $(1-\alpha)$ percent confidence interval for the population proportion is

$$\bar{p} \pm z_{\alpha/2}\sqrt{\bar{p}(1 - \bar{p})/n}$$

The sampling error is given by $E = z_{\alpha/2}\sqrt{\bar{p}(1 - \bar{p})/n}$.
Solving this equation for n provides the following formula for the sample size:

$$n = (z_{\alpha/2})^2\bar{p}(1 - \bar{p})/E^2$$

If a good value of $\bar{p}$ is not known, use $\bar{p} = 0.5$ because this value provides the largest sample size recommendation that guarantees the required level of precision.

Data Summarization

Raw data need to be organized, summarized, and visualized to turn them into information. **Information** is data in context of a business or organization. Common means of summarizing data are to calculate means, standard deviations, and other statistical measures. Graphs and charts provide a convenient way of visualizing and communicating information. The capabilities of today's spreadsheet and database software, such as Microsoft Excel and Access, make this easy to do by nearly any employee. In this section, we present some elementary tools for data summarization. The next chapter focuses on more sophisticated statistical methods used in the Analysis phase of DMAIC.

Descriptive Statistics

When we deal with data sets, it is important to understand the nature of the data in order to select the appropriate statistical tool or procedure. One classification of data is the following:

1. Type of data
   - *Cross-sectional*—data that are collected over a single period of time
   - *Time series*—data collected over time
2. Number of variables
   - *Univariate*—data consisting of a single variable
   - *Multivariate*—data consisting of two or more (often related) variables

Most performance measures used in Six Sigma are time series, because business processes operate over time. It is also common to find multivariate data because numerous factors influence business performance. Descriptive statistics provide basic understanding of data collected from a process.

A *population* is a complete set or collection of objects of interest; a *sample* is a subset of objects taken from the population. Characteristics of a population, such as the mean μ, standard deviation σ, or proportion π, are generally known as *parameters* of the population. In statistical notation, they are written as follows:

$$\text{Population mean: } \mu = \frac{1}{N}\sum_{i=1}^{N} x_i$$

$$\text{Population standard deviation: } \sigma = \sqrt{\frac{\sum_{i=1}^{N}(x_i - \mu)^2}{N}}$$

$$\text{Population proportion: } \pi = \frac{Q}{N}$$

where x_i is the value of the *i*th observation, N is the number of items in a population, and Q is the number of items exhibiting a criterion of interest, such as manufacturing defects or on-time departures of aircraft.

The sample mean, sample standard deviation, and sample proportion are computed as follows:

$$\text{Sample mean: } \bar{x} = \frac{1}{n}\sum_{i=1}^{n} x_i$$

$$\text{Sample standard deviation: } s = \sqrt{\frac{\sum_{i=1}^{n}(x_i - \bar{x})^2}{n - 1}}$$

$$\text{Sample proportion: } p = \frac{q}{n}$$

where n is the number of items in a sample, and q is the number of items in a sample exhibiting a criterion of interest.

Most data collected in Six Sigma projects represent samples. The purpose of sampling is to gain knowledge about the characteristics of the population from the information contained in a sample. For instance, the sample statistic $\bar{x}$ is generally used as a point estimator for the population parameter μ, s as a point estimator for σ, and p as a point estimator for π. The actual numerical values of $\bar{x}$, s and p, which represent the single "best guess" for each unknown population parameter, are called *point estimates*. Other useful statistics to describe a set of data include the median, range, and coefficient of skewness.

Statistical Calculations with Microsoft Excel

Spreadsheets are the most useful tools for managers and analysts. We will use Microsoft Excel whenever appropriate to perform statistical calculations and display graphs or charts. The disk accompanying this book contains all of the major spreadsheets used in examples in this book that will help you in working many end-of-chapter problems. The files available on the disk are identified by their name (NAME.XLS) in the text.

Microsoft Excel provides a set of data analysis tools, called the Analysis ToolPak, that are useful in complex statistical analyses. You provide the data and parameters for each analysis; the tool uses the appropriate statistical functions and then displays the results in an output table. Some tools generate charts in addition to output tables. To view a list of available analysis tools, click Data Analysis on the Tools menu. If the Data Analysis command is not on the Tools menu, run the Setup program to install the Analysis ToolPak. After you install the Analysis ToolPak, you must select it in the Add-In Manager. Excel also provides many other statistical worksheet functions. To see a list of available functions, click Edit Formula on the formula bar, and then click the down-arrow in Insert Function. We strongly encourage you to learn how to use the capabilities of Excel for quality assurance applications. Much more information can be found in the Help files available with Excel.

To illustrate basic statistical analysis, Table 4.1 shows a set of measurements of the width of U-bolts used in automobile assemblies. We will assume that this sample is representative of the population from which they were drawn. These data were entered into an Excel spreadsheet in the range A2:A121. Figure 4.5 shows the Descriptive Statistics dialog box that is displayed after choosing Descriptive Statistics from the Tools/Data Analysis options. See the Help files in Excel for an explanation of the features of this dialog. Figure 4.6 shows the results of applying the Descriptive Statistics tool to the data in Table 4.1.

TABLE 4.1 MEASUREMENTS OF U-BOLTS (U-BOLT DATA.XLS)

10.65	10.70	10.65	10.65	10.85
10.75	10.85	10.75	10.85	10.65
10.75	10.80	10.80	10.70	10.75
10.60	10.70	10.70	10.75	10.65
10.70	10.75	10.65	10.85	10.80
10.60	10.75	10.75	10.85	10.70
10.60	10.80	10.70	10.75	10.75
10.75	10.80	10.65	10.75	10.70
10.65	10.80	10.85	10.85	10.75
10.60	10.70	10.60	10.80	10.65
10.80	10.75	10.90	10.50	10.85
10.85	10.75	10.85	10.65	10.70
10.70	10.70	10.75	10.75	10.70
10.65	10.70	10.85	10.75	10.60
10.75	10.80	10.75	10.80	10.65
10.90	10.80	10.80	10.75	10.85
10.75	10.70	10.85	10.70	10.80
10.75	10.70	10.60	10.70	10.60
10.65	10.65	10.85	10.65	10.70
10.60	10,60	10.65	10.55	10.65
10.50	10.55	10.65	10.80	10.80
10.80	10.65	10.75	10.65	10.65
10.65	10.60	10.65	10.60	10.70
10.65	10.70	10.70	10.60	10.65

FIGURE 4.5   MICROSOFT EXCEL DESCRIPTIVE STATISTICS DIALOG BOX

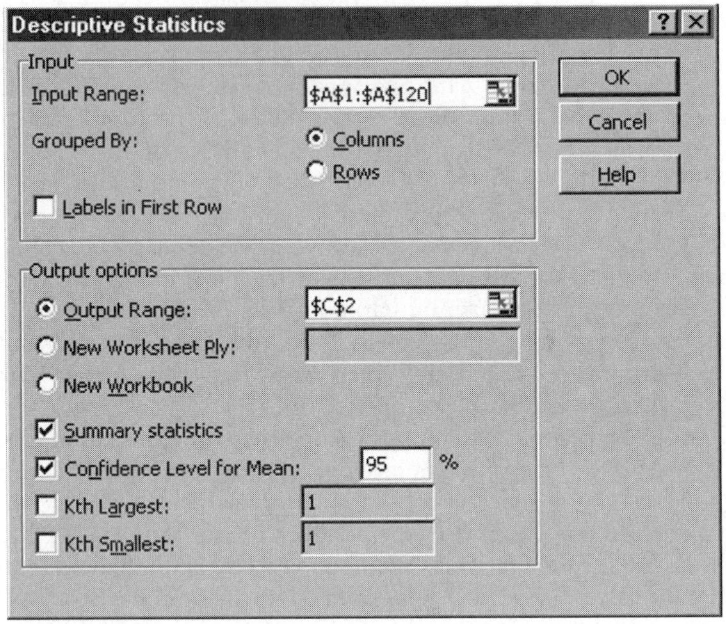

Descriptive Statistics   `? X`

Input
Input Range: `$A$1:$A$120`   OK

Grouped By: ⦿ Columns   Cancel
                      ○ Rows
                                                              Help
☐ Labels in First Row

Output options
⦿ Output Range: `$C$2`
○ New Worksheet Ply:
○ New Workbook

☑ Summary statistics
☑ Confidence Level for Mean: 95   %
☐ Kth Largest: 1
☐ Kth Smallest: 1

FIGURE 4.6   MICROSOFT EXCEL DESCRIPTIVE STATISTICS RESULTS

	A	B	C	D
1	10.65			
2	10.75		*Column1*	
3	10.75			
4	10.60		Mean	10.71708333
5	10.70		Standard Error	0.007927716
6	10.60		Median	10.7
7	10.60		Mode	10.65
8	10.75		Standard Deviation	0.086843778
9	10.65		Sample Variance	0.007541842
10	10.60		Kurtosis	-0.53752485
11	10.80		Skewness	-0.0420018
12	10.85		Range	0.4
13	10.70		Minimum	10.5
14	10.65		Maximum	10.9
15	10.75		Sum	1286.05
16	10.90		Count	120
17	10.75		Confidence Level(95.0%)	0.015697649

Histograms

A **histogram** is a basic statistical tool that graphically shows the frequency or number of observations of a particular value or within a specified group. Histograms provide clues about the characteristics of the parent population from which a sample is taken.

FIGURE 4.7 MICROSOFT EXCEL HISTOGRAM DIALOG BOX

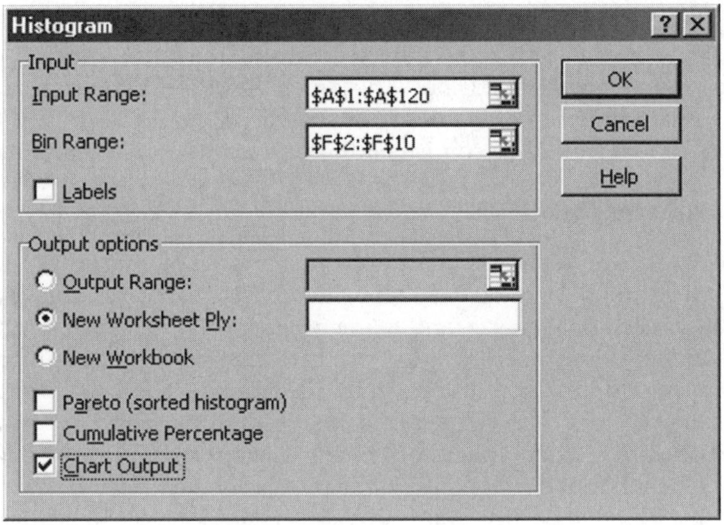

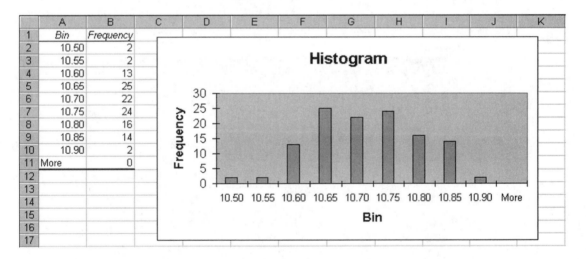

FIGURE 4.8 HISTOGRAM AND FREQUENCY DISTRIBUTION

Bin	Frequency
10.50	2
10.55	2
10.60	13
10.65	25
10.70	22
10.75	24
10.80	16
10.85	14
10.90	2
More	0

Patterns that would be difficult to see in an ordinary table of numbers become apparent. The check sheet in Figure 4.2, for example, was designed to provide the visual appeal of a histogram as the data are tallied. For these data, one can easily determine the proportion of observations that fell outside the specification limits.

Microsoft Excel provides a tool for creating histograms, the Histogram tool. Figure 4.7 shows the Excel dialog box for this option. See the Excel Help files for specific information on using this tool. Figure 4.8 shows the frequency distribution and histogram generated using the Histogram tool. We will use these results in another example later in this chapter.

Some cautions should be heeded when interpreting histograms. First, the data should be representative of typical process conditions. If a new employee is now operating the equipment, or some aspect of the equipment, material, or method has changed, then new data should be collected. Second, the sample size should be large enough to provide good conclusions. The larger, the better. Various guidelines exist, but a suggested minimum of at least 50 observations should be drawn. Finally, any conclusions drawn should be confirmed through further study and analysis.

Charts and Graphs

Microsoft Excel offers a variety of options to express data visually. These options include vertical and horizontal bar charts, line charts, pie charts, area charts, scatter plots, three-dimensional charts, and many other special types of charts. The Excel Chart Wizard provides an easy way to create charts within a spreadsheet. The Excel Chart Wizard is accessed from either the Insert . . . Chart . . . menu selection or by clicking on the Chart Wizard icon (the colored bar chart on the menu bar). The Chart Wizard guides you through four dialog boxes; the first is shown in Figure 4.9. The following steps outline the process of creating a chart:

1. Select the chart type from the list (for example, *Bar*) and then click on the specific chart subtype option. Click Next or press Enter to continue.

FIGURE 4.9   EXCEL CHART WIZARD DIALOG BOX

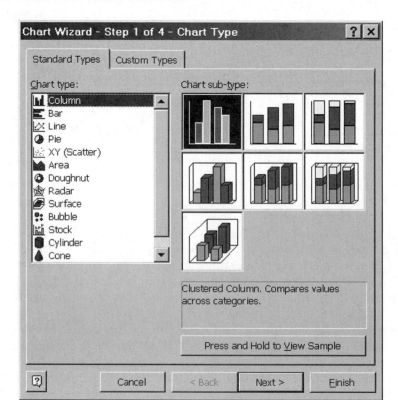

2. The second dialog box asks you to define the data to plot. You may enter the data range directly or highlight it in your spreadsheet with your mouse. You also need to define whether the data are stored by rows or columns. (Note: If the data you wish to plot are not stored in contiguous columns, hold down the Ctrl key while selecting each block of data; then start the Chart Wizard.) The Series tab allows you to check and modify the names and values of the data series in your chart.

3. The third dialog box allows you to specify details to customize the chart and make it easy to read and understand. You may specify titles for the chart and each axis, axis labels, style of gridlines, placement of the legend to describe the data series, data labels, and even a data table of values from which the chart is derived.

4. Finally, the last dialog box allows you to specify whether to place the chart as an object in an existing worksheet or as a new sheet in the workbook.

We encourage you to use these features of Excel while working with data in Six Sigma applications.

MEASUREMENT SYSTEM EVALUATION

Accurately assessing Six Sigma performance depends on reliable measurement systems. Measuring quality characteristics generally requires the use of the human senses—seeing, hearing, feeling, tasting, and smelling—and the use of some type of instrument or gauge to measure the magnitude of the characteristic. Common types of measuring instruments used in manufacturing today fall into two categories: low technology and high technology. Low-technology instruments are primarily manual devices that have been available for many years; high-technology instruments describe those that depend on modern electronics, micro-processors, lasers, or advanced optics.

Metrology

Gauges and instruments used to measure quality characteristics must provide correct information, which is assured through **metrology**—the science of measurement. Originally, metrology only measured the physical attributes of an object. Today, metrology is defined broadly as the collection of people, equipment, facilities, methods, and procedures used to assure the correctness or adequacy of measurements, and is a vital part of global competitiveness. In testifying before the U.S. Congress, the director of the Office of Standards Services at the National Institute of Standards and Technology noted that efficient national and international trade requires weights and measures organizations that assure uniform and accurate measures used in trade, national, or regional measurement standards laboratories, standards development organizations, and accredited and internationally recognized calibration and testing laboratories.[6]

The need for metrology stems from the fact that every measurement is subject to error. Whenever variation is observed in measurements, some portion is due to measurement system error. Some errors are systematic (called bias); others are random. The size of the errors relative to the measurement value can significantly affect the quality of the data and resulting decisions. The evaluation of data obtained from inspection and measurement is not meaningful unless the measurement instruments are accurate, precise, and reproducible.

Accuracy is defined as the closeness of agreement between an observed value and an accepted reference value or standard. The lack of accuracy reflects a systematic bias in the measurement such as a gauge out of calibration, worn, or used improperly by the operator. Accuracy is measured as the amount of error in a measurement in proportion to the total size of the measurement. One measurement is more accurate than another if it has a smaller relative error.

Precision is defined as the closeness of agreement between randomly selected individual measurements or results. Precision, therefore, relates to the variance of repeated measurements. A measuring instrument with a low variance is more precise than another having a higher variance. Low precision is due to random variation that is built into the instrument, such as friction among its parts. This random variation may be the result of a poor design or lack of maintenance.

For example, suppose that two instruments measure a dimension whose true value is 0.250 inch. Instrument A may read 0.248 inch, while instrument B may read 0.259 inch. The relative error of instrument A is $(0.250 - 0.248)/0.250 = 0.8\%$; the relative error of instrument B is $(0.259 - 0.250)/0.250 = 3.6\%$. Thus, instrument A is said to be more accurate than instrument B. Now suppose that each instrument measures the dimension three times. Instrument A records values of 0.248, 0.246, and 0.251; instrument B records values of 0.259, 0.258, and 0.259. Instrument B is more precise than instrument A because its values are clustered closer together.

A measurement system may be precise but not necessarily accurate at the same time. The relationships between accuracy and precision are summarized in Figure 4.10. The figure illustrates four possible frequency distributions of 10 repeated measurements of some quality characteristic. In Figure 4.10 (a), the average measurement is not close to the true value. Moreover, a wide range of values falls around the average. In this case, the measurement is neither accurate nor precise. In Figure 4.10 (b), even though the average measurement is not close to the true value, the range of variation is small. Thus, the measurement is precise but not accurate. In Figures 4.10 (c) and (d), the average value is close to the true value—that is, the measurement is accurate—but in 4.10 (c) the distribution is widely dispersed and therefore not precise, while the measurement in 4.10 (d) is both accurate and precise. Thus, Figure 4.10 demonstrates the vital nature of properly calibrating and maintaining all instruments used for quality measurements.

When a technician measures the same unit multiple times, the results will usually show some variability. **Repeatability**, or **equipment variation**, is the variation in multiple measurements by an individual using the same instrument. This measure indicates how precise and accurate the equipment is. **Reproducibility**, or **operator variation**, is the variation in the same measuring instrument when different individuals use it to measure the same parts, and indicates how robust the measuring process is to the operator and environmental conditions. Causes of poor reproducibility might be poor training of the operators in the use of the instrument or unclear calibrations on the gauge dial. Statistical approaches can be used to quantify and evaluate equipment and operator variation.

FIGURE 4.10 ACCURACY VERSUS PRECISION

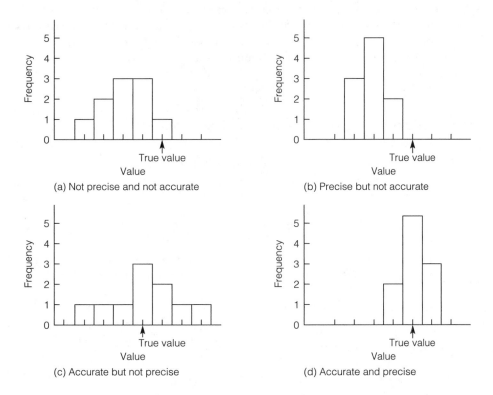

(a) Not precise and not accurate

(b) Precise but not accurate

(c) Accurate but not precise

(d) Accurate and precise

The importance of measurement analysis is summed up by the following equation:

$$\sigma^2_{total} = \sigma^2_{process} + \sigma^2_{measurement}$$

which states that the total observed variation in production output is the sum of the true process variation (which is what we actually want to measure) plus variation due to measurement. If the measurement variation is high, the observed results will be biased, and process capability measurements, for example, may look worse than they actually are. Thus, an objective of quality control is to reduce measurement error as much as possible.

Measurement System Evaluation and Verification

The accuracy, repeatability, and reproducibility of any measurement system must be quantified and evaluated. Accuracy can be measured by comparing the observed average of a set of measurements to the true value of a reference standard. Repeatability and reproducibility require a study of variation and can be addressed through statistical analysis. A repeatability and reproducibility study is conducted in the following manner.[7]

1. Select m operators and n parts. Typically at least 2 operators and 10 parts are chosen. Number the parts so that the numbers are not visible to the operators.

2. Calibrate the measuring instrument.
3. Let each operator measure each part in a random order and record the results. Repeat this procedure for a total of r trials. At least two trials must be used. Let M_{ijk} represent the kth measurement of operator i on part j.
4. Compute the average measurement for each operator:

$$\bar{x}_j = \left(\sum_j \sum_k M_{ijk} \right)/nr$$

The difference between the largest and smallest average is

$$\bar{x}_D = \max_i\{\bar{x}_i\} - \min_i\{\bar{x}_i\}$$

5. Compute the range for each part and each operator:

$$R_{ij} = \max_k\{M_{ijk}\} - \min_k\{M_{ijk}\}$$

These values show the variability of repeated measurements of the same part by the same operator. Next, compute the average range for each operator:

$$\bar{R}_i = \left(\sum_j R_{ij} \right)/n$$

The overall average range is then computed as

$$\bar{\bar{R}} = \left(\sum_i \bar{R}_i \right)/m$$

6. Calculate a control limit on the individual ranges R_{ij}:

$$\text{control limit} = D_4\bar{\bar{R}}$$

where D_4 is a constant that depends on the sample size (number of trials, r) and can be found in Appendix B at the end of this book. Any range value beyond this limit might result from some assignable cause, not random error. Possible causes should be investigated and, if found, corrected. The operator should repeat these measurements using the same part. If no assignable cause is found, these values should be discarded and all statistics in step 5 as well as the control limit should be recalculated.

Once these basic calculations are made, an analysis of repeatability and reproducibility can be performed. The repeatability, or equipment variation (EV) is computed as

$$EV = K_1\bar{\bar{R}}$$

Reproducibility, or operator (or appraisal) variation (AV) is computed as

$$AV = \sqrt{(K_2\bar{x}_D)^2 - (EV^2/nr)}$$

The constants K_1 and K_2 depend on the number of trials and number of operators, respectively. Some values of these constants are given in Table 4.2. These constants provide a 99 percent confidence interval on these statistics.

An overall measure of repeatability and reproducibility (R&R) is given by

$$R\&R = \sqrt{(EV)^2 + (AV)^2}$$

Repeatability and reproducibility are often expressed as a percentage of the tolerance of the quality characteristic being measured. The American Society for Quality suggests the following guidelines for evaluating these measures of repeatability and reproducibility:

- Under 10 percent error: This rate is acceptable.
- 10 to 30 percent error: This rate may be acceptable based on the importance of the application, cost of the instrument, cost of repair, and so on.
- Over 30 percent error: Generally, this rate is not acceptable. Every effort should be made to identify the problem and correct it.

To illustrate a gauge repeatability and reproducibility study, suppose that a gauge used to measure the thickness of a gasket having a specification of 0.50 to 1.0 mm is to be evaluated. Ten parts have been selected for measurement by three operators. Each part is measured twice with the results as shown in the spread-sheet in Figure 4.11. (Slight rounding differences from manual calculations may be evident.)

The average measurement for each operator, $\bar{x}_j$, is

$$\bar{x}_1 = 0.830 \quad \bar{x}_2 = 0.774 \quad \bar{x}_3 = 0.829$$

Thus, $\bar{x}_D = 0.830 - 0.774 = 0.056$. The average range for each operator is

$$\bar{R}_1 = 0.037 \quad \bar{R}_2 = 0.034 \quad \bar{R}_3 = 0.017$$

The overall average range is $\bar{\bar{R}} = (0.037 + 0.034 + 0.017)/3 = 0.0293$. From Appendix B at the end of the book, $D_4 = 3.267$ because the two trials were conducted. Hence, the control limit is $(3.267)(0.0293) = 0.096$. Because all range values fall below this limit, no assignable causes of variation are suspected. Compute the repeatability and reproducibility measures:

$$EV = (4.56)(0.0293) = 0.134$$
$$AV = \sqrt{[(0.056)(2.70)]^2 - (0.134)^2/(10)(2)} = 0.147$$
$$R\&R = \sqrt{(0.134)^2 + (0.147)^2} = 0.199$$

TABLE 4.2 VALUES OF K_1 AND K_2

Number of Trials	2	3	4	5
K_1	4.56	3.05	2.50	2.21
Number of Operators	2	3	4	5
K_2	3.65	2.70	2.30	2.08

FIGURE 4.11 SPREADSHEET FOR REPEATABILITY AND REPRODUCIBILITY ANALYSIS (R&R.XLS)

	A	B	C	D	E	F	G	H	I	J	K	L	M	N
1	Gauge Repeatability and Reproducibility													
2	This spreadsheet is designed for up to three operators, three trials, and ten samples. Enter data ONLY in yellow shaded cells.													
3														
4	Number of operators			3		Upper specification limit				1				
5	Number of trials			2		Lower specification limit				0.5				
6	Number of samples			10										
7														
8	Data		Operator 1				Operator 2				Operator 3			
9			Trial				Trial				Trial			
10	Sample #	1	2	3	Range	1	2	3	Range	1	2	3	Range	
11	1	0.630	0.590		0.040	0.560	0.560		0.000	0.510	0.540		0.030	
12	2	1.000	1.000		0.000	1.040	0.960		0.080	1.050	1.010		0.040	
13	3	0.830	0.770		0.060	0.800	0.760		0.040	0.810	0.810		0.000	
14	4	0.860	0.940		0.080	0.820	0.780		0.040	0.810	0.810		0.000	
15	5	0.590	0.510		0.080	0.430	0.430		0.000	0.460	0.490		0.030	
16	6	0.980	0.980		0.000	1.000	1.040		0.040	1.040	1.000		0.040	
17	7	0.960	0.960		0.000	0.940	0.900		0.040	0.950	0.950		0.000	
18	8	0.860	0.830		0.030	0.720	0.740		0.020	0.810	0.810		0.000	
19	9	0.970	0.970		0.000	0.980	0.940		0.040	1.030	1.030		0.000	
20	10	0.640	0.720		0.080	0.560	0.520		0.040	0.840	0.810		0.030	
21	Range average				0.037				0.034				0.017	
22	Sample average				0.830				0.774				0.829	
23														
24												Tolerance analysis		
25	Average range	0.029			Repeatability (EV)					0.134		26.75%		
26	X-bar range	0.056			Reproducibility (AV)					0.147		29.37%		
27					Repeatability and Reproducibility (R&R)					0.199		39.73%		
28					Control limit for individual ranges					0.096				
29					Note: any ranges beyond this limit may be the result									
30					of assignable causes. Identify and correct. Discard									
31					values and recompute statistics.									

If the tolerance of the gasket is $1.00 - 0.50 = 0.50$, these measures expressed as a percent of tolerance are:

$$\text{Equipment variation} = 100(0.134)/0.50 = 26.8\%$$

$$\text{Operator variation} = 100(0.147)/0.50 = 29.4\%$$

$$\text{Total R\&R variation} = 100(0.199)/0.50 = 39.8\%$$

Even though individually the equipment and operator variation may be acceptable, their combined effect is not. Efforts should be made to reduce the variation to an acceptable level.

Calibration

One of the most important functions of metrology is **calibration**—the comparison of a measurement device or system having a known relationship to national standards against another device or system whose relationship to national standards is unknown. Measurements made using uncalibrated or inadequately calibrated equipment can lead to erroneous and costly decisions. For example, suppose that an inspector has a micrometer that is reading 0.002 inch too low. When measurements are made close to the upper limit, parts that are as much as 0.002 inch over the maximum tolerance limit will be accepted as good, while those at the lower tolerance limit or that are as much as 0.002 inch above the limit will be rejected as nonconforming. A typical calibration system involves the following activities:

- Evaluation of equipment to determine its capability
- Identification of calibration requirements
- Selection of standards to perform the calibration
- Selection of methods and procedures to perform the calibration
- Establishment of calibration frequency and rules for adjusting this frequency
- Establishment of a system to ensure that instruments are calibrated according to schedule
- Implementation of a documentation and reporting system
- Evaluation of the calibration system through an established auditing process

The National Institute of Standards and Technology (NIST) maintains national measurement standards, and provides technical advice on making measurements consistent with national standards. NIST works with various metrology laboratories in industry and government to assure that measurements made by different people in different places yield the same results. Thus, the measurement of "voltage" or "resistance" in an electrical component has a precise and universal meaning. This process is accomplished in a hierarchical fashion. NIST calibrates the reference-level standards of those organizations requiring the highest level of accuracy. These organizations calibrate their own working-level standards and those of other metrology laboratories. These working-level standards are used to calibrate the measuring instruments used in the field. The usual recommendation is that equipment be calibrated against working-level standards that are 10 times as accurate as the equipment. When possible, at least a four-to-one accuracy ratio between the reference and working-level standards is desired; that is, the reference standards should be at least four times as accurate as the working-level standards.

Many government regulations and commercial contracts require regulated organizations or contractors to verify that the measurements they make are *traceable* to a reference standard. For example, world standards exist for length, mass, and time. For other types of measurement, such as chemical measurements, industry standards exist. Organizations must be able to support the claim of traceability by keeping records that their own measuring equipment has been calibrated by laboratories or testing facilities whose measurements can be related to appropriate standards, generally national or international standards, through an unbroken chain of comparison. The purpose of requiring traceability is to ensure that measurements are accurate representations of the specific quantity subject to measurement, within the uncertainty of the measurement. Not only should there be an unbroken chain of comparisons, each measurement should be accompanied by a statement of uncertainty associated with the farthest link in the chain from NIST, that is, the last facility providing the measurement value. This accountability can be assured by purchasing an instrument that is certified against a higher level (traceable) standard, or contracting with a calibration agency that has such standards to certify the instrument.

PROCESS CAPABILITY EVALUATION

Process capability is the range over which the natural variation of a process occurs as determined by the system of common causes, that is, what the process can achieve under stable conditions. Process capability is important to both product designers and manufacturing engineers, and is critical to achieving Six Sigma performance. Knowing process capability allows one to predict, quantitatively, how well a process will meet specifications and to specify equipment requirements and the level of control necessary. For example, suppose that the inside diameter of a bushing that supports a steel shaft must be between 1.498 and 1.510 inches for an acceptable fit. If the diameter is too small, it can be enlarged through a rework process. However if it is too large, the part must be scrapped. If the variation in the machining process results in diameters that typically range from 1.495 and 1.515 inches, we would say that the process is not capable of meeting the specifications. Management then faces three possible decisions: (1) measure each piece and either rework or scrap nonconforming parts, (2) develop a better process by investing in new technology, or (3) change the design specifications.

Unfortunately, product design often takes place in isolation, with inexperienced designers applying tolerances to parts or products while having little awareness of the capabilities of the production process to meet these design requirements. Even experienced designers may be hard-pressed to remain up-to-date on the capabilities of processes that involve constant equipment changes, shifting technology, and difficult-to-measure variations in methods at scores of plants located hundreds or thousands of miles away from a centralized product design department. Process capability should be carefully considered in determining design specifications in a Six Sigma environment.

Process Capability Studies

A **process capability study** is a carefully planned study designed to yield specific information about the performance of a process under specified operating conditions. Typical questions that are asked in a process capability study include the following:

- Where is the process centered?
- How much variability exists in the process?
- Is the performance relative to specifications acceptable?
- What proportion of output will be expected to meet specifications?
- What factors contribute to variability?

Many reasons exist for conducting a capability study. Manufacturing may wish to determine a performance baseline for a process, to prioritize projects for quality improvement, or to provide statistical evidence of quality for customers. Purchasing might conduct a study at a supplier plant to evaluate a new piece of equipment or to compare different suppliers. Engineering might conduct a study to determine the adequacy of R&D pilot facilities or to evaluate new processes.

Three types of studies are often conducted.

1. A *peak performance study* determines how a process performs under ideal conditions.
2. A *process characterization study* is designed to determine how a process performs under actual operating conditions.
3. A *component variability study* assesses the relative contribution of different sources of total variation.

The methods by which each study is conducted vary. A peak performance study is conducted under carefully controlled conditions over a short time interval to ensure that no special causes can affect variation. A process characterization study is performed over a longer time interval under actual operating conditions to capture the variations in materials and operators. A component variability study uses a designed experiment to control the sources of variability. Although this section considers a process characterization study, the general approach applies to a peak performance study with appropriate modifications.

The six steps in a process capability study are similar to those of any systematic study and include the following:

1. Choose a representative machine or segment of the process.
2. Define the process conditions.
3. Select a representative operator.
4. Provide materials that are of standard grade, with sufficient materials for uninterrupted study.
5. Specify the gauging or measurement method to be used.
6. Provide for a method of recording measurements and conditions, in order, on the units produced.

To obtain useful information, the sample size should be fairly large, generally at least 100. Process capability only makes sense if all special causes of variation have been eliminated and the process is in a state of statistical control (we will discuss this further in Chapter 7). For this discussion, we assume that the process is in control.

Two statistical techniques are commonly used to evaluate process capability. One is the frequency distribution and histogram, the other is the control chart. The use of frequency distributions and histograms is covered in this section, but the discussion of control charts is deferred to Chapter 7.

To illustrate the evaluation of process capability, let us consider the U-bolt previously discussed in Table 4.1. Using basic statistical calculations, we calculated the basic descriptive statistics for these data, and constructed a frequency distribution and histogram shown earlier in Figures 4.6 and 4.8. To recap, we saw that the mean dimension is $\bar{x} = 10.7171$, and the sample standard deviation $s = 0.0868$. The histogram suggests that the data are approximately normally distributed. Using this information, we can analytically estimate the yield of conforming product for various manufacturing specifications.

One of the properties of a normal distribution is that 99.73 percent of the observations will fall within three standard deviations from the mean. Thus, a process that is in control can be expected to produce a large percentage of output between

$\mu - 3\sigma$ and $\mu + 3\sigma$, where μ is the process average. Therefore, the *natural tolerance limits* of the process are $\mu \pm 3\sigma$. A six standard deviation spread is commonly used as a measure of process capability. Thus, for the example, nearly all U-bolt dimensions are expected to fall between $10.7171 - 3(0.0868) = 10.4566$ and $10.7171 + 3(0.0868) = 10.9766$. These calculations tell the production manager that if the design specifications are between 10.45 and 11.00, for instance, the process will be capable of producing nearly 100 percent conforming product.

Not all process output will fit neatly into a normal curve; one can usually obtain important capability information directly from the histogram. Figure 4.12 shows some typical examples of process variation histograms that might result from a capability study. Figure 4.12 (a) shows an ideal situation in which the natural variation is well within the specified tolerance limits. In Figure 4.12 (b), the variation and tolerance limits are about equal; any shift of the distribution will result in nonconformances. The histogram in Figure 4.12 (c) shows a distribution with a natural variation greater than the specification limits; in this case, the process is not capable of meeting specifications. The histograms in Figures 4.12 (d), (e), and (f) correspond to those in Figures 4.12 (a), (b), and (c), except that the process is off-center from the specified tolerance limits. The capability of each is the same as in Figures 4.12 (a), (b), and (c), but the shift in the mean of the distribution results

FIGURE 4.12   EXAMPLES OF PROCESS VARIATION HISTOGRAMS AND SPECIFICATIONS

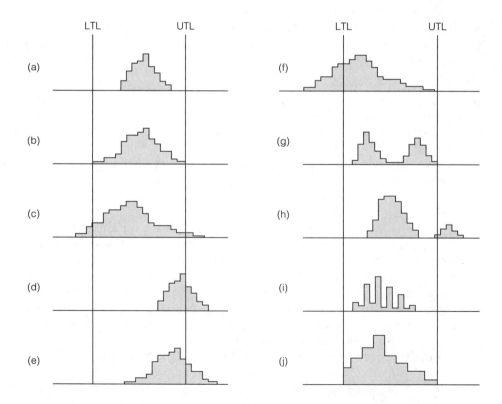

in a higher level of nonconformance. Thus, in Figure 4.12 (d), the process is capable; it is simply not adjusted correctly to the center of the specifications. In Figure 4.12 (g), the bimodal shape suggests that perhaps the data were drawn from two different machines or that two different materials or products were involved. The small distribution to the right in Figure 4.12 (h) may be the result of including pieces from a trial setup run while the machine was being adjusted. The strange distribution in Figure 4.12 (i) might be the result of the measurement process, such as inadequate gauging or rounding of data, and not inherent in the process itself. Finally, the truncated distribution in Figure 4.12 (j) is generally the result of sorting nonconforming parts; one would expect a smoother tail of the distribution on the left. Therefore, one must be careful to ensure that observed variation comes from the process itself, not from external influences. Thus, a good control system is a necessity, because a histogram alone will not provide complete information.

An important issue that is often ignored in process capability studies is the error resulting from using the sample standard deviation, s, rather than the true standard deviation, σ. A simple table can be constructed to find confidence intervals on the true value for σ for a given sample size. Such a table is shown in Table 4.3 and is easily explained by an example. For a given sample size, σ will be

TABLE 4.3 RATIO OF POPULATION TO SAMPLE STANDARD DEVIATION

Number of Samples	Fraction of Population Less Than or Equal to Value in Table							
	0.005	0 010	0.025	0 050	0.100	0 950	0.975	0 995
2	0.356	0.388	0.446	0.510	0.608	15.952	31.911	159.516
3	0.434	0.466	0.521	0 578	0.659	4.407	6.287	14.142
4	0.483	0.514	0.567	0.620	0.693	2.919	3.727	6.468
5	0.519	0.549	0.599	0.649	0.717	2.372	2.875	4.396
6	0.546	0.576	0.624	0.672	0.736	2.090	2.453	3.494
7	0.569	0.597	0.644	0.690	0.751	1.918	2.202	2.979
8	0.588	0.616	0.661	0.705	0.763	1.797	2.035	2.660
9	0.604	0.631	0.675	0 718	0.774	1.711	1.916	2.440
10	0.618	0.645	0.688	0 729	0.783	1.645	1.826	2.278
11	0.630	0.656	0.699	0.739	0.791	1.593	1.755	2.154
12	0.641	0.667	0.708	0.748	0.798	1.551	1.698	2.056
13	0.651	0.677	0.717	0.755	0.804	1.515	1.651	1.976
14	0.660	0.685	0.725	0.762	0.810	1.485	1.611	1.910
15	0.669	0.693	0.732	0 769	0.815	1.460	1.577	1.854
16	0.676	0.700	0.739	0.775	0.820	1.437	1 548	1.806
17	0.683	0.707	0.745	0.780	0.824	1.418	1.522	1.764
18	0.690	0.713	0.750	0.785	0.828	1.400	1.499	1.727
19	0.696	0.719	0.756	0.790	0.832	1.385	1.479	1.695
20	0.702	0.725	0.760	0.794	0.836	1.370	1.461	1.666
21	0.707	0.730	0.765	0.798	0.839	1.358	1.444	1.640
22	0.712	0.734	0.769	0.802	0.842	1.346	1.429	1.617
23	0.717	0.739	0.773	0.805	0.845	1.335	1.415	1.595
24	0.722	0.743	0.777	0.809	0.848	1.325	1.403	1.576
25	0.726	0.747	0.781	0.812	0.850	1.316	1.391	1.558

TABLE 4.3   *(continued)*

26	0.730	0.751	0.784	0.815	0.853	1.308	1.380	1.542
27	0.734	0.755	0.788	0.818	0.855	1.300	1.370	1.526
28	0.737	0.758	0.791	0.820	0.857	1.293	1.361	1.512
29	0.741	0.762	0.794	0.823	0.859	1.286	1.352	1.499
30	0.744	0.765	0.796	0.825	0.861	1.280	1.344	1.487
31	0.748	0.768	0.799	0.828	0.863	1.274	1.337	1.475
36	0.762	0.781	0.811	0.838	0.872	1.248	1.304	1.427
41	0.774	0.792	0.821	0.847	0.879	1.228	1.280	1.390
46	0.784	0.802	0.829	0.854	0.885	1.212	1.260	1.361
51	0.793	0.810	0.837	0.861	0.890	1.199	1.243	1.337
61	0.808	0.824	0.849	0.871	0.898	1.179	1.217	1.299
71	0.820	0.835	0.858	0.879	0.905	1.163	1.198	1.272
81	0.829	0.844	0.866	0.886	0.910	1.151	1.183	1.250
91	0.838	0.852	0.873	0.892	0.915	1.141	1.171	1.233
101	0.845	0.858	0.879	0.897	0.919	1.133	1.161	1.219

Source: Thomas D. Hall, "How Close is s to s?" *Quality*, December 1991, 45. Note: The table published in this article was incorrect. An error notice was published in a subsequent issue and the correct table was made available by *Quality* magazine, and is shown here. Reprinted with permission of *Quality* magazine.

less than or equal to s times the factor in that row with probability p, where p is the column heading. Thus, for a sample size of 30, $\sigma \leq 0.744s$ with probability 0.005; $\sigma \leq 1.280s$ occurs 95 percent of the time; and so on. A 90 percent confidence interval for σ can be found by using the factors in the columns corresponding to $p = 0.050$ and $p = 0.950$. Thus, for a sample size of 30, a 95 percent confidence interval would be $(0.825s, 1.280s)$. The interpretation of process capability information should be tempered by such an analysis.

Process Capability Indexes

The relationship between the natural variation and specifications is often quantified by a measure known as the process capability index. The **process capability index,** C_p (sometimes called the process potential index), is defined as the ratio of the specification width to the natural tolerance of the process. C_p relates the natural variation of the process with the design specifications in a single, quantitative measure.

In numerical terms, the formula is

$$C_p = \frac{UTL - LTL}{6\sigma}$$

where

UTL = upper tolerance limit

LTL = lower tolerance limit

σ = standard deviation of the process

Two important facts about the C_p index should be pointed out. One relates to process conditions and the other relates to interpretation of the values that have been calculated. First, the calculation of the C_p has no meaning if the process is not under statistical control. The natural spread (6σ) should be calculated using a sufficiently large sample to get a meaningful estimate of the population standard deviation (σ). Second, a C_p of 1.00 would require that the process be perfectly centered on the mean of the tolerance spread to prevent some units from being produced outside the limits. The goal of all units being produced within specifications with a C_p of 1.33 is much easier to achieve, and still easier with a C_p of 2.00. Based on the experience of a number of practitioners, they have suggested a "safe" lower limit C_p of 1.5. A value above this level will practically guarantee that all units produced by a controlled process will be within specifications. Many firms require C_p values of 1.66 or greater from their suppliers.

The previous discussion assumed that the process was centered; clearly the value of C_p does not depend on the mean of the process. To include information on process centering, one-sided indexes are often used. One-sided process capability indexes are as follows:

$$C_{pu} = \frac{\text{UTL} - \mu}{3\sigma} \quad \text{(called the upper one-sided index)}$$

$$C_{pl} = \frac{\mu - \text{LTL}}{3\sigma} \quad \text{(called the lower one-sided index)}$$

$$C_{pk} = \min(C_{pl}, C_{pu})$$

To illustrate these computations for the U-bolt example, we found a mean of 10.7171. Thus,

$$C_{pl} = \frac{10.7171 - 10.50}{3(.0868)} = .83$$

$$C_{pu} = \frac{11.0 - 10.7171}{3(.0868)} = 1.086$$

$$C_{pk} = \min\{.83, 1.086\} = .83$$

We see that the process is more capable of satisfying the upper specification limit than the lower specification limit. The low value of C_{pk} indicates that the worst case is unacceptable. This index is often used in specifying quality requirements in purchasing contracts. Figure 4.13 shows a spreadsheet, available on the CD-ROM accompanying this book, designed to compute these indexes.

We note that Six Sigma performance corresponds to process variation equal to half the design tolerance, or a C_p value of 2.0 (see Chapter 2, Figure 2.1). However, because Six Sigma allows a mean shift of up to 1.5 standard deviations from the target, C_{pk} must be held to 1.5.

It is important to remember that C_p and C_{pk} are simply point estimates from some unknown distribution because they are based on samples. A confidence interval for C_{pk} can be expressed as

$$C_{pk} \pm z_{\alpha/2}\sqrt{\frac{1}{9n} + \frac{C_{pk}^2}{2n - 2}}$$

For example, suppose the point estimate is 1.15 and the sample size $n = 45$. Using this formula, a 95 percent confidence interval is (0.89, 1.41). Although 1.15 may seem good, it is quite possible that the true population parameter is less than one because of sampling error. If a sample size of 400 were used instead to obtain the

FIGURE 4.13   SPREADSHEET FOR PROCESS CAPABILITY CALCULATIONS (PROCESS_CAPABILITY.XLS)

	A	B	C	D	E	F	G	H	I	J	K	L	M	N	O	P
1	Process Capability Analysis															
2																
3	This spreadsheet is designed to handle up to 150 observations. Enter data ONLY in yellow-shaded cells.															
4																
5	Nominal specification				10.75		Average			10.7171			Cp	0.96		
6	Upper tolerance limit				11		Standard deviation			0.0868			Cpl	0.833		
7	Lower tolerance limit				10.5								Cpu	1.086		
8													Cpk	0.833		
9																
10	DATA	1	2	3	4	5	6	7	8	9	10	11	12	13	14	15
11	1	10.650	10.800	10.500	10.800	10.700	10.800	10.750	10.650	10.850	10.650	10.800	10.650			
12	2	10.750	10.850	10.800	10.800	10.700	10.700	10.850	10.700	10.800	10.550	10.700	10.850			
13	3	10.750	10.700	10.650	10.800	10.650	10.650	10.750	10.650	10.500	10.800	10.750	10.800			
14	4	10.600	10.650	10.700	10.600	10.700	10.750	10.800	10.850	10.650	10.650	10.700	10.600			
15	5	10.700	10.750	10.700	10.750	10.550	10.700	10.850	10.700	10.750	10.600	10.750	10.700			
16	6	10.600	10.900	10.850	10.750	10.650	10.650	10.600	10.750	10.750	10.600	10.650	10.650			
17	7	10.600	10.750	10.800	10.700	10.600	10.850	10.850	10.850	10.800	10.850	10.850	10.800			
18	8	10.750	10.750	10.700	10.700	10.700	10.600	10.650	10.850	10.750	10.650	10.700	10.650			
19	9	10.650	10.650	10.750	10.800	10.650	10.900	10.650	10.750	10.700	10.750	10.700	10.700			
20	10	10.600	10.600	10.750	10.800	10.750	10.850	10.750	10.750	10.700	10.650	10.600	10.650			

same point estimate, the confidence interval would be (1.06, 1.24), providing a better indication that the capability is indeed good.

Process capability indexes depend on the assumption that the distribution of output is normal. When a normal distribution does not apply, such as in the chemical industry, when suppliers often pick and choose material that will meet the specifications of customers (which often results in a uniform distribution), or when output is affected by tool wear and exhibits a highly skewed distribution, process capability indexes can be below one even though all measurements are within specification limits. Finally, process capability may be affected by measurement error. If the measurement error is large, then process capability indexes must be viewed with caution.

BENCHMARKING

The development and realization of improvement objectives, particularly stretch objectives that often accompany Six Sigma projects, is often aided through the process of benchmarking. **Benchmarking** is defined as "measuring your performance against that of best-in-class companies, determining how the best-in-class achieve those performance levels, and using the information as a basis for your own company's targets, strategies, and implementation,"[8] or more simply, "the search of industry best practices that lead to superior performance."[9] The term **best practices** refers to approaches that produce exceptional results, are usually innovative in terms of the use of technology or human resources, and are recognized by customers or industry experts.

Through benchmarking, a company discovers its strengths and weaknesses and those of other industry leaders and learns how to incorporate the best practices into its own operations. Benchmarking can provide motivation to achieve stretch goals by helping employees to see what others can accomplish. For example, to meet a stretch target of reducing the time to build new 747 and 767 airplanes at Boeing from 18 months (in 1992) to 8 months, teams studied the world's best producers of everything from computers to ships. By 1996 the time had been reduced to 10 months.[10]

The concept of benchmarking is not new.[11] In the early 1800s Francis Lowell, a New England industrialist, traveled to England to study manufacturing techniques at the best British mill factories. Henry Ford created the assembly line after taking a tour of a Chicago slaughterhouse and watching carcasses hung on hooks mounted on a monorail, move from one workstation to another. Toyota's just-in-time production system was influenced by the replenishment practices of U.S. supermarkets. Modern benchmarking was initiated by Xerox and has since become a common practice among leading firms.

An organization may decide to engage in benchmarking for several reasons. It eliminates "reinventing the wheel" along with associated wasted time and resources. It helps identify performance gaps between an organization and competitors, leading to realistic goals. It encourages employees to continuously innovate. Finally, because it is a process of continuous learning, benchmarking emphasizes sensitivity to the changing needs of customers.[12]

Three major types of benchmarking have emerged in business. **Competitive benchmarking** involves studying products, processes, or business performance of competitors in the same industry to compare pricing, technical quality, features, and other quality or performance characteristics of products and services. For example, a television cable company might compare its customer satisfaction rating or service response time to other cable companies; a manufacturer of TVs might compare its unit production costs or field failure rates against competitors. Significant gaps suggest key opportunities for improvement. Competitive benchmarking was refined into a science by Xerox during the 1970s and 1980s.

Process benchmarking emerged soon after. It centers on key work processes such as distribution, order entry, or employee training. This type of benchmarking identifies the most effective practices in companies that perform similar functions, no matter in what industry. For example, Xerox adapted the warehousing and distribution practices of L.L. Bean for its spare parts distribution system. Texas Instruments studied the kitting (order preparation) practices of six companies, including Mary Kay Cosmetics, and designed a process that captured the best practices of each of them, cutting kitting cycle time in half. A General Mills plant in Lodi, California, had an average machine changeover time of three hours. Then somebody said, "From three hours to 10 minutes!" Employees went to a NASCAR track and videotaped the pit crews, and studied the process to identify how the principles could be applied to the production changeover processes. Several months later, the average time fell to 17 minutes.[13] The U.S. Marine Corps studied companies such as Wal-Mart and United Parcel Service to improve its supply chain processes, changing its inventory policies and learning to employ modern technology like handheld computers. Thus, companies should not aim benchmarking solely at direct competitors or similar organizations;

in fact, they would be mistaken to do so. If a company simply benchmarks within its own industry, it may merely be competitive and have a slight edge in those areas in which it is the industry leader. However, if benchmarks are adopted from outside the industry, a company may learn ideas and processes as well as new applications that allow it to surpass the best within its own industry and to achieve distinctive superiority.

Finally, **strategic benchmarking** examines how companies compete and seeks the winning strategies that have led to competitive advantage and market success. The typical benchmarking process can be described by the process used at AT&T.

1. *Project conception:* Identify the need and decide to benchmark.
2. *Planning:* Determine the scope and objectives, and develop a benchmarking plan.
3. *Preliminary data collection:* Collect data on industry companies and similar processes as well as detailed data on your own processes.
4. *Best-in-class selection:* Select companies with best-in-class processes.
5. *Best-in-class collection:* Collect detailed data from companies with best-in-class processes.
6. *Assessment:* Compare your own and best-in-class processes and develop recommendations.
7. *Implementation planning:* Develop operational improvement plans to attain superior performance.
8. *Implementation:* Enact operational plans and monitor process improvements.
9. *Recalibration:* Update benchmark findings and assess improvements in processes.[14]

PROJECT REVIEW—MEASURE PHASE

A project review of the Measure phase should ensure that

- Team members have received any necessary "just-in-time" training.
- Key metrics for all CTQ characteristics have been defined.
- The team has determined what aspects of the problem need to be measured, including both process and results measures.
- Operational definitions of all measurements have been developed.
- All appropriate sources of data have been investigated, and a data collection plan established before data is collected.
- Data collection forms have been tested and validated.
- Sample sizes required for statistical precision have been identified.
- Data have been collected in an appropriate fashion, according to plan.
- The data are accurate and reliable.
- Measurement systems have been evaluated using R&R studies or other appropriate tools.
- Process capability has been addressed as appropriate.
- Benchmarks and best practice information have been collected.

CASE STUDY

Measurement for Process Improvement at Middletown Regional Hospital[15]

Middletown Regional Hospital (MRH) is a licensed 310-bed acute care hospital located in Middletown, Ohio, a southwestern Ohio city about 35 miles from Cincinnati. The parent, MRHS Corporation, includes a major hospital and 20 offsite locations. MRH employs approximately 1,700 people across a four county area and provides all major medical services with the exception of open-heart surgery.

CEO Douglas W. McNeill has led MRH to become a quality-driven organization. This drive for continuous improvement can be seen from the top management down to the frontline employee. Dedication to quality is also evident in the mission, vision, and value statements. Every department at MRH is required to develop annual performance improvement goals and indicators. All employees are trained annually in tools and approaches developed by the Quality Management department. Because of these efforts, the hospital has received a number of quality awards and recognition, including winning the first Codman Award, presented by the Joint Commission on Accreditation of Healthcare Organizations (JCAHO) for quality in a health-care organization, and being named one of the 100 top hospitals in the United States.

Even though MRH does not formally call their improvement initiative "Six Sigma," it employs many of the tools and ideas. Measurement is the key to driving process improvement as well as monitoring and controlling daily operations in every department and area at MRH. A casual visitor who is there seeing a sick relative or friend might not notice the charts and graphs that are in back offices or inconspicuous places, but college classes and professional groups that occasionally take "behind the scenes" tours are struck by the type and amount of measurement that is visible. Variables such as mean time between repairs in instrument maintenance, frequency of use of restraints in the psychiatric nursing unit, and numbers of procedures performed in the phlebotomy (blood-testing) department are charted and analyzed. Over a dozen improvement teams are in operation at any one time. Once a year they come to a continuous improvement day and share their statistics, lessons learned, best practices, and success stories with associates in the hospital community.

An example of the efforts to improve daily operations at MRH is found in Maintenance and Environmental Services, whose director is Jim Faze. This division consists of two departments—the 20-person Maintenance department, which is responsible for the power plant, grounds, and the general maintenance of the 650,000-square foot main facility and the 20 offsite locations; and the Environmental Services (EVS) department, which employs 56 people and is responsible for linen, waste management, and cleaning services for the main facility. To focus on improving services to its internal and external customers, EVS has developed a Customer Service Monitoring System (CSMS) with three distinct parts: the Press Ganey Customer Satisfaction Survey, written customer comments that MRH receives from the survey, and a 7-Step Quality Improvement Process.

Patients fill out the Press Ganey Customer Satisfaction Survey after receiving services. This survey asks a full range of questions relating to all aspects of care the patient received while at any facility. The survey is divided into four major service sectors: Inpatient Services, Ambulatory Services, Outpatient Surgery, and Emergency Services. A direct question about the cleanliness of the hospital is asked for all sectors except Emergency Services. Results of the questionnaire are ranked against all hospitals in the nationwide Press Ganey database for each sector. The data are also sorted by geographic region and hospital size for additional comparative analysis. Approximately 450 hospitals nationwide use this survey so it can also be used as a benchmarking tool. MRH receives the report quarterly.

The second portion of the CSMS consists of written customer comments from the survey. These comments are forwarded to the Guest Relations department and then to the specific departments for action. MRH receives both positive and negative comments from this source. EVS formally praises employees with positive comments and retrains those who receive negative comments.

The third element of the CSMS is a structured and disciplined improvement process. Any time a major problem is encountered, MRH associates apply a seven-step process, which was developed and implemented by an external management consultant group, and is taught and reinforced during the annual employee training sessions. The steps of this process are:

1. Activate organizational awareness.
2. Seek environmental transformation.
3. Identify and define the process.
4. Determine measurements.
5. Collect data using statistical process control (SPC).
6. Analyze and make recommendations.
7. Remeasure to assess improvement.

One problem EVS recognized was that "A significant gap exists between the current level of perceived customer satisfaction and the management goal, as measured by the Press Ganey Customer Satisfaction Survey. The objective is to find ways to eliminate the gap between the current level of 69th percentile ranking and the management goal of 85th percentile."

At the time of this study, MRH had been using the Press Ganey Customer Satisfaction Survey for 11 quarters. One question pertained to the cleanliness of the facility; thus, the key issue for EVS was "How clean was the facility?" Two factors created difficulties in attacking this problem. First, MRH's management only monitored the percentile ranking in the Press Ganey Survey for each division, but no one had the responsibility for completely analyzing all of the survey data. The second factor was the speed at which MRH received the data. MRH and the EVS department had no opportunity for service recovery because the patients were no longer at the facility when MRH received their complaints.

The return rates on the customer surveys had remained fairly constant at 24 percent over the past three years. Return rates for the hospital's three service sectors were: Inpatient Services—26 percent, Ambulatory Services—30 percent, and Outpatient Surgery—16 percent. Three key outcomes were measured: the percentile rank, the mean score, and correlation coefficients. The percentile ranks and mean scores had remained very consistent over time. The correlation coefficients measure the relative importance of a specific question to the overall score. The higher the correlation, the more likely that the overall satisfaction score will go up when the question's score goes up. Revealing information was discovered about correlation coefficient differences among the three service areas. The correlation coefficients for the Ambulatory Services and the Outpatient Surgery are much higher than for Inpatient Services. This result shows that the cleanliness question has less of an impact on the overall score of the inpatient section than in Outpatient Services.

Over a two-year period, EVS teams tried three different approaches to improving the survey scores: implementing a computerized cleaning assignment system, tracking and addressing responses to comments received on customer surveys, and developing and deploying a daily room checklist to be filled out by housekeepers. The computerized cleaning assignment system helped improve the Press Ganey scores early in the process, but had more of an impact on the internal customers. The survey comments suggested that customers did not know what services to expect on a daily basis. MRH formed a team that developed tent cards similar to the ones used in the hotel industry. The tent card serves to let customers know what their room should look like when they arrive, what daily services they can expect, and a phone number to contact EVS if their expectations are not being met. The name of the housekeeper and encouragement to contact the housekeeper about any cleaning issues is also on the card. This approach reduced the number of negative written comments MRH receives. EVS uses the daily room checklist to provide documentation on what services have been performed and to hold housekeepers accountable to get the work done right the first time.

Management and associates in EVS at MRH continue to search for ways to continually improve service levels in their quest to reach the elusive 85th percentile level on the Press Ganey survey, which is management's long-term goal.

REVIEW QUESTIONS

1. Why do organizations need performance measures?
2. Explain the types of measures commonly used for product and service quality.
3. What are the differences between discrete and continuous metrics?
4. What are the basic questions organizations must ask in order to collect accurate data?
5. Describe different types of check sheets that are useful in quality improvement.
6. Discuss the basic questions that must be addressed in a sampling study.
7. Describe the different methods of sample selection and provide an example in which each would be most appropriate.
8. What are the sources of systematic error in sampling, and how can systematic error be overcome?
9. What are the benefits of good data and information systems?
10. Describe the science of metrology.

11. What is the difference between accuracy, precision, and reproducibility?

12. What is calibration and why is it important to a good quality assurance system?

13. Explain the term *process capability*. How can process capability generally be improved?

14. Define the process capability indexes, C_p, C_{pl}, and C_{pu}, and explain how they may be used to establish or improve quality policies in operating areas or with suppliers.

15. List and describe the three major types of benchmarking.

DISCUSSION QUESTIONS

1. How can measurement be used to control and improve the daily operations of your college or university?

2. How does the adoption of a Six Sigma approach within an organization change the amount and types of data that may be gathered routinely, as well as for specific projects?

3. What types of defects or errors might the following organizations measure and improve as part of a Six Sigma initiative?
   a. A metropolitan bus company
   b. A local department store
   c. An electric power company
   d. Walt Disney World or a regional amusement park like Paramount or Six Flags
   e. Your college or university

4. The Cincinnati Water Works (CWW) serves approximately one million customers.[16] Its billing system allows customer service representatives (CSRs) to retrieve information from customer accounts quickly using almost any piece of data such as customer name, address, phone number, social security number, and so on. Besides a customer's account history, the system contains everything that was said in a call, including documentation of past problems and their resolution. An integrated voice response system provides automated phone support for bill paying and account balances, tells customers of the approximate wait time to speak to a CSR, and allows the customers to leave a message for a CSR to return a call. An information board in the department shows the number of customers waiting, average length of time waiting, and the number of CSRs that are busy and doing post-call work. A pop-up screen provides CSRs with customer data before the phone rings so that he or she will have the customer's information before the customer even says hello. Work orders taken by CSRs, such as a broken water main or leaking meter, are routed automatically to a field service supervisor for immediate attention. This system is also used internally to allocate maintenance workers when a problem arises at a pumping station or treatment facility. A geographic information system is used for mapping the locations of water mains and fire hydrants, and provides field service employees, meter readers, and

contractors exact information to accomplish their work. Handheld meter readers are used to locate meters and download data into computers. Touch pad devices provide exterior connections to inside meters, eliminating the necessity to enter a house or building. CWW is also investigating automated meter readers and radio frequency devices that simply require a company van to drive by the building to automatically obtain readings. Explain the role of measurement in this operation. What might a dashboard or scorecard look like in this organization?

5. In the case study in this chapter, how do MRH's continuous improvement tools and practices compare to the DMAIC improvement steps?

6. In the case study in this chapter, what message is sent to associates by the visible use of measurement at MRH?

THINGS TO DO

1. Interview black belts or project champions in an organization that has adopted a Six Sigma approach. Discuss their requirements for data and find out how easy or difficult it is to gather the data needed to support their teams and recommendations to management.

2. Conduct an R&R study with a team of your fellow students to measure a set of sharpened pencils of various sizes. Use both an ordinary ruler and a metric ruler. What conclusions do you reach?

3. Visit several of the following metrology Web sites (and identify some others) and summarize new ideas, concepts, or findings that are not discussed in this chapter.
   www.uktm.external.hp.com
   www.kinematics.com
   www.sandia.gov/psl
   www.asq.org/measure
   www.boulder.nist.gov
   www.nist.gov
   www.gecals.com

4. Visit a local machine shop, bakery, or similar factory to determine what type of measurements they perform, what instruments they use, how they use the data, and how they ensure the precision and accuracy of their instruments and gauges. Write a report of your findings.

5. Identify some of the major processes a student encounters in a college or university. What types of noneducational institutions perform similar processes and might be candidates for benchmarking?

PROBLEMS

1. Apply the descriptive statistics and the histogram analysis tools in the Excel spreadsheet utility to compute the mean, standard deviation, and other relevant statistics, as well as a frequency distribution and histogram for the

data in the student CD-ROM for *Prob. 4-1.* Interpret your results for managerial purposes.

2. The data (*Prob. 4-2* in *Ch4Dataset.xls* on the student CD-ROM) represent the weight of castings (in kilograms) being made in the Harrison Metalwork foundry. Based on this sample of 100 castings, compute the mean, standard deviation and other relevant statistics, as well as a frequency distribution and histogram. What do you conclude from your analysis?

3. You are asked by a motel owner to develop a customer satisfaction survey to determine the percentage of customers who are dissatisfied with service. The motel serviced 20,000 customers in the past year. The manager desires a 95 percent level of confidence with an allowable statistical error of ± 0.02. From past estimates, the manager believes that about 7 percent of customers have expressed dissatisfaction. What sample size should you use for this survey?

4. A utility requires service operators to answer telephone calls from customers in an average time of 0.1 minute or less, and either respond to them or refer the customer to the proper department within 0.5 minute. The manager is interested in estimating the actual overall time for both components, in total. A pilot study sample of 30 actual operator times was drawn, and the results are given in the following table. If the service manager wants to be 95 percent confident that the overall time is correctly estimated, with a 3 percent probability of error, what size sample should be taken?

Component	Mean Time	Standard Deviation
Answer	0.1023	0.0183
Service	0.5290	0.0902

5. For the data from Fujiyama Electronics on the student CD-ROM, *Ch4Dataset* file for *Prob.4-5*, the upper specification limit was USL = 6.75, and the lower specification limit was LSL = 3.25. Compute the process capability and discuss its meaning in managerial terms.

6. A machining process has a required dimension on a part of 0.575 ± 0.007 inches. Twenty-five parts were measured as found in the *Ch4Dataset* file for *Prob.4-6* on the student CD-ROM. What is its capability for producing within acceptable limits?

7. Adjustments were made in the process discussed in Problem 6 and 25 more samples were taken. The results are given in the *Ch4Dataset* file for *Prob.4-7* on the student CD-ROM. What can you observe about the process? What is its capability for producing within acceptable limits now?

8. From the data for *Prob.4-8* for Kermit Theatrical Products on the student CD-ROM, calculate summary statistics and construct a histogram. If the specifications are 24 ± 0.03, compute C_p, C_{pu}, and C_{pl}.

9. Suppose that a process with a normally distributed output has a mean of 55.0 and a variance of 4.0.
   a. If the specifications are 55.0 ± 4.00, compute C_p, C_{pk}, and C_{pm}.
   b. Suppose the mean shifts to 53.0 but the variance remains unchanged. Recompute and interpret these process capability indexes.

c. If the variance can be reduced to 40 percent of its original value, how do the process capability indices change (using the original mean of 55.0)?

10. A gauge repeatability and reproducibility study at Frankford Brake Systems collected the data found in the *Ch4Dataset* file for *Prob.4-10* on the student CD-ROM. After analyzing these data, what should be done? The part specification for the collar that was measured was 1.0 ± 0.06 mm.

ENDNOTES

1. Greg Brue, *Design for Six Sigma* (New York: McGraw-Hill, 2003).

2. Glenn E. Hayes and Harry G. Romig, *Modern Quality Control* (Encino, CA: Benziger, Bruce & Glencoe, 1977).

3. U.S. Office of Management and Budget, "How to Develop Quality Measures That Are Useful in Day-to-Day Measurement," U.S. Department of Commerce, National Technical Information Service, January 1989.

4. "The Tools of Quality Part V: Check Sheets," *Quality Progress* 23, no. 10, October 1990, 53.

5. Kaoru Ishikawa, *Guide to Quality Control*, 2nd rev. ed. (Tokyo: Asian Productivity Organization, 1986). UNIPUB/Quality Resources, White Plains, NY 10601. Used with permission.

6. Statement made by Belinda Collins before the House Subcommittee on Technology, Committee on Science, June 29, 1995.

7. *ASQC Automotive Division Statistical Process Control Manual* (Milwaukee, WI: American Society for Quality Control, 1986). © 1986, American Society for Quality. Reprinted with permission.

8. Lawrence S. Pryor, "Benchmarking: A Self-Improvement Strategy," *Journal of Business Strategy*, November/December 1989, 28–32.

9. Robert C. Camp, *Benchmarking: The Search for Industry Best Practices That Lead to Superior Performance* (Milwaukee, WI: ASQC Quality Press and UNIPUB/Quality Resources, 1989).

10. Shawn Tully, "Why to Go for Stretch Targets," *Fortune*, November 14, 1994, 45–58.

11. Christopher E. Bogan and Michael J. English, "Benchmarking for Best Practices: Winning Through Innovative Adaptation," *Quality Digest*, August 1994, 52–62.

12. Cathy Hill, "Benchmarking and Best Practices," *ASQ's 54th Annual Quality Congress Proceedings*, 2000.

13. John Hackl, "New Beginnings: Change is Here to Stay," *Quality Progress*, February 1998, 5.

14. AT&T Consumer Communication Services Summary of 1994 Application for the Malcolm Baldrige National Quality Award.

15. Appreciation is expressed to one of the author's students, Jim Faze, who wrote the paper on which this case is based, as part of the requirements for MGT 640, Total Quality Management, 2001, at Northern Kentucky University.

16. Adapted from a student project by one of the author's students, Tim Planitz, December 2001.

5

Process Analysis

The third step in DMAIC is *Analysis*. **Analysis** refers to an examination of processes, facts, and data to gain an understanding of why problems occur and where opportunities for improvement exist. This stage might include flow-charting a process, brainstorming among project team members for root causes, stratifying and charting data, or conducting formal experiments and statistical tests. The analysis phase focuses on understanding the relationship between the response variable Y and the input variables X in the relationship $Y = f(X)$ that we introduced in Chapter 2 and expanded on in Chapter 4, particularly to identify the most important factors that influence the results.

Statistics, in particular, provides many useful tools to facilitate data analysis. A solid foundation of statistical principles and methodology is vital to everyone engaged in Six Sigma projects. Statistics provides the means to draw rigorous, quantitative conclusions about data and is one of the most important tools in Six Sigma practice and studies. Six Sigma has, in fact, elevated the importance of statistics in business. Readers of this text are assumed to have prior knowledge of elementary statistics. Although we provide a brief review of some important statistical concepts and applications in Six Sigma, this discussion is not intended to replace a rigorous treatment of statistical methods.

STATISTICAL METHODS IN SIX SIGMA

Statistics is the science concerned with "the collection, organization, analysis, interpretation, and presentation of data."[1] Some examples of data analyses used in Six Sigma include:

- Examining patterns, trends, and changes over time
- Making comparisons relative to other business units, competitor performance, or best-in-class benchmarks
- Seeking to understand relationships among different metrics

For example, simple descriptive statistics and charts can be used to examine patterns and trends, the significance of comparative data might be analyzed with hypothesis tests, and correlation and regression analysis can be used to understand relationships among variables.

Statistical methods have applications in many areas of Six Sigma, including product and market analysis, product and process design, process control, testing and inspection, identification and verification of process improvements, and reliability analysis. Evidence suggests that organizations that use more sophisticated statistical tools for analysis tend to have better results.

Figure 5.1 summarizes the basic statistical methodology used in Six Sigma. The first major component of statistical methodology is the efficient collection, organization, and description of data, commonly referred to as **descriptive statistics**. We discussed the fundamentals of descriptive statistics in Chapter 4.

The second component of statistical problem solving is **statistical inference**. Statistical inference is the process of drawing conclusions about unknown characteristics of a population from which data were taken. Techniques used in this phase include confidence intervals, hypothesis testing, and experimental design. For example, a chemical manufacturer might be interested in determining the effect of temperature on the yield of a new manufacturing process. Because of variation in

FIGURE 5.1   STATISTICAL METHODOLOGY FOR SIX SIGMA

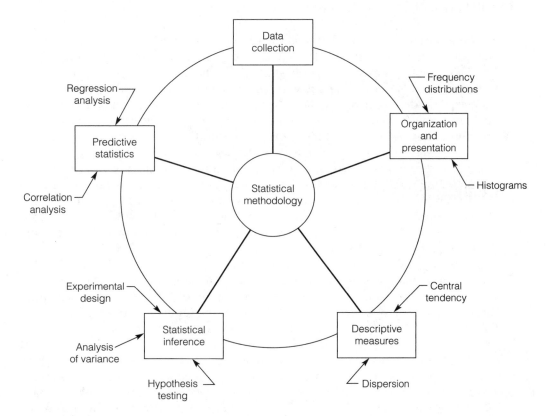

yields, a confidence interval might be constructed to quantify the uncertainty of sample data. In a controlled experiment, the manufacturer might test the hypothesis that the temperature has an effect on the yield against the alternative hypothesis that temperature has no effect. If the temperature is, in fact, a critical variable, the manufacturer will require steps to maintain the temperature at the proper level and to draw inferences as to whether the process remains under control, based on samples taken from it. Experimental design (also known as design of experiments, or DOE) is important for helping to understand the effects of process factors on performance and for optimizing systems. DOE plays a critical role in Design for Six Sigma and will be discussed in Chapter 9.

The third component in statistical methodology is **predictive statistics**, the purpose of which is to develop predictions of future values based on historical data. Correlation analysis and regression analysis are two useful techniques. Frequently, these techniques can clarify the characteristics of a process as well as predict future results. For example, in quality assurance, correlation is frequently used in test instrument calibration studies. In such studies, an instrument is used to measure a standard test sample that has known characteristics. The actual results are compared to standard results, and adjustments are made to compensate for errors.

PROBABILITY DISTRIBUTIONS

Random variables and probability distributions are the foundation for understanding statistical methods. The collectively exhaustive set of outcomes from an experiment makes up a *sample space*. A mathematical function that assigns numerical values to every possible outcome in a sample space is called a *random variable*. A random variable can be either discrete or continuous, depending on the specific numerical values it may assume. A *discrete random variable* can take on only finite values. An example would be the number of defects observed in a sample. A *continuous random variable* can take on any real value over a specified interval of real numbers. An example would be the diameters of bearings being manufactured in a factory. Of course, the actual observed values for the variable are limited by the precision of the measuring device. Hence, only a finite number of actual observations would occur. In theory, this result would still be a continuous random variable. Random variables are the key component used in the development of probability distributions.

A *probability distribution* represents a theoretical model of the relative frequency of a random variable. Relating probability distributions to the random variables that they represent allows a classification of the distributions as either discrete or continuous. You are undoubtedly quite familiar with the normal distribution and its use as a common assumption in statistical models. Unfortunately, most business processes do not produce normal distributions.[2] Lack of a normal distribution often results from the tendency to control processes tightly, which eliminates many sources of natural variation, as well as from human behavior, physical laws, and inspection practices. For example, data on the number of days customers take to pay bills typically show that many customers like to prepay; others send payments that arrive just after the due date. This behavior causes spikes in the distribution that do not conform to normality. In a hot-dip galvanizing process, a zinc layer forms when the base material reaches the temperature of molten zinc. However, if the part is removed before the critical temperature is reached, no zinc will adhere at all. Thus, all parts will have some minimum zinc thickness and the left side of the distribution will not tail off gradually as does a normal distribution. Measuring perpendicularity as the absolute deviation from 90 degrees instead of the actual angle can easily lead to non-normality. Therefore, it is important to fully understand the nature of your data before applying statistical theory that depends on normality assumptions.

Important Probability Distributions

Certain discrete distributions describe many natural phenomena and have broad applications in Six Sigma. Two of them are the binomial distribution and the Poisson distribution, discussed next. Later, some important continuous probability distributions are introduced.

Binomial Distribution

The **binomial distribution** describes the probability of obtaining exactly x "successes" in a sequence of n identical experiments, called trials. A *success* can be any one of two possible outcomes of each experiment. In some situations, it might represent a defective item, in others, a good item. The probability of success in each trial is a constant value p. The binomial probability function is given by the following formula:

$$f(x) = \binom{n}{x} p^x (1 - p)^{n-x}$$

$$= \frac{n!}{x!(n - x)!} p^x (1 - p)^{n-x} \quad x = 0, 1, 2, \ldots, n$$

where p is the probability of a success, n is the number of items in the sample, and x is the number of items for which the probability is desired $(0, 1, 2, \ldots, n)$. The expected value, variance, and standard deviation of the binomial distribution are

$$E(p) = \mu = np$$
$$\sigma^2 = np(1 - p)$$
$$\sigma = \sqrt{np(1 - p)}$$

Poisson Distribution

The second discrete distribution often used in quality control is the **Poisson distribution**. The Poisson probability distribution is given by

$$f(x) = \frac{e^{-\mu} \mu^x}{x!}$$

where μ = expected value or average number of occurrences, $x = 0, 1, 2, 3, \ldots$, and $e \approx 2.71828$, a constant.

The Poisson distribution is also used to calculate the number of occurrences of an event over a specified interval of time or space, such as the number of scratches per square inch on a polished surface. The Poisson distribution is closely related to the binomial distribution. It is derived by allowing the sample size (n) to become very large (approaching infinity) and the probability of success or failure (p) to become very small (approaching zero) while the expected value (np) remains constant. Thus, when n is large relative to p, the Poisson distribution can be used as an approximation to the binomial. A common rule of thumb is if $p \leq 0.05$ and $n \geq 20$, the Poisson will be a good approximation with $\mu = np$. If the conditions for the Poisson approximation cannot be met, a normal approximation to the binomial, discussed in the next section, may be of use.

Normal Distribution

The probability density function of the normal distribution is represented graphically by the familiar bell-shaped curve. However, not every symmetric, unimodal curve is a normal distribution, nor can all data from a sample or population be assumed to fit a normal distribution. However, data are often assumed to be normally distributed to simplify certain calculations. In most cases, this assumption makes little difference in the results but is important from a theoretical perspective. The probability density function for the normal distribution is as follows:

$$f(x) = \frac{1}{\sqrt{2\pi\sigma^2}} e^{-(x-\mu)^2/2\sigma^2} \quad -\infty < x < \infty$$

where

μ	=	the mean of the random variable x
σ^2	=	the variance of x
e	=	2.71828 . . .
π	=	3.14159 . . .

If a normal random variable has a mean $\mu = 0$ and a standard deviation $\sigma = 1$, it is called a **standard normal distribution**. The letter z is usually used to represent this particular random variable. By using the constants 0 and 1 for the mean and standard deviation, respectively, the probability density function for the normal distribution can be simplified as

$$f(z) = \frac{1}{\sqrt{2\pi}} e^{-z^2/2}$$

This standard normal distribution function is shown in Figure 5.2. Because $\sigma = 1$, the scale on the z-axis is given in units of standard deviations. Special tables of areas under the normal curve have been developed as an aid in computing probabilities. Such a table is given in Appendix A. Fortunately, any normal distribution involving a random variable x with a known (or estimated) mean and standard deviation is easily transformed into a standard normal distribution using the following formula:

$$z = \frac{x - \mu}{\sigma}$$

This formula takes the value of the variable of interest (x), subtracts the mean value (μ), and divides by the standard deviation (σ). This calculation yields a random variable z, which has a standard normal distribution. Probabilities for this variable can then be found in the table in Appendix A.

The area under the curve that corresponds to one standard deviation from the mean is 0.3413; therefore, the probability that the value of a normal random

FIGURE 5.2 STANDARD NORMAL DISTRIBUTION

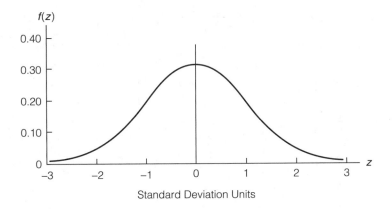

Standard Deviation Units

variable falls within one standard deviation ($\pm 1\sigma$) from the mean is 0.6826. The corresponding x-values are often called 1-sigma limits in statistical quality control terminology. Two standard deviations on one side of the mean correspond to 0.4772 area under the curve, so the probability that a normal random variable falls within a 2-sigma limit is twice that figure, or 0.9544. Three standard deviations encompass an area of 0.4986 under the curve on either side of the mean, or a total area of 0.9972. Hence, the 3-sigma limit encompasses nearly all of the normal distribution. These concepts form the basis for control charts.

Normal Approximation to the Binomial

Although the binomial distribution is extremely useful, it has a serious limitation when dealing with either small probabilities or large sample sizes—it is tedious to calculate. The discussion of the Poisson approximation to the binomial showed that when the probability of success or failure becomes small, the Poisson distribution permits calculation of similar probability values more easily than the binomial. Also, as the sample size gets large (approaches infinity), the binomial distribution approaches the normal distribution as a limit. Hence, for large sample sizes, good approximations of probabilities that would have been calculated using the binomial distribution can be obtained by using the normal distribution. The normal approximation holds well when $np \geq 5$ and $n(1 - p) \geq 5$.

Exponential Distribution

Another continuous distribution commonly used in quality assurance is the exponential distribution. The exponential distribution is used extensively in reliability estimation. The probability density function for the exponential distribution is much simpler than the one for the normal distribution. Therefore, direct evaluation is easier, although tabulated values for the exponential distribution are also readily available. The formula for the exponential probability density function is

$$f(x) = \frac{1}{\mu} e^{-x/\mu}, \quad x \geq 0$$

FIGURE 5.3 SUMMARY OF COMMON PROBABILITY DISTRIBUTIONS

Distribution	Form	Probability Function	Comments on Application
Normal		$y = \dfrac{1}{\sigma\sqrt{2\pi}}\,\theta^{-\frac{(x-\mu)^x}{2\sigma}}$ μ = Mean σ = Standard deviation	Applicable when a concentration of observations falls about the average and when observations are equally likely to occur above and below the average. Variation in observations is usually the result of many small causes.
Exponential		$y = \dfrac{1}{\mu}\,e^{-\frac{x}{\mu}}$	Applicable when more observations are likely to occur below the average than above.
Poisson	$p = 0.1$ $p = 0.3$ $p = 0.5$ x	$y = \dfrac{e^{-\mu}\mu^x}{x!}$ n = Number of trials p = Probability of occurrence x = Number of occurrences $\mu = np$	Same as binomial but particularly applicable when many opportunities for occurrence of an event are possible but have a low probability (less than 0.10) on each trial.
Binomial	$p = 0.1$ $p = 0.3$ $p = 0.5$ x	$y = \dfrac{n!}{x!(n-x)!}\,p^x q^{n-x}$ n = Number of trials x = Probability of occurrence p = Number of occurrences $q = 1 - p$	Applicable in defining the probability of x occurrences in n trials of an event that has a constant probability of occurrence on each independent trial.

Source: Adapted from J. M. Juran and F. M. Gryna, Jr., Instructor's Manual to accompany *Quality Planning and Analysis* (New York: McGraw-Hill, 1980), 125. © 1980 by McGraw-Hill, Inc. Used with permission.

where
- μ = mean value for the distribution
- x = time or distance over which the variable extends
- e = 2.71828 . . .

The cumulative distribution function is

$$F(x) = 1 - e^{-x/\mu}$$

Figure 5.3 summarizes these four important distributions.

BASIC STATISTICAL METHODS

The discipline of statistics encompasses a wide variety of tools and techniques, far too numerous to survey in this book. Some of the more important techniques in Six Sigma are reviewed in this section.

Statistical Inference

Statistical inference is concerned with drawing conclusions about populations based on sample data. To be able to make probability statements about the relationship between sample statistics and population parameters and draw inferences, we first need to understand sampling distributions.

Sampling Distributions

Different samples will produce different estimates of the population parameters. Therefore, sample statistics such as $\bar{x}$, s, and p are random variables that have their own probability distribution, mean, and variance. These probability distributions are called sampling distributions. In Six Sigma applications, the sampling distributions of $\bar{x}$ and p are of the most interest.

When using simple random sampling, the expected value of $\bar{x}$ is the population mean μ, or

$$E(\bar{x}) = \mu$$

The standard deviation of $\bar{x}$ (often called the **standard error of the mean**) is given by the formula

$$\sigma_{\bar{x}} = \frac{\sigma}{\sqrt{n}} \qquad \text{for infinite populations or sampling with replacement from an infinite population}$$

$$\sigma_{\bar{x}} = \sqrt{\frac{N-n}{N-1}} \frac{\sigma}{\sqrt{n}} \qquad \text{for finite populations}$$

When $n/N \leq 0.05$, $\sigma_{\bar{x}} = \sigma/\sqrt{n}$ provides a good approximation for finite populations.

The last step is to characterize the form of the probability distribution of $\bar{x}$. If the true population distribution is unknown, the central limit theorem (CLT) can provide some useful insights: If simple random samples of size n are taken from any population having a mean μ and a standard deviation of σ, the probability distribution of the sample mean approaches a normal distribution with mean μ and standard deviation (standard error) $\sigma_{\bar{x}} = \sigma/\sqrt{n}$ as n becomes very large. In more precise mathematical terms: As $n \to \infty$ the distribution of the random variable $z = (\bar{x} - \mu)/(\sigma/\sqrt{n})$ approaches that of a standard normal distribution. For samples as small as five, the sampling distribution begins to develop into the symmetric bell-shaped form of a normal distribution. Also, the variance decreases as the sample size increases. The approximation to a normal distribution can be assumed for sample sizes of 30 or more. If the population is *known* to be normal, the sampling distribution of $\bar{x}$ is normal for any sample size.

Next, consider the sampling distribution of p, in which the expected value of p, $E(p) = \pi$. Here π is used as the population parameter and is not related to the *number* $\pi \approx 3.14159$. The standard deviation of p is

$$s_p = \sqrt{\frac{\pi(1-\pi)}{n}}$$

for infinite populations.

For finite populations, or when $n/N > 0.05$, modify s_p by

$$s_p = \sqrt{\frac{N-n}{N-1}} \sqrt{\frac{\pi(1-\pi)}{n}}$$

In applying the central limit theorem (CLT) to p, the sampling distribution of p can be approximated by a normal distribution for large sample sizes. Consider the following example to illustrate the application of sampling distributions.

The mean length of shafts produced on a lathe has historically been 50 inches, with a standard deviation of 0.12 inch. If a sample of 36 shafts is taken, what is the probability that the sample mean would be greater than 50.04 inches?

The sampling distribution of the mean is approximately normal with mean 50 and standard deviation of $0.12/\sqrt{36}$. Thus,

$$z = \frac{\bar{x}-\mu}{\sigma/\sqrt{n}} = \frac{50.04-50}{0.12/\sqrt{36}} = 2.0$$

In the standard normal table, the value of 2.0 yields the probability of 0.4772 between the mean and this value. The area for $z \geq 2.0$ then is found by

$$P(z \geq 2.0) = 0.5000 - 0.4772 = 0.0228$$

Thus, the probability of a value equal to or greater than 50.04 inches as the mean of a sample of 36 items is only 0.0228 if the population mean is 50 inches. The applicability of sampling distributions to statistical quality is that "shifts" in the population mean can quickly be detected using small representative samples to monitor the process.

Similarly, if a sample size of 64 is used, $\sigma/\sqrt{n} = 0.12/8 = 0.015$ and

$$z = \frac{\bar{x}-\mu}{\sigma/\sqrt{n}} = \frac{50.04-50}{0.015} = 2.67$$

and $P(z \geq 2.67) = 0.5000 - 0.4962 = 0.0038$. As the sample size increases, it is less likely that a mean value of at least 50.04 will be observed purely by chance. If it was found, some special cause would likely be present.

Confidence Intervals

A confidence interval (CI) is an interval estimate of a population parameter that also specifies the likelihood that the interval contains the true population parameter. This probability is called the **level of confidence**, denoted by $1 - \alpha$, and is usually expressed as a percentage. For example, we might state that "a 90 percent CI for the mean is 10 ± 2." The value 10 is the point estimate calculated from the sample data, and 2 can be thought of as a margin for error. Thus, the interval estimate is [8, 12]. However, this interval may or may not include the true population mean. If we take a different sample, we will most likely have a different point estimate, say 11.4, which determines the interval estimate [8.4, 12.4]. Again, this interval may or may not include the true population mean. If we chose 100 samples, leading to 100 different interval estimates, we would expect that 90 percent of them—the level of confidence—would contain the true population mean. We would say we are 90 percent confident that the interval we obtain from sample data contains the true population mean. Commonly used confidence levels are 90, 95, and 99 percent; the higher the confidence level, the more assurance we have that the interval contains the true population parameter. As the confidence level increases, the confidence interval becomes larger to provide higher levels of assurance.

Some common confidence intervals are

- Confidence interval for the mean, standard deviation known, sample size $= n$:

$$\bar{x} \pm z_{\alpha/2}\sigma/\sqrt{n}$$

- Confidence interval for the mean, standard deviation unknown, sample size $= n$:

$$x \pm t_{\alpha/2,n-1}(s/\sqrt{n})$$

- Confidence interval for a proportion, sample size $= n$:

$$p \pm z_{\alpha/2}\sqrt{\frac{p(1-p)}{n}}$$

- Confidence interval for difference between two means, independent samples, equal variance, sample sizes $= n_1$ and n_2:

$$x_1 - x_2 \pm (t_{\alpha/2,n_1+n_2-2})s_p\sqrt{\frac{1}{n_1} + \frac{1}{n_2}}$$

- Confidence interval for differences between two proportions, sample sizes $= n_1$ and n_2:

$$p_1 - p_2 \pm z_{\alpha/2}\sqrt{\frac{p_1(1-p_1)}{n_1} + \frac{p_2(1-p_2)}{n_2}}$$

Hypothesis Testing

Hypothesis testing involves drawing inferences about two contrasting propositions (hypotheses) relating to the value of a population parameter, one of which is assumed to be true in the absence of contradictory data. For instance, suppose that a company is testing out a prototype process that is designed to reduce manufacturing cycle time. They can evaluate the proposed process by testing a hypothesis that the mean cycle time is the same as the current process.

A hypothesis test involves the following steps:

1. Formulate the hypotheses to test.
2. Select a level of significance that defines the risk of drawing an incorrect conclusion about the assumed hypothesis that is actually true.
3. Determine a decision rule on which to base a conclusion.
4. Collect data and calculate a test statistic.
5. Apply the decision rule to the test statistic and draw a conclusion.

To illustrate hypothesis testing, let us examine a producer of computer-aided design software for the aerospace industry that receives numerous calls for technical support. Tracking software is used to monitor response and resolution times. The company has a service standard of four days for the mean resolution time. However, the manager of the technical support group has been receiving some complaints of long resolution times. During one week, a sample of 44 customer calls resulted in a sample mean of 5.23 and standard deviation of 13.5. Even though the sample mean exceeds the four-day standard, does the manager have sufficient evidence to conclude that the mean service time exceeds four days, or is this sample mean simply a result of sampling error?

The hypothesis tested is

$$H_0: \text{Mean response time} \leq 4$$
$$H_1: \text{Mean response time} > 4$$

The appropriate test statistic is

$$t = \frac{\bar{x} - 4}{s/\sqrt{n}}$$

The decision rule is to reject H_0 if $t > t_{n-1,\,\alpha}$. We compute the value of the test statistic as

$$t = \frac{\bar{x} - 4}{s/\sqrt{n}} = \frac{5.23 - 4}{13.5/\sqrt{44}} = \frac{1.23}{2.035} = 0.604.$$

Because $t_{43,\,.05} = 1.6811$, we cannot reject the null hypothesis. Therefore, the manager finds no sufficient statistical evidence that the mean response time exceeds four days.

Enumerative and Analytic Studies

One of the biggest mistakes that people make in using statistical methods is confusing data that are sampled from a static population (cross-sectional data) with data sampled from a dynamic process (time series data). A static population, such as employees in a company or its customer base, can be analyzed to estimate population parameters such as the mean, variance, or proportion. Confidence intervals and hypothesis tests can be applied. However, the purpose of sampling from a process is generally to predict the future. The characteristics of the population may change over time as a plot of sample means or variances might show. In such cases, confidence intervals and hypothesis tests are not appropriate *unless the time series can be shown to be stationary*, that is, have a constant mean and variance over time. Examining a trend chart of the data over time can usually provide more stationary parameters. Deming called the analysis of a static population an **enumerative study**, and the analysis of a dynamic time series an **analytic study**. Applying classical statistical inferences to an analytic study is not appropriate because they provide no basis for prediction. Thus, it is important to understand how to apply statistical tools properly.

In the hypothesis testing example, for instance, we need to assume that the data are stationary during the week over which they were collected to apply this tool correctly. If we sampled the data over a long period of time and the characteristics of the population (mean or variance) changed over that time, then conducting a hypothesis test would not be appropriate.

Regression and Correlation

Regression analysis is a tool for building statistical models that characterize relationships between a dependent variable and one or more independent variables, all of which are numerical. The relationship may be linear, one of many types of nonlinear forms, or there may be no relationship at all. A regression model that involves a single independent variable is called *simple regression*. A regression model that involves several independent variables is called *multiple regression*. To develop a regression model, you first must specify the type of function that best describes the data. This step is important, because using a linear model for data that are clearly nonlinear, for instance, would probably lead to poor business decisions and results.

A visual indication of the type of relationship between two variables can usually be seen in a **scatter diagram**, and we always recommend that you create one first to gain some understanding of the nature of any potential relationship before conducting regression analysis. Typically, the variables in question represent possible cause-and-effect relationships. For example, if a manufacturer suspects that the percentage of an ingredient in an alloy is influencing the ability to meet hardness specifications, a scatter diagram can easily show if hardness seems to change when the percentage of the ingredient is changed. Scatter diagrams can be plotted easily on a Microsoft Excel chart.

Correlation is a measure of a linear relationship between two variables, X and Y, and is measured by the (population) correlation coefficient. Correlation coefficients will range from -1 to $+1$. A correlation of 0 indicates that the two variables have no linear relationship to each other. Thus, if one changes, we cannot reasonably predict what the other variable might do using a linear equation (we might, however, have a well-defined nonlinear relationship). A correlation coefficient of $+1$ indicates a perfect positive linear relationship; as one variable increases, the other will also increase. A correlation coefficient of -1 also shows a perfect linear relationship, except that as one variable increases, the other decreases.

To illustrate regression, we will use a common issue in quality that we will discuss again in a later chapter—ensuring that instruments are properly calibrated. In principle, it is a simple matter to check calibration. One connects the instrument to a known source, such as an extremely accurate voltage generator to check a voltmeter or a precision gauge block to check a micrometer. A reading is then obtained to determine whether the instrument is capable of accurately measuring the known variable. In practice, numerous sources of variation in the process may make calibration difficult.

The data in Figure 5.4 represent actual readings obtained from the calibration of a voltmeter versus the standard source readings from an accurate voltage generator. The source readings were purposely not set in even integer increments so as to minimize possible bias of the inspector taking the actual readings. To determine whether the instrument is accurate, we can develop a regression equation for the data. Using the Regression tool in Microsoft Excel, we obtain the results shown in Figure 5.4. The estimated regression equation is $Y = 0.0265 + .9914X$. The value of R^2 is 0.9999, indicating an excellent fit. Note also that the value of the intercept is close to 0 and the slope is close to 1, which is where they should be. We would conclude that the instrument is in near perfect calibration, as the scatter chart and fitted regression line in Figure 5.5 also indicate.

FIGURE 5.4   MICROSOFT EXCEL REGRESSION EXAMPLE

	A	B	C	D	E	F	G	H	I	J
1	**Voltmeter Calibration**									
2				SUMMARY OUTPUT						
3	Actual (Y)	Source (X)								
4	1.09	1.05		*Regression Statistics*						
5	2.12	2.15		Multiple R	0.999967043					
6	3.08	3.12		R Square	0.999934087					
7	4.09	4.08		Adjusted R Square	0.999925848					
8	5.11	5.11		Standard Error	0.027282724					
9	6.08	6.07		Observations	10					
10	7.2	7.23								
11	8.3	8.34		ANOVA						
12	9.59	9.66			*df*	*SS*	*MS*	*F*	*Significance F*	
13	10.41	10.49		Regression	1	90.33725522	90.33726	121364.4	5.16118E-18	
14				Residual	8	0.005954776	0.000744			
15				Total	9	90.34321				
16										
17					*Coefficients*	*Standard Error*	*t Stat*	*P-value*	*Lower 95%*	*Upper 95%*
18				Intercept	0.02648404	0.018447595	1.435636	0.189028	-0.016056219	0.069024299
19				Source (X)	0.991364042	0.002845689	348.374	5.16E-18	0.984801867	0.997926217

FIGURE 5.5   SCATTER CHART AND FITTED REGRESSION LINE OF VOLTMETER CALIBRATION READINGS

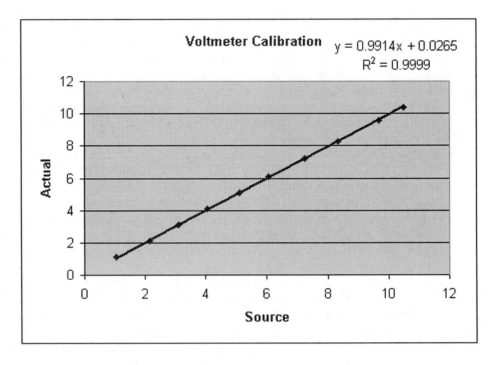

Analysis of Variance (ANOVA)

Because of Six Sigma, practitioners have "rediscovered" many long-standing statistical techniques such as analysis of variance, or ANOVA. ANOVA is a methodology for drawing conclusions about equality of means of multiple populations. In its simplest form—one-way ANOVA—we are interested in comparing means of observed responses of several different levels of a single factor.

ANOVA tests the hypothesis that the means of all populations are equal against the alternative hypothesis that at least one mean differs from the others. To conduct an ANOVA, we need to

1. Carefully define the purpose and assumptions of the experiment.
2. Gather data related to the factor levels of interest.
3. Compute ANOVA statistics.
4. Interpret the meaning of the data.
5. Take action.

Let us suppose that an analyst was interested in determining whether any significant differences exist in the performance between various brands of batteries (the factor levels) in a product. Understanding possible differences in battery performance could be a first step in examining whether other factors such as connector type or temperature might have an effect on product performance. Table 5.1 shows discharge times for three different brands of batteries, gathered through a measurement process.

Microsoft Excel provides a simple procedure to conduct a one-way ANOVA. Select ANOVA: Single Factor from the Tools/Data Analysis options. In the dialog box that pops up, enter the input range of the data in your spreadsheet and check whether it is stored in rows or columns. Table 5.2 shows the results of applying this tool. What does it tell us?

The objective of ANOVA is to statistically test the differences between the means of the groups (the time to discharge for the various brands of batteries) to determine whether they are the same or at least one mean is different. To make this determination, ANOVA partitions the total variability of the data into two parts, the variation between groups and the variation within groups. If the total variation between groups is relatively small compared to the variation within groups, it suggests that the populations are essentially the same. A relatively large variation between groups, however, suggests that differences exist in the unknown population means. The variation in the data is computed as a sum of squared (SS) deviations from the appropriate sample mean, and scaled as a variance measure, or "mean square" (MS). By dividing the mean square between groups by the mean square within groups, an F statistic is computed. If this value is larger than a critical value, $F_{crit,}$ then the data suggest that a difference in means exist.

An examination of the Summary section in Table 5.2 shows that Group A's mean value and variance are considerably larger than the others. In the ANOVA part of the table, the mean square between groups is significantly larger than the mean square within groups, resulting in an F statistic of

TABLE 5.1 BATTERY DISCHARGE TIME DATA BY BRAND

		Brand	
Observation	A	B	C
1	493	108	94
2	490	95	75
3	489	115	93
4	612	82	72

TABLE 5.2   RESULTS OF MICROSOFT EXCEL ANOVA PROCEDURE

Summary

Groups	Count	Sum	Average	Variance
A	4	2084	521	3683.333
B	4	400	100	212.6667
C	4	334	83.5	135

ANOVA

Source of Variation	SS	df	MS	F	P-value	F crit
Between Groups	491892.67	2	245946.33	183.0412	5.13E-08	4.256492
Within Groups	12093	9	1343.6667			
Total	503985.67	11				

183.0412. When this value is compared to the critical F value (4.256), for 2 and 9 degrees of freedom at a 0.05 level of significance (from an F-table, available in any statistics text), we can reject the hypothesis that the means for the three battery types are the same. In fact, $F = 183$ is so much larger than 4.256, that we only have a 5.13×10^{-8} probability (the p-value in the output) that we could be wrong and should have failed to reject the hypothesis! The analyst could conclude that a significant difference exists between the battery types. Other statistical tests are available to demonstrate what factor levels differ from the others (although in this case, it is fairly obvious). The next step might be to explore other variables (connector type, battery temperature) to see how they might affect battery discharge time. It would require more sophisticated ANOVA methods. We encourage you to consult more complete statistics books, such as Montgomery or Lipson and Sheth.[3]

You can probably identify many applications of ANOVA in Six Sigma projects, when differences among critical quality characteristics must be explored. However, ANOVA requires that some statistical assumptions be satisfied for proper interpretation of the results, namely that the populations from which the samples are drawn are normally distributed and have equal variances, and that the data are randomly and independently obtained. These assumptions should be validated if possible.

TOOLS FOR PROCESS ANALYSIS

We introduced the notion of processes in Chapter 1; in this section we present approaches for understanding processes, why variation occurs in them and how statistical thinking can help to understand variation, and drilling down to the root cause of poor process performance.

Process Mapping

A **process map** or **flowchart** identifies the sequence of activities or the flow of materials and information in a process. Process maps help the people involved in the process understand it much better and more objectively by providing a picture of the steps needed to accomplish a task. They are best developed by having the people involved in the process—employees, supervisors, managers, and customers—construct them. A facilitator provides objectivity in resolving conflicts. The facilitator can guide the discussion through questions such as "What happens next?" "Who makes the decision at this point?" and "What operation is performed at this point?" Quite often, the group does not universally agree on the answers to these questions due to misconceptions about the process itself or a lack of awareness of the "big picture." Flowcharts can easily be created using Microsoft Excel using the features found on the Drawing toolbar.[4]

Process maps help team members understand how a process operates and who the key suppliers and customers are. Once a flowchart is constructed, it can be used to identify sources of errors or defects, unwanted variation, and opportunities for improvement. Questions such as "How does this operation affect the customer?" "Can we improve or even eliminate this operation?" or "Should we control a critical quality characteristic at this point?" trigger the identification of improvement opportunities.

One way of building a detailed process map is to start with the outputs, or customer requirements, and move backward through the process to identify the key steps needed to produce each output; stop when the process reaches the supplier input stage.

AT&T suggests the following steps:[5]

1. Begin with the process output and ask, "What is the last essential subprocess that produces the output of the process?"
2. For that subprocess, ask "What input does it need to produce the process output?" For each input, test its value to ensure that it is required.
3. For each input, identify its source. In many cases, the input will be the output of the previous subprocess. In some cases, the input may come from external suppliers.
4. Continue backward, one subprocess at a time, until each input comes from an external supplier.

This technique can be applied to each subprocess to create a more detailed process description.

The following example shows in more detail how Boise Cascade, Inc. exploited process mapping.[6] The Timber and Wood Products Division of Boise formed a team of 11 people with diverse backgrounds from manufacturing, administration, and marketing to improve a customer claims processing and tracking system that affected all areas and customers in its six divisions. Although external customer surveys indicated that the company was not doing badly, internal opinions of the operation were far more critical. The first eye-opener came when the process was flowcharted and the group discovered that more than 70 steps were performed for each claim. Figure 5.6 shows the original flowchart from the marketing and sales department. Combined division tasks numbered in the hundreds for a single claim; the marketing and sales portion of the flowchart alone consisted of up to 20 separate tasks and seven decisions, which sometimes took months to complete. Most of these steps added no value to the settlement outcome. During their improvement process, the group eliminated 70 percent of the steps for small claims.

FIGURE 5.6 FLOWCHART FOR BOISE CLAIMS PROCESS

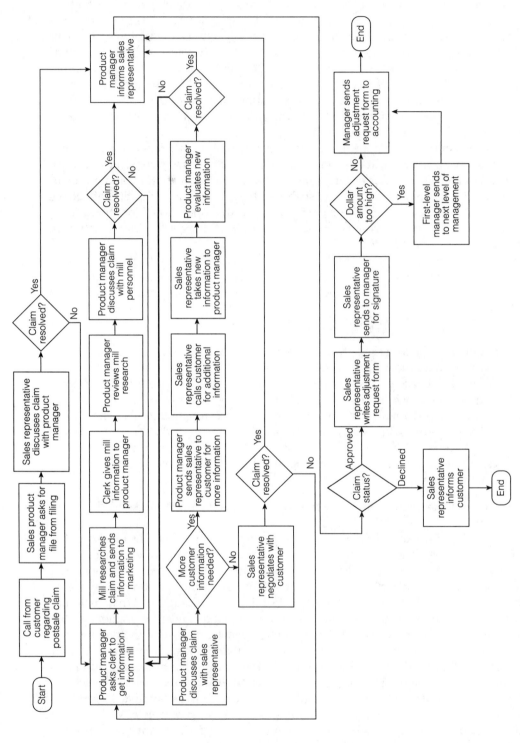

Source: Dwight Kirscht and Jennifer M. Tunnell. "Boise Cascade Stakes a Claim on Quality," *Quality Progress*, 26, 11, November, 1993. © 1993 American Society for Quality. Reprinted with permission.

Value Stream Mapping

A special type of process map is a **value stream map**. The value stream refers to all activities involved in designing, producing, and delivering goods and services to customers. These activities include the flow of materials throughout the supply chain, transformation activities in the manufacturing or service delivery process, and the flow of information needed to support these activities. A value stream map shows the process flows in a manner similar to an ordinary process map; however, the difference lies in that value stream maps highlight value-added versus non-value-added activities, and include times that activities take. This aspect allows one to measure the impact of value-added and non-value-added activities on the total lead time of the process, and compare this to the **takt time**— which is the ratio of the available work time to the required production volume necessary to meet customer demand. If the value stream is faster than the takt time, it generally means that waste in the form of overproduction is occurring; when it is less, the firm cannot meet customer demand. Value stream maps might also include other information such as machine uptime and reliability, process capacity, and size of batches moving through the process. All this information provides a more factual basis for identifying improvements in the Improve phase of DMAIC. Value stream maps are an important tool in lean enterprise methods that we discuss further in Chapter 7.

Statistical Thinking for Understanding Process Variation

The relationship between statistics and processes is embodied in the concept of statistical thinking. **Statistical thinking** is a philosophy of learning and action based on these principles:

1. All work occurs in a system of interconnected processes.
2. Variation exists in all processes.
3. Understanding and reducing variation are keys to success.[7]

The late W. Edwards Deming promoted the concepts of statistical thinking, using two simple, yet powerful experiments, the Red Bead and Funnel experiments, in his four-day management seminars.

The Red Bead experiment proceeds as follows. A Foreman (usually Deming) selects several volunteers from the audience: Six Willing Workers, a Recorder, two Inspectors, and a Chief Inspector. The materials for the experiment include 4,000 wooden beads—800 red and 3,200 white—and two Tupperware boxes, one slightly smaller than the other. Also, a paddle with 50 holes or depressions is used to scoop up 50 beads, which is the prescribed workload. In this experiment, the company is "producing" beads for a new customer who needs only white beads and will not take red beads. The Foreman explains that everyone will be an apprentice for three days to learn the job. During apprenticeship, the workers may ask questions. Once production starts, however, no questions are allowed. The procedures are rigid; no departures from procedures are permitted so that no variation in performance will occur. The Foreman explains to the Willing Workers that their jobs depend on their performance and if they are dismissed, many others are willing to replace them. Furthermore, no resignations are allowed. The company's work standard, the Foreman explains, is 50 beads per day.

The production process is simple: Mix the raw material and pour it into the smaller box. Repeat this procedure, returning the beads from the smaller box to the larger one. Grasp the paddle and insert it into the bead mixture. Raise the paddle at a 44-degree angle so that every depression will hold a bead. The two Inspectors count the beads independently and record the counts. The Chief Inspector checks the counts and announces the results, which are written down by the Recorder. The Chief Inspector then dismisses the worker. When all six Willing Workers have produced the day's quota, the Foreman evaluates the results. During "production" Deming would berate the poor performers and reward the good performers. He would try to motivate them to do better, knowing, of course, that they would not be able to affect the results.

This experiment leads to several important lessons about statistical thinking:

- *Variation exists in systems and, if stable, can be predicted.* If we plot the fraction of red beads produced by each worker each day, we can observe this variation easily. Figure 5.7 is a typical plot of the fraction of red beads produced over time during the experiment. In this case, all points fluctuate about the overall average, which is 0.21, falling roughly between 0.10 and 0.40. In Chapter 7 we will learn to calculate *statistical limits of variation* (0.04 and 0.38)—limits between which we would expect results from a stable system to fall. This variation shows that the system of production is indeed stable; that is, the variation arises from common causes. Although the exact number of red beads in any particular paddle is not predictable, we can describe statistically what we expect from the system.
- *All the variation in the production of red beads, and the variation from day to day of any Willing Worker, came entirely from the process itself.* Clearly, the output from this process is completely random and dependent solely on the mix of beads in the "raw material." In this experiment, Deming deliberately eliminated the source of variability that managers usually believe is the most significant: people. Each worker was basically identical, and no evidence showed that any one of them was better than another. They could not control the number of red beads produced, and could do no better than the system would allow. Neither motivation nor threats had any influence. Unfortunately, many managers believe that all variation is controllable and place blame on those who cannot do anything about it.
- *Numerical goals are often meaningless.* A Foreman who gives out merit pay and puts people on probation, supposedly as rewards and punishment of performance, actually rewards and punishes the performance of the process, not the Willing Workers. To rank or appraise people arbitrarily is demoralizing, especially when workers cannot influence the outcomes. No matter what the goal is, it has no effect on the actual number of red beads produced. Exhorting workers to "Do their best" only leads to frustration. Management has no basis to assume that the best Willing Workers of the past will be the best in the future.

FIGURE 5.7 CHART OF FRACTION OF RED BEADS PRODUCED

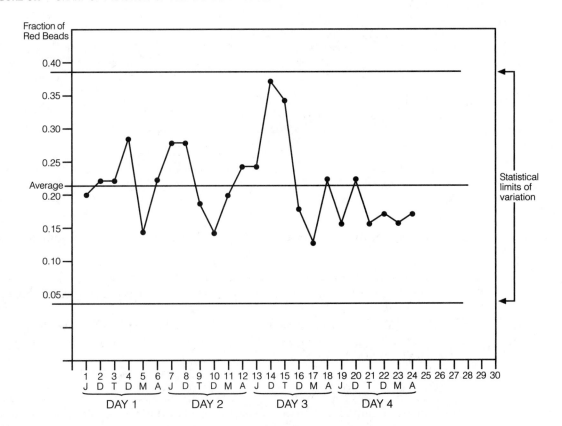

- *Management is responsible for the system.* The experiment shows bad management. Procedures are rigid. The Willing Workers have no say in improving the process. Management is responsible for the incoming material, but does not work with the supplier to improve the inputs to the system. Management designed the production system and decided to rely on inspection to control the process. These decisions have far more influence on the outcomes than the efforts of the workers. Three inspectors are probably as costly as the six workers and add practically no value to the output.

Deming's second experiment is the Funnel Experiment. Its purpose is to show that people can and do affect the outcomes of many processes and create unwanted variation by "tampering" with the process, or indiscriminately trying to remove common causes of variation. In this experiment, a funnel is suspended above a table with a target drawn on a tablecloth. The goal is to hit the target. Participants drop a marble through the funnel and mark the place where the marble eventually lands. Rarely will the marble rest on the target. This variation is due to common causes in the process. One strategy is to simply leave the funnel alone, which creates some variation of points around the target. This may be called *Rule 1*. However, many people believe they can improve the results by

FIGURE 5.8 TWO RULES FOR ADJUSTING THE FUNNEL

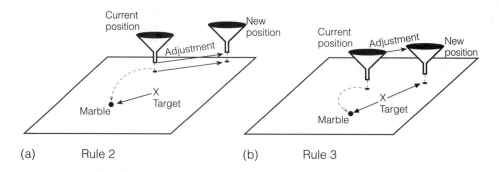

(a)   Rule 2   (b)   Rule 3

adjusting the location of the funnel. Three other possible rules for adjusting the funnel are:

> *Rule 2. Measure the deviation from the point at which the marble comes to rest and the target. Move the funnel an equal distance in the opposite direction from its current position [Figure 5.8(a)].*
>
> *Rule 3. Measure the deviation from the point at which the marble comes to rest and the target. Set the funnel an equal distance in the opposite direction of the error from the target [Figure 5.8(b)].*
>
> *Rule 4. Place the funnel over the spot where the marble last came to rest.*

Figure 5.9 shows a computer simulation of these strategies. Clearly the first rule—leave the funnel alone—results in the least variation. People use these rules inappropriately all the time, causing more variation than would normally occur. An amateur golfer who hits a bad shot tends to make an immediate adjustment. If the last manufactured part is off-specification, adjust the machine. If a schedule was not met last month, change the process. If the last quarter's earnings report was less than expected, dump the stock. If an employee's performance last week was subpar (or exceptional), punish (or reward) the employee. In all these cases, the error is usually compounded by an inappropriate reaction. All of these policies stem from a lack of understanding of variation, which originates from not understanding the process. Understanding processes and statistical thinking provides the context for determining the effects of variation and how to establish consistent, predictable processes, analyze them, and improve them.

Any process contains many sources of variation, as illustrated in Figure 5.10. In manufacturing, for example, different lots of material vary in strength, thickness, or moisture content. Cutting tools have inherent variation in their strength and composition. During manufacturing, tools experience wear, vibrations cause changes in machine settings, and electrical fluctuations cause variations in power. Operators do not position parts on fixtures consistently, and physical and emotional stress affect operators' consistency. In addition, measurement gauges and human inspection capabilities are not uniform. Even when measurements of several items by the same instrument are the same, it is due

FIGURE 5.9   RESULTS OF THE FUNNEL EXPERIMENT

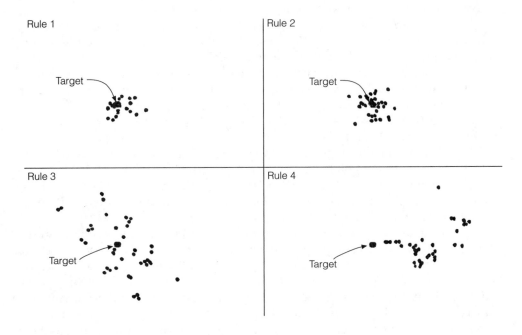

FIGURE 5.10   SOURCES OF VARIATION IN A PROCESS

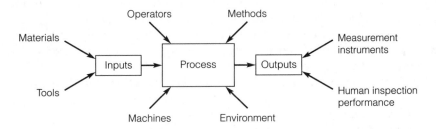

to a lack of precision in the measurement instrument; extremely precise instruments always reveal slight differences. Similar variation occurs in services, particularly as a result of inconsistency in human performance and the interface with technology.

The complex interactions of these variations in materials, tools, machines, operators, and the environment are not easily understood. Variation due to any of these individual sources appears at random; individual sources cannot be identified or explained. However their combined effect is stable and can usually be predicted statistically. These factors are present as a natural part of a process and are referred to as **common causes** of variation. Common causes are a result of the design of the product and production system and generally account for about 80 to 95 percent of the observed variation in the output of a production process. Therefore, common cause variation can only be reduced if the product is redesigned, or if better technology or training is provided for the production process.

As an example of common cause variation in a process, suppose that boards are to be cut to the precise length of 55 inches. If the worker is provided with only a handsaw, a table, and a 12-inch ruler, it will be virtually impossible for him or her to cut lengths of this precision consistently, and a significant amount of measurable variation will exist. However, suppose that a 60-inch metal tape measure, a fixture for holding the boards, and an electric saw are available, and workers are trained in how to use them properly. Clearly, the output from this system will have less variability and more consistent quality.

As a more practical example, Wilson Sporting Goods acknowledged that small irregularities in golf balls could cause the heavier core of golf balls to be off center, resulting in balls that don't roll straight, with up to 1 in 12 high-end balls having this problem. To solve the problem, Wilson introduced a new ball design, the True ball, with a lighter core and heavier cover.[8]

The remaining variation in a production process is the result of **special causes**, often called **assignable causes** of variation. Special causes arise from external sources that are not inherent in the process. They appear sporadically and disrupt the random pattern of common causes. Hence, they tend to be easily detectable using statistical methods, and usually economical to correct. For instance, the worker cutting boards may be distracted by a supervisor and mark the boards incorrectly before cutting, resulting in several pieces that may be an inch too short. Common factors that lead to special causes are a bad batch of material from a supplier, a poorly trained substitute machine operator, a broken or worn tool, or miscalibration of measuring instruments. Unusual variation that results from such isolated incidents can be explained or corrected. A system governed only by common causes is called a **stable system**. Understanding a stable system and the differences between special and common causes of variation is essential for managing any system.

Some of the operational problems created by variation include the following:[9]

- *Variation increases unpredictability*. If we don't understand the variation in a system, we cannot predict its future performance.
- *Variation reduces capacity utilization*. If a process has little variability, then managers can increase the load on the process because they do not have to incorporate slack into their production plans.
- *Variation contributes to a "bullwhip" effect*. This well-known phenomenon occurs in supply chains; when small changes in demand occur, the variation in production and inventory levels becomes increasingly amplified upstream at distribution centers, factories, and suppliers, resulting in unnecessary costs and difficulties in managing material flow.
- *Variation makes it difficult to find root causes*. Process variation makes it difficult to determine whether problems are due to external factors such as raw materials or reside within the processes themselves.
- *Variation makes it difficult to detect potential problems early*. Unusual variation is a signal that problems exist; if a process has little inherent variation, then it is easier to detect when a problem actually does occur.

Root Cause Analysis

Too often, we want to jump to a solution without fully understanding the nature of the problem and identifying the source, or root cause, of the problem. NCR Corporation defines **root cause** as "that condition (or interrelated set of conditions) having allowed or caused a defect to occur, which once corrected properly, permanently prevents recurrence of the defect in the same, or subsequent, product or service generated by the process."[10] As with a medical analogy, eliminating symptoms of problems usually provides only temporary relief; eliminating root causes provides long-term relief.

A useful approach for identifying the root cause is the "5 Why" technique.[11] This approach forces one to redefine a problem statement as a chain of causes and effects to identify the source of the symptoms by asking why, ideally five times. In a classic example at Toyota, a machine failed because a fuse blew. Replacing the fuse would have been the obvious solution; however, this action would have only addressed the symptom of the real problem. Why did the fuse blow? Because the bearing did not have adequate lubrication. Why? Because the lubrication pump was not working properly. Why? Because the pump axle was worn. Why? Because sludge seeped into the pump axle, which was the root cause. Toyota attached a strainer to the lubricating pump to eliminate the sludge, thus correcting the problem of the machine failure.

Cause-and-Effect Diagrams

Variation in process output can occur for a variety of reasons as we have noted. A **cause-and-effect diagram** is a simple graphical method for hypothesizing a chain of causes and effects and for sorting out potential causes and organizing relationships between variables.

Kaoru Ishikawa introduced the cause-and-effect diagram in Japan, so it is also called an Ishikawa diagram. Because of its structure, it is often called a *fishbone diagram*. The general structure of a cause-and-effect diagram is shown in Figure 5.11. At the end of the horizontal line, a problem is listed. Each branch pointing into the main stem represents a possible cause. Branches pointing to the causes are contributors to those causes. The diagram identifies the most likely causes of a problem so that further data collection and analysis can be carried out.

Cause-and-effect diagrams are constructed in a brainstorming atmosphere. Everyone can get involved and feel they are an important part of the problem-solving process. Usually small groups drawn from operations areas or management work with a trained and experienced facilitator. The facilitator guides attention to discussion of the problem and its causes, not opinions. As a group technique, the cause-and-effect method requires significant interaction between group members. The facilitator who listens carefully to the participants can capture the important ideas. A group can often be more effective by thinking of the problem broadly and considering environmental factors, political factors, employee issues, and even government policies, if appropriate.

To illustrate a cause-and-effect diagram, a major hospital was concerned about the length of time required to get a patient from the emergency department to an inpatient bed. Significant delays appeared to be caused by beds not being available. A quality improvement team tackled this problem by developing a cause-and-effect diagram. They identified four major causes: environmental

FIGURE 5.11   GENERAL STRUCTURE OF A CAUSE-AND-EFFECT DIAGRAM

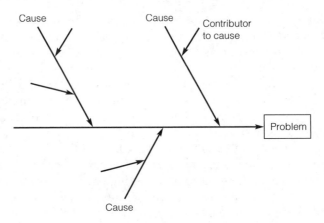

FIGURE 5.12   CAUSE-AND-EFFECT DIAGRAM FOR HOSPITAL EMERGENCY ADMISSION PROBLEM

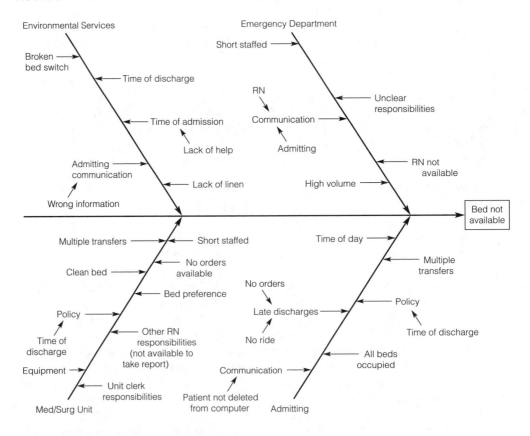

services, emergency department, medical/surgery unit, and admitting. Figure 5.12 shows the diagram with several potential causes in each category. It served as a basis for further investigations of contributing factors and data analysis to find the root cause of the problem.

PROJECT REVIEW—ANALYZE PHASE

A project review of the Analyze phase should ensure that

- Team members have received any necessary "just-in-time" training
- Team members understood how to use analysis tools appropriately and effectively
- The data collected in the Measure phase have been fully understood and studied
- Appropriate statistical tools have been used to conduct the analyses of data
- Variation is thoroughly understood
- Root causes and hypotheses that explain problems have been identified
- Data provide confirmation of key conclusions and validation of root causes
- Process maps are accurate and representative of actual or desired process flow (in the case of a redesign activity)
- The process has been studied to identify bottlenecks, sources of error, and non-value-added activities
- Preliminary improvement or redesign goals have been set

 CASE STUDY

Applying Statistical Analysis in a Six Sigma Project at GE Fanuc[12]

GE Fanuc Automation in Charlottesville, Virginia, is a joint venture between General Electric and Fanuc Ltd. of Japan, a company that specializes in computer numerical control (CNC) and robotic technology. The division has annual sales of about $700 million from the manufacture and sale of factory automation products, which serve the automotive, food processing and packaging, paper, pharmaceutical, robotics, chemical, and energy markets. The headquarters and main manufacturing plant is at its Charlottesville facility, and includes more than 500,000 square feet of floor space divided among seven buildings on 50 acres of land. GE Fanuc implemented their Six Sigma program in 1996, shortly after Jack Welch announced the quality initiative for the entire company.

In mid-2002 a team at the GE Fanuc manufacturing plant in Charlottesville, Virginia, led by Six Sigma black belt Donald Splaun was given the go-ahead to investigate Black Belt Project #P52320. The objective of the project was to evaluate Printed Wire Board (PWB) Fabricated Board Finishes to determine if the high-priced nickel-gold (Ni-Au) finished boards that were being used were necessary as mounting platforms for fine pitch surface-mounted devices (SMDs) or for fine pitched Ball Grid Array (BGA) electronic controller boards. SMDs are electronic components, such as microprocessors, that are placed on the top of electronic circuit boards (fabricated boards) and then have their electrical wire leads soldered into place. Fine pitch SMDs don't have much space between their electrical wire leads, making it difficult to put just the right amount of solder on them to make the proper electrical connection to the circuit boards on which they are mounted. The completed boards with all components properly mounted on them are then used in electrical assemblies to control the operations of industrial machinery.

Splaun had seven people on his analysis team, plus a financial representative to verify the dollar costs and savings; a master black belt reviewer, who would evaluate the project to prevent obvious gaps in the analysis; and perhaps most importantly from a managerial standpoint, a champion/sponsor, who would ensure project visibility and that resources were allocated to complete the project. Team members and their job functions were:

Team Members Titles and Functions

Team leader and black belt
Process engineer and fabricated board expert
Advanced manufacturing engineer responsible for SMD board assembly
Sourcing agent who purchases the boards
Test engineer who tests and evaluates boards
Producibility engineer who works with design teams
Production line operator who runs boards
Supplier quality analysis technician responsible for incoming board quality

Outside Resources

Financial representative to assist in cost calculations
Champion/Sponsor
Reviewer and master black belt

After being formed, the team used a 12-step DMAIC process developed by GE Fanuc, to guide them through the project (see Table 5.3). The first three pre-project definition substeps (A, B, and C) required them to identify project CTQs, develop a team charter and have it approved, and define a process map.

Project team members identified the CTQs by using a standard cause-and-effect matrix, and weighted rankings of CTQ factors to prioritize them. The team determined there were three CTQs, two of which were business factors and the other a project factor:

- *Business CTQ factors:* Variable cost productivity (VCP) improvement, composed of the CTQs of internal cost reduction and contribution margin improvement
- *Project CTQ factor:* Benefits associated with additional Ni-Au cost of $190,000 per year, suspected to be unnecessary

The team developed their charter to define the problem and working relationships. The problem clearly and succinctly stated as: *GE Fanuc currently specifies Ni-Au on fine pitch SMD and BGA boards. The purpose of this project is to evaluate if this specification is necessary.*

The team also identified tools and databases that were to be used in the study, not only to ensure that everyone was working from a common source, but also to take advantage of the training that had been provided to team members. The tools included two statistical/spreadsheet software packages (Minitab and Excel) and a plantwide integrated database (SAP) that contained information on board characteristics, usage, specifications, costs, and so on.

TABLE 5.3 GE Fanuc 12-Step DMAIC Process

Step	Description	Tools	Deliverables
Define			
A	Identify project CTQs		Project CTQs (1)
B	Develop team charter		Approved charter (2)
C	Define process map		High-level process map (3)
Measure			
1	Select CTQ characteristics	Customer, QFD, FMEA	Project Y (4)
2	Define performance standards	Customer, Blueprints	Performance standard for Project Y (5)
3	Measurement system analysis	Continuous Gage R&R, Test/Retest, Attribute R&R	Data collection plan and MSA (6), Data for Project Y (7)
Analyze			
4	Establish process capability	Capability indices	Process capability— Project Y (8)
5	Define performance objectives	Team, Benchmarking process and graphical Analysis, Hypothesis tests	Improvement goal for Project Y (9)
6	Identify variation sources		Prioritized list of all Xs (10)
Improve			
7	Screen potential causes	DOE-screening	List of vital few Xs (11)
8	Discover variable relationships	Factorial designs	Proposed solution (12)
9	Establish operating tolerances	Simulation	Piloted solution (13)
Control			
10	Define and validate measurement system on Xs (independent variables) in actual application	Continuous Gage R&R, MSA Test/Retest, Attribute R&R	
11	Determine process capability	Capability indices	Process capability Y, X (14)
12	Implement process control	Control charts, Mistake proof, FMEA	Sustained solution (15), Documentation (16)

Based on a 29-step process flowchart, it was decided that the analysis would require the use of a moderately complex experimental design. This design was required to determine the effects of supplier differences and finishes, because relatively few defects were being observed in manufacturing the boards. Data would have to be gathered from the experiment and from supplier surveys to help the team track potential causes that could have a bearing on the functionality and cost of each of the alternative boards or board materials being considered.

The experiment was designed to sample and test 288 CX3A1 boards:

- 96 hot air solder leveled (HASL) boards, 32 from each supplier
- 96 nickel-gold (Ni-Au) boards, 32 from each supplier
- 96 silver (Ag) boards, 32 from each supplier and to evaluate three suppliers

The three suppliers were:

- Vendor G, Singapore/China (one or two GE Fanuc production suppliers)
- Vendor P, Taiwan/China (second major GE Fanuc supplier)
- Vendor D, USA (current prototype/fast turn supplier)

The cause-and-effect matrix identified 13 characteristics (Xs, or independent variables) that were considered important to measure during the experiment for each of the three finish types (Ys, or dependent variables). The primary hypothesis was that no significant differences in numbers of defects would be incurred, regardless of finish. In addition, a hypothesis that no significant interaction effects existed between suppliers, coatings, and any of the 13 characteristics considered essential for quality board functioning was investigated. The data collection and analysis process consisted of eight carefully defined steps conducted over a six-day period, involving almost $37,500 worth of boards and hard-to-measure production delays while the test boards were run on what are normally high speed, highly automated production machines.

After the data were collected, numerous ANOVA computer runs were made to pinpoint problem areas and test hypotheses. It was especially important to test the capabilities of each of the three types of board finishes to determine whether they were equivalent to the current, and very expensive, Ni-Au finished boards. It was also necessary to get some data to prove or disprove hypotheses about supplier capabilities as well. Table 5.4 shows a typical computer printout and analysis of one of the 13 variables that was tested, called "Wave Solder Skips."

Of 15 ANOVA analysis runs performed on the 13 experimental variables that were measured, eight showed no significance, primarily because those variables had zero defects. Other findings included:

- Ni-Au boards are not significantly different from or better than horizontally processed HASL or silver boards for fine pitch SMD processing, therefore the firm can save money by switching from Ni-Au to HASL or silver.
- The company should not use Vendor D for production. Results and suggestions for improvement of their prototype quality should be discussed with them.
- Ni-Au is worse for wave soldering, based on a defect measure of "insufficient solder fill."
- Vendor G was found to have an issue with a defect measure of "GR False Failures" (to be reviewed with the supplier).
- The GE Fanuc PWB Fab Specifications should be changed to reflect these conclusions.

From these analyses, the summary conclusion was that GE Fanuc did not need nickel-gold boards for fine pitch SMD.

The estimated savings from this project ranged from 7.1 percent on two-layer boards to 22.8 percent on four-layer boards, with an average of 14.3 percent savings on these 89 board types, and total estimated savings of $190,000 per year.

TABLE 5.4 TYPICAL ANOVA OUTPUT FOR VENDOR AND FINISH ANALYSIS

Solder Skips, Analysis All
Two-Way Analysis of Variance
Analysis of Variance for Wave Solder Skips

Source	DF	SS	MS	F	P
Vendors	2	36.55	18.27	15.27	0.000
Finish	2	16.44	8.22	6.87	0.001
Interaction	4	23.39	5.85	4.89	0.001
Error	279	333.94	1.20		
Total	287	410.32			

Process Variable Averages

Manufacturers	Mean Number of Defects
Vendor C	0.03
Vendor D	0.80
Vendor G	0.06

Finish	
HASL	0.271
Ni-Au	0.021
Silver	0.604

REVIEW QUESTIONS

1. What is statistical analysis? Why is it important to Six Sigma?
2. Discuss the differences between the three major components of statistical methodology (descriptive statistics, statistical inference, and predictive statistics). Why might this distinction be important to a manager?
3. Provide some examples of discrete and continuous random variables in a quality management context.
4. Define a population and a sample. What are their major characteristics?
5. Explain the difference between the standard deviation and the standard error of the mean. How are they related?
6. State the meaning of the central limit theorem in your own words. How important is it to the development and use of statistical quality control techniques?
7. What is the difference between an enumerative and an analytic study?
8. What are the requirements of a hypothesis test, as related to enumerative and analytic studies?
9. How do scatter diagrams assist in finding solutions to quality problems?
10. Explain the differences between correlation and regression. How are they related?
11. What is the statistical basis for ANOVA; that is, what is it designed to test, statistically?

12. What types of questions might one ask to identify opportunities for improvement with a process flowchart?
13. Contrast the differences between an ordinary process map and a value stream map.
14. What is statistical thinking? Why is it important to managers and workers at all levels of an organization?
15. What are the lessons of the Red Bead and Funnel experiments?
16. Explain the difference between common and special causes of variation.
17. What are some of the operational problems caused by variation?
18. What is a root cause? How does the "5 Why" technique help uncover the root cause?
19. Describe the structure of a cause-and-effect diagram.

DISCUSSION QUESTIONS

1. Can you cite any examples in your experience where someone acted counter to the lessons in the Red Bead Experiment?
2. In the GE-Fanuc case, why did the experimental design have to be so complex? Why were so many individuals involved in this project?
3. What might have been some contributing factors that caused GE-Fanuc to select the Ni-Au over the cheaper boards in the past?
4. From Table 5.4 in the case study, what can you conclude, given the F values and the p-values in the table? What steps should the team take, regarding use of vendors and further testing for this particular independent variable?

THINGS TO DO

1. A computer version of Deming's Funnel exercise is available (free) at: http://www.qualitystation.com/Funnel-Free.htm. Download and run the funnel simulation. Does it simulate the same rules as described in this chapter?
2. Devise an experiment similar to the battery example in Table 5.1 to test different levels of some factor and conduct a statistical analysis using ANOVA on the results. Write up your experiment and results in a report along with the conclusions that you reach from the analysis. You might wish to consult a standard statistics text that explains ANOVA in slightly more detail.
3. Develop a flowchart of the process you use to study for an exam. How might you improve this process?
4. In small teams, develop cause-and-effect diagrams for the following problems:
   a. Poor exam grade
   b. No job offers
   c. Late for work or school

PROBLEMS

1. Kiwi Blend is sold in 950-milliliter (ml) cans. The mean volume of juice placed in a can is 945 ml with a standard deviation of 15 ml. Assuming a normal distribution, what is the probability that the filling machine will cause an overflow of a can, that is, the probability that more than 945 ml will be placed in the can?

2. Outback Beer bottles have been found to have a standard deviation of 5 ml. If 5 percent of the bottles contain less than 535 ml, what is the average filling volume of the bottles?

3. The standard deviation of the weight of filled salt containers is 0.4 ounce. If 2.5 percent of the containers contain less than 16 ounces, what is the mean filling weight of the containers?

4. In filling bottles of L&E Cola, the average amount of overfilling should be kept as low as possible. If the mean fill volume is 12.1 ounces and the standard deviation is 0.05 ounce, what percentage of bottles will have less than 12 ounces? More than 12.1 ounces (assuming no overflow)?

5. A utility requires service operators to answer telephone calls from customers in an average time of 0.1 minute or less. A sample of 30 actual operator times was drawn, and the results are given in the following table. In addition, operators are expected to determine customer needs and either respond to them or refer the customer to the proper department within 0.5 minute. Another sample of 30 times was taken for this job component and is also given in the table. If these variables can be considered to be independent, is the average time taken to perform each component statistically different from the standard?

Component	Mean Time	Standard Deviation
Answer	0.1023	0.0183
Service	0.5290	0.0902

6. An independent outplacement service helps unemployed executives find jobs. One of the major activities of the service is preparing resumes. Three word-processing employees (called "word processors") work at the service typing resumes and cover letters. They are assigned to individual clients, currently numbering about 120. Turnaround time for typing is expected to be 24 hours. The word-processing operation begins with clients placing work in the assigned word processor's bin. When the word processor picks up the work (in batches), it is logged in using a time clock stamp, and the work is typed and printed. After the batch is completed, the word processor returns the documents to the clients' bins, logs in the time delivered, and picks up new work. A supervisor tries to balance the workload for the three word processors. Lately, many of the clients have been complaining about errors in their documents— misspellings, missing lines, wrong formatting, and so on. The supervisor told the word processors to be more careful, but the errors still persist.

   a. Develop a cause-and-effect diagram that might clarify the source of errors.

   b. What tools might the supervisor use to study ways to reduce the number of errors?

7. The Monterey Fiesta Mexican Restaurant is trying to determine if its popular Pan Con Mucho Sabor breadsticks are correlated with the sales of margaritas. It has data on sales of breadstick baskets and margaritas for 25 weeks, shown in the *Ch5Dataset* file for *Prob. 5-7* on the CD-ROM. Use the correlation utility, along with a scatter diagram, in Microsoft Excel to analyze these data. What do they indicate?

8. Apply descriptive statistics tools and construct a scatter diagram using the hypothetical data on use of patient restraints in the Psychiatric Nursing Unit at Middletown Hospital (see Middletown Regional Hospital case in Chapter 4 for background) shown in the *Ch5Dataset* file for *Prob. 5-8* on the Student CD. What can you conclude from these data?

9. A purchasing agent for Rapidtest Instrument Labs is trying to determine the best delivery provider to use for delivering instruments to customers after they have been repaired or recalibrated. She has developed an index, on a scale of 1–5 (5 is outstanding) that weights the key quality factors of time, service, and cost. Three delivery services, A, B, and C, are candidates for a long term blanket contract with Rapidtest. The data shown in the *Ch5Dataset* file for *Prob. 5-9* on the Student CD were gathered in test deliveries to 10 customers. What recommendation would you make, based on these data?

10. A process engineer at Sival Electronics was trying to determine whether three suppliers would be equally capable of supplying the mounting boards for the new "gold plated" components that she was testing. The *Ch5Dataset* file for *Prob. 5-10* on the Student CD shows the coded defect levels for the suppliers, according to the finishes that were tested. Lower defect levels are preferable to larger levels. Using one-way ANOVA, analyze these results. What conclusion can be reached, based on these data?

ENDNOTES

1. J. M. Juran and Frank M. Gryna, Jr., *Quality Planning and Analysis*, 2nd ed. (New York: McGraw-Hill, 1980), 35.

2. Thomas Pyzdek, "Non-Normal Distributions in the Real World," *Quality Digest*, December 1999, 36–41.

3. Douglas C. Montgomery, *Design and Analysis of Experiments* (New York: John Wiley & Sons 1996); Charles Lipson and Narendra J. Sheth. *Statistical Design and Analysis of Engineering Experiments* (New York: McGraw-Hill Book Co., 1973).

4. Daniel R. Heiser and Paul Schikora, "Flowcharting with Excel," *Quality Management Journal* 8, no. 3, 2001, 26–35.

5. AT&T Quality Steering Committee, *Reengineering Handbook*, AT&T Bell Laboratories, 1991, 45.

6. Adapted from Dwight Kirscht and Jennifer M. Tunnell, "Boise Cascade Stakes a Claim on Quality," *Quality Progress* 26, no. 11, November 1993, 91–96. © 1993 American Society for Quality. Used with permission.

7. Adapted from Galen Britz, Don Emerling, Lynne Hare, Roger Hoerl, and Janice Shade, "How to Teach Others to Apply Statistical Thinking," *Quality Progress*, June 1997, 67–79.

8. Kimberly Weisul, "So Your Lie May Always Be True," *Business Week*, February 25, 2002, 16.

9. Steven A. Melnyk and R. T. Christensen, "Variance Is Evil," *APICS: The Performance Advantage*, June 2002, 19.

10. "NCR Corporation," in *Profiles in Quality* (Needham Heights, MA: Allyn and Bacon, 1991).

11. Howard H. Bailie, "Organize Your Thinking with a Why-Why Diagram," *Quality Progress* 18, no. 12, December 1985, 22–24.

12. Courtesy of Donald B. Splaun, Jr., Manager, Advanced Manufacturing Technology, GE-Fanuc, Inc.

6

Process Improvement

The goal of Six Sigma is to accelerate improvements and achieve unprecedented performance levels by focusing on characteristics that are critical to customers and identifying and eliminating causes of errors or defects in processes.[1] *Improve* is the fourth step in DMAIC, and the one that is more difficult to accomplish because it is more of an art than a science. Thinking of the $Y = f(X)$ relationship, the goal is to "fine-tune" the Xs that will deliver the performance in the Ys expected by customers. While improvement is a highly creative effort, it must be accomplished within the Six Sigma project management structure.

Looking back at the Project Life Cycle Accountability Matrix in Table 3.2, this step is the foundation of the Project Assurance stage. Each of the key members of the project team has various tasks that need to be accomplished in order to complete the DMAIC Improve step. At this project stage, core team members are working to screen potential causes, find and verify root causes, discover variable relationships, and establish operating tolerances using a variety of tools such as design of experiments and simulation. They should be thinking about process changes and talking to the project manager about them. The external customer (or process owner) is typically involved in obtaining approvals for changes in processes. During all this activity, the project manager must ensure that these process improvement requirements are communicated to the black belt, project champion, and the customer/process owner; if not, then subsequent testing, verification, implementation, and control activities could be delayed. The project champion must approve or reject process improvements and clear obstacles, as needed, and the black belt must continue to mentor the project manager, and provide expertise in the design of process improvements. In addition, he or she must continue to share good ideas and approaches between project teams to enhance project and organizational learning.

PRINCIPLES OF PROCESS IMPROVEMENT

The concept of improvement in business dates back many years. One of the earliest examples in the United States was at National Cash Register Company (NCR). After a shipment of defective cash registers was returned in 1894, the company's founder discovered unpleasant and unsafe working conditions. He made many changes, including better lighting, new safety devices, ventilation, lounges, and lockers. The company offered extensive evening classes to improve employees' education and skills, and instituted a program for soliciting suggestions from factory workers. Workers received cash prizes and other recognition for their best ideas; by the 1940s the company was receiving an average of 3,000 suggestions each year.

Over the years, many other companies such as Lincoln Electric and Procter & Gamble developed innovative and effective improvement approaches. However, many of these approaches focused almost exclusively on productivity and cost. A focus on quality improvement, on the other hand, is relatively recent, stimulated by the success of the Japanese. Toshiba in 1946, Matsushita Electric in 1950, and Toyota in 1951 initiated some of the earliest formal improvement programs. Toyota, in particular, pioneered just-in-time (JIT), which showed that companies could make products efficiently with virtually zero defects. JIT established a philosophy of continuous improvement, which the Japanese call **kaizen**, and which has been adopted by many organizations around the world.

It is important to note that although Six Sigma can result in significant benefits for an organization, it is not a substitute for continuous improvement. Because of Six Sigma's reliance on specialists—the black belts who lead the high-profile projects—it becomes quite easy to ignore simple improvements that can be achieved at the process-owner level. In fact, it can easily alienate process owners who, instead of seeking continuous improvements, leave them to the specialists. Thus, the objectives are somewhat different, yet both approaches can easily support one another. Process owners should be trained in Six Sigma methods and be involved in formal Six Sigma projects, but still have responsibility for continuous improvement on a daily basis.

Six Sigma project selection, as we discussed in Chapter 3, focuses on improvement opportunities that have a verifiable financial return. Such opportunities include the obvious reductions in manufacturing defects. A good illustration is Dell, Inc. Although it has had some of the highest quality ratings in the PC industry, CEO Michael Dell became obsessed with finding ways to reduce machine failure rates. He concluded that failures were related to the number of times a hard drive was handled during assembly, and insisted that the number of "touches" be reduced from an existing level of more than 30 per drive. Production lines were revamped and the number was reduced to fewer than 15. Soon after, the reject rate of hard drives fell by 40 percent and the overall failure rated dropped by 20 percent.[2] In addition, opportunities for Six Sigma projects involve improving the design of products with features that better meet customers' critical-to-quality needs and that can achieve higher performance, higher reliability, and other market-driven dimensions of quality (we will cover this more in Part III of this book); improving the efficiency of manufacturing systems by reducing unnecessary processing steps and workers' idle time; improving the operations infrastructure by reducing unnecessary inventory, transportation, material handling, scrap, and rework; and improving support services such as financial transaction processing, and employee recruiting and training.

Flexibility and Cycle Time Reduction

Flexibility refers to the ability to adapt quickly and effectively to changing requirements. It might mean rapid changeover from one product to another, rapid response to changing demands, or the ability to produce a wide range of customized services. Success in globally competitive markets requires a capacity for rapid change and flexibility. Electronic commerce, for instance, requires more rapid, flexible, and customized responses than traditional market outlets. Flexibility might demand special strategies such as modular designs, sharing components, sharing manufacturing lines, and specialized training for employees. It also involves outsourcing decisions, agreements with key suppliers, and innovative partnering arrangements. Many Six Sigma projects focus on improving organizational flexibility.

One important business metric that complements flexibility is cycle time. **Cycle time** refers to the time it takes to accomplish one cycle of a process (for example, the time from when a customer orders a product to the time that it is delivered, or the time to introduce a new product). Reductions in cycle time serve two purposes. First, they speed up work processes so that customer response is improved. Second, reductions in cycle time can only be accomplished by streamlining and simplifying processes to eliminate non-value-added steps such as rework. This approach forces improvements in quality by reducing the potential for mistakes and errors. By reducing non-value-added steps, costs are reduced as well. Thus, cycle time reductions often drive simultaneous improvements in organization, quality, cost, and productivity. Significant reductions in cycle time cannot be achieved simply by focusing on individual subprocesses; cross-functional processes must be examined across the organization. Through these activities, the company comes to understand work at the organizational level and to engage in cooperative behaviors.

Agility is a term that is commonly used to characterize flexibility and short cycle times. Agility is crucial to such customer-focused strategies as mass customization, which requires rapid response and flexibility to changing consumer demand. Enablers of agility include close relationships with customers to understand their emerging needs and requirements, empowering employees as decision makers, effective manufacturing and information technology, close supplier and partner relationships, and breakthrough improvement (discussed next).

Breakthrough Improvement

Breakthrough improvement refers to discontinuous change, as opposed to a gradual, continuous improvement philosophy that is more reflective of traditional quality management approaches. Six Sigma projects are usually oriented toward achieving such breakthrough improvements. Breakthrough improvements result from innovative and creative thinking; often these are motivated by **stretch goals**, or **breakthrough objectives**. Stretch goals force an organization to think in a radically different way, and to encourage major improvements as well as incremental ones. When a goal of 10 percent improvement is set, managers or engineers can usually meet it with some minor improvements. However, when the goal is 1,000 percent improvement, employees must be creative and think "outside of the box." The seemingly impossible is often achieved, yielding dramatic improvements and boosting morale. Motorola's initial Six Sigma thrust was driven by a goal of improving product and services quality 10 times within two years, and at least 100-fold within four years. For stretch goals to be successful, they must derive unambiguously from corporate strategy. Organizations must not set goals that result in unreasonable stress to employees or punish failure. In addition, they must provide appropriate help and tools to accomplish the task.

One approach for breakthrough improvement that helps companies achieve stretch goals is known as **reengineering**, which has been defined as "the fundamental rethinking and radical redesign of business processes to achieve dramatic improvements in critical, contemporary measures of performance, such as cost, quality, service, and speed."[3] Reengineering involves asking basic questions about business processes: why do we do it and why is it done this way? Such questioning often uncovers obsolete, erroneous, or inappropriate assumptions. Radical redesign involves tossing out existing procedures and reinventing the process, not just incrementally improving it. The goal is to achieve quantum leaps in performance. For example, IBM Credit Corporation cut the process of financing IBM computers, software, and services from seven days to four hours by rethinking the process. Originally, the process was designed to handle difficult applications and required four highly trained specialists and a series of handoffs. The actual work took only about 1.5 hours; the rest of the time was spent in transit or delay. By questioning the assumption that every application was unique and difficult to process, IBM Credit Corporation was able to replace the specialists by a single individual supported by a user-friendly computer system that provided access to all the data and tools that the specialists would use.

Successful reengineering requires fundamental understanding of processes, creative thinking to break away from old traditions and assumptions, and effective use of information technology. PepsiCo has embarked on a program to reengineer all of its key business processes, such as selling and delivery, equipment service and repair, procurement, and financial reporting. In the selling and delivery of its products, for example, customer reps typically experience stockouts of as much as 25 percent of product by the end of the day, resulting in late-day stops not getting full deliveries and the need to return to those accounts. Many other routes return with overstock of other products, increasing handling costs. By redesigning the system to include handheld computers, customer reps can confirm and deliver that day's order and also take a future order for the next delivery to that customer.[4]

TOOLS FOR PROCESS IMPROVEMENT

Effective implementation of Six Sigma improvement strategies requires a disciplined application of statistical principles and various tools for implementing the

DMAIC process. While some consultants and practitioners have suggested that Six Sigma is unique in its approach to improvement, it is important to understand that the "Six Sigma toolbox" is simply a collection of proven methods that have been used successfully for many years in all types of quality management and improvement initiatives.

Many different tools and techniques exist to facilitate Six Sigma projects. The basic techniques for measurement and analysis we described in the previous two chapters are useful in the improvement phase of DMAIC. Other statistical techniques, such as design of experiments and Taguchi methods, are also important. These tools are central to Design for Six Sigma and will be discussed in a later chapter. Here we introduce a number of other tools and approaches that support the improvement phase of DMAIC.

Analyzing Process Maps

Perhaps the first place to begin identifying improvements is with a process or value stream map. Several fundamental questions can be asked:

- Are the steps in the process arranged in logical sequence?
- Do all steps add value? Can some steps be eliminated and should others be added in order to improve quality or operational performance? Can some be combined? Should some be resequenced?
- Are capacities of each step in balance; that is, do bottlenecks exist for which customers will incur excessive waiting time?
- What skills, equipment, and tools are required at each step of the process? Should some steps be automated?
- Where are the critical points of customer contact?
- At which points in the system might errors occur that would result in customer dissatisfaction, and how might these errors be corrected?
- At which point or points should quality be measured?
- Where interaction with the customer occurs, what procedures and guidelines should employees follow to present a positive image?

In analyzing the times for activities in value stream maps, we can easily determine the amount of time that value-added work is actually being done and also measure the cycle time. Often, the actual work time is a relatively small percentage of the cycle time, maybe as low as 15–20 percent; this indicates that considerable delays and non-value-added steps that might be eliminated or improved exist in the process.

Process mapping is a powerful tool to stimulate improvement. Using process mapping, Motorola reduced manufacturing time for pagers from 40 days to less than one hour. Citibank adopted this approach and reduced internal callbacks in its Private Bank group by 80 percent and the credit process time by 50 percent. Its Global Equipment Finance division, which provides financing and leasing services to Citibank customers, lowered the credit decision cycle from three days to one. Copeland Companies, subsidiaries of Travelers Life & Annuity, reduced the cycle time of processing statements from 28 days to 15 days.[5]

One example of how process mapping helped in a cycle time reduction project is Procter & Gamble's over-the-counter (OTC) clinical division, which conducts clinical studies that involve testing drugs, health care products, or treatments in humans.[6] Such testing requires rigorous stages of design, conduct, analysis, and summarization of data. P&G had at least four different ways to perform a clinical study and needed to find the best way to meet its research and development needs. They chose to focus on cycle time reduction. The improvement team found that final reports took months to prepare. Only by mapping the existing process did they fully understand the causes of long production times and the amount of rework and recycling during review and signoff. By restructuring the activities from sequential to parallel work and identifying critical measurements to monitor the process, they were able to reduce the time to less than four weeks. Figure 6.1 shows the process maps that helped them achieve this improvement.

Kaizen Blitz

A **kaizen blitz** is an intense and rapid improvement process in which a team or a department throws all its resources into an improvement project over a short time period, as opposed to traditional kaizen applications, which are performed on a part-time basis. Blitz teams are generally comprised of employees from all areas involved in the process who understand it and can implement changes on the spot. Improvement is immediate, exciting, and satisfying for all those involved in the process. Some examples of using kaizen blitz at Magnivision include the following:[7]

- The molded lens department ran two shifts per day, using 13 employees, and after 40 percent rework, yielded 1,300 pieces per day. The production line was unbalanced and work piled up between stations, which added to quality problems as the work-in-process was often damaged. After a three-day blitz, the team reduced the production to one shift of six employees and a balanced line, reducing rework to 10 percent and increasing yield to 3,500 per day, saving more than $179,000.
- In Retail Services, a blitz team investigated problems that continually plagued employees, and discovered that many were related to the software system. Some of the same customer information had to be entered in multiple screens, sometimes the system took a long time to process information, and sometimes it was difficult to find specific information quickly. Neither the programmers nor the engineers were aware of these problems. By getting everyone together, some solutions were easily determined. Estimated savings were $125,000.

Poka-Yoke (Mistake-Proofing)

Human beings tend to make mistakes inadvertently.[8] Such errors can arise from the following factors:

- Forgetfulness due to lack of concentration
- Misunderstanding because of the lack of familiarity with a process or procedures
- Poor identification associated with lack of proper attention

FIGURE 6.1 FINAL REPORT "IS" AND "SHOULD" PROCESS MAP EXAMPLE

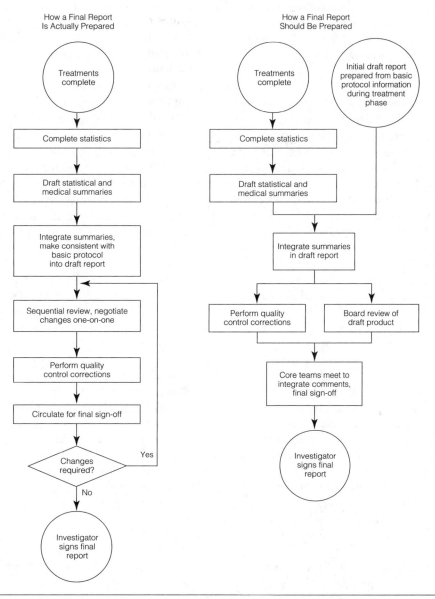

Source: David A. McCamey, Robert W. Bogs, and Linda M. Bayuk, "More, Better, Faster From Total Quality Effort," *Quality Progress,* Aug. 1999, 43–50. © 1999. American Society for Quality. Reprinted with permission.

- Lack of experience
- Absentmindedness
- Delays in judgment when a process is automated
- Equipment malfunctions

Typical mistakes in production are omitted processing, processing errors, setup errors, missing parts, wrong parts, and adjustment errors. Once mistakes are identified, one might use a cause-and-effect diagram or other analysis tools to identify the reasons for their occurrence. For example, an assembly error might be due to poor training of the worker, bad design of the part, complexity of a work task, different parts that look alike, and so on. The next step is to try to prevent them from occurring in the first place.

Blaming workers not only discourages them and lowers morale, but also does not solve the problem. **Poka-yoke** (POH-kah YOH-kay) is an approach for mistake-proofing processes using automatic devices or methods to avoid simple human error. The poka-yoke concept was developed and refined in the early 1960s by the late Shigeo Shingo, a Japanese manufacturing engineer who developed the Toyota production system.[9] Shingo visited a plant and observed that the plant was not using any type of measurement or statistical process control system for tracking defects. When asked why, the manager replied that they did not make any defects to track! His investigation led to the development of a mistake-proofing approach called Zero Quality Control, or ZQC. ZQC is driven by simple and inexpensive inspection processes, such as successive checking, in which operators inspect the work of the prior operation before continuing, and self-checking, in which operators assess the quality of their own work. Poka-yokes are designed to facilitate this process or remove the human element completely.

Poka-yoke is focused on two aspects: (1) prediction, or recognizing that a defect is about to occur and providing a warning, and (2) detection, or recognizing that a defect has occurred and stopping the process. Many applications of poka-yoke are deceptively simple, yet creative. Usually, they are inexpensive to implement. One of Shingo's first poka-yoke devices involved a process at the Yamada Electric plant in which workers assemble a switch having two push buttons supported by two springs.[10] Occasionally, a worker would forget to insert a spring under each button, which led to a costly and embarrassing repair at the customer's facility. In the old method, the worker would take two springs out of a large parts box and then assemble the switch. To prevent this mistake, the worker was instructed first to place two springs in a small dish in front of the parts box, and then assemble the switch. If a spring remains in the dish, the operator knows immediately that an error has occurred. The solution was simple, cheap, and provided immediate feedback to the operator.

Many other examples can be cited:

- Machines have limit switches connected to warning lights that tell the operator when parts are positioned improperly on the machine.
- A device on a drill counts the number of holes drilled in a work piece; a buzzer sounds if the work piece is removed before the correct number of holes has been drilled.
- Cassette covers were frequently scratched when the screwdriver slipped out of the screw slot and slid against the plastic covers. The screw design was changed as shown in Figure 6.2 to prevent the screwdriver from slipping.
- A metal roller was used to laminate two surfaces bonded with hot melted glue. The glue tended to stick to the roller and cause defects in the laminate surface.

FIGURE 6.2 A POKA-YOKE EXAMPLE OF SCREW REDESIGN

Old Design   New Design

An investigation showed that if the roller were dampened, the glue would not stick. A secondary roller was added to dampen the steel roller during the process, preventing the glue from sticking.

- One production step at Motorola involves putting alphabetic characters on a keyboard, and then checking to make sure each key is placed correctly. A group of workers designed a clear template with the letters positioned slightly off center. By holding the template over the keyboard, assemblers can quickly spot mistakes.
- Computer programs display a warning message if a file that has not been saved is to be closed.
- A 3.5-inch diskette is designed so that it cannot be inserted unless the disk is oriented correctly (try it!). These disks are not perfectly square, and the beveled right corner of the disk allows a stop in the disk drive to be pushed away if it is inserted correctly.
- Power lawn mowers now have a safety bar on the handle that must be engaged in order to start the engine.
- A proxy ballot for an investment fund will not fit into the return envelope unless a small strip is detached. The strip asks the respondent to check to see whether the ballot is signed and dated.

From this discussion and examples, we see three levels of mistake-proofing with increasing costs associated with them:

1. *Designing potential errors out of the product or process.* Clearly, this approach is the most powerful form of mistake-proofing because it eliminates any possibility that the error or defect might occur and has no direct cost in terms of time or rework and scrap.
2. *Identifying potential defects and stopping a process before the defect is produced.* Although this approach eliminates any cost associated with producing a defect, it does require the time associated with stopping a process and taking corrective action.
3. *Finding defects that enter or leave a process.* This approach eliminates wasted resources that would add value to nonconforming work, but clearly results in scrap or rework.

It is not always possible to achieve the highest level in designing or improving a process, but it is certainly advantageous to try.

Richard B. Chase and Douglas M. Stewart suggest that the same concepts can be applied to services.[11] The major differences are that service mistake-proofing must account for the customers' activities as well as those of the producer, and fail-safe methods must be set up for interactions conducted directly or by phone, mail, or other technologies, such as ATM. Chase and Stewart classify service poka-yokes by the type of error they are designed to prevent: server errors and customer errors. Server errors result from the task, treatment, or tangibles of the service. Customer errors occur during preparation, the service encounter, or during resolution.

Task errors include doing work incorrectly, work not requested, work in the wrong order, or working too slowly. Some examples of poka-yoke devices for task errors are computer prompts, color-coded cash register keys, measuring tools such as McDonald's french-fry scoop, and signaling devices. Hospitals use trays for surgical instruments that have indentations for each instrument, preventing the surgeon from leaving one of them in the patient.

Treatment errors arise in the contact between the server and the customer, such as lack of courteous behavior, and failure to acknowledge, listen, or react appropriately to the customer. A bank encourages eye contact by requiring tellers to record the customer's eye color on a checklist as they start the transaction. To promote friendliness at a fast-food restaurant, trainers provide the four specific cues for when to smile: when greeting the customer, when taking the order, when telling about the dessert special, and when giving the customer change. They encourage employees to observe whether the customer smiled back, a natural reinforcer for smiling.

Tangible errors are those in physical elements of the service, such as unclean facilities, dirty uniforms, inappropriate temperature, and document errors. Hotels wrap paper strips around towels to help the housekeeping staff identify clean linen and show which ones should be replaced. Spell-checkers in word processing software eliminate document misspellings (provided they are used!).

Customer errors in preparation include the failure to bring necessary materials to the encounter, to understand their role in the service transaction, and to engage the correct service. A computer manufacturer provides a flowchart to specify how to place a service call. By guiding the customers through three yes-or-no questions, the flowchart prompts them to have the necessary information before calling.

Customer errors during an encounter can be due to inattention, misunderstanding, or simply a memory lapse, and include failure to remember steps in the process or to follow instructions. Poka-yoke examples include height bars at amusement rides that indicate rider size requirements, beepers that signal customers to remove cards from ATM machines, and locks on airplane lavatory doors that must be closed to turn on the lights. Some cashiers at restaurants fold back the top edge of credit card receipts, holding together the restaurant's copies while revealing the customer's copy.

Customer errors at the resolution stage of a service encounter include failure to signal service inadequacies, to learn from experience, to adjust expectations, and to execute appropriate post-encounter actions. Hotels might enclose a small gift certificate to encourage guests to provide feedback. Strategically placed tray-return stands and trash receptacles remind customers to return trays in fast-food facilities.

Mistake-proofing a service process requires identifying when and where failures generally occur. Once a failure is identified, the source must be found. The final step is to prevent the mistake from occurring through source inspection, self-inspection, or sequential checks.

Creative Thinking

Poka-yoke, and in fact, all improvement approaches, require a high degree of creativity. Many tools and techniques for enhancing creative thinking have been developed, and Six Sigma participants are well advised to study them.

One of the difficulties in trying to identify ideas for improvement is the natural instinct to prejudge them before thoroughly evaluating them. Most people have a natural fear of proposing a "silly" idea or looking foolish. However, such ideas may actually form the basis for a creative and useful solution. Effective problem solvers must learn to defer judgment and develop the ability to generate a large number of ideas at this stage of the process. A number of processes and tools to facilitate idea generation can be used. One of the most popular is brainstorming.

Brainstorming, a useful group problem-solving procedure for generating ideas, was proposed by Alex Osborn[12] "for the sole purpose of producing checklists of ideas" that can be used in developing a solution to a problem. With brainstorming, no criticism is permitted, and people are encouraged to generate a large number of ideas through combination and enhancement of existing ideas. Wild ideas are encouraged and frequently trigger other good ideas from somewhere else. The process often works in the following manner. Each individual in the group suggests an idea relating to the problem at hand, working in a round-robin fashion. If a person cannot think of anything, he or she passes. A facilitator writes down all ideas on a blackboard or easel so that everyone can see them. Each individual presents only one idea at a time. The process is repeated until no further ideas can be generated. By writing down the ideas in plain view of the group, new ideas are usually built from old ones by combining or extending previous suggestions.

For example, suppose that a group is examining the problem of the reasons for damage in the course of parts handling. The first individual might suggest "lack of storage"; the second, "poor placement of machines"; the third, "poor design of racks." The next individual might combine the previous two ideas and suggest "poor placement of parts on racks." In this fashion, one individual's idea might spawn a new idea from someone else. Checklists are often used as a guide for generating ideas. Osborn proposed about 75 fundamental questions based on the following principles:

- Put to other uses?
- Adapt?
- Modify?
- Magnify?
- Minify?
- Substitute?
- Rearrange?
- Reverse?
- Combine?

By consciously seeking ideas based on this list, one can generate many unusual and often useful ideas.

Several other methods for generating ideas have been suggested. One is to change the wording of a problem statement. Simple modification of a single word can dramatically change the meaning. For example, consider this statement: "In what ways might this company reduce quality costs by 30 percent?" Dropping the qualifier "by 30 percent" broadens the problem and potential solutions. Relaxing the "by 30 percent" to "by 5 percent" produces a similar effect. Changing the action verb or goal can also change the problem perspective. Turning a negative statement into a positive one leads to different ideas, such as "reducing quality costs" to "increasing quality value." Reversing the focus of the problem is another technique. For instance, "how to reduce costs due to scrap" can be reversed to "how to use scrap to reduce costs" (by recycling, for example).

SIX SIGMA AND LEAN PRODUCTION

Lean production refers to approaches initially developed by Toyota that focus on the elimination of waste in all forms, including defects requiring rework, unnecessary processing steps, unnecessary movement of materials or people, waiting time, excess inventory, and overproduction. A simple way of defining it is "getting more done with less."[13] It involves identifying and eliminating non-value-added activities throughout the entire value chain to achieve faster customer response, reduced inventories, higher quality, and better human resources. As one article about Toyota observed, to see the Toyota production system in action is to "behold a thing of beauty."[14]

Lean production is facilitated by a focus on measurement and continuous improvement, cross-trained workers, flexible and increasingly automated equipment, efficient machine layout, rapid setup and changeover, just-in-time delivery and scheduling, realistic work standards, worker empowerment to perform inspections and take corrective action, supplier partnerships, and preventive maintenance. Some of the benefits claimed by proponents of lean production include the following:

- At least 60 percent reduction in cycle times
- 40 percent improvement in space utilization
- 25 percent greater throughput
- 50 percent reduction in work-in-process and finished goods inventories
- 50 percent improvement in quality
- 20 percent improvements in working capital and worker productivity

However, as one industry expert observed, it takes "an incredible amount of detailed planning, discipline, hard work, and painstaking attention to detail."[15] Surveys have noted that midsized and large companies are likely to be familiar with lean principles and have systems in place; however, few small manufacturing shops have much familiarity with the principles. Thus, considerable opportunity exists for this important economic sector.

Some of the key tools used in lean production include:

- *The 5S's.* The 5S's are derived from Japanese terms: *seiri* (sort), *seiton* (set in order), *seiso* (shine), *seiketsu* (standardize), and *shitsuke* (sustain). They define a system for workplace organization and standardization. Sort refers to ensuring that each item in a workplace is in its proper place or identified as unnecessary and removed. Set in order means to arrange materials and equipment so that they are easy to find and use. Shine refers to a clean work area. Not only is this important for safety, but as a work area is cleaned, maintenance problems such as oil leaks can be identified before they cause problems. Standardize means to formalize procedures and practices to create consistency and ensure that all steps are performed correctly. Finally, sustain means to keep the process going through training, communication, and organizational structures.
- *Small batch or single-piece flow.* To minimize inventory and reduce cycle times, small production batches (ideally a single piece) should be used, making the process flow in a more continuous fashion. This also makes it easier to find defects and correct them early, thus reducing rework later in the process.
- *Visual controls.* Visual controls are indicators for tools, parts, and production activities that are placed in plain sight of all workers so that everyone can understand the status of the system at a glance. Thus, if a machine goes down, or a part is defective or delayed, immediate action can be taken.
- *Efficient layout and standardized work.* The layout of equipment and processes is designed according to the best operational sequence, by physically linking and arranging machines and process steps most efficiently, often in a cellular arrangement. Standardizing the individual tasks by clearly specifying the proper method reduces wasted human movement and energy.
- *Pull production.* In this system (also described as *kanban* or *just-in-time*), upstream suppliers do not produce until the downstream customer signals a need for parts.
- *Single minute exchange of dies (SMED).* SMED refers to rapid changeover of tooling and fixtures in machine shops so that multiple products in smaller batches can be run on the same equipment. Reducing setup time adds value to the operation and facilitates smoother production flow.
- *Total productive maintenance.* Total productive maintenance is designed to ensure that equipment is operational and available when needed.
- *Source inspection.* Inspection and control by process operators guarantees that product passed onto the next production stage conforms to specifications.
- *Continuous improvement.* Continuous improvement provides the link to Six Sigma. In order to make lean production work, one must get to the root causes of problems and permanently remove them. Teamwork is an integral part of continuous improvement in lean environments. Many techniques that we discuss in subsequent chapters are used.

One example of the application of lean concepts is found at Sunset Manufacturing, Inc., of Tualatin, Oregon, a 35-person, family-owned machine shop.[16] Because of competitive pressures and a business downturn, Sunset began to look for ways to simplify operations and cut costs. They established a lean steering committee to coordinate and drive the process. The committee chartered a kaizen team to reduce setup time on vertical milling machines by 50 percent. The team used SMED and the 5S's approach as their basic tools. Several actions were taken, including (1) standardizing parts across milling machines, (2) reorganizing the tool room, (3) incorporating the SMED approach in machine setups, and (4) implementing what was termed "dance cards," which gave operators the specific steps required for the SMED of various machines and products. The results were impressive. Tool preparation time dropped from an average of 30 minutes to less than 10 minutes, isolation and identification of worn tools was improved, improved safety and appearance in the tool room due to 5S's application was apparent, and machine setup time was reduced from an average of 216 minutes to 36 minutes (an 86 percent improvement). Estimated savings were $33,000 per year, with an implementation cost of less than half of that amount. The net impact was to allow smaller lots to be run, a 75 percent reduction in setup scrap, emergence of a more competitive organization, and a morale boost for team members.

Six Sigma is a useful and complementary approach to lean production. For example, a cycle time reduction project might involve aspects of both. Lean tools might be applied to streamline an order entry process. This application could lead to the discovery that significant rework occurs because of incorrect addresses, customer numbers, or shipping charges and results in high variation of processing time. Six Sigma tools might then be used to drill down to the root cause of the problems and identify a solution. Because of these similarities, many industry training programs and consultants have begun to focus on "Lean Six Sigma," drawing on the best practices of both approaches. Both are driven by customer requirements, focus on real dollar savings, have the ability to make significant financial impacts on the organization, and can be used in non-manufacturing environments.

However, some differences clearly exist between lean production and Six Sigma. First, they attack different types of problems. Lean production addresses visible problems in processes, for example, inventory, material flow, and safety. Six Sigma is more concerned with less visible problems, for example, variation in performance. Another difference is that lean tools are more intuitive and easier to apply by anybody in the workplace, while many Six Sigma tools require advanced training and expertise of black belt or master black belt specialists, or consultant equivalents. For example, the concept of the 5S's is easier to grasp than statistical methods. Thus, organizations might be well advised to start with basic lean principles and evolve toward more sophisticated Six Sigma approaches.

Lean Six Sigma and Services

Lean production can easily be applied to non-manufacturing environments. Pure service firms such as banks, hospitals, and restaurants have benefited from lean principles. In these contexts, lean production is often called **lean enterprise**. For example, banks operate on low margins and require quick response and efficiency. Many of their processes, such as check sorting and mortgage approval, are systematic and repeatable processes that are natural candidates for lean enterprise solutions. Handling of paper checks and credit card slips, for instance, involves a physical process that is similar to a manufacturing operation. The faster a bank moves checks through its system, the sooner it can collect its funds and improve its returns on invested capital.

One North American financial institution applied lean enterprise principles to check processing operations.[17] They documented the check handling process from start to finish, and recorded the time spent in actual processing and in waiting, rework, and handling. They found that almost half of the bank's processing capacity was consumed by nonprocessing activities such as fixing jams and setting up machines. Further investigation revealed wide variations in the way individual operators performed their task, which lowered overall productivity. They also found that the flow of incoming checks was not well matched to processing capacity, creating bottlenecks. Using just-in-time principles, they reduced batch sizes and spread the check flow evenly through the day. The analysis also revealed that all checks presented for morning processing were sorted three times. These extra steps made it difficult to process the morning check volume in time to meet the account-posting deadline. However, many of the checks did not need to be completed by the morning deadline, and once the sorting of these low-priority items was shifted to later in the day when volumes were lower, capacity increased by 122 percent. By freeing up capacity that had previously been taken up by waiting time, maintenance, and rework, they were able to increase actual capacity by more than 25 percent without investing in additional equipment, and more than doubled the margin contributed by the operation.

A medical laboratory had been improving cycle time from test sample receipt to shipment for several years and had achieved a 30 percent reduction, primarily by using new technology. However, doctors were still asking for faster responses. Using performance benchmarking, the lab quality coordinator found some examples of manufacturing plants that had reduced cycle time by as much as 90 percent with little capital investment. The coordinator discovered that these improvements were not achieved simply by making each step work faster, but also by identifying and reducing waste that existed between the process steps, such as movement, waiting, and inventory. By learning about lean production techniques and changing the flow of test samples in the lab, the organization was able to reduce cycle time by another 20 percent within seven months.[18]

Six Sigma is being successfully implemented in local government settings. Consider the case of the city of Fort Wayne, Indiana.[19] Before he was elected mayor of the city, Graham Richard had founded a quality learning network in 1991. Thanks to the TQM Network, more than 40 small- and medium-sized companies, nonprofit organizations, and local governments now provide Six Sigma training to their employees. When he took office in January 2000, Mayor Richard quickly enrolled the city of Fort Wayne into membership in the Northeast Indiana TQM Network. Michele Hill was appointed to the city's newly created position of quality enhancement manager, and was assisted by Roger Hirt, a Six Sigma master black belt formerly with General Electric. Ten city employees from a variety of departments initially received Six Sigma black belt training and each completed a city-approved project. As a result of some of these projects, the city reduced larcenies by 19 percent in a targeted area, increased fire code re-inspections by 23 percent, reduced the time to re-inspect by 17 days, and increased the amount of transportation engineering change orders within an accepted tolerance by 21 percent.

Perhaps the most shining example of Six Sigma's potential in a municipal setting comes from a most unglamorous process: waste activated sludge. Cheryl Cronin, of the Fort Wayne's Water Pollution Control Plant, set her sights on increasing the amount of waste activated sludge processed through the plant's centrifuge. It might not sound exciting, but the results were impressive. As a direct result of Cronin's project, the city avoided $1.7 million in improvements to the WPC Plant's digester, the digester's use of alternative fuels dropped 98 percent, and the operating time on the process decreased by four hours per day. "With tools like Six Sigma in the hands of City workers, we can not only provide quality training for our employees, but now we can also measure and improve customer satisfaction," Cronin said. "This is a win-win situation for everyone living in Fort Wayne or using services offered by the city."

IMPLEMENTATION PLANNING

Simply identifying a good solution is insufficient; a Six Sigma team must also plan for implementing it. This might include a pilot project to determine whether the proposed idea is feasible and will accomplish the improvement objective, as well as preparing budgets, training, facility or procedure changes, and so on.

The Deming Cycle

The **Deming cycle** is a simple methodology for improvement. It was originally called the *Shewhart cycle* after its founder, Walter Shewhart, but was renamed the Deming cycle by the Japanese in 1950. The Deming cycle is composed of four stages: *plan, do, study,* and *act* (PDSA) as illustrated in Figure 6.3. Overall, the Deming cycle is similar to DMAIC. However, much of the focus of the Deming cycle is on implementation and learning, so it complements the Improve phase of DMAIC quite well.

FIGURE 6.3 THE DEMING CYCLE

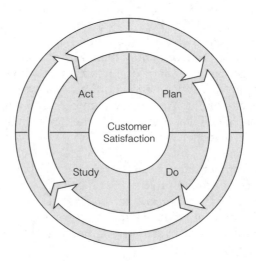

The Plan stage consists of studying the current situation and describing the process: its inputs, outputs, customers, and suppliers; understanding customer expectations; gathering data; identifying problems; testing theories of causes; and developing solutions and action plans. Essentially, the Plan stage covers most everything in "DMAI" that we have already discussed. The remaining steps provide useful approaches for testing and implementing Six Sigma improvement ideas.

In the Do stage, the plan is implemented on a trial basis, for example, in a laboratory, pilot production process, or with a small group of customers, to evaluate a proposed solution and provide objective data. Data from the experiment are collected and documented. The Study stage determines whether the trial plan is working correctly by evaluating the results, recording the learning, and determining whether any further issues or opportunities need be addressed. Often, the first solution must be modified or scrapped. New solutions are proposed and evaluated by returning to the Do stage. Statistical hypothesis testing can be used to verify whether a proposed improvement does indeed improve performance, and cost-benefit analysis might be applied to ensure that the improvement is fiscally responsible. In the last stage, Act, the improvements become standardized and the final plan is implemented as a "current best practice" and communicated throughout the organization. As Figure 6.3 suggests, this process then leads back to the Plan stage for identification of other improvement opportunities.

The Seven Management and Planning Tools

A set of simple tools and techniques, known as the **seven management and planning tools**, are often used to assist in implementing improvement projects. They are:

1. *Affinity diagram*: A tool for organizing a large number of ideas, opinions, and facts relating to a broad problem or subject area. Essentially, affinity diagrams group ideas into similar categories, allowing for better understanding of themes (think of a wall full of sticky notes grouped together in a logical fashion). Cause-and-effect diagrams, discussed in the previous chapter, can be thought of as a graphical version of affinity diagrams.
2. *Interrelationship digraph*: A tool for identifying and exploring causal relationships among related concepts or ideas. Visualize drawing arrows between sticky notes placed on a wall to show the chains of relationships among factors to show which factors influence or "drive" others. Such a diagram can be helpful in drilling down to the root cause of a problem and for building a cause-and-effect diagram.
3. *Tree diagram*: A tool to map out the paths and tasks necessary to complete a specific project or reach a specified goal. A tree diagram breaks up tasks into progressively smaller elements or subtasks. Essentially, this is a graphical version of a standard outline that you have undoubtedly used in preparing an essay or school report.
4. *Matrix diagram*: "Spreadsheets" that graphically display relationships between ideas, activities, or other dimensions in such a way as to provide

logical connecting points between each item. A specific example of a matrix diagram is the House of Quality that we will discuss in Chapter 8.

5. *Matrix data analysis*: A tool to take data and arrange them to display quantitative relationships among variables to make them more easily understood and analyzed. Scoring models, such as the one we discussed for project selection in Chapter 3, are essentially matrix data analysis tools.

6. *Process decision program chart*: A method for mapping out every conceivable event and contingency that can occur when moving from a problem statement to possible solutions. A PDPC takes each branch of a tree diagram, anticipates possible problems, and provides countermeasures that will (1) prevent the deviation from occurring, or (2) be in place if the deviation does occur. Figure 6.4 shows one example for implementing a strategy to educate and train all employees to use a new computer system.

7. *Arrow diagrams*: These are essentially project management networks that have been used extensively to sequence and schedule project tasks. They show the sequence of activities in a project along with time estimates and are used to schedule and control projects.

The first two are particularly useful in the analysis and improvement phases of DMAIC; the remainder focus primarily on implementation. These tools had their roots in post–World War II operations research developments in the United States, but were combined and refined by several Japanese companies over the past several decades. They were popularized in the United States during the mid-1980s by the consulting firm GOAL/QPC, and have been used by many firms.

FIGURE 6.4 PROCESS DECISION PROGRAM CHART

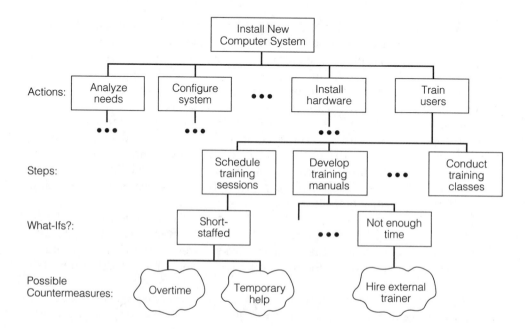

PROJECT REVIEW—IMPROVE PHASE

A project review of the Improve phase should ensure that

- Team members have received any necessary "just-in-time" training
- Process maps have been studied and evaluated in detail
- Ideas and suggestions from all the right people have been solicited and considered
- All reasonable alternatives have been identified
- Both incremental and breakthrough improvements have been considered
- Criteria for evaluating alternatives have been developed
- Alternatives have been thoroughly evaluated for feasibility and improvement potential
- Improvements identified align with the project metrics ("vital few" independent variables) and goals
- Mistake-proofing has been incorporated into improvement ideas
- Impacts of proposed changes have been tested and verified through experimentation or a pilot project

 CASE STUDY

An Application of Six Sigma to Reduce Medical Errors[20]

Medication administration and laboratory processing/results reporting are examples of complex systems in health care that are known to be error prone. As described in the report of the National Academy of Sciences/Institute of Medicine, medication errors are a substantial source of preventable errors in hospitals, but result in part from poorly designed complex systems. At Froedtert Hospital in Milwaukee, Wisconsin, errors with IV medication drips and laboratory processing and results reporting were well documented. Additionally, errors in ordering, transporting, analyzing, and reporting clinical laboratory tests were known to be a significant source of error at the hospital. It is for these reasons that these two areas were targeted for initial study.

A consortium was created by four Milwaukee-based organizations committed to the development of an approach to reduce errors and improve patient safety. The consortium members include the Medical College of Wisconsin, Froedtert Memorial Lutheran Hospital, the American Society for Quality, and SecurTrac, a company formed specifically to develop technologies to improve patient safety. The consortium is currently addressing three major efforts: (1) improved identification and reporting of health-care errors, (2) deployment of the Six Sigma methodology to reduce errors, and (3) testing and implementation of technical solutions to improve patient safety. At the center of this approach is the effort to determine whether the Six Sigma error-reduction methodology can be successfully applied in health care.

Using Six Sigma methods and selected statistical tools, Froedtert Hospital's processes for medication delivery were evaluated with the goal of designing an approach that would decrease the likelihood of errors. The design employed the classic Six Sigma process steps. A multidisciplinary group of physicians, nurses, pharmacists, and administrators identified medication delivery by continuous IV infusions as a process subject to substantial error. Continuous IV infusions are used in many clinical settings and errors can severely impact patient well-being. Initially, the focus was on five specific IV medications. Soon it was realized that the number was too small to permit quantification of error rates. The scope of the project was expanded to 22 medications delivered by continuous IV infusion. Team members developed a process map (flowchart) to delineate each step in the procedure for continuous IV medication infusion. The process map revealed nine steps: (1) physician order, (2) order review, (3) pharmacist order entry, (4) dose preparation, (5) dose dispensing, (6) infusion rate calculation, (7) IV pump setup, (8) pump programming, and (9) pump monitoring.

Each of the steps was subjected to failure modes and effect analysis (FMEA—see Chapter 8) and scored on a scale of 1 to 10 for three categories: frequency of occurrence, detectability, and severity. The scores were multiplied together to yield a risk priority number (RPN) for each step. Eighteen months of retrospective medication error reports were reviewed to provide additional data for the RPN calculation. This review confirmed the FMEA results that IV rate calculations and IV pump setup were the two most error-prone steps in the IV infusion process. Initial efforts to delineate and reduce errors focused on these two steps.

Because it was not known how often errors went unrecognized or unreported, an audit was conducted to determine whether the prescribed dose rate matched the actual infusion rate. Two weeks of audit data were collected and the resulting 124 data points were rated on a discrepancy scale of 1 to 3 (1 for a $\leq$ 1 ml/hr discrepancy, 2 for a 1–5 ml/hr discrepancy, 3 for a $\geq$ 5ml/hr discrepancy). Ten of the audits were rated at level 2 and four were rated at level 3. Root cause analysis was employed to determine the cause of the discrepancies. Work was then begun to affect the accuracy of infusion rates.

Using Six Sigma methods and statistical tools, the team also examined the hospital's clinical laboratory process. Key elements in the acquisition, laboratory analysis, and reporting of patient specimens were identified. The steps included (1) physician order, (2) order entry, (3) matching the order to the patient, (4) collecting the specimen, (5) labeling the specimen, (6) transporting the specimen, (7) analyzing the specimen, (8) reporting the results, and (9) entering the results into the patient's chart. Each of these steps is subject to error. Applying Six Sigma analysis, the steps subject to the most errors were identified. These steps were: order entry by the unit clerical staff, transportation of the specimens to the lab, and analysis of specimens in the lab. To identify, define, and reduce these errors, a laboratory error reduction task force was established. It included members from administration, lab, nursing, clerical staff, information systems, and quality management. The task force first developed a process map so that all members could appreciate the complexity and vulnerability of the entire process. The process map provided the task force with the tools to analyze the clinical laboratory problem in depth. The FMEA technique was employed to arrive at an RPN so that steps in the laboratory analysis process could be prioritized in terms of their vulnerability to error. Again, order entry, transportation, and analysis of specimens were identified. Statistical tools, including correlation and regression, analysis of variance, confidence intervals, and hypothesis testing, were employed to evaluate the laboratory process further.

The analysis of medication delivery by IV infusions served as a good example of deployment of Six Sigma methodology to reduce error and improve patient safety in a health-care setting. Significant variability in the ordering and processing of IV drips was identified. Lack of standardization in many steps of the process posed the greatest risk for system failure. Those steps with the highest degree of variability and the greatest chance for error were

1. MD ordering practices (that is, lack of standardization in medication description, dosage, concentration, etc.)
2. IV drip preparation (lack of standardization by pharmacy and nursing of IV bag concentrations)
3. RN labeling and documentation of IV concentrations

In these three areas, a multidisciplinary task force created standards to reduce variation. Specific interventions included implementation of standardized physician order sheets, a policy requiring preparation of all IV medications in a standard concentration, and use of color-coded labels when nonstandard concentrations were in use. Thirty days after implementation, measurable improvement was evident. Level 1 discrepancies fell from 47.4 percent to 14 percent. Level 2 discrepancies fell from 21.1 percent to 11.8 percent and level 3 discrepancies fell from 15.8 percent to 2.9 percent. Though far from achieving a 6-sigma level of performance, substantial efforts continue to move toward that goal.

The laboratory project proved to be more complex. It was evident early on that the scope of this complex system was too broad for an initial effort. The project was broken down into smaller individual steps of the larger process. Once refocused, the appointed task force identified opportunities to reduce variation in select steps of the laboratory process: Alternate means of identifying specimens, changes in the approach to "point of care" laboratory analysis, decentralization of some laboratory tests, and a revised system to order and process satisfaction improvement. The goal is that at least the stat lab tests would be put into place. Effectiveness monitoring continues, as does measurement of sustainable error reductions. These efforts marked the beginning of a long laboratory redesign process aimed at driving out error, reducing turnaround time, and improving patient safety.

REVIEW QUESTIONS

1. Explain the Japanese concept of kaizen. How does it differ from traditional Western approaches to improvement?
2. What is flexibility and why is it important to a modern organization?
3. What are the key impacts of cycle time reduction?
4. What is a stretch goal? How can stretch goals help an organization?
5. What is reengineering? How does it relate to Six Sigma practices?
6. What are the fundamental questions that should be asked when analyzing a process using a process map?

7. What is a kaizen blitz? How does it differ from traditional kaizen applications?
8. Why do people make inadvertent mistakes? How does poka-yoke help prevent such mistakes?
9. List and explain the three levels of mistake-proofing.
10. Describe the types of errors that service poka-yokes are designed to prevent.
11. List and explain some of the tools and approaches used in "lean" organizations. How does the lean operating concept relate to Six Sigma?
12. What are some reasons why the lean approach appeals to small organizations?
13. What is the Deming cycle? Explain the four steps.
14. List and explain the seven management and planning tools.

DISCUSSION QUESTIONS

1. A good improvement philosophy seeks to encourage suggestions, not to find excuses for failing to improve. Typical excuses are "If it's not broken, don't fix it," "I'm too busy to work on it," and "It's not in the budget." Think of at least five other excuses why people don't try to improve.
2. How can lean concepts be applied in a classroom?
3. Maintaining accuracy of books on the shelves in a college library is an important task. Consider the following problems that are often observed.
    a. Books are not placed in the correct shelf position. This process includes those books that have been checked out and returned, as well as those taken off the shelves for use within the library by patrons.
    b. New or returned books are not checked in and consequently, the online catalog does not show their availability.
    What procedures or poka-yokes might you suggest for mitigating these problems? You might wish to talk to some librarians or administrators at your college library to see how they address such problems.
4. Referring to the case study, how did the team use process mapping as a key part of the Six Sigma process? What value did process mapping have?
5. In the case, why were the teams and task forces multidisciplinary in nature? What benefits does this approach have?

THINGS TO DO

1. Design a process for the following activities:
    a. Preparing for an exam
    b. Writing a term paper
    c. Planning a vacation
    d. Making breakfast for your family
    e. Washing your car
    Draw a flowchart for each process and discuss how ways in which both quality and cycle time might be improved.

2. Research several companies to identify the type of problem solving and improvement approaches (such as Six Sigma or lean principles) they use. Compare and contrast their approaches. Which, if any, of the approaches described in the chapter are they most similar to?

3. Work with your school administrators to identify an important quality-related problem they face. Outline a plan for improvement. If time permits, apply some of the problem-solving tools to collect data, identify the root cause, and generate ideas for solving the problem or improving the situation.

4. Describe a personal problem you face and how you might use the Deming cycle and QC tools to address it.

5. Work with teachers at a local high school or grade school to identify some students who are having difficulties in school. Apply quality tools to help find the source of the problems and create an improvement plan.

6. Identify several sources of errors as a student or in your personal life. Develop some poka-yokes that might prevent them.

7. Interview a plant manager or quality professional at one or more local companies to see if they have used any poka-yoke approaches to mistake-proof their operations.

8. Check out the Web site www.freequality.org. This contains descriptions and examples of the use of quality improvement tools. Find some that have not been discussed in this chapter and develop a short tutorial for using them.

9. Search the Internet for John Grout's poka-yoke Web site. Read several of the interesting articles available there and write a report on the information you discovered.

PROBLEMS

1. A flowchart for a fast-food drive-through window is shown in Figure 6.5. Determine the important quality characteristics inherent in this process and suggest possible improvements, using the Deming cycle.

2. A catalog order-filling process for personalized printed products can be described as follows:[21] Telephone orders are taken over a 12-hour period each day. Orders are collected from each person at the end of the day and checked for errors by the supervisor of the phone department, usually the following morning. The supervisor does not send each one-day batch of orders to the data processing department until after 1:00 P.M. In the next step—data processing—orders are invoiced in the one-day batches. Then, they are printed and matched back to the original orders. At this point, if the order is from a new customer, it is sent to the person who did the customer verification and setup of new customer accounts. This process must be completed before the order can be invoiced. The next step—order verification and proofreading—occurs after invoicing is completed. The orders, with invoices attached, are given to a person who verifies that all required information is present and correct to permit typesetting. If the verifier has any questions, they are checked by computer or by calling the customer.

FIGURE 6.5 FLOWCHART FOR PROBLEM 1

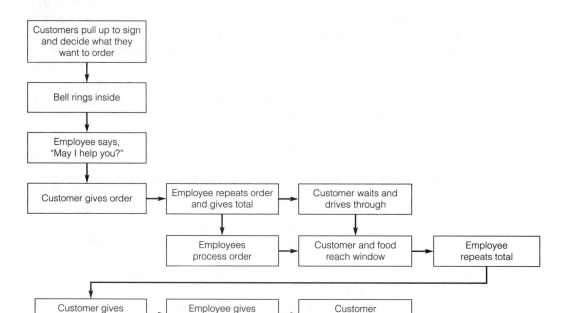

Finally, the completed orders are sent to the typesetting department of the print shop.

a. Develop a flowchart for this process.

b. Identify opportunities for improving the quality of service in this situation, using the Deming cycle.

3. Rick Hensley owns an automotive dealership. Service is a major part of the operation. Rick and his service team have spent considerable time in analyzing the service process and have developed a flowchart, shown in Figure 6.6 that describes the typical activities in servicing a customer's automobile. Rick wants to ensure that customers receive superior service and are highly satisfied; thus, he wants to establish poka-yokes for any possible failures that may occur. Your assignment is to identify any possible failure in the service process that may be detrimental to customer satisfaction and suggest poka-yokes to eliminate these failures.

4. Figure 6.7 shows a medication administration process in a hospital. The administrative staff of the hospital is getting concerned about frequent medication errors. By examining this flowchart, discuss possible sources of errors, the types of individuals responsible (for example, physicians, nurses, pharmacists, other) and poka-yokes that might be used to mitigate these errors.

5. "Let's plan a graduation party for our seniors," suggested Jim Teacher, president of the Delta Mu Zeta fraternity at State U. Everyone on the fraternity council thought that it was a good idea, so they agreed to brainstorm ideas for the party.

FIGURE 6.6 AUTOMOBILE SERVICE FLOWCHART

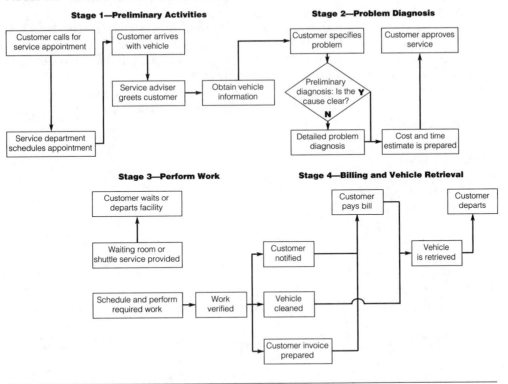

FIGURE 6.7 MEDICAL ADMINISTRATION PROCESS

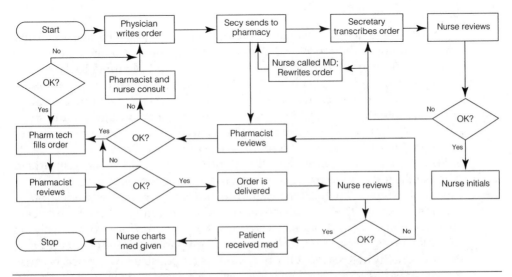

"First, we have to pick a date," suggested Joe. "It'll have to be after final exams are over, but before graduation."

"That narrows it down pretty quickly to June 8, 9, or 10. The 11th is a Sunday and the 12th is graduation day," said Jim. "I propose that we try for Thursday the 8th, with the alternate date of Friday, the 9th. We'll have to take a vote at the fraternity meeting tomorrow."

"Now, let's list things that have to be done in order to get ready for the party, " suggested Amber. They quickly produced the following list (not in any order).

Pick date
Plan menu
Get food delivered
Estimate costs
Locate and book a hall
Determine budget
Select music
Hire a DJ
Plan decorations
Setup, decorate hall
Determine how much can be paid from treasury and what the cost of the special assessment will be for each member
Design and print invitations
Set up mailing list
Dress rehearsal (day before party) "dummy activity"
Mail invitations
Plan ceremony for seniors
Rehearse ceremony
Plan after-party cleanup and bill paying
Have the party
Cleanup and pay bills

Next, they selected Joe as the "project manager" since he had fraternity party planning experience and was taking a quality management course where he was exposed to the seven management and planning tools.

a. Put yourself in Joe's position. Develop an interrelationship digraph for the party planners. Draw arrows from one activity to the next one that must occur. Note that the activities that have the most arrows going into them will tend to be the long-range results. Activities having the most arrows originating from them will tend to be the initial activities.

b. What can you conclude from the graph? How would this digraph help make the job of organizing the party easier for the project team?

6.   Creative Design Group (CDG) designs brochures for companies, trade groups, and associations. Their emphasis on customer service is based on speed, quality, creativity, and value. They want each brochure to "wow" the customer in its design, meet or exceed the preparation deadline, and be of superior quality at a reasonable price. Value is emphasized over price, because the president, Trendy Art, believes that CDG's experienced staff should

emphasize high quality and creativity instead of price. They accomplish their primary objectives 97 percent of the time.

To carry out their objectives, the small company has four designers, a customer service/estimator (CSE), and Trendy, who is the creative director and strategic visionary. The work environment, in a converted garage behind Trendy's house, features modern (though not always state-of-the-art) computer hardware and software, excellent lighting, and modern communications for sending design documents to clients and printers. Designers generally work independently of each other, consulting with the CSE when there are requests for status updates or client-initiated changes. They also consult with Trendy, who signs off on the creative design, after consultation with each client. A casual dress code and work policies, and a number of perks for workers, such as health insurance, flextime, generous vacation and sick leave benefits, a 401(k) retirement plan, competitive wages, etc. have, in the past, made it easy to attract and retain talented people. However, with fewer talented people graduating from design schools in the area, and more competitive firms bidding up salaries, turnover has become an issue.

The CSE, Green Ishied, is the contact point for all projects, of which there may be 10–20 active at any one time. He must ensure that projects are carefully estimated and prepare proposals, track progress of each project, and communicate with clients on status and change requests. He is also responsible for advertising and promotion of the firm.

Trendy's husband, Hy, is a CPA and part-time accountant for the company. He has noticed recently that costs are increasing, the percentage of bids accepted is decreasing, and the ROI is slipping.

Develop an affinity diagram that captures the major organizational features and issues. How could this diagram help Trendy develop a 3–5 year strategic plan for CDG?

7. Given the situation in problem 6, Trendy has determined several long-range objectives, among which are outdistancing the competition so as to grow the business by 10 percent per year for each of the next 5 years (a 61 percent compound growth rate), and adding a new designer every two years. These elements should be the key ingredients for her goal of increasing her profitability by 10 percent per year. To accomplish her objectives, she must deal with the two major issues of the increasing competition and improving employee recruitment and retention in order to develop effective action plans to support her long-range plan. Develop a tree diagram, starting with "Develop action plans" as the main theme. At the next level, include the two main issues. One, for example, is "Develop a plan to meet competition." Then, break out each of the issues into two or three feasible proposals, such as "Make advertising more effective," under the previous item of "Develop a plan to meet competition." Finally, add another level of specificity with 2–4 items, such as: "Place ads in business newspaper," "Redesign web page," etc. under the "Make advertising more effective" item.

8. Jim Teacher (see problem 5) was able to get some estimating information from the president of another fraternity that had planned and carried out a

similar party for graduating seniors last year. They had not kept financial information, but they did have the actual hours that it took to complete each activity. From these data, Jim obtained the following time estimates for Delta Mu Zeta.

Activity	Time Estimate (days)
Pick date	1
Plan menu	2
Get food delivered	1
Estimate costs	3
Locate and book a hall	5
Determine budget	3
Select music	2
Select and hire a DJ	3
Plan decorations	2
Set up, decorate hall	1
Dress rehearsal (day before party) "dummy activity"	0
Determine how much can be paid from treasury and what the cost of the special assessment will be for each member	1
Design and print invitations	3
Set up mailing list	5
Mail invitations	1
Plan ceremony for seniors	2
Rehearse ceremony	1
Plan after-party cleanup and bill paying	2
Have the party	1
Cleanup and pay bills	1

    a. You are Joe, the project manager. Use the interrelationship digraph developed in problem 5 to draw an arrow diagram, making sure that activities are sequenced in the correct order.

    b. If you are familiar with PERT/CPM through other courses, use the data above to calculate the minimum time that the project will take; that is, compute the critical path.

9. Given Creative Design Group's (CDG) situation in problem 6 and Trendy's development of strategic objectives in Problem 7, she decided that, along with improving her recruiting processes for new and replacement hiring, it was time to replace the computer system with state-of-the-art hardware and software. Knowing that she and her staff did not have the expertise to design the type of system that they needed, Trendy looked around, analyzed three competing firms' proposals, and finally settled on Creative Computer Group (CCG) to act as consultants and system integrators. Before signing the contract, Trendy decided to ask Hy and Green Ishied (the CSE) to meet with her and the CEO of CCG to clarify the system design requirements and the wording of the contract.

Trendy, Hy, and Green all agreed that the system needed to be completely integrated, with the capability to gather cost and scheduling data directly from the designers, and to produce all necessary business reports, as well as having graphics capability. Both cost and design information would have to be available to everyone in the firm. Therefore, the network should be capable of interfacing Macintosh and PC desktops via USB connections, with common printers. It should also provide for high bandwidth Internet access and capability to send and receive graphic and text data files. Charlie Nerd, the president of CCG, said that all of those requirements could be met by the system that he would design. This was such an important project for his company that he would personally be the project manager for the installation and testing of the new system. After outlining the plans for the system, Charlie asked if there were any questions that they had. Trendy, High, and Green had no immediate questions, but promised to get back to Charlie within three days.

Supplier Char-acteristics	Weights	Rating for CCG	Rating for COG	Rating for COW	Weighted Value CCG	Weighted Value COG	Weighted Value COW
System design reliability	0.3	8	6	5			
Delivery timelines	0.2	7	4	9			
Cost	0.2	5	7	6			
System service	0.2	9	6	4			
Experience	0.1	4	9	6			
Total	1.0						

Note: Independent ratings on a scale of 1–10 (where 10 is best) were performed by the Small Business Council of Qualdale, where CDG is located.
Suppliers: CCG = Creative Computer Group
                    COG = Computer Organizational Group
                    COW = Operations Workgroup

a. Given the above information, perform a matrix data analysis to determine why (or if) CCG should get the contract to install the computer system. Justify your analysis.
b. What questions would you suggest that Trendy, Hy, and Green get back to Charlie on?
c. Construct a process decision program chart, similar to Figure 6.4 in the chapter, but closely reflecting CCG's training needs. What special consider-ations would need to be included in training graphic designers with little business knowledge and business-oriented people (such as Hy and Green) with little artistic design knowledge, about each other's areas of work in order to use an integrated system?

ENDNOTES

1. Ronald D. Snee, "Why Should Statisticians Pay Attention to Six Sigma?" *Quality Progress*, September 1999, 100–103.
2. Andrew E. Serwer, "Michael Dell Turns the PC World Inside Out," *Fortune*, September 8, 1997, 76–86.
3. Michael Hammer and James Champy, *Reengineering the Corporation* (New York: HarperBusiness, 1993), 177–178.
4. P. Kay Coleman, "Reengineering Pepsi's Road to the 'Right Side Up' Company," *Insights Quarterly* 5, no. 3, Winter 1993, 18–35.
5. Rochelle Rucker, "Six Sigma at Citibank," available at http://www.insidequality.wego.net.
6. David A. McCamey, Robert W. Bogs, and Linda M. Bayuk, "More, Better, Faster From Total Quality Effort," *Quality Progress*, August 1999, 43–50.
7. Eleanor Chilson, "Kaizen Blitzes at Magnivision: $809,270 Cost Savings," *Quality Management Forum* 29, no. 1, Winter 2003.
8. For an interesting, albeit academic discussion of the psychology of human error and its relationship to mistake-proofing, see Douglas M. Stewart and Richard B. Chase, "The Impact of Human Error on Delivering Service Quality," *Production and Operations Management* 8, no. 3, Fall 1999, 240–263; and Douglas M. Stewart and John R. Grout, "The Human Side of Mistake Proofing," *Production and Operations Management* 10, no. 4, Winter 2001, 440–459.
9. From *Poka-Yoke: Improving Product Quality by Preventing Defects*. Edited by NKS/Factory Magazine, English translation copyright © 1988 by Productivity Press, Inc., P.O. Box 3007, Cambridge, MA 02140, 800-394-6868. Reprinted by permission.
10. Harry Robinson, "Using Poka-Yoke Techniques for Early Defect Detection," Paper presented at the Sixth International Conference on Software Testing and Analysis and Review (STAR '97).
11. Excerpts reprinted from Richard B. Chase and Douglas M. Stewart, "Make Your Service Fail-Safe," *Sloan Management Review* 35, no. 3, Spring 1994, 35–44. © 1994 by the Sloan Management Review Association. All rights reserved.
12. A. F. Osborn, *Applied Imagination*, 3rd ed. (New York: Scribner's, 1963).
13. Gary Conner, "Benefiting from Six Sigma," *Manufacturing Engineering*, 130, no. 2, February, 2003, 53–59.
14. Alex Taylor III, "How Toyota Defies Gravity," *Fortune*, December 8, 1997, 100–108.
15. Joseph Orlicky, *Material Requirements Planning* (New York: McGraw-Hill, 1975).
16. Gary Conner, "Benefiting from Six Sigma," *Manufacturing Engineering*, 130, no. 2, February 2003, 53–59.
17. Anthony R. Goland, John Hall, and Devereaux A. Clifford, "First National Toyota," *The McKinsey Quarterly* no. 4, (1998), 58–66.
18. Duke Okes, "Organize Your Quality Toolbelt," *Quality Progress*, July 2002, 25–29.
19. Source: http://www.usmayors.org/uscm/us_mayor_newspaper/documents/06_11_01/ft_wayne_best_practice.asp
20. Adapted from Cathy Buck, "Application of Six Sigma to Reduce Medical Errors," *Proceedings of the 55th Annual Quality Congress of the American Society for Quality*, 2001 (CD-ROM). © 2001, American Society for Quality. Reprinted with permission.
21. Adapted from Ronald G. Conant, "JIT in a Mail Order Operation Reduces Processing Time from Four Days to Four Hours," *Industrial Engineering* 20, no. 9, September 1988, 34–37.

Process Control

CONTROL SYSTEMS

Control is the last step of the Six Sigma DMAIC process, and is the activity of ensuring that project improvements will be sustained by tracking key performance measures and CTQs. This requires monitoring the process and results, and taking corrective action when necessary to correct problems and bring the process back to stable performance. Control is important for two reasons. First, it is the basis for effective daily management of work at all levels of an organization. Second, long-term improvements cannot be made to a process unless the process is first brought under control.

Any control system has three components:

1. A standard or goal
2. A means of measuring accomplishment
3. Comparison of actual results with the standard, along with feedback to form the basis for corrective action

Goals and standards establish what is supposed to be accomplished. These goals and standards are reflected by measurable quality characteristics, such as dimensions of machined parts, numbers of defectives, customer complaints, or waiting times. For example, golf balls must meet five standards to be considered as conforming to the Rules of Golf: minimum size, maximum weight, spherical symmetry, maximum initial velocity, and overall distance.[1] Methods for measuring these quality characteristics may be automated or performed manually by the workforce. Golf balls are measured for size by trying to drop them through a metal ring—a conforming ball sticks to the ring while a nonconforming ball falls through; digital scales measure weight to one-thousandth of a gram; and initial velocity is measured in a special machine by finding the time it takes a ball struck at 98 mph to break a ballistic screen at the end of a tube exactly 6.28 feet away.

Measurements supply the information concerning what has actually been accomplished. Workers, supervisors, or managers then assess whether the actual results meet the goals and standards. If not, then remedial action must be taken. For example, workers might check the first few parts after a new production setup (called setup verification) to determine whether they conform to specifications. If not, the worker adjusts the setup. Sometimes this process occurs automatically. For instance, in the production of plastic sheet stock, thickness depends on temperature. Sensors monitor the sheet thickness; if it begins to go out of tolerance, the system can adjust the temperature in order to change the thickness.

However, in many industries, data are collected through some type of manual inspection process. Such processes rely on visual interpretation of product characteristics or manual reading of gauges and instruments and may encounter error rates of from 10 to 50 percent. This high rate occurs for several reasons:

- *Complexity:* The number of defects caught by an inspector decreases with more parts and less orderly arrangement.
- *Defect rate:* When the product defect rate is low, inspectors tend to miss more defects than when the defect rate is higher.
- *Inspection rate:* The inspector's performance degrades rapidly as the inspection rate increases.[2]

These factors can be mitigated by using automated technology, or at the very least, minimizing the number of quality characteristics that must be inspected, reducing time pressures, using repeated inspections (if the same item is inspected by several people, a higher percentage of total defects will be caught), and improving the design of the workspace to facilitate the inspection task.

Short-term corrective action generally should be taken by those who own the process and are responsible for doing the work, such as machine operators, order fulfillment workers, and so on. Long-term remedial action is the responsibility of management. The responsibility for control can be determined by checking the three components of control systems. Process owners must have the means of knowing what is expected (the standard or goal) through clear instructions and specifications; they must have the means of determining their actual performance, typically through inspection and measurement; and they must have a means of making corrections if they discover a variance between what is expected of them and their actual performance. If any of these criteria is not met, then the process is the responsibility of management, not the process owner.

If process owners are held accountable for, or expected to act on problems beyond their control, they become frustrated and end up playing games with management. Juran and Deming stated that the majority of quality problems are management-controllable—the result of common cause variation. For the smaller proportion of problems resulting from special causes, process owners must be given the tools to identify them and the authority to take action. This philosophy shifts the burden of assuring quality from inspection departments and "quality control" personnel to workers on the shop floor and in customer-contact positions. For example, DaimlerChrysler manufactures the PT Cruiser at the company's Toluca Assembly Plant in Mexico. To ensure quality, the Toluca plant verifies parts, processes, fit, and finish every step of the way, from stamping and body to paint and final assembly. The control practices include visual management through quality alert systems, which are designed to call immediate attention to abnormal conditions. The system provides visual and audible signals for each station for tooling, production, maintenance, and material flow.[3]

Documentation and Audits

Effective control systems include documented procedures for all key processes; a clear understanding of the appropriate equipment and working environment; methods for monitoring and controlling critical quality characteristics; approval processes for equipment; criteria for workmanship, such as written standards, samples, or illustrations; and maintenance activities. Dashboards and scorecards, which we introduced earlier in the book, are often used to summarize performance in a control plan.

To ensure that processes are performed correctly, many companies use **standard operating procedures (SOPs)**, which clearly document how each step of a process should be carried out. Often, a **quality manual** serves as a permanent reference for documenting and maintaining a quality control system. A quality manual need not be complex; a small company might need only a dozen pages while a large organization might need manuals for all key functions. Sufficient records should be maintained to demonstrate conformance to requirements and verify that the quality system is operating effectively. Typical records that might be maintained are inspection reports, test data, audit reports, and calibration data. They should be readily retrievable for analysis to identify trends and monitor the effectiveness of corrective actions.

Cincinnati Fiberglass, a small manufacturer of fiberglass parts for trucks, uses a control plan for each production process that includes the process name, tool used, standard operating procedure, tolerance, inspection frequency, sample size, person responsible, reporting document, and reaction plan. Of particular importance is the ability to trace all components of a product back to key process equipment and operators and to the original material from which it was made. Process control also includes monitoring the accuracy and variability of equipment, operator knowledge and skills, the accuracy of measurement results and data used, and environmental factors such as time and temperature.

Finally, the control system itself needs to be maintained and kept up to date. This maintenance can be facilitated through **internal audits**, which focus on identifying whether documented procedures are being followed and are effective, and reporting the issues to management for corrective action. Internal audits generally include a review of process records, training records, complaints, corrective actions, and previous audit reports. A typical internal audit begins by asking those who perform a process regularly to explain how it works.[4] Their statements are compared to written procedures, and compliance and deviations are noted. Next, the trail of paperwork or other data are examined to determine whether the process is consistent with the intent of the written procedure and the worker's explanation. Internal auditors also need to analyze whether the process is meeting its intent and objectives, thus focusing on continuous improvement.

Control in Services

Many people think that process control applies only to manufacturing. This assumption could not be further from the truth. The approach used by The Ritz-Carlton Hotel Company to control quality is proactive because of their intensive personalized service environment.[5] Systems for collecting and using quality-related measures are widely deployed and used extensively throughout the organization. Each hotel tracks service quality indicators on a daily basis. The Ritz-Carlton recognizes that many customer requirements are sensory, and thus, difficult to measure. However, by selecting, training, and certifying employees in their knowledge of The Ritz-Carlton Gold Standards of service, they are able to assess their work through appropriate sensory measurements—taste, sight, smell, sound, and touch—and take appropriate actions.

The company uses three types of control processes to deliver quality:

1. Self-control of the individual employee based on their spontaneous and learned behavior.
2. Basic control mechanism, which is carried out by every member of the workforce. The first person who detects a problem is empowered to break away from routine duties, investigate and correct the problem immediately, document the incident, and then return to their routine.
3. Critical success factor control for critical processes. Process teams use customer and organizational requirement measurements to determine quality, speed, and cost performance. These measurements are compared against benchmarks and customer satisfaction data to determine corrective action and resource allocation.

In addition, The Ritz-Carlton conducts both self-audits and outside audits. Self-audits are carried out internally at all levels, from one individual or function to an entire hotel. Process walk-throughs occur daily in hotels while senior leaders assess field operations during formal reviews at various intervals. Outside audits are performed by independent travel and hospitality rating organizations. All audits must be documented, and any findings must be submitted to the senior leader of the unit being audited. They are responsible for action and for assessing the implementation and effectiveness of recommended corrective actions.

The most common quality characteristics in services, time (waiting time, service time, delivery time) and number of nonconformances, can be measured rather easily. Insurance companies, for example, measure the time to complete different transactions such as new issues, claim payments, and cash surrenders. Hospitals measure the percentage of infections and the percentage of unplanned re-admissions to the emergency room, intensive care, or operating room within, say, 48 hours. Other quality characteristics are observable. They include the types of errors (wrong kind, wrong quantity, wrong delivery date, etc.) and behavior (courtesy, promptness, competency, and so on). Hospitals might monitor the completeness of medical charts and the quality of radiology readings, measured by a double-reading process.

Simple data collection procedures capture the measurements for service quality control. Time is easily measured by taking two observations: starting time and finishing time. Many observed data assume only "yes" or "no" values. For example, a survey of pharmaceutical operations in a hospital might include the following questions:

- Are drug storage and preparation areas within the pharmacy under the supervision of a pharmacist?
- Are drugs requiring special storage conditions properly stored?
- Are drug emergency boxes inspected on a monthly basis?
- Is the drug emergency box record book filled out completely?

Even though human behavior is easily observable, the task of describing and classifying the observations is far more difficult. The major obstacle is developing operational definitions of behavioral characteristics. For example, how does one define courteous versus discourteous, or understanding versus indifference? Defining such distinctions is best done by comparing behavior against understandable standards. For instance, a standard for "courtesy" might be to address the customer as "Mr." or "Ms." Failure to do so is an instance of an error. "Promptness" might be defined as greeting a customer within five seconds of entering the store, or answering letters within two days of receipt. These behaviors can easily be recorded and counted.

STATISTICAL PROCESS CONTROL

Statistical process control (SPC) is a methodology for monitoring a process to identify special causes of variation and signals the need to take corrective action when it is appropriate. When special causes are present, the process is deemed to be *out of control*. If the variation in the process is due to common causes alone, the process is said to be *in statistical control*. A practical definition of statistical control is that both the process averages and variances are constant over time.[6] Because SPC requires processes to show measurable variation, it is ineffective for quality levels approaching 6-sigma, but is quite useful in early stages of Six Sigma efforts.

SPC Metrics

Measures and indicators used in SPC fall into one of two categories. An **attribute** is a performance characteristic that is either present or absent in the product or service under consideration. For example, a dimension is either within tolerance or out of tolerance, an order is complete or incomplete, or an invoice can have one, two, three, or any number of errors. Thus, attribute data are discrete and tell whether the characteristic conforms to specifications. Attributes can be measured by visual inspection, such as assessing whether the correct ZIP code was used in shipping an order; or by comparing a dimension to specifications, such as whether the diameter of a shaft falls within specification limits of 1.60 ± 0.01 inch. Attribute measurements are typically expressed as proportions or rates, for example, the fraction of nonconformances in a group of items, number of defects per unit, or rate of errors per opportunity.

The second type of performance characteristic is called a **variable**. Variable data are continuous (for example, length or weight). Variable measurements are concerned with the *degree* of conformance to specifications. Thus, rather than

TABLE 7.1 EXAMPLES OF ATTRIBUTES AND VARIABLES MEASUREMENTS

Attributes

Percentage of accurate invoices
Number of lost parcels
Number of complaints
Mistakes per week
Percentage of on-time shipments
Errors per thousand lines of code
Percentage of absenteeism

Variables

Time waiting for service
Hours per week correcting documents
Time to process travel expense accounts
Days from order receipt to shipment
Cost of engineering changes per month
Time between system crashes
Cost of rush shipments

determining whether the diameter of a shaft simply meets a specification of 1.60 ± 0.01 inch, a measure of the actual value of the diameter is recorded. Variable measurements are generally expressed with such statistics as averages and standard deviations. Table 7.1 provides additional examples of both attributes and variables measurements.

Collecting attribute data is usually easier than collecting variable data because the assessment can usually be done more quickly by a simple inspection or count, whereas variable data require the use of some type of measuring instrument. In a statistical sense, attribute inspection is less efficient than variable inspection; that is, it does not provide as much information. This difference means that attribute inspection requires a larger sample than variable inspection to obtain the same amount of statistical information. The difference can become significant when inspection of each item is time-consuming or expensive. Most quality characteristics in services are attributes, which is perhaps one reason why service organizations have been slow to adopt measurement-based quality management approaches.

Run Charts and Control Charts

Control charts provide a visual representation of the state of control of a process over time. Control charts are an extension of simple **run charts**, which are line graphs in which data are plotted over time. The vertical axis represents a measurement; the horizontal axis is the time scale. The daily newspaper usually includes several examples of run charts, such as the Dow Jones Industrial Average. They can be used to track such things as production volume, costs, and customer satisfaction indexes.

The first step in constructing a run chart is to identify the measurement or indicator to be monitored. In some situations, one might measure the quality characteristics for each individual unit of process output. For low-volume processes, such as chemical production or surgeries, this approach would be appropriate. However, for high-volume production processes or services with large numbers of customers or transactions, it would be impractical. Instead, samples taken on a periodic basis provide the data for computing basic statistical measures such as the mean, range or standard deviation, proportion of items that do not conform to specifications, or number of nonconformances per unit.

Constructing the chart consists of the following steps:

Step 1. Collect the data. If samples are chosen, compute the relevant statistic for each sample, such as the average or proportion.

Step 2. Examine the range of the data. Scale the chart so that all data can be plotted on the vertical axis. Provide additional room for new data as they are collected.

Step 3. Plot the points on the chart and connect them. Use graph paper if the chart is constructed by hand; a spreadsheet program is preferable.

Step 4. Compute the average of all plotted points and draw it as a horizontal line through the data. This line denoting the average is called the center line (CL) of the chart.

Run charts can be used as a basic control mechanism. If the plotted points fluctuate in a stable pattern around the center line, with no large spikes, trends, or shifts, they indicate that the process is apparently under control. If unusual patterns exist, then the cause for lack of stability should be investigated and corrective action should be taken. However, run charts lack a statistical basis for drawing such conclusions.

A **control chart** is simply a run chart to which two horizontal lines, called **control limits** are added: the **upper control limit (UCL)** and **lower control limit (LCL)**, as illustrated in Figure 7.1. Walter Shewhart at Bell Laboratories first proposed control charts in the 1920s and Deming strongly advocated them. Control limits are chosen statistically to provide a high probability (generally

FIGURE 7.1 STRUCTURE OF A CONTROL CHART

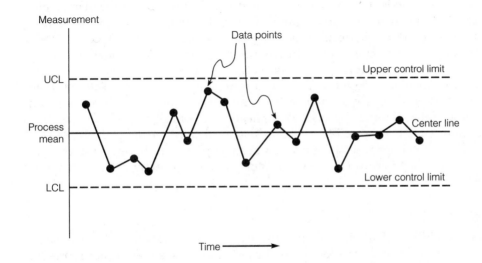

TABLE 7.2   CONTROL CHART APPLICATIONS IN SERVICE ORGANIZATIONS

Organization	Quality Measure
Hospital	Lab test accuracy
	Insurance claim accuracy
	On-time delivery of meals and medication
Bank	Check-processing accuracy
Insurance company	Claims-processing response time
	Billing accuracy
Post Office	Sorting accuracy
	Time of delivery
	Percentage of express mail delivered on time
Ambulance	Response time
Police Department	Incidence of crime in a precinct
	Number of traffic citations
Hotel	Proportion of rooms satisfactorily cleaned
	Checkout time
	Number of complaints received
Transportation	Proportion of freight cars correctly routed
	Dollar amount of damage per claim
Auto service	Percentage of time work completed as promised
	Number of parts out of stock

greater than 0.99) that points will fall between these limits if the process is in control. Control limits make it easier to interpret patterns in a run chart and draw conclusions about the state of control.

If sample values fall outside the control limits or if nonrandom patterns occur in the chart, then special causes may be affecting the process, the process is not stable. The process should be examined and corrective action taken as appropriate. If evaluation and correction are done in real time, then the chance of producing nonconforming product is minimized. Thus, as a control tool, control charts allow process owners to identify problems as they occur. Of course, control charts alone cannot determine the source of the problem. Operators, supervisors, and engineers may have to resort to other problem-solving tools to seek the root cause.

Although control charts were first developed and used in a manufacturing context, they are easily applied to service organizations. Table 7.2 lists just a few of the many potential applications of control charts for services. The key is in defining the appropriate quality measures to monitor. Most service processes can be improved through the appropriate application of control charts.

Control charts can provide a feedback loop in the DMAIC process. After a process has been improved, a control chart can help to identify further opportunities for improving performance and reducing variation, leading to new Six Sigma projects.

Capability and Control

Process capability calculations make little sense if the process is not in statistical control because the data are confounded by special causes that do not represent

TABLE 7.3   THIRTY SAMPLES OF QUALITY MEASUREMENTS

Sample	Observations					Mean
1	0.682	0.689	0.776	0.798	0.714	0.732
2	0.787	0.860	0.601	0.746	0.779	0.755
3	0.780	0.667	0.838	0.785	0.723	0.759
4	0.591	0.727	0.812	0.775	0.730	0.727
5	0.693	0.708	0.790	0.758	0.671	0.724
6	0.749	0.714	0.738	0.719	0.606	0.705
7	0.791	0.713	0.689	0.877	0.603	0.735
8	0.744	0.779	0.660	0.737	0.822	0.748
9	0.769	0.773	0.641	0.644	0.725	0.710
10	0.718	0.671	0.708	0.850	0.712	0.732
11	0.787	0.821	0.764	0.658	0.708	0.748
12	0.622	0.802	0.818	0.872	0.727	0.768
13	0.657	0.822	0.893	0.544	0.750	0.733
14	0.806	0.749	0.859	0.801	0.701	0.783
15	0.660	0.681	0.644	0.747	0.728	0.692
16	0.816	0.817	0.768	0.716	0.649	0.753
17	0.826	0.777	0.721	0.770	0.809	0.781
18	0.828	0.829	0.865	0.778	0.872	0.834
19	0.805	0.719	0.612	0.938	0.807	0.776
20	0.802	0.756	0.786	0.815	0.801	0.792
21	0.876	0.803	0.701	0.789	0.672	0.768
22	0.855	0.783	0.722	0.856	0.751	0.793
23	0.762	0.705	0.804	0.805	0.809	0.777
24	0.703	0.837	0.759	0.975	0.732	0.801
25	0.737	0.723	0.776	0.748	0.732	0.743
26	0.748	0.686	0.856	0.811	0.838	0.788
27	0.826	0.803	0.764	0.823	0.886	0.820
28	0.728	0.721	0.820	0.772	0.639	0.736
29	0.803	0.892	0.740	0.816	0.770	0.804
30	0.774	0.837	0.872	0.849	0.818	0.830

the inherent capability of the process. Consider Table 7.3, which shows 30 samples measurements of a quality characteristic from a manufacturing process with specifications 0.75 ± 0.25. Each row corresponds to a sample size 5 taken every 15 minutes. The mean of each sample is also given in the last column. A frequency distribution and histogram of these data is shown in Figure 7.2. The data form a relatively symmetric distribution with a mean of 0.762 and standard deviation 0.0738. Using these values, we find that $C_{pk} = 1.075$, indicating that the process capability is at least marginally acceptable. Because the data were taken over an extended period of time, we cannot determine whether the process remained stable.

In a histogram, the dimension of time is not considered. Thus, histograms do not allow you to distinguish between common and special causes of variation. It is unclear whether any special causes of variation are influencing the capability index. If we plot the mean of each sample against the time at which the sample was taken (because the time increments between samples are equal, the sample number is an appropriate surrogate for time), we obtain the

FIGURE 7.2 FREQUENCY DISTRIBUTION AND HISTOGRAM

Frequency distribution	
Upper limit	*Frequency*
0.55	1
0.6	1
0.65	10
0.7	14
0.75	40
0.8	31
0.85	37
0.9	14
0.95	1
1	1
More	0
Average	0.762
Std. Dev.	0.0738

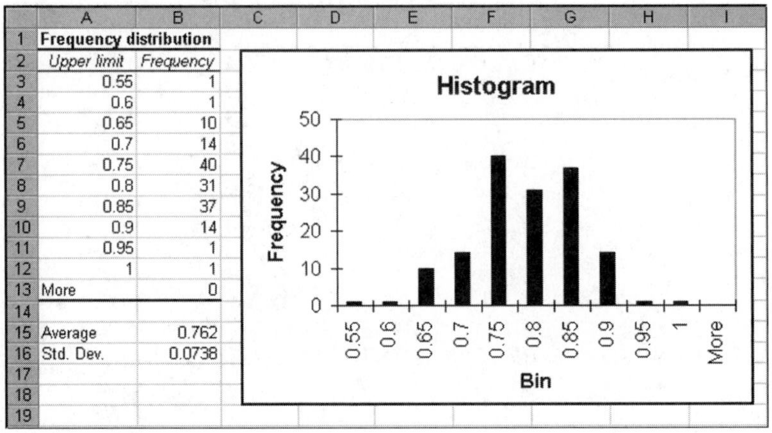

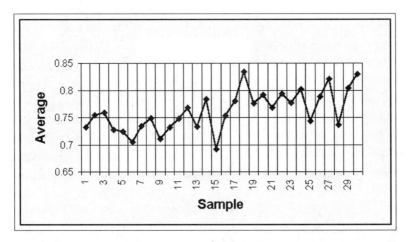

FIGURE 7.3 RUN CHART OF SAMPLE MEANS

run chart shown in Figure 7.3. It indicates that the mean has shifted up at about sample 17. In fact, the process average for the first 16 samples is only 0.738 while the average for the remaining samples is 0.789. Therefore, although the overall average is close to the target specification, at no time was the actual process average centered near the target. We should conclude that this process is not in statistical control, and we should not pay much attention to the process capability calculations.

CONSTRUCTING AND USING CONTROL CHARTS

Control charts can be used for three purposes: (1) to help identify special causes of variation and establish a state of statistical control, (2) to monitor a process and signal when the process goes out of control, and (3) to determine process capability. The following is a summary of the steps required to develop and use control charts. Steps 1 through 4 focus on establishing a state of statistical control; in step 5, the charts are used for ongoing monitoring; and finally, in step 6, the data are used for process capability analysis.

1. Preparation
   a. Choose the variable or attribute to be measured.
   b. Determine the basis, size, and frequency of sampling.
   c. Set up the control chart.
2. Data collection
   a. Record the data.
   b. Calculate relevant statistics: averages, ranges, proportions, and so on.
   c. Plot the statistics on the chart.
3. Determination of trial control limits
   a. Draw the center line (process average) on the chart.
   b. Compute the upper and lower control limits.
4. Analysis and interpretation
   a. Investigate the chart for lack of control.
   b. Eliminate out-of-control points.
   c. Recompute control limits if necessary.
5. Use as a problem-solving tool
   a. Continue data collection and plotting.
   b. Identify out-of-control situations and take corrective action.
6. Determination of process capability using the control chart data

Although many different charts exist, they differ only in the type of measurement for which the chart is used; the methodology previously described applies to each of them. We will illustrate the basic types of control charts used for variable and attribute data, and then briefly describe other types of charts available. A more complete treatment of these charts may be found in more advanced textbooks.

Control Charts for Variable Data

The charts most commonly used for variable data are the $\bar{x}$-chart ("x-bar" chart) and the R-chart (range chart). The $\bar{x}$-chart is used to monitor the centering of the process, and the R-chart is used to monitor the variation in the process. The range is used as a measure of variation simply for convenience, particularly when frontline workers perform control chart calculations by hand. For large samples and when data are analyzed by computer programs, the standard deviation is a better measure of variability.

The first step in developing $\bar{x}$- and R-charts is to gather data. Usually, about 25 to 30 samples are collected. Samples between size 3 and 10 are generally used, with 5 being the most common. The number of samples is indicated by k, and n denotes the sample size. For each sample i, the mean, denoted $(\bar{x}_i)$, and the range (R_i) are computed. These values are then plotted on their respective control charts. Next, the *overall mean* and *average range* calculations are made. These values specify the center lines for the $\bar{x}$- and R-charts, respectively. The overall mean is the average of the sample means $\bar{x}_i$:

$$\bar{\bar{x}} = \frac{\sum_{i=1}^{k} \bar{x}_i}{k}$$

The average range is similarly computed, using the formula:

$$\overline{R} = \frac{\sum\limits_{i=1}^{k} R_i}{k}$$

The average range and average mean are used to compute control limits for the R- and $\overline{x}$-charts. Control limits are easily calculated using the following formulas:

$$\text{UCL}_R = D_4\overline{R} \qquad \text{UCL}_{\overline{x}} = \overline{\overline{x}} + A_2\overline{R}$$

$$\text{LCL}_R = D_3\overline{R} \qquad \text{LCL}_{\overline{x}} = \overline{\overline{x}} - A_2\overline{R}$$

where the constants D_3, D_4, and A_2 depend on the sample size and can be found in Appendix B.

The control limits represent the range between which all points are expected to fall if the process is in statistical control. If any points fall outside the control limits or if any unusual patterns are observed, then some special cause has probably affected the process. The process should be studied to determine the cause. If special causes are present, then they are *not* representative of the true state of statistical control, and the calculations of the center line and control limits will be biased. The corresponding data points should be eliminated, and new values for $\overline{\overline{x}}, \overline{R}$, and the control limits should be computed.

In determining whether a process is in statistical control, the R-chart is always analyzed first. Because the control limits in the $\overline{x}$-chart depend on the average range, special causes in the R-chart may produce unusual patterns in the $\overline{x}$-chart, even when the centering of the process is in control. Once statistical control is established for the R-chart, attention may turn to the $\overline{x}$-chart.

To illustrate these charts, we present an example for the thickness of silicon wafers used in the production of semiconductors. The tolerance of one such product is specified as ±0.0050 inches. In one production facility, three wafers were selected each hour and the thickness measured carefully to within one ten-thousandth of an inch. Figure 7.4 shows the results obtained for 25 samples entered manually on a data sheet (available from the American Society for Quality). For example, the mean of the first sample is $(41 + 70 + 22)/3 = 133$ and the range of sample 1 is $70 - 22 = 48$. (*Note:* Calculations are rounded to the nearest integer for simplicity.)

The average range is the sum of the sample ranges (676) divided by the number of samples (25); the overall mean is the sum of the sample averages (1,221) divided by the number of samples (25). Because the sample size is 3, the factors used in computing the control limits are $A_2 = 1.023$ and $D_4 = 2.574$. (For sample sizes of 6 or less, factor $D_3 = 0$; therefore, the lower control limit on the range chart is 0.) We suggest that you draw the center lines and control limits directly on Figure 7.4.

Examining the range chart first, it appears that the process is in control. All points lie within the control limits and no unusual patterns exist. In the $\overline{x}$-chart, however, sample 17 lies above the upper control limit. On investigation, some defective material had been used. These data should be eliminated from the control chart calculations. You should verify that the new overall mean is 47.0, average range is 27.6, control limits for the $\overline{x}$-chart are UCL = 75.2 and LCL = 18.8, and control

FIGURE 7.4 SILICON WAFER THICKNESS DATA

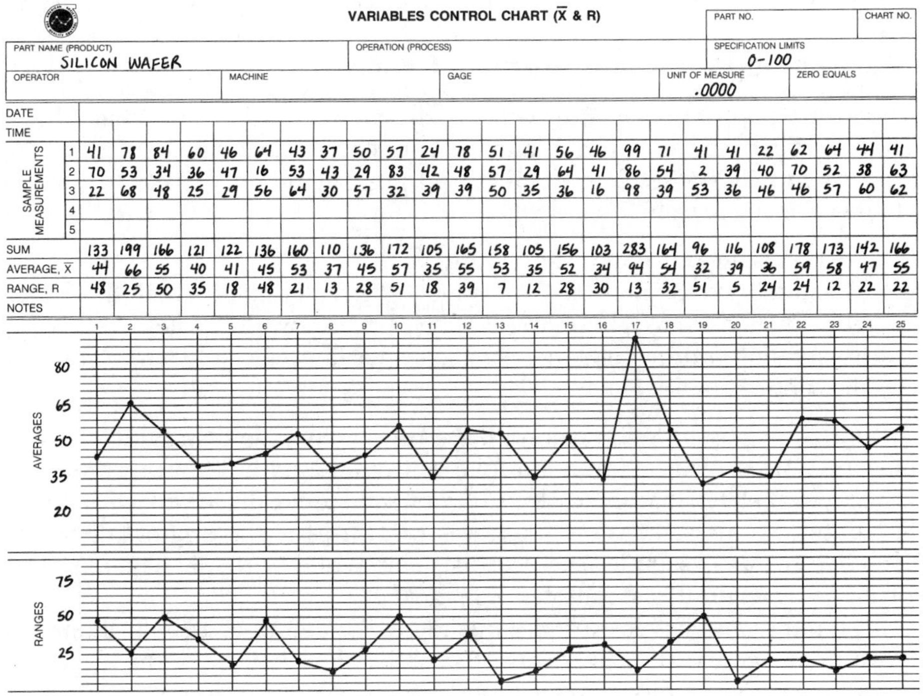

VARIABLES CONTROL CHART ($\bar{X}$ & R)

PART NO. | CHART NO.

PART NAME (PRODUCT): SILICON WAFER | OPERATION (PROCESS) | SPECIFICATION LIMITS: 0-100

OPERATOR | MACHINE | GAGE | UNIT OF MEASURE: .0000 | ZERO EQUALS

	1	2	3	4	5	6	7	8	9	10	11	12	13	14	15	16	17	18	19	20	21	22	23	24	25
DATE																									
TIME																									
SAMPLE MEASUREMENTS 1	41	78	84	60	46	64	43	37	50	57	24	78	51	41	56	46	99	71	41	41	22	62	64	44	41
2	70	53	34	36	47	16	53	43	29	83	42	48	57	29	64	41	86	54	2	39	40	70	52	38	63
3	22	68	48	25	29	56	64	30	57	32	39	39	50	35	36	16	98	39	53	36	46	46	57	60	62
4																									
5																									
SUM	133	199	166	121	122	136	160	110	136	172	105	165	158	105	156	103	283	164	96	116	108	178	173	142	166
AVERAGE, $\bar{X}$	44	66	55	40	41	45	53	37	45	57	35	55	53	35	52	34	94	54	32	39	36	59	58	47	55
RANGE, R	48	25	50	35	18	48	21	13	28	51	18	39	7	12	28	30	13	32	51	5	24	24	12	22	22
NOTES																									

Source: Adapted from ASQ's Control chart form. ©American Society for Quality. Used with permission.

limits for the R-chart are UCL = 71.0 and LCL = 0. Using these values and eliminating sample 17, you should verify that the resulting charts appear to be in control.

Microsoft Excel Templates

Microsoft Excel templates for many common types of control charts are available on the CD-ROM accompanying this book. The template includes an automatic plot of the $\bar{x}$- and R-charts and calculation of process capability indexes. Some scaling of the chart display ranges may be necessary for certain problems. Please note the following:

- The recalculation option for the spreadsheets is set to manual. Therefore, to recalculate any spreadsheet after making changes, press the F9 key or set the recalculation option to automatic in the Calculation tab from the Tools/Options menu.
- To rescale the vertical axis in a chart, to widen the range of the plotted data for instance, double-click on the y-axis, and select the Scale tab in the dialog box that appears. Change the "min" and "max" parameters as appropriate.
- When deleting special cause data and re-computing control limits, be sure to update the number of samples used in the calculations to compute the statistics.

- When a sample is deleted from a data set in the templates, do not enter zero for the data; instead, leave the cells blank. The charts are set up to interpolate between non-missing data points in the Tools/Options/Chart tab.

Interpreting Patterns in Control Charts

When a process is in statistical control, the points on a control chart fluctuate randomly between the control limits with no recognizable pattern. The following checklist provides a set of general rules for examining a process to determine whether it is in control:

1. No points are outside control limits.
2. The number of points above and below the center line is about the same.
3. The points seem to fall randomly above and below the center line.
4. Most points, but not all, are near the center line, and only a few are close to the control limits.

The underlying assumption behind these rules is that the distribution of sample means is normal. This assumption follows from the central limit theorem of statistics, which states that the distribution of sample means approaches a normal distribution as the sample size increases regardless of the original distribution. Of course, for small sample sizes, the distribution of the original data must be reasonably normal for this assumption to hold.

The upper and lower control limits are computed to be three standard deviations from the overall mean. Thus, the probability that any sample mean falls outside the control limits is small. This probability is the origin of rule 1. Because the normal distribution is symmetric, about the same number of points fall above as below the center line. Also, because the mean of the normal distribution is the median, about half the points fall on either side of the center line. Finally, about 68 percent of a normal distribution falls within one standard deviation of the mean; thus, most—but not all—points should be close to the center line. These characteristics will hold provided that the mean and variance of the original data have not changed during the time the data were collected; that is, the process is stable. The most common indicators of an out-of-control condition are summarized below.

One Point Outside Control Limits
A single point outside the control limits is usually produced by a special cause. Often, the R-chart provides a similar indication. Once in a while, however, such points are a normal part of the process and occur simply by chance. A common reason for a point falling outside a control limit is an error in the calculation of $\bar{x}$ or R for the sample. You should always check your calculations whenever this occurs. Other possible causes are a sudden power surge, a broken tool, measurement error, or an incomplete or omitted operation in the process.

Sudden Shift in the Process Average
An unusual number of consecutive points falling on one side of the center line is usually an indication that the process average has suddenly shifted. Typically, this occurrence is the result of an external influence that has affected the process, which would be considered a special cause. In both the $\bar{x}$- and R-charts, possible

causes might be a new operator, a new inspector, a new machine setting, or a change in the setup or method.

If the shift is up in the R-chart, the process has become less uniform. Typical causes are carelessness of operators, poor or inadequate maintenance, or possibly a fixture in need of repair. If the shift is down in the R-chart, the uniformity of the process has improved. This shift might be the result of improved workmanship or better machines or materials. As mentioned, every effort should be made to determine the reason for the improvement and to maintain it.

Three rules of thumb are used for early detection of process shifts. A simple rule is that if eight consecutive points fall on one side of the center line, one could conclude that the mean has shifted. Second, divide the region between the center line and each control limit into three equal parts. Then if (1) two of three consecutive points fall in the outer one-third region between the center line and one of the control limits or (2) four of five consecutive points fall within the outer two-thirds region, one would also conclude that the process has gone out of control.

Cycles

Cycles are short, repeated patterns in the chart, alternating high peaks and low valleys. These patterns are the result of causes that come and go on a regular basis. In the $\bar{x}$-chart, cycles may be the result of operator rotation or fatigue at the end of a shift, different gauges used by different inspectors, seasonal effects such as temperature or humidity, or differences between day and night shifts. In the R-chart, cycles can occur from maintenance schedules, rotation of fixtures or gauges, differences between shifts, or operator fatigue.

Trends

A trend is the result of some cause that gradually affects the quality characteristics of the product and causes the points on a control chart to gradually move up or down from the center line. As a new group of operators gains experience on the job, for example, or as maintenance of equipment improves over time, a trend may occur. In the $\bar{x}$-chart, trends may be the result of improving operator skills, dirt or chip buildup in fixtures, tool wear, changes in temperature or humidity, or aging of equipment. In the R-chart, an increasing trend may be due to a gradual decline in material quality, operator fatigue, gradual loosening of a fixture or a tool, or dulling of a tool. A decreasing trend often is the result of improved operator skill or work methods, better materials, or improved or more frequent maintenance.

After a process is determined to be in control, the charts should be used on a routine basis to monitor performance, identify any special causes that might arise, and make corrections only as necessary. Control charts indicate when to take action, and more importantly, when to leave a process alone. Unnecessary adjustments to a process result in nonproductive labor, reduced production, and increased variability of output.

The data in a control chart may also be used to estimate short-term process capability. This approach is not as accurate as that described in Chapter 4 because it uses the average range rather than the estimated standard deviation of the original data. Nevertheless, it is a quick and useful method, provided that the distribution of the original data is reasonably normal. Under the normality assumption, the standard deviation of the original data can be estimated as follows:

$$\hat{\sigma} = \overline{R}/d_2$$

where d_2 is a constant that depends on the sample size and is also given in Appendix B. Process capability is therefore given by $6\hat{\sigma}$. The natural variation of individual measurements is given by $\overline{\overline{x}} \pm 3\hat{\sigma}$.

Control Charts for Attributes

Attribute data assume only two values—good or bad, pass or fail, and so on. Attributes usually cannot be measured, but they can be observed and counted and are useful in many practical situations. For instance, in printing packages for consumer products, color quality can be rated as acceptable or not acceptable, or a sheet of cardboard either is damaged or is not. Usually, attribute data are easy to collect, often by visual inspection. Many accounting records, such as percent scrapped, are readily available. However, one drawback in using attribute data is that large samples are necessary to obtain valid statistical results.

Several different types of control charts are used for attribute data. One of the most common is the p-chart. Other types of attribute charts are also used. One distinction that we must make is between the terms *defects* and *defectives*. A **defect** is a single nonconforming quality characteristic of an item. An item may have several defects. The term **defective** refers to items having one or more defects. Because certain attribute charts are used for defectives while others are used for defects, one must understand the difference. The term *nonconforming* is often used instead of *defective*.

A **p-chart** monitors the proportion of nonconforming items produced in a lot. Often it is also called a **fraction nonconforming** or **fraction defective chart**. As with variable data, a p-chart is constructed by first gathering 25 to 30 samples of the attribute being measured. The size of each sample should be large enough to have several nonconforming items. If the probability of finding a nonconforming item is small, a large sample size is usually necessary. Samples are chosen over time periods so that any special causes that are identified can be investigated.

Suppose that k samples, each of size n, are selected. If y represents the number nonconforming in a particular sample, the proportion nonconforming is y/n. Let p_i be the fraction nonconforming in the ith sample; the average fraction nonconforming for the group of k samples then is

$$\overline{p} = \frac{p_1 + p_2 + \ldots + p_k}{k}$$

This statistic reflects the average performance of the process. One would expect a high percentage of samples to have a fraction nonconforming within three standard deviations of $\overline{p}$. An estimate of the standard deviation is given by

$$s_{\overline{p}} = \sqrt{\frac{\overline{p}(1 - \overline{p})}{n}}$$

Therefore, upper and lower control limits are given by

$$UCL_p = \bar{p} + 3s_{\bar{p}}$$

$$LCL_p = \bar{p} - 3s_{\bar{p}}$$

If LCL_p is less than zero, a value of zero is used.

Analysis of a p-chart is similar to that of an $\bar{x}$- or R-chart. Points outside the control limits signify an out-of-control situation. Patterns and trends should also be sought to identify special causes. However, a point on a p-chart below the lower control limit or the development of a trend below the center line indicates that the process might have improved, based on an ideal of zero defectives. Caution is advised before such conclusions are drawn, because errors may have been made in computation.

To illustrate the construction of a p-chart, suppose that the operators of automated sorting machines in a post office must read the ZIP code on a letter and divert the letter to the proper carrier route. Over one month's time, 25 samples of 100 letters were chosen, and the number of errors was recorded. This information is shown in the Excel template in Figure 7.5. The fraction nonconforming is found by dividing the number of errors by 100. The average fraction nonconforming, $\bar{p}$, is determined to be

$$\bar{p} = \frac{0.03 + 0.01 + \ldots + 0.01}{25} = 0.022$$

FIGURE 7.5 DATA AND CALCULATIONS FOR THE ZIP CODE READER EXAMPLE

	A	B	C	D	E	F	G	H	I	J	K	L	M
1	Fraction Nonconforming (p) Chart												
2	This spreadsheet is designed for up to 50 samples. Enter data ONLY in yellow-shaded cells.												
3	Click on the sheet tab to display the control chart (some rescaling may be needed).												
4													
5	Average (p-bar)			0.022									
6	Avg. sample size			100									
7										Approximate Control Limits Using			
8			Sample	Fraction		Standard				Average Sample Size Calculations			
9	Sample	Value	Size	Nonconforming	Deviation	LCLp	CL	UCLp		LCLp	CL	UCLp	
10	1	3	100	0.0300	0.01467	0	0.022	0.066		0	0.022	0.066	
11	2	1	100	0.0100	0.01467	0	0.022	0.066		0	0.022	0.066	
12	3	0	100	0.0000	0.01467	0	0.022	0.066		0	0.022	0.066	
13	4	0	100	0.0000	0.01467	0	0.022	0.066		0	0.022	0.066	
14	5	2	100	0.0200	0.01467	0	0.022	0.066		0	0.022	0.066	
15	6	5	100	0.0500	0.01467	0	0.022	0.066		0	0.022	0.066	
16	7	3	100	0.0300	0.01467	0	0.022	0.066		0	0.022	0.066	
17	8	6	100	0.0600	0.01467	0	0.022	0.066		0	0.022	0.066	
18	9	1	100	0.0100	0.01467	0	0.022	0.066		0	0.022	0.066	
19	10	4	100	0.0400	0.01467	0	0.022	0.066		0	0.022	0.066	
20	11	0	100	0.0000	0.01467	0	0.022	0.066		0	0.022	0.066	
21	12	2	100	0.0200	0.01467	0	0.022	0.066		0	0.022	0.066	
22	13	1	100	0.0100	0.01467	0	0.022	0.066		0	0.022	0.066	
23	14	3	100	0.0300	0.01467	0	0.022	0.066		0	0.022	0.066	
24	15	4	100	0.0400	0.01467	0	0.022	0.066		0	0.022	0.066	
25	16	1	100	0.0100	0.01467	0	0.022	0.066		0	0.022	0.066	
26	17	1	100	0.0100	0.01467	0	0.022	0.066		0	0.022	0.066	
27	18	2	100	0.0200	0.01467	0	0.022	0.066		0	0.022	0.066	
28	19	5	100	0.0500	0.01467	0	0.022	0.066		0	0.022	0.066	
29	20	2	100	0.0200	0.01467	0	0.022	0.066		0	0.022	0.066	
30	21	3	100	0.0300	0.01467	0	0.022	0.066		0	0.022	0.066	
31	22	4	100	0.0400	0.01467	0	0.022	0.066		0	0.022	0.066	
32	23	1	100	0.0100	0.01467	0	0.022	0.066		0	0.022	0.066	
33	24	0	100	0.0000	0.01467	0	0.022	0.066		0	0.022	0.066	
34	25	1	100	0.0100	0.01467	0	0.022	0.066		0	0.022	0.066	

The standard deviation is computed as

$$s_{\bar{p}} = \sqrt{\frac{0.022(1 - 0.022)}{100}} = 0.01467$$

Thus, the upper control limit, UCLp, is $0.022 + 3(0.01467) = 0.066$, and the lower control limit, LCL$_p$, is $0.022 - 3(0.01467) = -0.022$. Because this latter figure is negative, 0 is used. The control chart for this example is shown in Figure 7.6. The sorting process appears to be in control. Any values found above the upper control limit or evidence of an upward trend might indicate the need for more experience or training of the operators.

Attributes Charts with Variable Sample Size

Often 100 percent inspection is performed on process output during fixed sampling periods; however, the number of units produced in each sampling period may vary. In this case, the p-chart would have a variable sample size. One way of handling this variation is to compute a standard deviation for each individual sample. Thus, if the number of observations in the ith sample is n_i, control limits are given by

$$\bar{p} \pm 3\sqrt{\frac{\bar{p}(1 - \bar{p})}{n_i}}$$

where $\bar{p} = \dfrac{\Sigma \text{number nonconforming}}{\Sigma n_i}$

The data given in Figure 7.7 represent 20 samples with varying sample sizes. The value of $\bar{p}$ is computed as

$$\bar{p} = \frac{18 + 20 + 14 + \ldots + 18}{137 + 158 + 92 + \ldots + 160} = \frac{271}{2,980} = 0.0909$$

FIGURE 7.6   P-CHART FOR THE ZIP CODE READER EXAMPLE

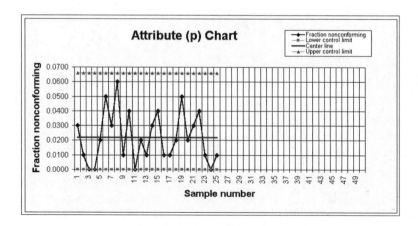

FIGURE 7.7   DATA AND CALCULATIONS FOR VARIABLE SAMPLE SIZE EXAMPLE

Sample	Value	Sample Size	Fraction Nonconforming	Standard Deviation	LCLp	CL	UCLp		LCLp	CL	UCLp
1	18	137	0.1314	0.02456	0.017	0.091	0.165		0.02028	0.09094	0.1616
2	20	158	0.1266	0.02287	0.022	0.091	0.160		0.02028	0.09094	0.1616
3	14	92	0.1522	0.02998	0.001	0.091	0.181		0.02028	0.09094	0.1616
4	6	122	0.0492	0.02603	0.013	0.091	0.169		0.02028	0.09094	0.1616
5	11	86	0.1279	0.03100	0.000	0.091	0.184		0.02028	0.09094	0.1616
6	22	187	0.1176	0.02103	0.028	0.091	0.154		0.02028	0.09094	0.1616
7	6	156	0.0385	0.02302	0.022	0.091	0.160		0.02028	0.09094	0.1616
8	9	117	0.0769	0.02658	0.011	0.091	0.171		0.02028	0.09094	0.1616
9	14	110	0.1273	0.02741	0.009	0.091	0.173		0.02028	0.09094	0.1616
10	12	142	0.0845	0.02413	0.019	0.091	0.163		0.02028	0.09094	0.1616
11	8	140	0.0571	0.02430	0.018	0.091	0.164		0.02028	0.09094	0.1616
12	13	179	0.0726	0.02149	0.026	0.091	0.155		0.02028	0.09094	0.1616
13	5	196	0.0255	0.02054	0.029	0.091	0.153		0.02028	0.09094	0.1616
14	15	163	0.0920	0.02252	0.023	0.091	0.159		0.02028	0.09094	0.1616
15	25	140	0.1786	0.02430	0.018	0.091	0.164		0.02028	0.09094	0.1616
16	12	135	0.0889	0.02475	0.017	0.091	0.165		0.02028	0.09094	0.1616
17	16	186	0.0860	0.02108	0.028	0.091	0.154		0.02028	0.09094	0.1616
18	12	193	0.0622	0.02070	0.029	0.091	0.153		0.02028	0.09094	0.1616
19	15	181	0.0829	0.02137	0.027	0.091	0.155		0.02028	0.09094	0.1616
20	18	160	0.1125	0.02273	0.023	0.091	0.159		0.02028	0.09094	0.1616

Fraction Nonconforming (p) Chart. This spreadsheet is designed for up to 50 samples. Enter data ONLY in yellow-shaded cells. Click on the sheet tab to display the control chart (some rescaling may be needed). Average (p-bar) 0.090939597. Avg. sample size 149. Approximate Control Limits Using Average Sample Size Calculations.

The control limits for sample 1 are

$$LCL_p = 0.0909 - 3\sqrt{\frac{0.0909(1 - 0.0909)}{137}} = 0.017$$

$$UCL_p = 0.0909 + 3\sqrt{\frac{0.0909(1 - 0.0909)}{137}} = 0.165$$

Because the sample sizes vary, the control limits are different for each sample. The p-chart is shown in Figure 7.8(a). Note that points 13 and 15 are outside the control limits.

An alternative approach is to use the average sample size, $\bar{n}$, to compute approximate control limits. Using the average sample size, the control limits are computed as

$$UCL_p = \bar{p} + 3\sqrt{\frac{\bar{p}(1 - \bar{p})}{\bar{n}}}$$

and

$$LCL_p = \bar{p} - 3\sqrt{\frac{\bar{p}(1 - \bar{p})}{\bar{n}}}$$

These result in an approximation to the true control limits. For the data in Figure 7.7, the average sample size is $\bar{n} = 2{,}980/20 = 149$. Using this value, the upper control limit is calculated to be 0.1616, and the lower control limit is 0.0202. However, this approach has several disadvantages. Because the control limits are

FIGURE 7.8(A)   P-CHART FOR VARIABLE SAMPLE SIZE EXAMPLE (TRUE QUALITY LIMITS)

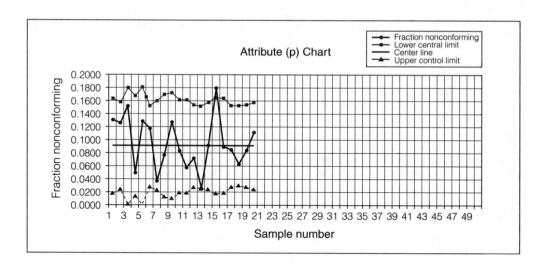

only approximate, points that are actually out of control may not appear to be so on this chart. Second, runs or nonrandom patterns are difficult to interpret because the standard deviation differs between samples as a result of the variable sample sizes. Hence, this approach should be used with caution. Figure 7.8(b) shows the control chart for this example with approximate control limits using the average sample size. Note the difference in sample 13; this chart shows that it is in control, whereas the true control limits show that this point is out of control.

As a general guideline, use the average sample size method when the sample sizes fall within 25 percent of the average. For this example, 25 percent of 149 is 37.25. Thus, the average could be used for sample sizes between 112 and 186. This guideline would exclude samples 3, 6, 9, 11, 13, and 18, whose control limits should be computed exactly. If the calculations are performed on a computer, sample size is not an issue.

Other Types of Control Charts

Several alternatives to the popular $\bar{x}$-, R-, and p-charts are available and others are used for different types of data. We briefly review some of these; more complete discussions may be found in the references in the bibliography.

s-Charts

An alternative to using the R-chart along with the $\bar{x}$-chart is to compute and plot the standard deviation s of each sample. The range involves less computational effort and is easier for shop-floor personnel to understand, making it advantageous. However, the sample standard deviation is a more sensitive and better indicator of process variability than the range, especially for larger sample sizes. Thus, when tight control of variability is required, s-charts should be used. With

FIGURE 7.8(B)   P-CHART FOR VARIABLE SAMPLE SIZE EXAMPLE (APPROXIMATE CONTROL LIMITS)

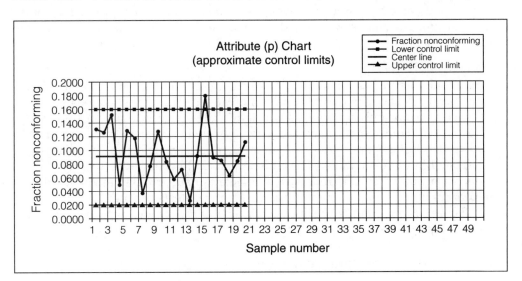

the availability of modern calculators and personal computers, the computational burden of computing s is reduced or eliminated, and s has thus become a viable alternative to R-charts.

Individual (x) Charts

With the development of automated inspection for many processes, manufacturers can now easily inspect and measure quality characteristics on every item produced. Hence, the sample size for process control is $n = 1$, and a control chart for *individual measurements*—also called an *x-chart*—can be used. Other examples in which x-charts are useful include accounting data such as shipments, orders, absences, and accidents; production records of temperature, humidity, voltage, or pressure; and the results of physical or chemical analyses. Samples of size 1, however, do not furnish enough information for process variability measurement. Process variability can be determined by using a moving average of ranges, or a *moving range*, of n successive observations.

np-Charts

Instead of using a chart for the fraction nonconforming (p-chart), an equivalent alternative—a chart for the *number* of nonconforming items—is useful. Such a control chart is called an **np-chart**. The np-chart is a control chart for the number of nonconforming items in a sample. To use the np-chart, the size of each sample *must be constant*. Suppose that two samples of sizes 10 and 15 each have four nonconforming items. Clearly, the fraction nonconforming in each sample is different, which would be reflected in a p-chart. An np-chart, however, would indicate no difference between samples. Thus, equal sample sizes are necessary to have a common base for measurement. Equal sample sizes are not required for p-charts, because the fraction nonconforming is invariant to the sample size.

The np-chart is a useful alternative to the p-chart because it is often easier to understand for production personnel—the *number* of nonconforming items is more meaningful than a fraction. Also, it requires only a count, making the computations simpler.

Charts for Defects

Recall that a *defect* is a single nonconforming characteristic of an item, while a *defective* refers to an item that has one or more defects. In some situations, one may be interested not only in whether an item is defective but also in how many defects it has. For example, in complex assemblies such as electronics, the number of defects is just as important as whether the product is defective. Two charts can be applied in such situations. The **c-chart** is used to control the total number of defects per unit when subgroup size is constant. If subgroup sizes are variable, a **u-chart** is used to control the average number of defects per unit.

Figure 7.9 provides guidelines for selecting the proper type of chart in a control application.

Controlling Six Sigma Processes[7]

SPC is a useful methodology for processes that operate at a low sigma level, for example 3-sigma or less. However, when the rate of defects is extremely low, standard control charts are not effective. For example, in using a p-chart for a process with a high sigma level, few defectives will be discovered even with large sample sizes. For instance, if $p = 0.001$, a sample size of 500 will only have an expected number of $500(0.001) = 0.5$ defects. Hence, most samples will have only zero or one defect, and the chart will provide little useful information for control.

FIGURE 7.9 GUIDELINES FOR CONTROL CHART SELECTION

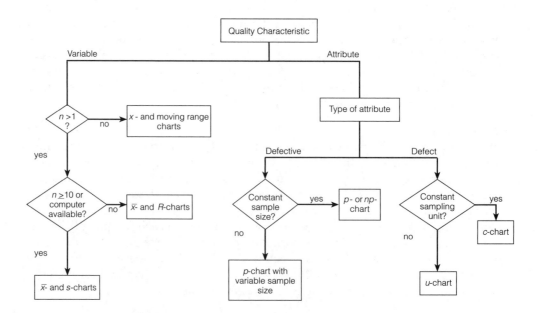

Using much larger sample sizes would only delay the timeliness of information and increase the chances that the process may have changed during the sampling interval. Small sample sizes will typically result in a conclusion that any observed defect indicates an out-of-control condition, thus, implying that a controlled process will have zero defects, which may be impractical. In addition, conventional SPC charts will have higher frequencies of false alarms and make it difficult to evaluate process improvements. These issues are important for Six Sigma green belts and black belts to understand.

One way of handling this situation is to use variable data rather than attribute data; however, this approach may be prohibitive from a cost or physical standpoint. An alternative for attribute data is to construct a **cumulative count of conforming (CCC) chart** to monitor the total number of conforming items until a defective item is found. The control limits for this type of chart are

$$LCL = \ln(1 - \alpha/2)/\ln(1 - p)$$
$$CL = \ln(0.5)/\ln(1 - p)$$
$$UCL = \ln(\alpha/2)/\ln(1 - p)$$

where α is the risk of a false alarm, for example, 0.0027, the value traditionally used for standard control charts. This level can be adjusted for different processes, depending on their criticality and costs of adjustment. A value that exceeds UCL indicates the process has likely improved; a value lower than LCL indicates deterioration of the process. Other advanced techniques are also available.

PROJECT REVIEW—CONTROL PHASE

A project review of the Control phase should ensure that

- Process changes have been adequately documented
- Documentation for new process has been completed
- Process owners have been assigned responsibility for ongoing control
- Process capability for new process has been determined
- Systems, such as statistical process control, have been developed to identify out-of-control performance
- Responsibility for control and adjustment has been given to appropriate process owners
- Senior management has been informed of the project results
- Team members have been thanked, rewarded, and given appropriate new assignments

CASE STUDY

Using a Control Chart in a Receiving Process[8]

CBT, Company is a distributor of electrical automation and power transmission products. One manager was eager to study the organization's receiving process because of a decrease in on-time deliveries. The manager suspected that the data entry person in the purchasing department was not entering data in the computer in a timely fashion; consequently, packages could not be properly processed for subsequent shipping to the customer. A preliminary analysis indicated that the manager's notion was inaccurate. In fact, the manager was able to see that the data entry person was doing an excellent job. The analysis showed that handling packages that were destined for a branch operation in the same fashion as other packages created significant delays. A simple process change of placing a branch designation letter in front of the purchase order number told the receiving clerk to place those packages on a separate skid for delivery to the branch.

However, this analysis revealed a variety of other problems. Generally, anywhere from 65 to 110 packing slips were processed each day. These slips were found to contain many errors in addition to the wrong destination designation that contributed to the delays. Errors included

- Wrong purchase order
- Wrong quantity
- Purchase order not on the system
- Original order not on the system
- Parts do not match
- Purchase order was entered incorrectly
- Double shipment
- Wrong parts
- No purchase order

Many packing slips contained multiple errors. Table 7.4 shows the number of packing slips and total errors during one period of time. Because the number of opportunities for errors (that is, number of packing slips) varied each day, a u-chart was constructed for each day to track the number of packing slip errors—defects—found. Thus, the statistic monitored was the number of errors per packing slip per day.

To construct the u-chart, we compute and plot $u_i = c_i/n_i$ for each day, where c_i = number of errors for day i and n_i = number of packing slips for day i. Then, compute the average number of errors per packing slip per day, called $\bar{u}$:

$$\bar{u} = \frac{c_1 + c_2 + \ldots + c_k}{n_1 + n_2 + \ldots + n_k}$$

The control limits for the u-chart are:

$$\text{UCL}_u = \bar{u} + 3\sqrt{\bar{u}/n_i}$$
$$\text{LCL}_u = \bar{u} - 3\sqrt{\bar{u}/n_i}$$

Figure 7.10 shows the u-chart that was constructed for this period. (This change in the branch designation took place on January 24, resulting in significant improvement, as shown on the chart.) Note that the control limits vary with the sample size as does a p-chart with variable sample size.

TABLE 7.4   CBT, Co. PACKING SLIP ERROR COUNTS

Date	Packing Slips	Errors	Date	Packing Slips	Errors
21 Jan	87	15	4 Mar	92	8
22 Jan	79	13	5 Mar	69	13
23 Jan	92	23	6 Mar	86	6
24 Jan	84	3	9 Mar	85	13
27 Jan	73	7	10 Mar	101	5
28 Jan	67	11	11 Mar	87	5
29 Jan	73	8	12 Mar	71	3
30 Jan	91	8	13 Mar	83	8
31 Jan	94	11	16 Mar	103	4
3 Feb	83	12	17 Mar	82	6
4 Feb	89	12	18 Mar	90	7
5 Feb	88	6	19 Mar	80	4
6 Feb	69	11	20 Mar	70	4
7 Feb	74	8	23 Mar	73	11
10 Feb	67	4	24 Mar	89	13
11 Feb	83	10	25 Mar	91	6
12 Feb	79	8	26 Mar	78	6
13 Feb	75	8	27 Mar	88	6
14 Feb	69	3	30 Mar	76	8
17 Feb	87	8	31 Mar	101	9
18 Feb	99	13	1 Apr	92	8
19 Feb	101	13	2 Apr	70	2
20 Feb	76	7	3 Apr	72	11
21 Feb	90	4	6 Apr	83	5
24 Feb	92	7	7 Apr	69	6
25 Feb	80	4	8 Apr	79	3
26 Feb	81	5	9 Apr	79	8
27 Feb	105	8	10 Apr	76	6
28 Feb	80	8	13 Apr	92	7
2 Mar	82	5	14 Apr	80	4
3 Mar	75	3	15 Apr	78	8

Although the chart shows that the process is in control (since the branch designation change), the average error rate of more than 9 percent still was not considered acceptable. After consolidating the types of errors into five categories, a Pareto analysis was performed. This analysis showed the following:

Category	Percentage
Purchase order error	35
Quantity error	22
No purchase order on system	17
Original order not on system	16
Parts error	10

The analysis is illustrated in Figure 7.11.

The first two categories accounted for more than half of the errors. The remedy for these problems was to develop a training module on proper purchasing methods to ensure that vendors knew the correct information needed on the

FIGURE 7.10 U-CHART FOR CBT, CO. PACKING SLIP ERRORS

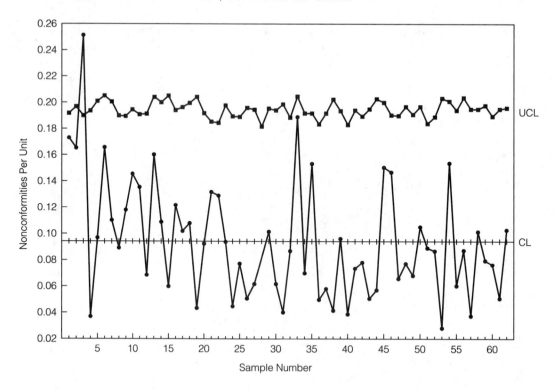

FIGURE 7.11 PARETO ANALYSIS OF PACKING SLIP ERRORS

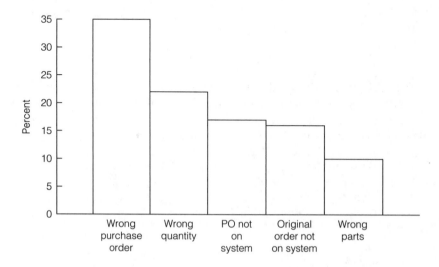

purchase orders. The third category—no purchase order on the computer system—caused receiving personnel to stage the orders until an investigation could find the necessary information. Because of this problem the company realized it needed to revamp the original order-writing process. Specifically, both the order-writing and purchase order activities needed to be improved.

An analysis of the control chart in Figure 7.10 shows that the average error rate has gradually improved. To a large extent, this improvement was due to the recognition of the problems and enhanced communication among the constituents. While the full training program had not been implemented at the time this case was written, the company believed that a significant reduction in the error rate would result once the training was completed.

REVIEW QUESTIONS

1. Describe the three components of any control system.
2. How can one check whether process owners have true responsibility for controlling a process?
3. Define *statistical process control* and discuss its advantages.
4. What does the term *in statistical control* mean? Explain the difference between capability and control.
5. Describe the difference between variable and attribute data. What types of control charts are used for each?
6. Discuss the three primary applications of control charts.
7. What are the disadvantages of simply using histograms to study process capability?
8. What does one look for in interpreting control charts? Explain the possible causes of different out-of-control indicators.
9. Explain the difference between *defects* and *defectives*.
10. Briefly describe the process of constructing a p-chart. What are the key differences in construction when compared with an $\bar{x}$-chart?
11. Why is the s-chart sometimes used in place of the R-chart?
12. Describe some situations in which a chart for individual measurements would be used.
13. Does an np-chart provide any different information than a p-chart? Why would an np-chart be used?
14. Explain the difference between a c-chart and a u-chart.
15. Explain briefly how a cumulative count of conforming (CCC) chart helps overcome some of the problems of conventional SPC charts when processes approach the 6-sigma performance level.

DISCUSSION QUESTIONS

1. In the case study, verify the computation of the center line and control limits in Figure 7.10.
2. In the case study, what information might a separate chart for each error category provide? Would you recommend spending the time and effort to make these additional computations?

THINGS TO DO

1. Visit a local production plant, a bank, or a mail processing facility (preferably one that is known to have a total quality or Six Sigma process) and determine whether they track processing information on any type of chart. Is it a standard control chart, or one that they have tailored to their plant or company? What do they do with the results? Do they use them for improvement, or just for information? Write a report of your findings.
2. Identify some of the processes a student encounters in a college or university. How might those processes be charted on a control chart and improved?
3. Investigate how political polls are conducted and tracked during a state or national campaign. Contact your congressman's (or congresswoman's) office to find leads on how to gather data for this project. Are control charts typically used? Why or why not? Write a report on your findings.
4. How might you design an automated system to "analyze" a control chart and provide conclusions about the state of control without human intervention? If you can program in a high-level computer language, develop a prototype.

 PROBLEMS

Note: Data sets for many problems in this chapter are available in the Excel workbook *Ch7Dataset.xls* on the CD-ROM that accompanies this textbook. Click on the appropriate worksheet tab as noted in the problem (for example, *Prob. 7-1*) to access the data. The Excel templates for control charts used in this chapter are also available in a separate folder on the CD-ROM.

1. Thirty samples of size 3 were taken from a Wilmer Machine Shop machining process over a 15-hour period. These data can be found in the worksheet *Prob. 7-1*.
   a. Compute the mean and standard deviation of the data.
   b. Compute the mean and range of each sample and plot them on control charts. Does the process appear to be in statistical control? Why or why not?
2. The data in worksheet *Prob. 7-2* list electrical resistance measure values for 50 samples of size 5 that were taken from Babbage Chips, Inc.'s computer chip-making process over a 25-hour period.
   a. Compute the mean and standard deviation of the data.
   b. Calculate the control limits and construct the $\bar{x}$- and R-charts, using the first 30 samples. Is the process under control at that point?
   c. After calculating the control limits, the last 20 samples were collected. When plotted using the control limits calculated earlier, does the process appear to be in statistical control? Why or why not? What should be done if it is not under control?
3. Fujiyama Electronics, Inc. has been having difficulties with circuit boards purchased from an outside supplier. Unacceptable variability occurs between two drilled holes that are supposed to be 5 cm apart on the circuit boards.

Thirty samples of four boards each were taken from shipments sent by the supplier as shown in the data listed in the worksheet *Prob. 7-3*.

a. Construct $\bar{x}$- and R-charts for these data.

b. If the supplier's plant quality manager admitted that they were experiencing quality problems for shipments 18, 19, and 21, how would that affect your control chart? Show this adjustment on revised $\bar{x}$- and R-charts for these data.

c. Ten more observations were taken, as shown in the second table in the worksheet. Using the revised $\bar{x}$- and R-charts from part (b), comment on what the chart shows after extending it with the new data.

4. Discuss the interpretation of each of the following control charts:

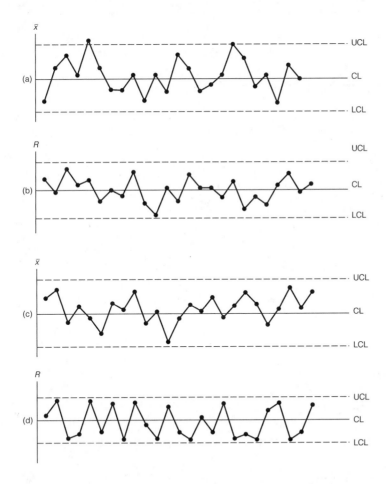

5. For each of the following control charts, assume that the process has been operating in statistical control for some time. What conclusions should the operators reach at this point?

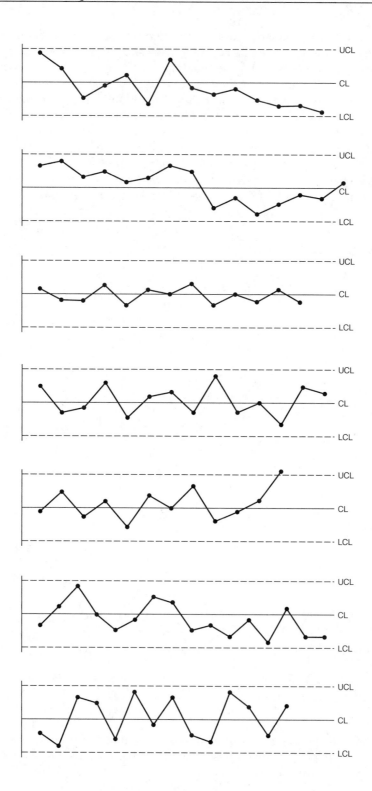

6. Consider the data for the time required to begin loading the home page in an Internet browser for Slowbay's Web site. Fifteen samples of size 5 are shown in the worksheet *Prob. 7-6*. Specifications are 0.076 ± 0.009.

   a. Compute control limits for an x chart (chart for individuals) using the statistic $\bar{R}/d_2$ as an estimate of the standard deviation and using the actual standard deviation for the data. Why might they be different?

   b. Construct the $\bar{x}$- and R-charts and an x-chart for individuals using the data. Interpret the results.

   c. Estimate the process capability by using the estimated sample standard deviation, available on the $\bar{x}$- and R-chart spreadsheet templates on the student CD-ROM.

7. The fraction defective for a folding process in a Quality Printing plant is given in the worksheet *Prob. 7-7* for 25 samples. Fifty units are inspected each shift.

   a. Construct a p-chart and interpret the results.

   b. After the process was determined to be under control, process monitoring began, using the established control limits. The results of 25 more samples are shown in the second part of the worksheet. Is there a problem with the process? If so, when should the process have been stopped, and steps taken to correct it?

8. One hundred insurance claim forms are inspected daily at Full Life Insurance Co. over 25 working days, and the number of forms with errors have been recorded in the worksheet *Prob. 7-8*. Construct a p-chart. If any points occur outside the control limits, assume that assignable causes have been determined. Then, construct a revised chart.

9. Edgewater Hospital surveys all outgoing patients by means of a patient satisfaction questionnaire. The number of patients surveyed each month varies. Control charts that monitor the proportion of dissatisfied patients for key questions are constructed and studied. Construct a p-chart for the data in the worksheet *Prob. 7-9*, which represent responses to a question on satisfaction with hospital meals.

10. AtYourService.com, an Internet service provider (ISP), is concerned that the level of access of customers is decreasing, due to heavier use. The proportion of peak period time when a customer is likely to receive busy signals is considered a good measure of service level. The percentage of times a customer receives a busy signal during peak periods varies. Using a sampling process, the ISP set up control charts to monitor the service level, based on proportion of busy signals received. Construct the p-chart using the sample data in the table in the worksheet *Prob. 7-10*. What does the chart show? Is the service level good or bad, in your opinion, based on the p-chart data?

ENDNOTES

1. "Testing for Conformity: An Inside Job," *Golf Journal*, May 1998, 20–25.
2. Douglas H. Harris and Frederick B. Chaney, *Human Factors in Quality Assurance* (New York: John Wiley & Sons, 1969).
3. "DaimlerChrysler's Quality Practices Pay Off for PT Cruiser," News and Analysis, Metrologyworld.com (accessed March 23, 2000).
4. Tom Taormina, "Conducting Successful Internal Audits," *Quality Digest*, June 1998, 44–47.
5. Adapted from The Ritz-Carlton Hotel Company, Application Summaries for the Malcolm Baldrige National Quality Award, 1992 and 1999.
6. Robert W. Hoyer and Wayne C. Ellis, "A Graphical Exploration of SPC, Part 1," *Quality Progress* 29, no. 5, May 1996, 65–73.
7. T. N. Goh and M. Xie, "Statistical Control of a Six Sigma Process," *Quality Engineering* 15, no. 4, 2003, 587–592.
8. We are grateful to Richard J. Casey for supplying this application.

P A R T

III

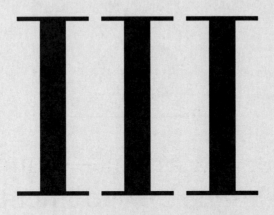

Design for Six Sigma

Chapter 8
Design for Six Sigma—
Concept and Design Development

Chapter 9
Design for Six Sigma—
Optimization and Verification

CHAPTER

8

Design for Six Sigma—Concept and Design Development

OVERVIEW OF DFSS

Design for Six Sigma (DFSS) represents a set of tools and methodologies used in product development for ensuring that goods and services will meet customer needs and achieve performance objectives, and that the processes used to make and deliver them achieve six sigma capability. While traditional Six Sigma applications focus on improving existing processes, DFSS focuses on predicting and improving quality and CTQ performance during the design phase of products and processes before prototypes have been developed or processes have been rolled out. Thus, DFSS is focused on prevention activities that might inhibit Six Sigma performance. This is a significant change in philosophy for many companies. However, it is consistent with the bottom line orientation of Six Sigma, because early design changes are much less expensive to make than after the product is rolled out or introduced into the market.

DFSS is relatively new and is rapidly becoming recognized and incorporated into traditional product development processes. It is not only applied to engineered products, but also to business transactions and production processes. Because DFSS is new, there is little universal agreement about what it means and how it should be implemented; companies view the concept in different ways and employ different approaches. Nevertheless, some features of DFSS include the following:

- A high-level architectural view of the design
- Use of CTQs with well-defined technical requirements
- Application of statistical modeling and simulation approaches
- Predicting defects, avoiding defects, and performance prediction using analysis methods

- Examining the full range of product performance using variation analysis of subsystems and components[1]

DFSS uses many tools including reliability analysis, multivariable optimization, design of experiments, statistical analysis, probabilistic simulation, and failure mode and effects analysis, many of which are discussed elsewhere in this book, as well as advanced engineering tools that we cannot address in a short introductory book. In this chapter and the next, we focus on some of the important and unique tools and techniques that support DFSS. Like Six Sigma itself, most tools for DFSS have been around for some time and developed in different disciplines; its uniqueness lies in the manner in which they are integrated into a formal methodology, driven by the Six Sigma philosophy, with clear business objectives in mind.

General Electric is one company that embraced DFSS. One of the early applications of DFSS was at GE's Medical Systems Division. The Lightspeed Computed Tomography (CT) System was the first GE product to be completely designed and developed using DFSS. Lightspeed allows doctors to capture multiple images of a patient's anatomy simultaneously at a speed six times faster than traditional scanners. As a result, productivity doubled while the images had much higher quality. Jack Welch announced that all GE products designed after that time would be designed using the DFSS approach.[2] In its 1998 annual report, GE stated that "Every new product and service in the future will be DFSS. . . . They were, in essence, designed by the customer, using all of the critical-to-quality performance features (CTQs) the customer wanted in the product and then subjecting these CTQs to the rigorous statistical Design for Six Sigma Process."

Some authors describe DFSS using a similar approach as DMAIC: **Define, Measure, Analyze, Design, and Verify (DMADV)**.[3] In the Define step, the goals of the design activity are established. The Measure step focuses on identifying CTQs using similar tools as the DMAIC process uses. The Analyze step consists of evaluating product concepts for their ability to satisfy or go beyond (excite and delight) customer expectations. The Design step focuses on optimizing the configuration of the features and specifications of the good or service as well as the processes that will produce it. Finally, the Verify step ensures that the new product performs as expected at the appropriate six sigma level of performance and meets all customer requirements.

Another way of characterizing DFSS is with the following four basic activities:[4]

1. *Concept development*, in which product concepts and functionality are determined based upon customer CTQs, technological capabilities, and economic realities
2. *Design development*, which focuses on evaluating and selecting specific product and process performance characteristics necessary to fulfill customer requirements and stay within budget and resource constraints
3. *Design optimization*, which seeks to minimize the impact of variation in production and use, creating a "robust" design
4. *Design verification*, which ensures that the capability of the production system meets the appropriate sigma level and prepare for full-scale production rollout

Both approaches are similar; in DMADV, the Define, Measure, and Analyze steps are part of the concept development process. The Design step is roughly equivalent to design development and optimization. Verification, of course, would be essentially the same as Control. Although the language is not standardized, the fundamental focus and approaches used for both are essentially the same. In this chapter, we focus on the first two activities, and in the next chapter, on the last two. However, we will barely scratch the surface of the full scope of DFSS, and we encourage you to refer to one or more of the many books that comprehensively treat this topic.

Concept Development

Concept development is the process of developing innovative ideas for a market opportunity that meet customer requirements and their CTQs. Good concepts respond to needs that currently do not exist and that customers might not even imagine. Common products today, such as the minivan, PDA, and MP3 player all began as vague and sometimes unusual concepts. Concept development should begin with a valid business case that establishes the market viability of the product, a financial analysis of future cash flows, and an analysis of risks. It then requires market research processes for determining specific features that would appeal to customers and potential demand estimates.

Concept development is a highly creative activity that can be enhanced by such techniques as brainstorming and brainwriting—a written form of brainstorming—and is focused first on identifying potential ideas. After potential ideas have been identified, they are evaluated using cost-benefit analysis, risk analysis, and other techniques. Finally, the best concept is selected, often using some type of scoring matrix to weight the selection criteria.

Understanding the Voice of the Customer

The first question one must ask during concept development is: What is the product (good or service) intended to do? Understanding the "voice of the customer" is the starting point for concept development. Recall that we briefly introduced this concept in Chapter 3. How the voice of the customer is translated into physical or operational specifications—Critical to Quality (CTQ) characteristics—and production processes for a product or service can mean the difference between a successful product and an outright failure. Table 8.1 provides a few examples.

For example, consumers expect a camera to take good pictures. In developing a new camera, Japanese engineers at one company studied pictures developed at photo labs and talked with customers to determine the major causes of poor pictures. The three biggest problems were underexposures, out of focus, and out of film (attempting to take pictures past the end of the roll). They developed the first camera that included a built-in flash to prevent underexposure, an autofocus lens, and an automatic rewind feature. Today, most popular models have these features to meet customer requirements. Other design considerations include the product's weight, size, appearance, safety, life, serviceability, and maintainability.

TABLE 8.1 CRITICAL-TO-QUALITY DIMENSIONS OF A MANUFACTURED PRODUCT AND SERVICE

Quality Dimension	Manufactured Product (Stereo Amplifier)	Service Product (Checking Account)
Performance	Signal-to-noise ratio; power	Time to process customer requests
Features	Remote control	Automatic bill paying
Conformance	Workmanship	Accuracy
Reliability	Mean time to failure	Variability of time to process requests
Durability	Useful life	Keeping pace with industry trends
Serviceability	Ease of repair	Resolution of errors
Aesthetics	Oak cabinet	Appearance of bank lobby

Source: Adapted from Paul E. Pisek, "Defining Quality at the Marketing/Development Interface," *Quality Progress* 20, no.6 (June 1987), 28–36. © 1987 American Society for Quality. Used with permission.

Technical requirements, sometimes called design characteristics, translate the voice of the customer into technical language, specifically into measures of product performance. For example, consumers might want portable stereos with "good sound quality." Technical aspects of a stereo system that affect sound quality include the frequency response, flutter (the wavering in pitch), and the speed accuracy (inconsistency affects the pitch and tempo of the sound). Technical requirements are actionable; they lead to design specifications such as the electrical properties of stereo system components.

When design decisions are dominated by engineering considerations rather than by customer requirements, poor designs that fail in the market are often the result. A powerful tool for developing appropriate design ideas is *concept engineering.*

CONCEPT ENGINEERING

Concept engineering (CE) emerged from a consortium of companies that included Polaroid and Bose along with researchers at MIT, and is promoted and taught by the Center for Quality of Management (http://www.cqm.org). CE is a focused process for discovering customer requirements and using them to select superior product or service concepts that meet those requirements. Although similar to QFD in many respects, it puts the voice of the customer into a broader context and employs numerous other techniques to ensure effective processing of qualitative data. Five major steps comprise the process:

1. *Understanding the customer's environment.* This step involves first project planning activities such as team selection, identifying fit with business strategy, and gaining team consensus on the project focus. It also includes collecting the voice of the customer to understand the customer's environment—physical, psychological, competitive, and so on.

2. *Converting understanding into requirements.* In this step, teams analyze the customer transcripts to translate the voice of the customer into more specific requirements. Essentially this step focuses on identifying the technical requirements we discussed in the context of QFD, selecting the most significant requirements, and "scrubbing" the requirements to refine them into clear and insightful statements.

3. *Operationalizing what has been learned.* This step involves determining how to measure how well a customer requirement is met. For example, a requirement developed for a project at Polaroid was "Document photographer delivers document photo quickly while the customer waits." The principal requirement is about throughput time, so the concept of "quickly" needs to be operationalized and measured.[5] Once potential metrics are defined, they are evaluated to reduce the number of metrics that need to be used while ensuring that they cover all key requirements. This evaluation usually requires some sort of customer questionnaire to identify the importance of the requirements and prioritize them.

4. *Concept generation.* This step focuses on generating ideas for solutions that will potentially meet customers' needs. One unique approach is to brainstorm ideas that might resolve each individual customer requirement, select the best ones, and then classify them under the more traditional functional product characteristics. This approach helps to develop a "market in" rather than a "product out" orientation. Creative thinking techniques are applied here to increase the number and diversity of potential ideas.

5. *Concept selection.* Finally, the potential ideas are evaluated with respect to meeting requirements, trade-offs are assessed, and prototyping may begin. The process ends with reflection on the final concept to test whether the decision "feels right" based on all the knowledge acquired.

As an example, Bose Corporation, a leader in high-end audio products, used concept engineering to improve its European delivery system while decreasing overhead cost to the company.[6] The delivery system included every activity from the time a dealer realizes that he or she needs a product from Bose until the product is delivered. In personal visits to dealers in France, Germany, Netherlands, Spain, Belgium, and the United Kingdom, Bose developed an interview guide that addressed the following:

1. How do you describe the perfect supplier?
2. Please describe your process of ordering.
3. Where does customer service fit into your business?
4. General questions about your impressions of Bose.

In processing the qualitative data obtained from the interviews, Bose focused on the question, "What scenes or images come to mind when you visualize a supplier's delivery system?" From an analysis of more than 100 customer requirements, 24 were selected as key requirements for a world-class delivery system. This analysis led the team to the conclusion that supplier reliability and system efficiency build confidence and create trusting relationships. Next, these requirements were stated in measurable terms and questionnaires were developed to ensure that the requirements truly reflected the opinions of the dealers. For example, a requirement might be "Have a simple and swift return policy for faulty or damaged products." This requirement might then be measured by the amount of information required to process a product return.

The team spent nearly three days generating potential solutions for each customer requirement. As they discussed the strengths of each idea, new ideas often emerged, even from seemingly bizarre ideas. The four strongest ideas were chosen, and the team wrote a story or scenario with specific changes that needed to be made to the delivery system as a way of presenting the solution; this form of presentation would enable those outside of the team to understand how the new systems would work in delighting the customer. Although the process was quite tedious, the team members agreed that it was an excellent approach for arriving at an effective solution and turned them "into believers."

Concept engineering leaves a strong audit trail back to the voice of the customer. This evidence makes it difficult for skeptics to challenge the results and easier to convert them. The process helps to build consensus and gives the team confidence in selling the concept to management. It takes a lot of discipline and patience, but the end result is well worth the effort.

DESIGN DEVELOPMENT

Design is a highly creative activity, but one that must be based on good customer research and understanding as well as scientific analysis. The fundamental question in design development is "What do I need to make the concept of the product, service, or process work and meet (or exceed) customer expectations?" The responses might include specifying product features such as materials, colors, style and form, information content, equipment and facilities, product packaging, or people skills. For example, when Procter & Gamble introduced Liquid Tide back in 1984, one of the most critical pieces of the product was the cap. It was designed to measure, pretreat, and have a self-draining device inside the package to minimize messes. While many might consider this a small issue as opposed the ability of the product to clean clothes, the functionality built into the cap delighted customers every time they opened the bottle.

Design development is the process of applying scientific, engineering, and business knowledge to produce a basic functional design that meets all CTQs—both customer needs and manufacturing or service delivery requirements. Design development usually starts with a **high-level design** and then moves toward more detail design of components or subsystems. The $Y = f(X)$ concept that we used in explaining Six Sigma for process improvement applies in DFSS also. The goal of design is to identify both the most appropriate Xs along with their features—material quality, quantity, frequency of service, and so on—and then to optimize their performance.

Developing a basic functional design involves translating customer requirements into measurable technical requirements and, subsequently, into detailed design specifications. Concurrently, one must consider how the manufacturing and/or service-delivery process will be designed to support the product. Usually, there are many different alternatives to consider, and trade-offs must invariably be made, for example, sacrificing size for reduced weight, or elaborate features for lower costs. An extremely useful tool to do this is quality function deployment, which we discuss next.

QUALITY FUNCTION DEPLOYMENT

A major problem with the traditional product development process is that customers and engineers speak different languages. A customer might express a desire to own a car that is easy to start. The translation of this requirement into technical language might be "car will start within 4 seconds of continuous cranking." Or, a requirement that "soap leaves my skin feeling soft" demands translation into pH or hardness specifications for the bar of soap. The actual intended message can be lost in the translation and subsequent interpretation by design or production personnel.

The Japanese developed an approach called **quality function deployment (QFD)** to meet customers' requirements throughout the design process and also in the design of production systems. The term, a translation of the Kanji characters used to describe the process, can sound confusing. QFD is a planning process to guide the design, manufacturing, and marketing of goods by integrating the voice of the customer throughout the organization. Through QFD, every design, manufacturing, and control decision is made to meet the expressed needs of customers. It uses a type of matrix diagram to present data and information.

QFD originated in 1972 at Mitsubishi's Kobe shipyard site. Toyota began to develop the concept shortly thereafter, and has used it since 1977 with impressive results. Between January 1977 and October 1979, Toyota realized a 20 percent reduction in start-up costs on the launch of a new van. By 1982, start-up costs had fallen 38 percent from the 1977 baseline, and by 1984, were reduced by 61 percent. In addition, development time fell by one-third at the same time quality improved. Xerox and Ford initiated the use of QFD in the United States in 1986 (at that time, more than 50 percent of major Japanese companies were already using the approach). Today, QFD is used successfully by manufacturers of electronics, appliances, clothing, and construction equipment, by firms such as General Motors, Ford, Mazda, Motorola, Xerox, Kodak, IBM, Procter & Gamble, Hewlett-Packard, and AT&T. The 1992 model Cadillac was planned and designed entirely with QFD. Two organizations, the American Supplier Institute, Inc., a nonprofit organization, and GOAL/QPC, a Massachusetts consulting firm, have publicized and developed the concept in the United States.

At the strategic level, QFD presents a challenge and the opportunity for top management to break out of its traditional narrow focus on results, which can only be measured after the fact, and to view the broader process of how results are obtained. Under QFD, all operations of a company are driven by the voice of the customer, rather than by edicts of top management or the opinions or desires of design engineers. At the tactical and operational levels, QFD departs from the traditional product planning process in which product concepts are originated by design teams or research and development groups, tested and refined, produced, and marketed. Often, a considerable amount of wasted effort and time is spent redesigning products and production systems until customer needs are met. If customer needs can be identified properly in the first place, then such wasteful effort is eliminated, which is the principal focus of QFD.

QFD benefits companies through improved communication and teamwork between all constituencies in the value chain, such as between marketing and design, between design and manufacturing, and between purchasing and suppliers. Product objectives are better understood and interpreted during the production process because all key design information is captured and synthesized. This approach helps to understand trade-offs in design, and promote consensus among managers. Use of QFD focuses on the drivers of customer satisfaction and dissatisfaction, making it a useful tool for competitive analysis of product quality by top management. Productivity as well as quality improvements generally follow QFD. Perhaps most significant, though, QFD reduces the time for new product development. QFD allows companies to simulate the effects of new design ideas and concepts. Through this benefit, companies can reduce product development time and bring new products into the market sooner, thus gaining competitive advantage. Details of the QFD process and its use are presented next.

The House of Quality

A set of matrixes is used to relate the voice of the customer to a product's technical requirements, component requirements, process control plans, and manufacturing operations. The first matrix, the customer requirement planning matrix shown in Figure 8.1, provides the basis for the QFD concept. The figure demonstrates why this matrix is often called the **House of Quality**.

Building the House of Quality consists of six basic steps:

1. Identify customer requirements.
2. Identify technical requirements.
3. Relate the customer requirements to the technical requirements.
4. Conduct an evaluation of competing products or services.
5. Evaluate technical requirements and develop targets.
6. Determine which technical requirements to deploy in the remainder of the production/delivery process.

To illustrate the development of the House of Quality and the QFD process, the task of designing a new fitness center in a community with two other competing organizations is presented.

Step 1: Identify customer requirements.
The voice of the customer is the primary input to the QFD process. Many methods can be used to gather valid customer information. The most critical and most difficult step of the process is to capture the essence of the customer's needs and expectations. The customer's own words are vitally important in preventing misinterpretation by designers and engineers. Figure 8.2 shows the voice of the customer in the House of Quality for the fitness center, perhaps based on a telephone survey or focus groups. They are grouped into five categories: programs and activities, facilities, atmosphere, staff, and other.

FIGURE 8.1 THE HOUSE OF QUALITY

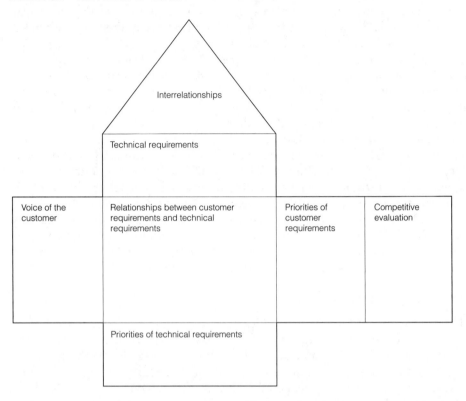

Step 2: List the technical requirements that provide the foundation for the product or service design.

Technical requirements are design characteristics that describe the customer requirements as expressed in the language of the designer or engineer. Essentially, they are the "hows" by which the company will respond to the "whats"—customer requirements. They must be measurable, because the output is controlled and compared to objective targets. For the fitness center, these requirements include the number and type of program offerings and equipment, times, staffing requirements, facility characteristics and maintenance, fee structure, and so on. Figure 8.3 adds this information to the House of Quality.

The roof of the House of Quality shows the interrelationships between any pair of technical requirements. Various symbols denote these relationships. A typical scheme uses the symbol ● to denote a very strong relationship, ○ for a strong relationship, and Δ to denote a weak relationship. These relationships indicate answers to questions such as "How does a change in a technical characteristic affect others?" For example, increasing program offerings will probably require more staff, a larger facility, expanded hours, and higher costs; hiring more maintenance staff, building a larger facility, and buying more equipment will probably result in a higher membership fee. Thus, design decisions cannot be viewed in isolation. This relationship matrix helps to assess trade-offs.

FIGURE 8.2   VOICE OF THE CUSTOMER IN THE HOUSE OF QUALITY

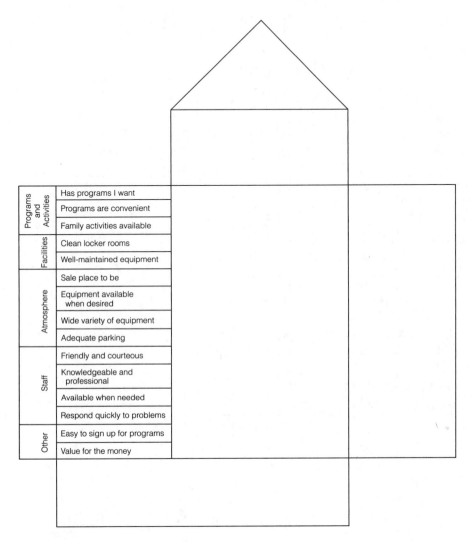

Programs and Activities	Has programs I want	
	Programs are convenient	
	Family activities available	
Facilities	Clean locker rooms	
	Well-maintained equipment	
Atmosphere	Sale place to be	
	Equipment available when desired	
	Wide variety of equipment	
	Adequate parking	
Staff	Friendly and courteous	
	Knowledgeable and professional	
	Available when needed	
	Respond quickly to problems	
Other	Easy to sign up for programs	
	Value for the money	

Step 3: Develop a relationship matrix between the customer requirements and the technical requirements.

Customer requirements are listed down the left column; technical requirements are written across the top. In the matrix itself, symbols indicate the degree of relationship in a manner similar to that used in the roof of the House of Quality. The purpose of the relationship matrix is to show whether the final technical requirements adequately address customer requirements. This assessment is usually based on expert experience, customer responses, or controlled experiments.

The lack of a strong relationship between a customer requirement and any technical requirement shows that the customer needs either are not addressed or

FIGURE 8.3 TECHNICAL REQUIREMENTS IN THE HOUSE OF QUALITY

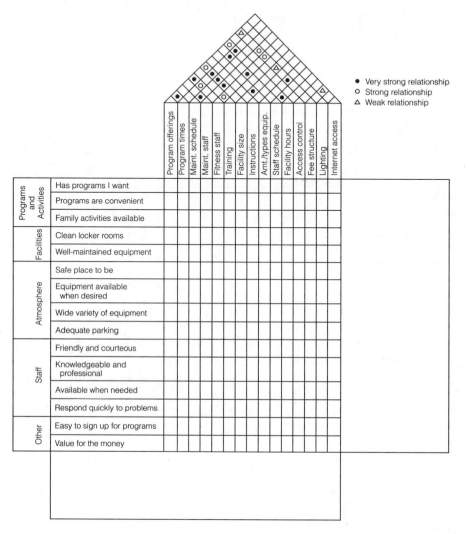

that the final design will have difficulty in meeting them. Similarly, if a technical requirement does not affect any customer requirement, it may be redundant or the designers may have missed some important customer need. For example, the customer requirement "clean locker rooms" bears a very strong relationship to the maintenance schedule and only a strong relationship to the number of maintenance staff. "Easy to sign up for programs" would probably bear a very strong relationship to Internet access and only a weak relationship to the hours the facility is open. Figure 8.4 shows an example of these relationships.

Step 4: Add competitor evaluation and key selling points.

This step identifies importance ratings for each customer requirement and evaluates competitors' existing products or services for each of them (see Figure 8.5).

FIGURE 8.4 RELATIONSHIP MATRIX

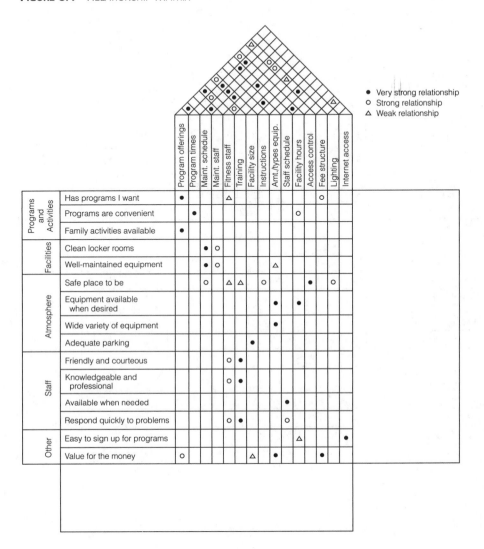

Customer importance ratings represent the areas of greatest interest and highest expectations as expressed by the customer. Competitive evaluation highlights the absolute strengths and weaknesses in competing products. By using this step, designers can discover opportunities for improvement. It also links QFD to a company's strategic vision and indicates priorities for the design process. For example, if an important customer requirement receives a low evaluation on all competitors' products (for instance, "family activities available"), then by focusing on this need a company might gain a competitive advantage. Such requirements become key selling points and the basis for formulating marketing strategies.

FIGURE 8.5 COMPETITIVE EVALUATION

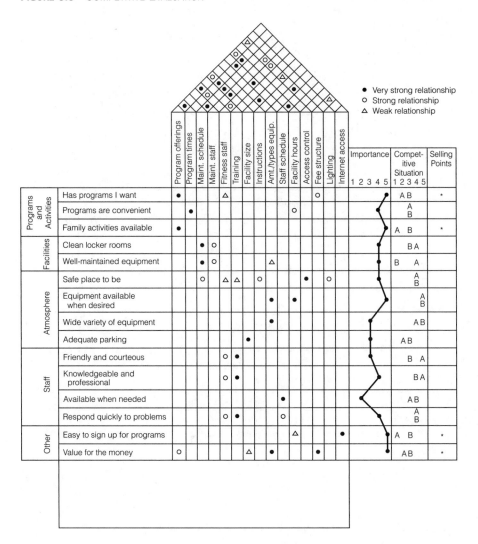

Step 5: Evaluate technical requirements of competitive products and services and develop targets.

This step is usually accomplished through intelligence gathering or product testing and then translated into measurable terms. These evaluations are compared with the competitive evaluation of customer requirements to determine inconsistencies between customer requirements and technical requirements. If a competing product is found to best satisfy a customer requirement but the evaluation of the related technical requirements indicates otherwise, then either the measures used are faulty or else the product has an image difference (either positive toward the competitor or negative toward the company's product), which affects customer perceptions. On the basis of customer importance ratings and existing product strengths and weaknesses, targets for each technical requirement

FIGURE 8.6 COMPLETED HOUSE OF QUALITY

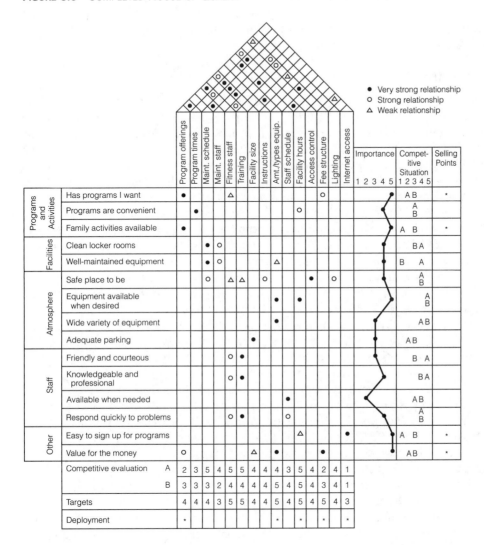

are set, as shown in Figure 8.6. For example, customers rated programs and family activities of high importance while competitive evaluation shows them to be quite low. Setting a higher target for these requirements will help to meet this critical need and be a source of competitive advantage.

Step 6: Select technical requirements to be deployed in the remainder of the process.

The technical requirements that have a strong relationship to customer needs, have poor competitive performance, or are strong selling points are identified during this step. These characteristics have the highest priority and need to be "deployed" throughout the remainder of the design and production process to maintain a responsiveness to the voice of the customer. Those characteristics not identified as critical do not need such rigorous attention. For example, program offerings, amount and types of equipment, facility hours, fee structure, and Internet access have been identified in Figure 8.6 as the key issues to address in designing the fitness center.

Beyond the House of Quality

The House of Quality provides the marketing function with an important tool to understand customer needs and gives top management strategic direction. However, it is only the first step in the QFD process. The voice of the customer must be carried throughout the production/delivery process. Three other "houses of quality" are used to deploy the voice of the customer to (in a manufacturing setting) component parts: characteristics, process plans, and quality control. These aspects apply the house of quality concepts to more detailed phases of the design process.

The second house is similar to the first house but applies to subsystems and components. The technical requirements from the first house are related to detailed requirements of subsystems and components (see Figure 8.7). At this stage, target values representing the best values for fit, function, and appearance are determined. For example, program offerings might be broken down into fitness programs, children's programs, family programs, and so on, each with its own unique set of design requirements, and hence, its own House of Quality.

In manufacturing, most of the QFD activities represented by the first two Houses of Quality are performed by product development and engineering functions. At the next stage, the planning activities involve supervisors and production line operators. In the third house, the process plan relates the component characteristics to key process operations, the transition from planning to execution. (For the fitness center, this step might involve creating a project plan for selecting, designing, and evaluating programs.) Key process operations are the basis for a *control point*. A control point forms the basis for a quality control plan delivering those critical characteristics that are crucial to achieving customer satisfaction, as specified in the last house of quality. At this point, for example, the fitness center might design membership surveys for evaluating programs, checklists for maintenance, performance appraisal approaches for the staff, and measures of equipment failures and problems. These activities are what must be measured and evaluated on a continuous basis to ensure that processes continue

FIGURE 8.7 THE FOUR HOUSES OF QUALITY

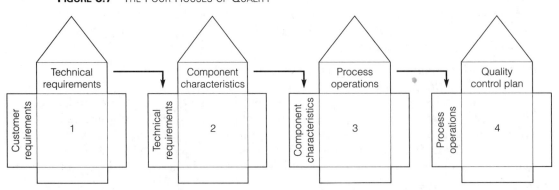

to meet the important customer requirements defined in the first House of Quality. Thus, the QFD process provides a thread from the voice of the customer, through design and production/delivery activities, to daily management and control. In that way, it provides the basis for more advanced methodologies such as design of experiments that we discuss in the next chapter, and for effective implementation of statistical process control.

DETAILED DESIGN AND ANALYSIS

After a high-level design is established and approved, a more detailed design process begins, with a focus on establishing specific product specifications, which represent the transition from a designer's concept to a producible design, while also ensuring that the product can be produced and delivered economically, efficiently, and with high quality—ideally at six sigma levels of performance. This step usually requires extensive engineering knowledge and experience. Many industries have "design rules" that guide engineers in these tasks. As noted earlier, the QFD process can be used to initiate detailed design activities by moving beyond the first House of Quality.

For manufactured goods, detailed design involves specifying an ideal target, or **nominal dimensions** and **tolerances**, which define permissible ranges of variation. To illustrate, consider a simple microprocessor. The drawing in Figure 8.8 shows some of the critical nominal dimensions and tolerances for the microprocessor. The "ratio" notation (0.514/0.588) denotes the permissible range of the dimension. Unless otherwise stated, the nominal dimension is the midpoint. Thus, the specification of 0.514/0.588 may be interpreted as a nominal dimension of (0.514 + 0.588)/2 = 0.551 with a tolerance of plus or minus 0.037. Usually, this is written as 0.551 ± 0.037. Specifications like these apply to services as well. For instance, at Starbucks, the well-known international chain of coffeehouses, milk must be steamed to at least 150 degrees Fahrenheit but never more than 170 degrees (milk begins to scald at that temperature), and every espresso shot must be pulled within 23 seconds of service or tossed.[7]

FIGURE 8.8 MICROPROCESSOR SPECIFICATIONS

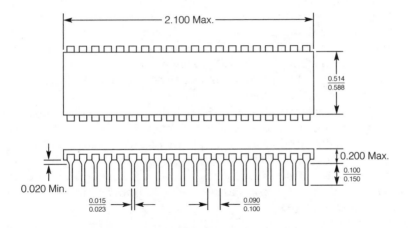

Simulation or other types of experimentation are often used to evaluate the performance of goods and services and to help establish the best parameters. This is part of design optimization, and will be discussed in the next chapter.

One of the more challenging tasks in design is setting appropriate tolerances. **Tolerance design** involves determining the permissible variation in a dimension. To design tolerances effectively, engineers must understand the necessary trade-offs in product functionality, manufacturability, and cost. Narrow tolerances tend to raise manufacturing costs but they also increase the interchangeability of parts within the plant and in the field, product performance, durability, and appearance. Also, a tolerance reserve or factor of safety is needed to account for engineering uncertainty regarding the maximum variation allowable and compatibility with satisfactory product performance. Wide tolerances, on the other hand, increase material utilization, machine throughput, and labor productivity, but have a negative impact on product characteristics, as previously mentioned. Thus, factors operating to enlarge tolerances include production planning requirements; tool design, fabrication, and setup; tool adjustment and replacement, process yield; inspection and gauge control and maintenance; and labor and supervision requirements.

Traditionally, tolerances are set by convention rather than scientifically. A designer might use the tolerances specified on previous designs or base a design decision on judgment from past experience. Setting inappropriate tolerances can be costly. For instance, in one company, a bearing seat had to be machined on a large part, costing more than $1,000. Because of the precision tolerance specified by design engineers, one or two parts per month had to be scrapped when the tolerance was exceeded. A study revealed that the bearings being used did not require such precise tolerances. When the tolerance was relaxed, the problem disappeared. This one design change resulted in approximately $20,000 in savings per year.

Design for Manufacturability

Simplifying a design can often improve manufacturing cost as well as reduce the potential for defects, thus raising six sigma performance. Designs with numerous parts increase the incidence of part mix-ups, missing parts, and test failures. Complicated assembly steps or tricky joining processes can cause incorrect, incomplete, unreliable, or otherwise faulty assemblies. Thus, product design must be closely integrated with process design. For example, some parts may be designed with features that make them difficult to manufacture with consistent quality. Others might lack features enabling assemblers to always insert them correctly (think of the poka-yoke concept). Parts that are fragile or susceptible to corrosion might be damaged in shipping or handling.

Design for manufacturability (DFM) is the process of designing a product for efficient production at the highest level of quality. DFM is intended to prevent product designs that simplify assembly operations but require more complex and expensive components, designs that simplify component manufacture while complicating the assembly process, and designs that are simple and inexpensive to produce but difficult or expensive to service or support. Some DFM guidelines include minimizing the number of parts, eliminating screws and loose fasteners, using proven "off-the shelf" components that have high reliability and are insensitive to environmental variation, making assembly foolproof, and eliminating the need for adjustment.

DFM is often supported by **design reviews**. The purpose of a design review is to stimulate discussion, raise questions, and generate new ideas and solutions to help designers anticipate problems before they occur. Generally, a design review is conducted in three major stages: preliminary, intermediate, and final. The preliminary design review establishes early communication between marketing, engineering, manufacturing, and purchasing personnel and provides better coordination of their activities. It usually involves higher levels of management and concentrates on strategic issues in design that relate to customer requirements and thus the ultimate quality of the product. A preliminary design review evaluates such issues as the function of the product, conformance to customer's needs, completeness of specifications, manufacturing costs, and liability issues. After the design is well established, an intermediate review takes place to study the design in greater detail to identify potential problems and suggest corrective action. Personnel at lower levels of the organization are more heavily involved at this stage. Finally, just before release to production, a final review is held. Materials lists, drawings, and other detailed design information are studied with the purpose of preventing costly changes after production setup.

Many statistical tools that we discuss in other chapters, including statistical inference, regression, and design of experiments, play an important role in design development. In this section we introduce two other general approaches: *design failure mode and effects analysis*, and *reliability prediction*.

DESIGN FAILURE MODE AND EFFECTS ANALYSIS

The purpose of **design failure mode and effects analysis (DFMEA)** is to identify all the ways in which a failure can occur, to estimate the effect and seriousness of the failure, and to recommend corrective design actions. A DFMEA usually consists of specifying the following information for each design element or function:

- *Failure modes*—ways in which each element or function can fail. This information generally takes some research and imagination. One way to start is with known failures that have occurred in the past. Documents such as quality and reliability reports, test results, and warranty reports provide useful information. For example, some failure modes for a computer on start-up might be a hard drive failure, software corruption, loose connections, failed motherboard, and so on. For a restaurant, a failure mode might be not having a menu item available, excessive customer wait time, or incorrect bill.
- *Effect of the failure on the customer*—such as dissatisfaction, potential injury or other safety issue, downtime, repair requirements, and so on. Maintenance records, customer complaints, and warranty reports provide good sources of

information. Consideration should be given to failures on the function of the end product, manufacturability in the next process, what the customer sees or experiences, and product safety.

- *Severity, likelihood of occurrence, and detection rating*—A computer boot failure will certainly cause extreme customer dissatisfaction, but a spark or fire would be more serious. Severity might be measured on a scale of 1 to 10, where a "1" indicates that the failure is so minor that the customer probably would not notice it, and a "10" might mean that the customer might be endangered. The frequency of occurrence based on service history or field performance provides an indication of the significance of the failure. Based on severity and likelihood, a risk priority can be assigned to identify critical failure modes that must be addressed.

- *Potential causes of failure*—Cause-and-effect diagrams can help to isolate specific causes. For a computer failure these might include a bad component, over-heating, or dust contamination. For a restaurant, lack of a menu item might result from a poor ordering process, supplier failure to deliver, or unusual weather conditions. Often, the root cause is the result of poor design. Design deficiencies can cause errors either in the field or in manufacturing and assembly. Identification of causes might require experimentation and rigorous analysis.

- *Corrective actions or controls*—These controls might include design changes, "mistake-proofing" (see Chapter 6), better user instructions, management responsibilities, and target completion dates.

DFMEA can be applied at the component, subsystem, or system levels of a product design as well as to production processes, and is a valuable tool for preventing problems from occurring, thus improving six sigma capability. Using DFMEA will not only improve product functionality and safety, but also reduce external failure costs—particularly warranty costs, as well as decrease manufacturing and service delivery problems. It can also provide a defense against frivolous lawsuits. DFMEA should be conducted early in the design process to save costs and reduce cycle times, and provide a knowledge base to improve subsequent design efforts. This approach can also be used for processes to identify hazardous conditions that may endanger a worker or operational problems that can disrupt a production process and result in scrap, downtime, or other non-value-added costs.

RELIABILITY PREDICTION IN DFSS

Reliability—the ability of a product to perform as expected over time—is a critical customer requirement and an important metric for Six Sigma. To achieve six sigma levels of performance, both products and processes must be designed for high reliability. Sophisticated equipment used today in such areas as transportation (airplanes), communications (satellites), and medicine (pacemakers) requires high reliability. High reliability can also provide a competitive advantage for many consumer goods. Japanese automobiles gained large market shares in the 1970s primarily because of their high reliability. As the overall quality of products continues to improve, consumers expect higher reliability with each purchase; they simply are not satisfied with products that fail unexpectedly. However, the increased complexity of modern products makes high reliability more difficult to achieve. Likewise in manufacturing, the increased use of automation, complexity of machines, low profit margins, and time-based competitiveness make reliability in production processes a critical issue for survival of the business.

Basic Concepts and Definitions

Like quality, reliability is often defined in a similar "transcendent" manner as a sense of trust in a product's ability to perform satisfactorily or resist failure. However, reliability is an issue that requires a more objective, quantitative treatment. Formally, reliability is defined as *the probability that a product, piece of equipment, or system performs its intended function for a stated period of time under specified operating conditions.* This definition has four important elements: probability, time, performance, and operating conditions.

First, reliability is defined as a *probability*, that is, a value between 0 and 1. Thus, it is a numerical measure with a precise meaning. Expressing reliability in this way provides a valid basis for comparison of different designs for products and systems. For example, a reliability of 0.97 indicates that, on average, 97 of 100 items will perform their function for a given period of time and under certain operating conditions. Often reliability is expressed as a percentage simply for descriptive purposes.

The second element of the definition is *time.* Clearly a device having a reliability of 0.97 for 1,000 hours of operation is inferior to one having the same reliability for 5,000 hours of operation, assuming that the mission of the device is long life.

Performance is the third element and refers to the objective for which the product or system was made. The term *failure* is used when expectations of performance of the intended function are not met. Two types of failures can occur: **functional failure** *at the start of product life due to manufacturing or material defects such as a missing connection or a faulty component,* and **reliability failure** *after some period of use.* Examples of reliability failures include the following: a device does not work at all (car will not start); the operation of a device is unstable (car idles rough); or the performance of a device deteriorates (shifting becomes difficult). Because the nature of failure in each of these cases is different, the failure must be clearly defined.

The final component of the reliability definition is *operating conditions,* which involves the type and amount of usage and the environment in which the product is used. For example, typical operating conditions and environments for a wristwatch are summarized in Table 8.2. Notice that reliability must include extreme environments and conditions as well as the typical on-the-arm use.

By defining a product's intended environment, performance characteristics, and lifetime, a manufacturer can design and conduct tests to measure the probability of product survival (or failure). The analysis of such tests enable better prediction of reliability and improved product and process designs.

TABLE 8.2 SOME TYPICAL WATCH ENVIRONMENTS

Environment	Condition	Quantifiable Characteristics	Exposure Time
Typical use	On-the-arm	31°C (88°F)	16 hours/day
Transportation	In packing box	Vibration and shock (−20°C to +80°C)	Specifications for truck/rail/air shipping
Handling accident	Drop to hard floor	1,200 g. 2 milliseconds	1 drop/year
Extreme temperature	Hot, closed automobile	85°C (185°F)	4–6 hours, 5 times/year
Humidity and chemicals	Perspiration, salt, soaps	35°C (95°F) with 90% pH, rain	500 hours/year
Altitude	Pike's Peak	15,000 feet, −40°C	1 time

Source: Adapted from William R. Taylor, "Quality Assessed in New Products Via Comprehensive Systems Approach," *Industrial Engineering* 13, no.3 (March 1981), 28–32. Reprinted with the permission of the Institute of Industrial Engineers, 3577 Parkway Lane, Suite 200, Norcross, GA 30092, 770-449-0461. Copyright © 1981.

Reliability engineers distinguish between **inherent reliability**, which is the predicted reliability determined by the design of the product or process, and the **achieved reliability**, which is the actual reliability observed during use. Actual reliability can be less than the inherent reliability due to the effects of the manufacturing process and the conditions of use. Inherent reliability should be predicted during design based on the type of components used and past failure rate experiences as a basis for evaluating alternatives and improving designs. Data on actual reliability can be gathered from customers out in the field.

Reliability Measurement

In practice, reliability is measured by the number of failures per unit time during the duration under consideration (called the **failure rate**). The reciprocal of the failure rate, which is measured in units of time per failure, is often used as an alternative measure. Some products must be scrapped and replaced on failure; others can be repaired. For items that must be replaced when a failure occurs, the reciprocal of the failure rate is called the **mean time to failure (MTTF)**. For repairable items, the **mean time between failures (MTBF)** is used.

In considering the failure rate of a product, suppose that a large group of items is tested or used until all fail, and that the time of failure is recorded for each item. Plotting the cumulative percentage of failures against time results in a curve such as the one shown in Figure 8.9. The slope of the curve at any point (that is, the slope of the straight line tangent to the curve) gives the instantaneous failure rate (failures per unit time) at any point in time. Figure 8.10 shows a plot of these failure rates, generally called a **product life characteristics curve**, corresponding to the cumulative failure curve in Figure 8.10. This curve was obtained by plotting the slope of the curve at every point. Notice that the slope of the curve and thus the instantaneous failure rate may change over time. Thus, in Figure 8.10, the failure rate at 500 hours is 0.02 failures per hour while the failure rate at 4,500 hours is 0.04 failures per hour. The average failure rate over any interval of time is the slope of the line between the two endpoints of the interval on the curve. As shown in Figure 8.11, the average failure rate over the entire 5,000-hour time period is

FIGURE 8.9   CUMULATIVE FAILURE CURVE OVER TIME

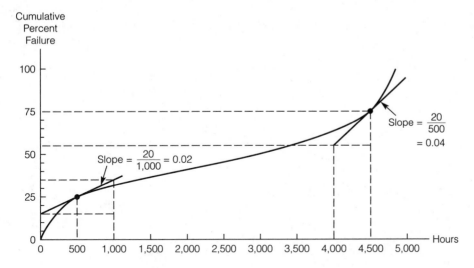

FIGURE 8.10   PRODUCT LIFE CHARACTERISTICS CURVE

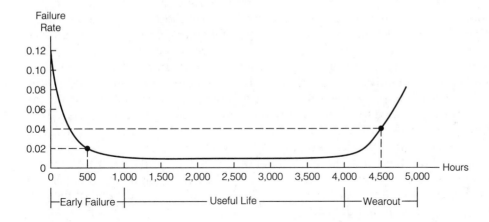

0.02 failures per hour. Many research institutes and large manufacturers conduct extensive statistical studies to identify distinct patterns of failure over time.

Gathering enough data about failures to generate as smooth a curve as is shown in Figure 8.11 is not always possible. If limited data are available, the failure rate is computed using the following formula:

$$\text{Failure rate} = \lambda = \frac{\text{Number of failures}}{\text{Total unit operating hours}}$$

or alternatively,

$$\lambda = \frac{\text{Number of failures}}{(\text{Units tested}) \times (\text{Number of hours tested})}$$

FIGURE 8.11 AVERAGE FAILURE RATE OVER A TIME INTERVAL

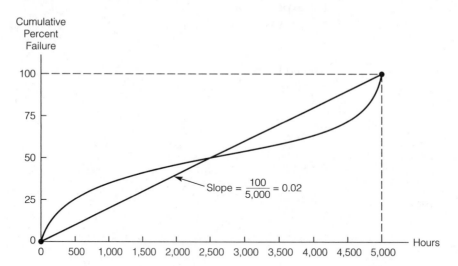

A fundamental assumption in this definition allows for different interpretations. Because the total unit operating hours equal the number of units tested times the number of hours tested, no difference occurs in total unit operating hours between testing 10 units for 100 hours or one unit for 1,000 hours. However, the difference in Figure 8.10 is clear because the failure rate varies over time. For example, if useful life began at 10 hours and the wearout period began at 200 hours, a failure would almost certainly occur before 1,000 hours, whereas a failure would not be likely to occur in 100-hour tests. During a product's useful life, however, the failure rate is assumed to be constant, and different test lengths during this period of time should show little difference. This assumption is the reason that time is an important element of the definition of reliability.

To illustrate the computation of λ, suppose that 10 units are tested over a 100-hour period. Four units failed with one unit each failing after 6, 35, 65, and 70 hours; the remaining six units performed satisfactorily until the end of the test. The total unit operating hours are

$$
\begin{array}{rcl}
1 \times 6 & = & 6 \\
1 \times 35 & = & 35 \\
1 \times 65 & = & 65 \\
1 \times 70 & = & 70 \\
1 \times 100 & = & \underline{600} \\
& & 776
\end{array}
$$

Therefore, $\lambda = (4 \text{ failures})/(776 \text{ unit operating hours}) = 0.00515$ failures per hour. In other words, in a one-hour period, about 0.5 percent of the units would be expected to fail. On the other hand, over a 100-hour period, about $(0.00515)(100) = 0.515$ or 51.5 percent of the units would be expected to fail. In the actual test, only 40 percent failed. The failure rate curve in Figure 8.9 is an example of a typical curve for such components as semiconductors.

Many electronic components commonly exhibit a high, but decreasing, failure rate early in their lives (as evidenced by the steep slope of the curve), followed by a period of a relatively constant failure rate, and ending with an increasing failure rate.

In Figure 8.10, three distinct time periods are evident: early failure (from 0 to about 1,000 hours), useful life (from 1,000 to 4,000 hours), and wearout period (after 4,000 hours). The first is the early failure period, sometimes called the **infant mortality period**. Weak components resulting from poor manufacturing or quality control procedures will often lead to a high rate of failure early in a product's life. This high rate usually cannot be detected through normal test procedures, particularly in electronic semiconductors. Such components or products should not be permitted to enter the marketplace. The second phase of the life characteristics curve describes the normal pattern of random failures during a product's useful life. This period usually has a low, relatively constant failure rate caused by uncontrollable factors, such as sudden and unexpected stresses due to complex interactions in materials or the environment. These factors are usually impossible to predict on an individual basis. However, the collective behavior of such failures can be modeled statistically. Finally, as age takes over, the wearout period begins, and the failure rate increases.

New car owners generally experience this phenomenon. During the first few months of ownership, owners may have to return their car to the dealer or remove the initial bugs caused by poor workmanship or manufacturing processes, such as wheel alignment or rattles. Such defects are monitored by J.D. Power's Initial Quality metrics of which you are probably aware. During its prime lifetime, the car may have few failures; however, as parts begin to wear out, the number and rate of failures begin to increase until replacement becomes desirable.

Knowledge of a product's reliability characteristics helps engineers predict behavior and make decisions accordingly. For instance, if a manufacturer knows that the early failure period for a microprocessor is 600 hours, it can test the chip for 600 hours (or more) under actual or simulated operating conditions before releasing the chip to the market. It is also useful in developing warranties. As an illustration, consider a tire manufacturer who must determine a mileage warranty policy for a new line of tires. From engineering test data, the reliability curve shown in Figure 8.12 was constructed. This graph shows the probability of tread separation within a certain number of miles. Half the tires will fail by 36,500 miles, 87 percent will wear out by 42,000 miles, and only 14 percent will wear out by 31,000 miles. Thus, if a 31,000-mile warranty is established, management can compute the expected cost of replacing 14 percent of the tires. On the other hand, these data may indicate a poor design in relation to similar products of competitors. Design changes might be necessary to improve reliability. Note that in this example time is not measured chronologically, but in terms of product usage.

FIGURE 8.12   CUMULATIVE PROBABILITY FOR TIRE MILEAGE

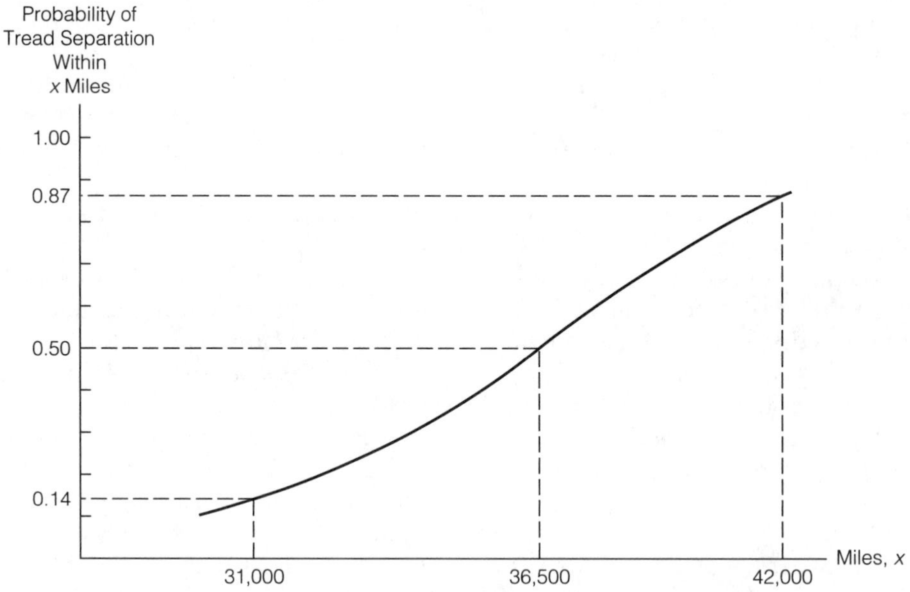

Reliability and the Exponential Distribution

Recall that during the useful life of a product, the failure rate is assumed to be constant. One can assume then that the probability of failure over time can be modeled mathematically by an exponential probability distribution. Not only is this model mathematically justified, but it has been empirically validated for many observable phenomena, such as failures of light bulbs, electronic components, and repairable systems such as automobiles, computers, and industrial machinery.

If λ is a constant failure rate, the probability of failure in the interval $(0, T)$ is given by the cumulative exponential distribution function

$$F(T) = 1 - e^{-\lambda T}$$

Because reliability is the probability of *survival*, the **reliability function** is

$$R(T) = 1 - F(T) = e^{-\lambda T}$$

This function represents the probability that the item will not fail within T units of time under the assumption of a constant failure rate.

Consider, for example, an item having a reliability of 0.97 for 100 hours of normal use. Determine the failure rate λ by solving the equation $R = e^{-\lambda T}$ for λ. Substituting $R = 0.97$ and $T = 100$ into this equation yields

$$0.97 = e^{-\lambda(100)}$$

$$\ln 0.97 = 100\lambda$$

TABLE 8.3 CUMULATIVE FRACTION FAILING AND SURVIVING

Time, T	Failures, $F(T)$	Survivors, $R(T)$
10	0.003	0.997
20	0.006	0.994
30	0.009	0.991
40	0.012	0.988
50	0.015	0.985
60	0.018	0.982
70	0.021	0.979
80	0.024	0.976
90	0.027	0.973
100	0.030	0,970

$$\lambda = -(\ln 0.97)/100$$

$$= 0.0304/100$$

$$= 0.0003 \text{ failure per hour}$$

Thus, the reliability function is $R(T) = e^{-0.0003T}$. The cumulative fraction of items that are expected to fail and survive after each 10-hour period may then be tabulated as given in Table 8.3. Note that the fraction failing in any 10-hour period is constant.

The reciprocal of the failure rate is often used in reliability computations. For non-repairable items, $\theta = 1/\lambda$ is defined as the *mean time to failure* (MTTF). Thus, in the preceding example for $\lambda = 0.0003$ failure per hour, $\theta = 1/0.0003 = 3{,}333$ hours. That is, one failure can be expected every 3,333 hours on the average. The probability distribution function of failures and the reliability function can be equivalently expressed using the MTTF as

$$F(T) = 1 - e^{-T/\theta}$$

and

$$R(T) = e^{-T/\theta}$$

Suppose, for example, that an electronic component has a failure rate of $\lambda = 0.0001$ failure per hour. The MTTF is $\theta = 1/0.0001 = 10{,}000$ hours. The probability that the component will not fail in 15,000 hours is

$$R(15{,}000) = e^{-15{,}000/10{,}000}$$

$$= e^{-1.5}$$

$$= 0.223$$

For repairable items, θ is usually called the *mean time between failures* (MTBF). For example, suppose that a machine is operated for 10,000 hours and experiences four failures that are immediately repaired. The mean time between failures is

$$\text{MTBF} = 10{,}000/4 = 2{,}500 \text{ hours}$$

and the failure rate is

$$\lambda = 1/2{,}500 = 0.0004 \text{ failure per hour}$$

Predicting System Reliability

Many systems (which could be products or manufacturing processes) are composed of individual components with known reliabilities. For example, engineers have accumulated vast knowledge of the reliability characteristics of electronic components such as transistors and resistors, and production methods such as soldering or fastening. The reliability data of individual components can be used to predict the reliability of the system at the design stage and help to evaluate alternative designs as to their ability to achieve Six Sigma performance levels. Systems of components may be configured in *series*, in *parallel*, or in some mixed combination. **Block diagrams**, which show the physical or logical relationships of components and subsystems, are useful ways to represent system configurations.

We first consider a **series system**, illustrated in Figure 8.13. In such a system, all components must function or the system will fail. If the reliability of component i is R_i, the reliability of the system is the product of the individual reliabilities, that is

$$R_S = R_1 R_2 \ldots R_n$$

This equation is based on the multiplicative law of probability. For example, suppose that a personal computer system is composed of the processing unit, modem, and printer with reliabilities of 0.997, 0.980, and 0.975, respectively. The reliability of the system is therefore given by

$$R_S = (0.997)(0.980)(0.975) = 0.953$$

Note that when reliabilities are less than one, system reliability decreases as additional components are added in series. Thus, the more complex a series system is, the greater the chance of failure.

FIGURE 8.13 SERIES SYSTEM

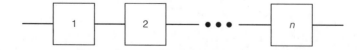

If the reliability function is exponential, for example, $R_i = e^{-\lambda_i T}$ then

$$R_S = e^{-\lambda_1 T} e^{-\lambda_2 T} \ldots e^{-\lambda_n T}$$

$$= e^{-\lambda_1 T - \lambda_2 T \ldots - \lambda_n T}$$

$$= e^{-\left(\sum\limits_{n-1}^{n} \lambda_i\right) T}$$

Suppose that a two-component series system has failure rates of 0.004 and 0.001 per hour. Then

$$R_S(T) = e^{-(0.004 + 0.001)T}$$

$$= e^{-0.005T}$$

The probability of survival for 100 hours would be

$$R_S(100) = e^{-0.005(100)}$$

$$= e^{-0.5}$$

$$= 0.6065$$

A parallel system is illustrated in Figure 8.14. In such a system, failure of an individual component is less critical than in series systems; the system will successfully operate as long as one component functions. Hence, the additional components are *redundant*. Redundancy is often built into systems to improve their reliability. However, as mentioned earlier, trade-offs in cost, size, weight, and so on must be taken into account.

The reliability of the parallel system in Figure 8.14 is derived as follows. If $R_1, R_2, \ldots, R_n$ are the reliabilities of the individual components, the probabilities of failure are $1 - R_1, 1 - R_2, \ldots, 1 - R_n$, respectively. Because the system fails only if each component fails, the probability of system failure is

$$(1 - R_1)(1 - R_2) \ldots (1 - R_n)$$

FIGURE 8.14 PARALLEL SYSTEM

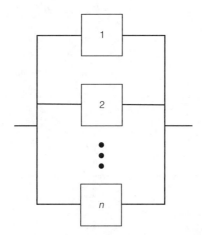

Hence, the system reliability is computed as

$$R_S = 1 - (1 - R_1)(1 - R_2) \ldots (1 - R_n)$$

If all components have identical reliabilities R, then

$$R_S = 1 - (1 - R)^n$$

The computers on the space shuttle were designed with built-in redundancy in case of failure. Five computers were designed in parallel. Thus, for example, if the reliability of each is 0.99, the system reliability is

$$R_S = 1 - (1 - 0.99)^5 = 0.9999999999$$

Most systems are composed of combinations of series and parallel systems. Consider the system shown in Figure 8.15(a). To determine the reliability of such a system, first compute the reliability of the parallel subsystem B:

$$R_B = 1 - (1 - 0.9)^3 = 0.999$$

This level of reliability is equivalent to replacing the three parallel components B with a single component B having a reliability of 0.999 in series with A, C, and D,

FIGURE 8.15   SERIES-PARALLEL SYSTEM AND EQUIVALENT PARALLEL SYSTEM EXAMPLE 1

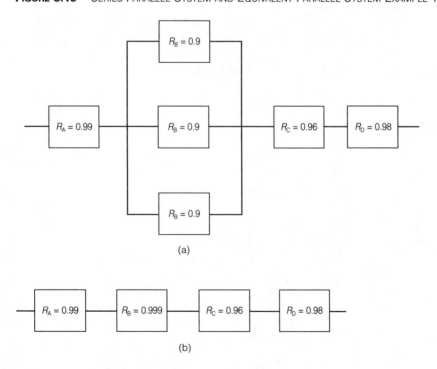

as shown in Figure 8.15(b). Next, compute the reliability of the equivalent series system:

$$R_S = (0.99)(0.999)(0.96)(0.98) = 0.93$$

A second type of series-parallel arrangement is shown in Figure 8.16(a). System reliability is determined by first computing the reliability of the series systems ABC and DE:

$$R_{ABC} = (0.95)(0.98)(0.99) = 0.92169$$
$$R_{DE} = (0.99)(0.97) = 0.9603$$

The result is an equivalent parallel system shown in Figure 8.16(b). The system reliability is then computed as

$$R_S = 1-(1-0.92169)(1-0.9603) = 0.9969$$

By appropriately decomposing complex systems into series and/or parallel components as shown in these examples, the system reliability can be easily computed. In DFSS, the designer may use these techniques to predict the performance of a particular design, and to evaluate the impacts of adding redundancy, substituting different components, or reconfiguring the design. This analysis helps to pinpoint weak areas and where improvements are needed.

FIGURE 8.16   SERIES-PARALLEL SYSTEM AND EQUIVALENT PARALLEL SYSTEM EXAMPLE 2

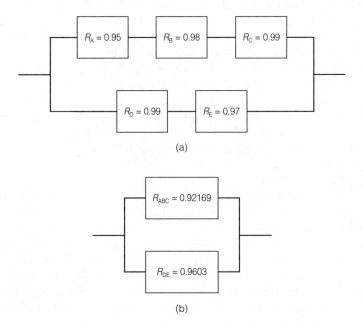

The PIVOT Initiative at Midwest Bank[8]

This case study is based on a real project; however the names and data are disguised to protect proprietary information.

Midwest, a bank holding company located in Ohio, provides a diverse line of banking and financial products and services regionally; and selected business activities are conducted nationally. Consumer, small business, and investment products and services are offered through a network of retail banking centers located primarily within Ohio and Kentucky. Midwest Bank also has a growing presence in Florida. Commercial banking products and services are offered through nine regional offices. Customers can also access this Midwest's financial and banking products and services 24 hours per day via its network of ATMs, a 24-hour telephone customer service center, or online. This bank has served the financial needs of its customers for 100 years, and currently 3,200 associates serve approximately 600,000 customers.

The PIVOT initiative, the name that Midwest gave its Six Sigma process improvement approach, started with the selection of three pilot projects, one of which was in the Commercial Processing Department (CPD) that works as Midwest Bank's cash vault. CPD already operated at a high level of sigma (4.26) as found early in Six Sigma training. CPD processes a high dollar volume of transactions. One costly error in the previous year resulted in a loss of over a quarter million dollars and brought the department to the forefront of change initiatives. Once the project was chosen, the bank selected six associates to run the first PIVOT project. A project coordinator working from the project office was selected as project manager for the Six Sigma functions of the project. An operations financial manager was in charge of financial impact analysis and equipment purchasing. The assistant vice president and team supervisor were subject matter experts from within CPD. Another project coordinator was brought on board for her bankwide knowledge and overall project support. The project analyst for CPD and five other areas was in charge of the departmental project management and was the Six Sigma analyst for the team. The Six Sigma analyst was responsible for data integrity, graphical analysis, and data stratification. After their weeklong Six Sigma course, the six team members ran the project from project definition to the control stage. The team followed the Six Sigma DMAIC process steps (Define, Measure, Analyze, Improve, Control) during the CPD PIVOT project to define the project and get it under way.

The senior vice president and vice president over CPD were the champions for this project and initially worked to establish the problem definition statement. These champions were responsible for the process every day and also held accountable for the errors in the department. Because the two largest potential sources of errors (strapping and deposit processing) did not influence each other in the process and had separate causes for creating errors, the champions separated them. The problem statement defined the number of errors the department was accountable for during the previous year and the dollar losses of these errors.

In this case study, the number of errors and the actual dollar losses are only approximate. The (disguised) problem statement was:

> In (the previous year) the number of internal and external defects for the CPD was 150, resulting in Bank losses of $400,000 as well as significant potential risk exposure. Included in the losses is an anomaly of $280,000. The remainder represents a gap of $120,000 versus the goal of $0 of total losses due to Commercial Processing Department operations. Our objective is to reduce the internal error ratio by December of the current year and the total amount of losses by over 50 percent in the following 12 months. Projects from this business case will reduce loss expense and risk exposure, while increasing customer satisfaction.

Much debate centered on whether to include the anomaly loss because it skewed the numbers considerably. However, the decision was finally made to include it. Support for the CPD PIVOT project centered on risk mitigation, which is difficult to quantify, and on dollar losses required to carry the project. Based on the potential reduction of approximately $400,000 in losses and the future risk mitigation, the steering committee approved the project launch, and the CPD PIVOT team moved onto the Measure stage.

The Measure stage demanded an intense data collection effort by the PIVOT team. They used a tool called an *XY matrix* (see example in Figure 8.17), designed to rank factors for potential error causes (Xs) and for customer outputs (Ys). The team gathered data and studied departmental process flows, seeking to find root causes of the problem, and to identify and agree on key CTQs that impact the customer. During the process, it was difficult for everyone, especially the subject matter experts (SMEs), to ignore their perceptions in speculating about possible causes of errors, which became known as "tribal knowledge." Six Sigma theory strongly discourages any attempt to let unproven assumptions creep into recommendations. All factors must be statistically proven through in-depth analysis to justify recommendations.

For CPD, the principal customer outputs selected were risk mitigation, error reduction, and reducing dollar loss, which were then stratified against potential error causes. The matrix was then used to calculate an overall ranking to guide the team toward the most probable causes of errors. After deciding to focus on the top seven potential causes, the CPD department's staff began the task of gathering data for each of them to verify their impact on errors in the process.

The Six Sigma analyst stratified the data collected across the potential error categories. During the Analysis stage, analysis of an extensive array of graphs developed from the data permitted the team to see trends in the process and to begin seeking strategic solutions. Construction of the graphs required more than 48 hours of team effort. Trends pointed to problems with the manual strapping process. However, the tribal knowledge suggested that errors were due to insufficient staffing, but the initial analysis of the data did not match this hypothesis. As a result, the team began to search for a way to prove or disprove the tribal knowledge.

It was suggested that the data were not properly stratified with regard to staffing and that analysis should be applied across a longer time frame. CPD set

FIGURE 8.17   EXAMPLE OF AN XY MATRIX

XY Matrix

Project: CDP Pivot

Output Variables (Ys)	Reduce Loss Potential	Mitigate Risk	Reduce Defects	Rank	% Rank
Output Rating	9	10	10		
Input Variables (Xs)	Association Table				
Customer Compliance	9	10	10	281	15.11%
Experience	10	10	9	280	15.05%
Manual Processes	10	9	10	280	15.05%
Human Factor	10	8	10	280	15.05%
Training	8	10	10	272	14.62%
Volume	9	9	10	271	14.57%
Interdepartmental Processing Flow	10	10	5	240	12.90%
Timeliness of Courier	3	5	8	157	8.44%
Timeliness Standards	3	3	9	147	7.90%
Staffing	5	3	6	135	7.26%
Theft	2	4	2	78	4.19%

out to collect more data from past months, and the Six Sigma analyst began developing the graphs needed to examine the new data. Over the next week, some 100 different graphs were created, depicting data in single strands and also paired with variables that interacted with one another. The team's Six Sigma training had emphasized the importance of *fully* exploring all data interactions, using graphs to illustrate relationships between variables. Despite the team's best efforts to find a relationship, staffing and volume did not appear to affect strapping errors. This finding disproved the tribal knowledge, while providing a multitude of additional graphs for analysis.

Strong correlations were seen in the graphs involving human factors and manual processes. CPD's processes called for numerous manual steps when handling cash. The graphs' trends suggested that whenever a manual process occurred, the number of errors increased, especially in the cash strapping area where, despite many years of experience, associates were making more than 100 errors each year. These errors caused the bank to lose thousands of dollars through miss-strapped cash. On the deposit side, manual errors created a much larger dollar loss per error. The one anomaly loss accounted for almost 280,000 dollars without any repercussions for the associate making the error. A manual process caused the error, but several team members felt that the overall attitude toward dollar errors was insufficient. Associates on the deposit side were far more concerned about quantity of deposit errors, than they were about the dollar losses from each error. These human factor elements began to cause the team great concern, because it was likely to be difficult to come to agreement on immediate solutions for such a complicated issue.

To further evaluate the process, the team decided to utilize an advanced Six Sigma tool called the failure modes and effects analysis (FMEA), seen in Figure 8.18. The FMEA paralleled the process map constructed in the Measure stage, but concentrated more on the inputs to the processes. Once the steps were laid out, the team brainstormed potential fallouts or errors from the process. Each of these errors was then charted until the potential effect of the individual problem was found. After the causes and effects were mapped out, each process step was then ranked on three categories: severity, occurrence, and detection, to create an overall ranking of potential failures (RPN) in the process and spearhead the team's efforts (see the example in Figure 8.18). The highest-ranking index of the team was strapping cash, with an RPN of 360. Of the top 10 potential errors, 77 percent involved human factors as the root cause of the problem. These issues focused the team on the need to alleviate the human interaction with the process, and especially on fixing strapping errors.

FIGURE 8.18   EXAMPLE FMEA SHOWING KEY PROCESS STEPS

#	Process Function (step)	Potential Failure Modes (process defects)	Potential Failure Effects (Ys)	SEV	Potential Causes of Failures (Xs)	OCC	Current Process Controls	DET	RPN	Recommended Actions	Responsible Person and Target Date	Taken Actions
2	Customer Makes Deposit	No deposit ticket	Deposited in wrong account	10	Human factor	3	Magnet verifies A/C# and name	8	180	Extensive customer ed. possible fee assessments	SMEs Sept.	
14	Check Deposits to Processing	Customer fraud	Bank takes loss	9	Bank takes loss	2	Currently verify payee/ systemic controls	10	180	Data collection concerning all deposited checks	SMEs	Verifying deposit ownership and check verify <15
24	Processor Verifies Deposit	Lost check	Bank takes loss	9	Human factor	2	Research and correct if possible	10	180	Dollar standard and dual control	Team 7/31/02	
31	Cash In Ticket/Ship Processing	Lost deposit	Bank takes loss	9	Human factor	1	Research and correct if possible	1	9	Explore possible upload w/FTP	Team 7/31/02	
33	Strap Cash	Lost cash	Bank takes loss	9	Human factor	4	Manual process	10	360	Automate process with a strapper	SME	Approval CBA submitted
51	Processing Completes Deposit	Miss post	Deposit delayed or bank loss	8	Human factor	4	Manual process	8	256	Explore possible upload w/FTP	Team 7/31/02	

FIGURE 8.19 COUNTERMEASURES TREE

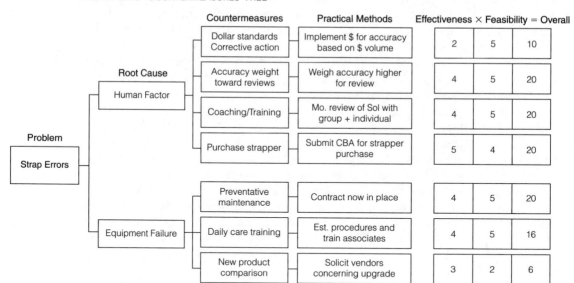

With statistically proven error causes available, the PIVOT team turned its attention to the Improve stage to develop corrective actions. One of the most beneficial tools used to find solutions to error causes was the *Countermeasures Matrix*. A portion of this matrix is shown in the form of the Countermeasures Tree Diagram in Figure 8.19. This diagram helped the team organize potential solutions to the most risky issues and to ensure that root causes were effectively addressed. The diagram categorized the proposed solutions by effectiveness and feasibility on a scale of 1 to 5, based on team opinion, statistical information, and cost estimates. Some of the solutions emerged in earlier stages of the process, while others came after intense scrutiny. After two or three potential solutions were identified for each root cause, the team disbanded to conduct individual research on the feasibility and effectiveness of each solution. These activities included bringing in vendors, visiting other cash vaults around the city, and researching literature and online sources. Five major countermeasures were recommended as part of the total package of seven recommendations to eliminate strapping errors, and 14 recommendations concerning deposit errors. The five were:

1. Purchase a cash strapping machine.
2. Assess a $5 charge to the clients for incorrect deposits.
3. Eliminate double keying of deposits in both CPD and Processing departments.
4. Implement a new vacation scheduling system for deposit processing associates to reduce the number of errors attributable to inexperienced personnel on the job.
5. Implement a dollar loss corrective action program to discourage associates from making large dollar errors in CPD's deposit section.

The potential advantages and barriers for each countermeasure are shown in Figure 8.20. None of them were likely to provide a perfect solution to the

FIGURE 8.20   COUNTERMEASURES SELECTION AND CONTROL

Countermeasure	Potential Advantage	Potential Barrier	Cost	Result
Purchase strapping machine	Eliminate 98.2% of strapping errors with 99.95% accuracy	Cost	Very high purchase cost	• Delayed in finding vendor • Currently only handles $20 bills
Assess $5 customer charge for incorrect deposits	Reduce 44% of deposit errors	Loss of customers	• Low out of pocket • Hard to quantify customer impact	After quantified risky study, has been implemented, with some concerns
Eliminate double keying of deposits	Reduce deposit data entry errors by 24%	IT must confirm current system can handle increased volumes	Moderate, $5,000	Await testing
New vacation schedule policy	Reduce the 79% of deposit errors when experienced associates on vacation	Employee dissatisfaction	No out of pocket cost	Implemented policy for one associate per group to be on vacation at a time
Dollar loss corrective action for associates	Reduce the magnitude of dollar losses, not just volume, in deposit sections	Supervisor and employee dissatisfaction	No out of pocket cost	Implemented policy based on similar branch bank policy

problem, but each could contribute substantially to meeting the goals of the project. The CPD PIVOT team started out slowly in the Control stage as many solutions were left to the subject matter experts to implement while some of the minor solutions were immediately implemented into daily CPD processes. Some of the recommended improvements were easy to sell and showed immediate results, while others were extremely difficult. A pilot study of the $5 charge for incorrect deposits showed promise for substantially reducing the 44 percent of deposit errors attributable to improper deposit preparation by large corporate clients. The large anomaly deposit loss had been due to an improperly completed deposit ticket.

The most difficult recommendation to handle was number 5. After the team began falling behind on execution of solutions, it took some negotiation between the champions and the department head to regain momentum in implementing countermeasures for the project. The corrective action plan for dollar losses mirrored the branch plan, as it was introduced to CPD associates. Its success had not been accurately measured.

The project has had a significant impact on errors within the department. Some of the solutions have proved to be effective. Overall errors are down by 30 percent. Although this percentage does not perfectly match the goal, several solutions are still in their infancy, with a strong potential for that number to be further reduced. The second metric involved dollar losses that the bank incurred. Dollar losses plummeted 57 percent from the same period last year. In a dollar-focused environment, these solutions proved to be essential to the survival of the business and a drive toward increased competitiveness within the banking market.

REVIEW QUESTIONS

1. What is Design for Six Sigma? Explain the four basic elements of DFSS and the various tools and methodologies that comprise this body of knowledge.
2. What are the principal benefits of quality function deployment (QFD)?
3. Outline the process of building the House of Quality for QFD. What departments and functions within the company should be involved in each step of the process?
4. Explain concept engineering. Why is it an important tool for assuring quality in product and process design activities?
5. Explain the difference between nominal dimensions and tolerances. How should tolerances be realistically set?
6. What is design failure mode and effects analysis (DFMEA)? Provide a simple example illustrating the concept.
7. How can product design affect manufacturability? Explain the concept and importance of design for manufacturability.
8. What is the importance of reliability and why has it become such a prominent area within the quality disciplines?
9. Explain the product life characteristics curve and how it can be used.
10. Define reliability. Explain the definition thoroughly.
11. What is the difference between a functional failure and a reliability failure?
12. What is the definition of failure rate? How is it measured?
13. Explain the differences and relationships between the cumulative failure rate curve and the failure rate curve.
14. How is the average failure rate over a time interval computed?
15. What is a reliability function? Discuss different ways of expressing this function.
16. Explain how to compute the reliability of series, parallel, and series-parallel systems.

DISCUSSION QUESTIONS

1. What factors in the Midwest Bank case do you think weighed in on the decision to include the $280,000 "anomoly" in the project justification? If you were the project champion, how would you assess this justification in deciding whether the project was significant enough to move forward?
2. In the case, how difficult did it appear to be to find the "root cause" of the errors? What do you think contributed to the difficulty?
3. What types of quantitative analysis would need to be done in order to justify the implementation of the case's five major recommendations?
4. For which of the adopted changes in the case would it be most difficult to "hold the gains"? Why?

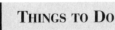

THINGS TO DO

1. Using whatever "market research" techniques are appropriate, define a set of customer attributes for:
    a. Purchasing books at your college bookstore
    b. A college registration process
    c. A hotel room used for business
    d. A hotel room used for family leisure vacations
    For each case, determine a set of technical requirements and construct the relationship matrix for the House of Quality.

2. (This exercise would best be performed in a group.) Suppose that you were developing a small pizza restaurant with a dining area and local delivery. Develop a list of customer requirements and technical requirements and try to complete a House of Quality. What service standards might such an operation have?

3. Most children (and many adults) like to assemble and fly balsa-wood gliders. From your own experiences or from interviews with other students, define a set of customer requirements for a good glider. (Even better, buy one and test it to determine these requirements yourself.) If you were to design and manufacture such a product, how would you define a set of technical requirements for the design? Using your results, construct a relationship matrix for a House of Quality.

4. Fill in the relationship matrix below (Figure 8.21) of a House of Quality for a screwdriver. By sampling your classmates, develop priorities for the customer attributes and use these and the relationships to identify key technical requirements to deploy.

FIGURE 8.21 SCREWDRIVER MATRIX

	Price	Interchangeable bits	Steel shaft	Rubber grip	Ratchet capability	Plastic handle
Easy to use						
Does not rust						
Durable						
Comfortable						
Versatile						
Inexpensive						
Priority						

5. Discuss and prepare a report with examples on how DFMEA might be used in a service application rather than in a pure product design application.

PROBLEMS

1. Bob's Big Burgers conducted consumer surveys and focus groups and identified the most important customer expectations as
   • Healthy food
   • Speedy service
   • An easy-to-read menu board
   • Accurate order filling
   • Perceived value

   Develop a set of technical requirements to incorporate into the design of a new facility and a House of Quality relationship matrix to assess how well your requirements address these expectations. Refine your design as necessary, based on the initial assessment.

2. Bob's Big Burgers (problem 1) acquired some additional information. It found that consumers placed the highest importance on healthy food, followed by value, followed by order accuracy and service. The menu board was only casually noted as an important attribute in the surveys. Bob faces three major competitors in this market: Grabby's, Queenburger, and Sandy's. Studies of their products yielded the information shown in Table 8.4. Results of the consumer panel ratings for each of these competitors are shown in Table 8.5 (a 1–5 scale, with 5 being the best). Using this information, modify and extend your House of Quality from problem 1 and develop a deployment plan for a new burger. On what attributes should the company focus its marketing efforts?

TABLE 8.4 COMPETITORS' PRODUCT INFORMATION

Company	Price	Size (oz.)	Calories	Sodium (mg)	Fat (%)
Grabby's	1.55	5.5	440	75	13
Queenburger	2.25	7.5	640	95	23
Sandy's	1.75	6.0	540	80	16

TABLE 8.5 CONSUMER PANEL RATINGS

Attribute	Grabby's	Queenburger	Sandy's
Menu board	4	4	5
Order accuracy	4	5	3
Healthy food	4	2	3
Speedy service	3	5	4
Taste appeal	2	4	3
Visual appeal	3	4	3
Value	5	3	4

3.   Fingerspring, Inc., is working on a design for a new personal digital assistant. They surveyed potential customers to determine the characteristics that the customers want and expect in a PDA. Fingerspring's studies have identified the most important customer expectations as
a. Initial cost
b. Reliability
c. Ease of use
d. Features
e. Operating cost
f. Compactness

Develop a set of technical requirements to incorporate into the design of a House of Quality relationship matrix to assess how well your requirements address these expectations. Refine your design as necessary, based on the initial assessment.

4.   Fingerspring, Inc. (problem 3), faces three major competitors in this market: Harespring, Springbok, and Greenspring. It found that potential consumers placed the highest importance on reliability (measured by such things as freedom from operating system crashes and battery life), followed by compactness (weight/bulkiness), followed by flexibility (features, ease of use, and types of program modules available). The operating cost was only occasionally noted as an important attribute in the surveys. Studies of their products yielded the information shown in Table 8.6. Results of the consumer panel ratings for these competitors are shown in Table 8.7 (a 1–5 scale, with 5 being

TABLE 8.6   COMPETITORS' PRODUCT INFORMATION

Company	Price	Wt. (oz.)	Size (In.)	Features	Operating Program	Battery life (hrs)	Opr. Cpsts (Batt./Prg/)
Harespring	575	4.0	4.8 × 3.2	15	PalmOS*	50	High
Springbok	195	7.5	5.1 × 3.3	9	Hardmark*	12	Low
Greenspring	450	8.8	5.3 × 3.3	12	Easyware**	25	Moderately high

Note: PalmOS® is one of the most recognized operating software programs for PDAs.
 * New unproven software, unique to Springbok
 ** Well-received proprietary software, used on many PDAs several years

TABLE 8.7   CONSUMER PANEL RATINGS

Attribute	Harespring	Springbok	Greenspring
Initial cost	3	5	4
Reliability	5	2	3
Ease of use	4	1	3
Features	4	2	3
Operating cost	5	3	4
Weight	5	3	3
Size	4	4	4

FIGURE 8.22 CUMULATIVE FAILURE CURVE

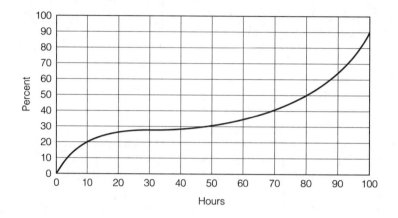

the best). Using this information, modify and extend your House of Quality from Problem 3 and develop a deployment plan for a new PDA. On what attributes should the company focus its marketing efforts?

5. Given the cumulative failure curve in Figure 8.22, sketch the failure rate curve.

6. Compute the average failure rate during the intervals 0 to 30, 30 to 60, and 60 to 90, and 0 to 100, based on the information in Figure 8.22.

7. The life of a watch battery is normally distributed with a mean of 1,000 days and standard deviation of 60 days.
   a. What fraction of batteries is expected to survive beyond 1,100 days?
   b. What fraction will survive fewer than 880 days?
   c. Sketch the reliability function.
   d. What length of warranty is needed so that no more than 10 percent of the batteries will be expected to fail during the warranty period?

8. Lifetred, Inc., makes automobile tires that have a mean life of 50,000 miles with a standard deviation of 3,000 miles.
   a. What fraction of tires is expected to survive beyond 56,000 miles?
   b. What fraction will survive fewer than 47,000 miles?
   c. Sketch the reliability function.
   d. What length of warranty is needed so that no more than 10 percent of the tires will be expected to fail during the warranty period?

9. Compute the failure rate for six transformers that were tested for 600 hours each, three of which failed after 100, 175, and 350 hours.

10. Assuming an exponential distribution, a particular light bulb has a failure rate of 0.002 units per hour. What is the probability of failure within 400 hours? What is the reliability function?

11. The MTBF of a circuit is 1,200 hours. Calculate the failure rate.

12. An electronic missile guidance system consists of the following components:

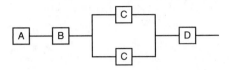

Components A, B, C, and D have reliabilities of 0.96, 0.98, 0.90, and 0.99, respectively. What is the reliability of the entire system?

13. A manufacturer of portable radios purchases major electronic components as modules. The reliabilities of components differ by supplier. Suppose that the configuration of the major components is given by:

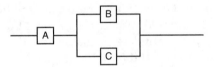

The components can be purchased from three different suppliers. The reliabilities of the components are as follows:

Component	Supplier 1	Supplier 2	Supplier 3
A	0.95	0.92	0.94
B	0.80	0.86	0.90
C	0.90	0.93	0.85

Transportation and purchasing considerations require that only one supplier be chosen. Which one should be selected if the radio is to have the highest possible reliability?

14. In a complex manufacturing process, three operations are performed in series. Because of the nature of the process, machines frequently fall out of adjustment and must be repaired. To keep the system going, two identical machines are used at each stage; thus, if one fails, the other can be used while the first is repaired (see figure, below).

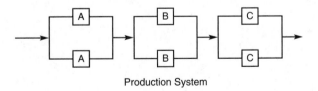

Production System

The reliabilities of the machines are as follows:

Machine	Reliability
A	0.80
B	0.90
C	0.98

a. Analyze the system reliability, assuming only one machine at each stage.

b. How much is the reliability improved by having two machines at each stage?

15. An automated production system consists of three operations: turning, milling, and grinding. Individual parts are transferred from one operation to the next by a robot. Hence, if one machine or the robot fails, the process stops.

a. If the reliabilities of the robot, turning center, milling machine, and grinder are 0.98, 0.94, 0.98, and 0.90, respectively, what is the reliability of the system?

b. Suppose that two grinders are available and the system does not stop if one fails. What is the reliability of the system?

ENDNOTES

1. This definition is adapted from Maurice L. Berryman, "DFSS and Big Payoffs," *Six Sigma Forum Magazine* 2, no. 1, November 2002, 23–28.

2. Charles Humber and Robert Launsby, "Straight Talk on DFSS," *Six Sigma Forum Magazine* 1, no. 4, August 2002.

3. Joseph A. De Feo and William W. Barnard, *Juran Institute's Six Sigma Breakthrough and Beyond* (New York: McGraw-Hill, 2004).

4. C. M. Creveling, J. L. Slutsky, and D. Antis, Jr., *Design for Six Sigma in Technology and Product Development* (Upper Saddle River, NJ: Prentice Hall, 2003).

5. Christina Hepner Brodie, "A Polaroid Notebook: Concept Engineering," *Center for Quality of Management Journal* 3, no. 2, 1994, 7–14.

6. Laura Horton and David Boger, "How Bose Corporation Applied Concept Engineering to a Service," *Center for Quality Management Journal*, 3, no. 2, 1994, 52–59.

7. Jennifer Reese, "Starbucks: Inside the Coffee Cult," *Fortune*, December 9, 1996, 190–200.

8. Appreciation is expressed to one of the author's students, Michael Wolf, who wrote the paper on which this case is based, as part of the requirements for MGT 699, Total Quality Management, 2002, at Northern Kentucky University, and Cathy Ernst, senior vice president at the bank.

CHAPTER

9

Design for Six Sigma—Optimization and Verification

DESIGN OPTIMIZATION AND VERIFICATION

Designers of products and processes should make every effort to optimize their designs. From a Six Sigma perspective and the fundamental equation $Y = f(X)$, this corresponds to finding the set of critical Xs that have the most significant effect on the response variable Y, and their best levels to optimize the performance. A good analogy for understanding this concept is to consider the task of a major league baseball manager who must design the best player lineup and pitching rotation. Although variation will be a factor among individuals as well as with the opposing team's defense, the manager would like to set the lineup that best plays to their strengths and overcomes their weaknesses. A second objective of designers is to design products and processes to be **robust**—that is, insensitive to variations in manufacturing or the use environment.

Many tools exist to facilitate design optimization. Some of the more useful approaches are the Taguchi methods and design of experiments, which we present in this chapter. We will also discuss some approaches for optimizing reliability.

The final phase of DFSS is verification of product and process designs. Design verification is necessary to ensure that designs will meet customer requirements and can be produced to specifications. Sometimes verification is required by government regulations or for legal concerns. For products, reliability evaluation provides a means for obtaining data about product performance as both a verification approach and a means for design improvement. Verifying measurement systems and the capability of processes to meet specifications are also important in achieving Six Sigma performance.

DESIGN OF EXPERIMENTS

Design of experiments (DOE), developed by R. A. Fisher in England, dates back to the 1920s. A designed experiment is a test or series of tests that enables the experimenter to compare two or more methods to determine which is better, or determine levels of controllable factors to optimize the yield of a process or minimize the variability of a response variable.[1] For example, a paint company might be interested in determining whether different additives have an effect on the drying time of paint in order to select the additive that results in the shortest drying time. As another example, suppose that two machines produce the same part. The material used in processing can be loaded onto the machines either manually or with an automatic device. The experimenter might wish to determine whether the type of machine and the type of loading process affect the number of defectives and then to select the machine type and loading process combination that minimizes the number of defectives.

As a practical tool for quality improvement, experimental design methods have achieved considerable success in many industries. In a celebrated case, Ina Tile Company, a Japanese ceramic tile manufacturer, had purchased a $2 million kiln from West Germany in 1953.[2] Tiles were stacked inside the kiln and baked. Tiles toward the outside of the stack tended to have a different average size and more variation in dimensions than those further inside the stack. The obvious cause was the uneven temperatures inside the kiln. Temperature was an uncontrollable factor, a noise factor. To try to eliminate the effects of temperature would require redesign of the kiln itself, a very costly alternative. A group of engineers, chemists, and others who were familiar with the manufacturing process brainstormed and identified seven major controllable variables that could affect the tile dimensions:

1. Limestone content
2. Fineness of additive
3. Content of agalmatolite
4. Type of agalmatolite
5. Raw material quantity
6. Content of waste return
7. Content of feldspar

The group designed and conducted an experiment using these factors. The experiment showed that the first factor, the limestone content, was the most significant factor; the other factors had smaller effects. By increasing the limestone content from 1 percent to 5 percent and choosing better levels for other factors, the percentage of size defects was reduced from 30 percent to less than 1 percent. Limestone was the cheapest material in the tile. In addition, the experiment revealed that a smaller amount of agalmatolite, the most expensive material in the tile, could be used without adversely affecting the tile dimension. Both the effect of the noise factor and the cost of the product were reduced at the same time! This discovery was a breakthrough in the ceramic tile industry.

As another example, ITT Avionics Division, a leading producer of electronic warfare systems, experienced a high defect rate when using a wave solder machine to solder assemblies on printed circuit boards.[3] The wave solder machine, developed to eliminate hand soldering, transports printed circuit boards through a wave of solder under computer control. A brainstorming session identified 14 process variables. From three sets of designed experiments, the subsequent data resulted in decisions that lowered the defect rate from 7 or 8 to 1.5 per board. With 2,500 solder connections per board, this translated to a defect rate of 600 defects per million connections.

Historically, experimental design was not widely used in industrial quality improvement studies because engineers had trouble working with the large number of variables and their interactions on many different levels in industrial problems. However, improved computer software and more sophisticated training have recently made experimental design an important tool for Six Sigma.

Factorial Experiments

One of the most common types of experimental designs is called a **factorial experiment**. In a factorial experiment, all combinations of levels of each factor (the X variables) are considered. For example, suppose that temperature and reaction time are identified as important factors in the yield of a chemical process. If the experiment is designed to analyze the effect of two levels of each factor (for instance, temperature at 100 and 120 degrees, and time at 60 and 75 minutes), then there would be $2^2 = 4$ possible combinations to test:

Temperature	Time
100 degrees	60 minutes
100 degrees	75 minutes
120 degrees	60 minutes
120 degrees	75 minutes

In general, an experiment with m factors at k levels would have k^m combinations. Each combination should be performed in a random fashion to eliminate any potential systematic bias.

The purpose of a factorial experiment is to estimate the effects of each factor. For instance, what is the effect of a 20-degree change in temperature? Of a 15-minute change in reaction time? These questions are answered easily by finding the differences of the averages at each level. For instance, suppose we obtained the following results:

Temperature	Time	Yield (%)
100 degrees	60 minutes	85
100 degrees	75 minutes	88
120 degrees	60 minutes	90
120 degrees	75 minutes	80

The average yield for a temperature of 100 degrees is $(85 + 88)/2 = 86.5$. The average yield for a temperature of 120 degrees is $(80 + 90)/2 = 85$. Thus, the average difference in yield from increasing the temperature from 100 to 120 degrees is $85 - 86.5 = -1.5$ percent. Similarly, the average difference in increasing the time from 60 to 75 minutes is $(88 + 80)/2 - (85 + 90)/2 = 84 - 87.5 = -3.5$ percent. These differences—how the changes in the level of one factor affect the response—are called *main effects*. Thus, we might conclude that increasing temperature or time decreases the yield of the process.

However, in many situations, the effect of changing one factor depends on the level of other factors. For example, the effect of temperature may depend on the reaction time. In this example, we see that if the temperature is held constant at 100 degrees, an increase in reaction time results in a higher yield. However, when the temperature is 120 degrees, an increase in reaction time decreases the yield. This *interaction* is easy to determine by graphing the results as shown in Figure 9.1. If the lines are nearly parallel, then no interaction exists. In this case, we see an interaction. We may quantify the interaction by taking the average of difference of the yield when the temperature is increased from 100 to 120 degrees at a constant reaction time of 60, and subtracting the average of difference of the yield when the temperature is increased from 100 to 120 degrees at a constant reaction time of 75:

Temperature $\times$ Time Interaction $= (90 - 85)/2 - (80 - 88)/2 = 6.5$ percent

The closer this quantity is to zero, the smaller the interaction effect. In this case, a significant interaction is apparent. When interactions are present, main effects have little meaning; individual factors must be interpreted relative to levels of the other factors. We see that higher temperature and lower time appear to optimize the yield.

FIGURE 9.1   INTERACTION EFFECTS

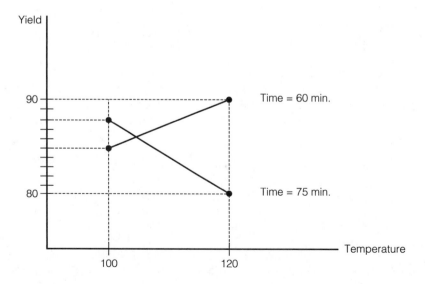

TAGUCHI METHODS FOR ROBUST DESIGN

Classical design of experiments can require many, often costly, experimental runs to estimate all main effects and interactions. A Japanese engineer, Dr. Genichi Taguchi, proposed another approach to DOE. He developed an approach to designing experiments that focused on the critical factors while deemphasizing their interactions, which greatly reduced the number of required experiments. However, Taguchi's approach violates some traditional statistical principles and has been criticized by the statistical community. Despite the controversy regarding statistical theory, numerous companies have used Taguchi's approaches effectively.

Taguchi's approach focuses on optimizing design parameters to reduce the variability caused by manufacturing variations. In most industrial processes, controlling variability is much harder than controlling the average value. Taguchi categorizes variables that affect product performance according to whether they are design parameters or sources of noise. Design parameters are simply the nominal dimensions chosen by the designer. Classical DOE focuses on these parameters. Sources of noise include all those variables that cause performance to deviate from target values. Taguchi's approach includes and systematically varies noise factors in a designed experiment.

A principal objective of a Taguchi experiment is to identify settings of the design parameters at which the effect of the noise factors on the response variable is at a minimum. This minimum effect is determined by systematically varying the settings of the design parameters in the experiment and comparing the results in the same fashion as is done with classical DOE. Other objectives include identifying design parameters that influence the mean value of the response variable but have no effect on its variation (these can be set at their optimum values), and identifying those parameters that have no detectable influence on the response variables (tolerances on these can be relaxed, thus improving Six Sigma performance).

One metric that Taguchi methods use is the **signal-to-noise (S/N) ratio**. This ratio measures the sensitivity of the effect (signal) to the noise factors. The signal is measured by the mean value, while the noise factors are measured by the standard deviation of the response variable. Thus, the S/N ratio essentially is the ratio of the mean to the standard deviation (in statistics, this is the reciprocal of the coefficient of variation). High S/N ratios mean that the sensitivity to noise factors is low. For example, the signal for a package delivery service might be on-time delivery of an undamaged package to its destination. Noise that might cause variations in the expected delivery time might include internal errors resulting in misrouted, damaged, or incorrectly coded packages. External noise might result from incomplete addresses furnished by the sender, weather-related delays, or aircraft breakdowns. By reducing the noise factors—the variability—the S/N ratio will clearly improve.

Setting Tolerances with the Taguchi Loss Function

Taguchi also maintained that the traditional concept of specification limits is inherently flawed. For example, suppose that a specification for some quality

FIGURE 9.2 TRADITIONAL ECONOMIC VIEW OF CONFORMANCE TO SPECIFICATIONS

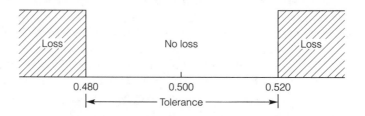

characteristic is 0.500 ± 0.020. Using this definition, the actual value of the quality characteristic can fall anywhere in a range from 0.480 to 0.520. This approach assumes that the customer, either the consumer or the next department in the production process, would accept any value within the 0.480 to 0.520 range, but not be satisfied with a value outside this tolerance range. Also, this approach assumes that costs do not depend on the actual value of the quality characteristic as long as it falls within the tolerance specified (see Figure 9.2).

But what is the real difference between 0.479 and 0.481? The former would be considered as "out of specification" and either reworked or scrapped while the latter would be acceptable. Actually, the impact of either value on the performance characteristic of the product would be about the same. Neither value is close to the nominal specification 0.500. The nominal specification is the ideal target value for the critical quality characteristic. Taguchi's approach assumes that the smaller the variation about the nominal specification, the better is the quality. In turn, products are more consistent, and total costs are lower.

All too often, tolerance settings fail to account for the impact of variation on product functionality, manufacturability, or economic consequences. In a review of Audi's TT Coupe when it was first introduced, automobile columnist Alan Vonderhaar noted, "There was apparently some problem with the second-gear synchronizer, a device that is supposed to ease shifts. As a result, on full-power upshifts from first to second, I frequently got gear clashes." He observed others with the same problem from Internet newsgroups and concluded, "It appears to be an issue that surfaces just now and again, here and there throughout the production mix, suggesting it may be a tolerance issue—sometimes the associated parts are close enough to specifications to get along well, other times they're at the outer ranges of manufacturing tolerance and cause problems."[4] Thus, optimal performance of a product requires design parameters to be at their nominal, or target, settings.

These insights form the basis for tolerance design optimization. Taguchi measures quality as the variation from the target value of a design specification, and then translates that variation into an economic "loss function" that expresses the cost of variation in monetary terms. Taguchi postulates that losses can be approximated by a quadratic function so that larger deviations from target correspond to increasingly larger losses. For the case in which a specific target value,

FIGURE 9.3 NOMINAL-IS-BEST LOSS FUNCTION

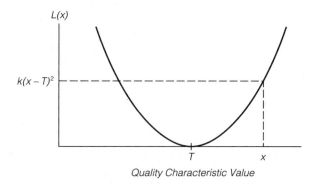

Quality Characteristic Value

T, is determined to produce the optimum performance, and in which quality deteriorates as the actual value moves away from the target on either side (called "nominal is best"), the loss function is represented by

$$L(x) = k(x - T)^2$$

where x is any actual value of the quality characteristic and k is some constant. Thus, $(x - T)$ represents the deviation from the target, and the loss increases by the square of the deviation. Figure 9.3 illustrates this function.

The constant k is estimated by determining the cost associated with a certain deviation from the target, as the following example illustrates. Assume that a certain quality characteristic has a specification of 0.500 ± 0.020. An analysis of company records reveals that if the value of the quality characteristic exceeds the target of 0.500 by the tolerance of 0.020 on either side, the product is likely to require an adjustment during the warranty period and cost \$50 for repair. Then,

$$50 = k(0.020)^2$$
$$k = 50/0.0004 = 125{,}000$$

Therefore, the loss function is $L(x) = 125{,}000(x - T)^2$. If the deviation is only 0.010, the estimated loss is $L(0.010) = 125{,}000(0.010)^2 = \$12.50$.

If the distribution of the variation about the target value is known, the average loss per unit can be computed by statistically averaging the loss associated with possible values of the quality characteristic. In statistical terminology, this average loss per unit is simply the expected value of the loss. To keep the mathematics simple, consider the following example.

Suppose that two processes, A and B, have the following distributions of a quality characteristic with specification 0.50 ± 0.02. In process A, the output of the process has values ranging from 0.48 to 0.52, all of which are equally likely. For process B, 60 percent of the output is expected to have a value of 0.50, 15 percent has a value of 0.49, and so

Value	Process A Probability	Process B Probability
0.47	0	0.02
0.48	0.20	0.03
0.49	0.20	0.15
0.50	0.20	0.60
0.51	0.20	0.15
0.52	0.20	0.03
0.53	0	0.02

Notice that the output from process A is spread equally over the range from 0.48 to 0.52 and lies entirely within specifications. In process B, output is concentrated near the target value, but does not entirely lie within specifications. Using the loss function

$$L(x) = 125{,}000 \, (x - 0.50)^2$$

the expected loss for each process can be computed as follows:

Value, x	Loss	Process A Probability	Weighted Loss	Process B Probability	Weighted Loss
0.47	112.5	0.00	0	0.02	2.25
0.48	50.0	0.20	10	0.03	1.50
0.49	12.5	0.20	2.5	0.15	1.875
0.50	0.0	0.20	0	0.60	0
0.51	12.5	0.20	2.5	0.15	1.875
0.52	50.0	0.20	10	0.03	1.50
0.53	112.5	0.00	0	0.02	2.25
		Expected loss	25.0		11.25

Clearly process B incurs a smaller total expected loss even though some output falls outside specifications. The expected loss is computed using a simple formula that involves the variance of the quality characteristic, σ^2, and the square of the deviation of the mean value from the target $D^2 = (\bar{x}-T)^2$. The expected loss is $EL(x) = k(\sigma^2 + D^2)$.

For instance, in process A, the variance of the quality characteristic is 0.0002 and $D^2 = 0$ because the mean value is equal to the target. Thus,

$$EL(x) = 125{,}000 \, (0.0002 + 0) = 25$$

A similar computation can be used to determine the expected loss for process B.

The expected loss provides a measure of variation that is independent of specification limits. Such a measure stresses continuous improvement rather than acceptance of the status quo simply because a product "conforms to specifications."

Not all quality characteristics have nominal targets with tolerances on either side. In some cases, such as impurities in a chemical process or fuel consumption, "smaller is better." In other cases, "larger is better" as with breaking strength or product life. The loss function for the smaller-is-better case is

$$L(x) = kx^2$$

and for the larger-is-better case is

$$L(x) = k(1/x^2)$$

These formulas can be applied in a manner similar to the previous examples.

The following example shows how the Taguchi loss function may be used to set tolerances. The desired speed of a cassette tape is 1.875 inches per second. Any deviation from this value causes a change in pitch and tempo and thus poor sound quality. Suppose that adjusting the tape speed under warranty when a customer complains and returns a cassette player costs a manufacturer $20. (This repair expense does not include other costs due to customer dissatisfaction and therefore is at best a lower bound on the actual loss.) Based on past information, the company knows the average customer will return a player if the tape speed is off the target by at least 0.15 inch per second. The loss function constant is computed as

$$20 = k(0.15)^2$$
$$k = 888.9$$

and thus the loss function is $L(x) = 888.9(x - 1.875)^2$. At the factory, the adjustment can be made at a much lower cost of $3, which consists of the labor to make the adjustment and additional testing. What should the tolerance be before an adjustment is made at the factory?

To use the loss function, set $L(x) = \$3$ and solve for the tolerance:

$$3 = 888.9 \text{ (one-half tolerance)}^2$$
$$\text{tolerance} = \pm\sqrt{3/888.9} = \pm 0.058$$

Therefore, if the tape speed is off by more than 0.058 inches per second, adjusting it at the factory is more economical. Thus, the specifications should be 1.875 ± 0.058 or 1.817 to 1.933.

DESIGN FOR RELIABILITY

As a fundamental dimension of quality, reliability must be *designed* into a product. The performance characteristics, operating conditions, and performance duration specified for the product or system drive the technical design. Variations in product performance arise because of the way it is used or because of environmental conditions. Changes take place over time because of chemical changes in components, vibration and stress, or expansion and contraction of materials due to fluctuations in temperature or humidity, for example. Sooner or later, products fail. Although consumers would like products to be 100 percent reliable, creating products that have perfect reliability under all conditions is impractical, if not impossible. The question is not whether a product will fail, but when. Designers must decide to what extent failure is acceptable and establish specifications for reliability.

High reliability results in lower costs to society in the context of Taguchi's loss function. To achieve high reliability, better materials and more precise manufacturing processes must be used. These improvements will increase manufacturing costs to the point that consumers are unwilling to pay the price. Thus, management must balance the economic factors and seek to minimize total cost, keeping in mind that too low reliability may damage the firm's reputation and result in lost sales or product liability suits. Such decisions must be addressed strategically in the context of DFSS.

Consumers will not always use a product correctly or follow suggested maintenance procedures. Designers must account for operating errors that will result in failure, and they must maintain safety when failure does occur. Fail-safe designs provide safety in the event of failure. An example is a railway signal that turns red when a failure occurs. Foolproof designs prevent operation in the event of an operating error, thus avoiding failure. An example is a temperature control that prevents overheating by not allowing a heating switch to be closed without prior closure of a fan switch.

Whatever is done in the manufacturing process can and does have an effect on the reliability of the final product sold to customers. To manufacture reliable products from good designs, companies must use good materials, well-maintained machines, and trained workers. The greater the capability of a process to conform to design specifications and targets, the more likely it is that the product will have high reliability. Preventive maintenance in manufacturing is crucial to equipment reliability.

Manufacturing, marketing, and financial managers must work together to ensure adequate time, schedules, and budgets for preventive maintenance activities. Operations control strategies such as just-in-time, the use of inspection, and statistical process control all contribute to the achievement of reliability objectives. Packaging and transportation cannot be neglected. Poor protection and handling can adversely affect the reliability of the product when it reaches the customer. Denton relates a situation in which one company inadvertently packed a half-full load of computers in a 40-foot truck.[5] The boxes dropped from 12-feet high and tumbled around inside the truck from South Carolina to Boston. The cartons were demolished and all the computers were believed to be destroyed. However, not one computer was damaged because of the careful attention to and testing of packaging.

Many techniques are used to improve designs and optimize the reliability of products. These include:

- *Standardization.* One method of ensuring high reliability is to use components with proven track records of reliability over years of actual use. If failure rates of components can be established, then standard components can be selected and used in the design process. The use of standardized components not only achieves higher reliability, but also reduces costs because standardized components are used in many different products.

- *Redundancy.* Redundancy provides backup components that can be used when the failure of any one component in a system can cause a failure of the entire system. The section on reliability prediction provided examples of how redundant components can increase reliability dramatically. Redundant components are designed either in a standby configuration or a parallel configuration. In a *standby system*, the standby unit is switched in when the operating unit fails; in the *parallel configuratio*n, both units operate normally but only one is required for proper functioning. Redundancy is crucial to systems in which failures can be extremely costly, such as aircraft or satellite communications systems. Redundancy, however, increases the cost, size, and weight of the system. Therefore, designers must trade off these attributes against increased reliability.
- *Physics of failure.* Many failures are due to deterioration because of chemical reactions over time, which may be aggravated by temperature or humidity effects. Understanding the physical properties of materials and their response to environmental effects helps to eliminate potential failures or to make the product robust with respect to environmental conditions that affect reliability. Reliability engineers must work closely with chemists, materials science engineers, and others who can contribute to a better understanding of failure mechanisms.

RELIABILITY EVALUATION

The reliability of a product is determined principally by the design and the reliability of the components of the product. However, reliability is such a complex issue that it cannot always be determined from theoretical analysis of the design alone. Hence, formal evaluation and testing for design verification are necessary, which involve simulating environmental conditions to determine a product's performance, operating time, and mode of failure.

Testing is useful for a variety of other reasons. Test data are often necessary for liability protection, as means for evaluating designs or vendor reliability, and in process planning and selection. Often, reliability test data are required in military contracts. Testing is necessary to evaluate warranties and to avoid high costs related to early field failure. Good testing leads to good reliability and hence good quality.

Product testing is performed by various methods. The purpose of *life testing*, that is, running devices until they fail, is to measure the distribution of failures to better understand and eliminate their causes. However, such testing can be expensive and time-consuming. For devices that have long natural lives, life testing is not practical. **Accelerated life testing** involves overstressing components to reduce the time to failure and find weaknesses. This form of testing might involve running a motor faster than typically found in normal operating conditions. However, failure rates must correlate well to actual operating conditions if accelerated life testing is to be useful. Other testing studies the robustness of products. For example, one company performed a variety of tests on its computers. Products were disassembled and destructive testing was performed on the electromechanical, mechanical, and physical properties of components. *Environmental testing* consisted of varying the temperature from $-40°F$ (the temperature inside trucks in the northern United States and Canada) to 165°F (the temperature inside trucks in the southwestern United States) to shock the product to see whether it could withstand extremes. Because old wiring exhibits a wide range of variation, AC power was varied from 105 to 135 volts. *Vibration and shock testing* were used to simulate trucks driving from the East to the West Coast to determine the product's ability to withstand rough handling and accidents.

Semiconductors are the basic building blocks of numerous modern products such as DVD players, automotive ignition systems, computers, and military weapons systems. Semiconductors have a small proportion of defects, called *latent defects*, that can cause them to fail during the first 1,000 hours of normal operation. After that, the failure rate stabilizes, perhaps for as long as 25 years, before beginning to rise again as components wear out. These infant mortalities can be as high as 10 percent in a new technology or as low as 0.01 percent in proven technologies. The sooner a faulty component is detected, the cheaper is its replacement or repair. A correction on an integrated circuit fabrication line costs about 50 cents; at the board level it might cost $5; at the system level about $50; and in the field, $500. If a printed circuit board contains 100 semiconductors, a failure rate of 0.01 percent would cause a board failure rate of 1 percent.

Burn-in, or *component stress testing*, involves exposing integrated circuits to elevated temperatures in order to force latent defects to occur. For example, a device that might normally fail after 300 hours at 25°C might fail in less than 20 hours at 150°C. Survivors are likely to have long, trouble-free operating lives. Studies and experience have demonstrated the economic advantages of burn-in. For example, a large-scale study of the effect of burn-in on enhancing reliability of certain memory chips was conducted in Europe. The failure rate without burn-in conditioning and testing to eliminate infant mortality was 0.24 percent per thousand hours, while burn-in and testing reduced the rate to 0.02 percent per thousand hours. When considering the cost of field service and warranty work, for instance, reduction of semiconductor failure rates in a large system by an order of magnitude translates roughly into an average of one repair call per year versus one repair call per month. Because burn-in requires considerable time—48 to 96 hours is common—designers attempt to produce equipment that can perform some functional tests during the burn-in cycle rather than after. Modern systems exist to test and burn-in integrated circuits. One system has the capacity of 18,000 DRAMs (dynamic random access memory) per load and is flexible in its burn-in and test procedures to accommodate future types without modification of the hardware. The system can accumulate and display information on the devices under test, both for real-time evaluation and for lot documentation.

SIMULATION IN DFSS

Simulation is an approach to building a logical model of a real business system, and experimenting with the model to obtain insight about the behavior of the system or to evaluate the impact of changes in assumptions or potential improvements to it. Simulation allows you to collect large amounts of real-time data that might take days or months to collect in minutes on a computer and avoid costly physical experiments. Two basic types of simulation modeling approaches are used in Six Sigma—process simulation and Monte-Carlo simulation. **Process simulation** models the dynamics and behavior over time of interacting elements in a system such as a manufacturing facility or a call center. **Monte-Carlo simulation** is based on repeated sampling from probability distributions of model inputs to characterize the distributions of model outputs, usually in a spreadsheet environment.

Process Simulation

Process simulation has been used routinely in business to address complex operational problems, so it is no wonder that it is a useful tool for Six Sigma applications, especially those involving customer service improvement, cycle time reduction, and reducing variability. Process simulation should be used when the process is highly complex and difficult to visualize, involves many decision points, or when the goal is to optimize the use of resources for a process.[6]

Building a process simulation model involves first describing how the process operates, normally using a process map. The process map includes all process steps, including logical decisions that route materials or information to different locations. Second, all key inputs such as how long it takes to perform each step of the process and resources needed must be identified. Typically the activity times in a process are uncertain and described by probability distributions, which normally makes it difficult to evaluate process performance and identify bottlenecks without simulation.

The intent is for the model to duplicate the real process so that what-if questions can easily be evaluated without having to make time consuming or costly changes to the real process. Once the model is developed, the simulation process repeatedly samples from the probability distributions of the input variables to create a distribution of potential outputs.

As an example, a common customer support process is the help desk or call center process responsible for answering and addressing customer questions and complaints.[7] Typically, customer satisfaction ratings of the help desk are low. Although this process is common, it is difficult to analyze with conventional Six Sigma tools. The measure phase usually identifies "time to resolve an issue" and "quality of the issue resolution" as the two CTQs. When these factors are measured, performance is generally less than a 1-sigma level, so significant improvement potential exists.

Help desks are much too complex to analyze using basic Six Sigma tools. Most help desks have two or three levels of support. When a call comes in, it often waits in a queue. When a level 1 person is available, he or she takes the call. If this person cannot resolve the issue, the call is forwarded to level 2. If the level 2 rep cannot resolve the call, it is forwarded to engineering or a similar support group. Between each of these levels, the call may end up waiting in several more queues, or the customer may be asked to wait for a callback.

By developing a process simulation model, a black belt can validate the model against the real process by collecting whatever data are available for model inputs, running the model, and statistically matching the results with data collected during the measure phase. Once the model is validated, analysis can begin. Most simulation packages provide operational output data for all the process steps, resource utilization data, and any additional variables tracked throughout the process. When the data are collected, it becomes a fairly straightforward task to analyze the data statistically, identify bottlenecks, develop proposed solutions, and rerun the simulation to confirm the results.

To provide a simple illustration, suppose that in a phone support center, incoming calls arrive on a random basis with an average time between calls of about 5 minutes and a support representative evaluates the nature of each problem.[8] Each call takes anywhere between 30 seconds and 4 minutes, although most can be handled in about 2 minutes. The representative is able to resolve 75 percent of the calls immediately. However, 25 percent of the calls require other support representatives to do research and make a return call to the customer. The research itself, combined with the return call, requires on average 20 minutes. This time may vary quite a bit, from as little as 5 minutes to more than 35 minutes. Figure 9.4 shows the process map for this situation, including the support representative resources.

It is difficult to perform a process simulation, even for such a simple process, without some type of commercial simulation software. For this example, we used a package called ProcessModel,[9] which facilitates the simulation process by allowing you to build the model by simply "dragging and dropping" the process map symbols on the computer screen, entering the appropriate data input descriptions, and running the model. As the model runs, ProcessModel provides a visual animation of the process, allowing you to see the buildup of calls at each support stage to gain insight into the system performance.

Standard output reports, such as the one shown in Figure 9.5, are generated automatically. By examining these results (see the circled entries in the figure), we see that support problems waited in the *Return Call inQ* activity an average of more than 496 minutes, and as many as 51 calls were waiting at any one time. Thus, this activity should be identified as a problem area suitable for process improvement efforts. In the RESOURCES section, we see that Support 1 was busy about half the time, while Support 2 was busy nearly 100 percent of the time. Any time human resource utilization is greater than 80 percent for extended periods,

FIGURE 9.4 PROCESS MAP FOR HELP DESK SIMULATION MODEL

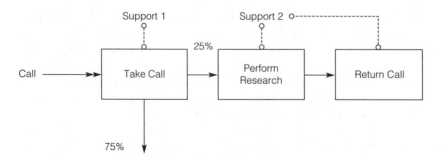

the system will most likely result in long waiting times and queue lengths, requiring more resources or changes in the assignment of resources. This evidence suggests that better allocation of resources should improve performance. To reduce the customer waiting time we might add additional support representatives or cross-train and share the existing representatives. The simulation model can easily be modified to incorporate these changes and the impacts on the results can be evaluated. Clearly, trying to simulate the real process would be costly and disruptive, with no guarantee that it will work.

FIGURE 9.5 PROCESSMODEL SIMULATION RESULTS

Scenario   = Normal Run
Replication   = 1 of 1
Simulation Time = 48 hr

ACTIVITIES

Activity Name	Scheduled Hours	Capacity	Total Entries	Average Minutes Per Entry	Average Contents	Maximum Contents	Current Contents	% Util
Take Call inQ	40	999	504	1.01	0.21	5	0	0.02
Take Call	40	1	504	2.17	0.45	1	0	45.62
Perform Research inQ	40	999	114	112.50	5.34	11	4	0.53
Perform Research	40	10	110	19.92	0.91	1	1	9.13
Return Call inQ	40	999	109	496.78	22.56	51	51	2.26
Return Call	40	1	58	3.00	0.07	1	0	7.25

ACTIVITY STATES BY PERCENTAGE (Multiple Capacity)

Activity Name	Scheduled Hours	% Empty	% Partially Occupied	% Full
Take Call inQ	40	84.85	15.15	0.00
Perform Research inQ	40	10.50	89.50	0.00
Perform Research	40	8.67	91.33	0.00
Return Call inQ	40	2.06	97.94	0.00

ACTIVITY STATES BY PERCENTAGE (Single Capacity)

Activity Name	Scheduled Hours	% Operation	% Idle	% Waiting	% Blocked
Take Call	40	45.62	54.38	0.00	0.00
Return Call	40	7.25	92.75	0.00	0.00

RESOURCES

Resource Name	Units	Scheduled Hours	Number of Times Used	Average Minutes Per Usage	% Util
Support 1	1	48	504	2.17	45.62
Support 2	1	48	168	14.08	98.58

RESOURCE STATES BY PERCENTAGE

Resource Name	Scheduled Hours	% In Use	% Idle	% Down
Support 1	40	45.62	54.38	0.00
Support 2	40	98.58	1.42	0.00

ENTITY SUMMARY (Times in Scoreboard time units)

Entity Name	Qty Processed	Average Cycle Time (Minutes)	Average VA Time (Minutes)	Average Cost
Call	398	4.19	2.18	0.43
HardCall	58	596.99	24.99	004

VARIABLES

Process simulation is a rich and complex topic. Many good books exist about process simulation and we encourage you to explore other references.

Monte-Carlo Simulation

The term *Monte-Carlo simulation* was coined by scientists who worked on the development of the atom bomb and is taken from the random behavior of casino games at Monte Carlo in Monaco. By randomly selecting model inputs and evaluating the outcomes, managers may construct a distribution of potential outcomes of key model variables along with their likelihood of occurrence. This simulation provides an assessment of the risk associated with a set of decisions that analytical methods generally cannot capture. By manipulating key decision variables and evaluating the risks associated with them, managers can use a simulation model to help identify good decisions. Monte-Carlo simulation using spreadsheets has gained an increasing amount of popularity in recent years because of the availability of powerful spreadsheet add-ins such as Crystal Ball™, which we will feature in this section.

Monte-Carlo simulation is currently being used in Six Sigma to analyze and understand the effects of uncertainty on the performance of processes and product designs. Common applications in DFSS include

- Identifying key parameters driving variation
- Understanding and reducing variation
- Obtaining early visibility into design performance
- Creating robust designs
- Optimizing parameters and tolerances[10]

Monte-Carlo simulation can be used in the design of experiments in the analysis of tolerances and reliability or to statistically assess the effect of individual tolerances on an assembly or process. It is also used to help establish tradeoffs between parameters in creating a product or assembly. Spreadsheet models are often used to characterize mathematical relationships between parameters, and which can be easily analyzed by changing the variables to understand their impact on cost and performance of the design.

Crystal Ball is a Microsoft Excel add-in that automates the complex tasks required in Monte-Carlo simulations, such as generating random outcomes from probability distributions, inserting them into the spreadsheet model, aggregating results, and computing statistics. The key features of Crystal Ball for Six Sigma applications are Monte-Carlo simulation, distribution fitting, sensitivity analysis, and optimization. Monte-Carlo simulation provides the ability to factor uncertainty into models using predefined or custom input distributions. With distribution fitting, an analyst can analyze the data collected during the Measure phase and automatically create assumptions that can be used as inputs in models. Sensitivity analysis helps understand which inputs are most critical and drive the uncertainty in the process or design. Crystal Ball optimization facilitates finding optimal solutions to a Six Sigma process or design model. A full description of Crystal Ball and a demonstration version can be found on the CD-ROM accompanying this book.

Applying Monte-Carlo Simulation in Six Sigma: Catapult Design[11]

A simple catapult is an excellent way of illustrating both principles of design of experiments and Monte-Carlo simulation in the context of DFSS. A catapult is shown in Figure 9.6. The objective of the design is to determine the best values of four factors to launch a weight a distance of 50 feet with a tolerance of ($\pm$2.50 feet):

1. Spring constant (k)—The spring constant is the force/foot required to pull back the catapult arm (in lbf/ft).
2. Pull Distance (x)—This is the distance in feet the arm is pulled back to launch the mass.
3. Mass (m)—This is the mass of the object in slugs (lbf/ft/sec^2).
4. Launch Angle (θ)—This is the angle in degrees to the horizontal at which the mass leaves the catapult.

Using some theory from physics, the distance that the mass will travel can be computed with the formula:

$$s = \frac{kx^2}{mg} \sin\theta \, \cos\theta$$

Note that the degree of the launch angle must be converted into radians for input to the Excel sine and cosine functions. (If you are not familiar with the mathematics here, the math is not necessary to follow the example.)

One way to find the best catapult design is to build a working prototype and experiment with the factors to identify the best combination that meets the design requirements. Design of experiments would be an appropriate approach for experimenting with different parameters to identify the best combination. Conducting a series of physical experiments, of course, would be quite time consuming. Experimenting on a computer would be much faster. Figure 9.7 shows a Microsoft Excel model for calculating the distances as a function of the design parameters. You can see that the parameters chosen in the spreadsheet meet the design specifications.

However, a complicating factor is that variability in materials and use would not yield consistent results. For example, a batch of springs purchased from the supplier might have some variability in the spring constants and the weights launched might also vary in mass. The user might not measure the launch angle correctly or consistently pull back the launcher the same pull distance. The only thing that is constant is gravity! The interaction of these factors would cause some variation in the actual distance that might not meet the required specifications. Would you want to explain to Attila the Hun why your catapult did not work? You can now understand the importance of trying to create robust designs for more practical products, such as electronics and other consumer goods.

Let us assume that the spring constant is normally distributed with a mean of 47.3 and a standard deviation of 0.1; the pull distance has a uniform distribution between 5.8 and 6.2; the mass is normally distributed, with a mean of 0.5, and a

FIGURE 9.6 CATAPULT DESIGN

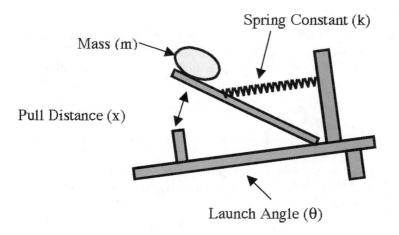

FIGURE 9.7 EXCEL MODEL FOR THE CATAPULT EXAMPLE

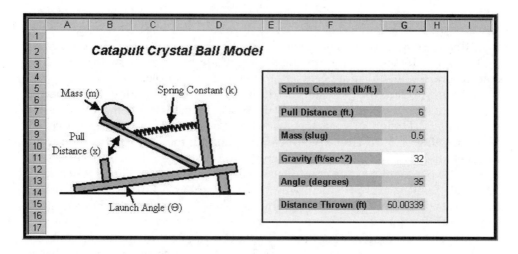

standard deviation of 0.1; and the launch angle is also normally distributed, with a mean of 35 and a standard deviation of 3.

These assumptions have been built into the Crystal Ball model. When the model is run, Crystal Ball will randomly sample from these distributions, insert the values into the model, and compile the results. Figure 9.8 shows the Crystal Ball forecast chart for a simulation of 2,500 trials using these assumptions. Although the mean distance is within the specification limits, you can see that considerable variability exists in the actual distances and that less than 60 percent of the trials met the specifications.

Crystal Ball has an option called the Sensitivity Chart that illustrates the effect of each input variable on the output variable. The sensitivity chart shown in Figure 9.9 shows that the pull distance and the launch angle contribute the most

FIGURE 9.8 CRYSTAL BALL FORECAST CHART

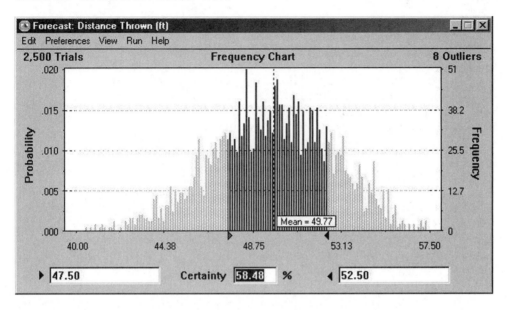

FIGURE 9.9 CRYSTAL BALL SENSITIVITY CHART

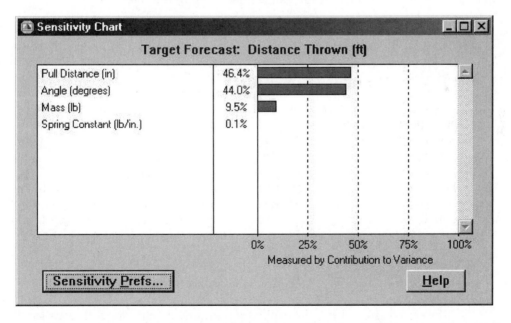

to the variation in the distance. This suggests that the designer should consider ways in which the variation in these parameters might be reduced. In terms of the physical product, can you think of any ideas? We leave it to you as a project to experiment with this model and try to find a design with at least a 3- to 4-sigma level of performance that works within the variation of the input variables.

Design Verification

The purpose of verification is to validate product and process designs and to prepare procedures and documentation for full-scale production rollout. A final design review should anticipate and mistake-proof potential failure modes for the production and delivery process. Verification is often facilitated by industrial engineering studies of production and assembly methods, statistical process control, and development of preventative maintenance strategies. It might also include evaluating process capability, supplier capability, and post-production services to support product delivery, and include worker training plans and a quality measurement plan. Many of these processes have been discussed in previous chapters.

Verification is often performed by doing a small-scale pilot run prior to full rollout. This provides the ability to assess whether standard operating procedures are effective, additional training is needed, or other critical changes to the production system must be made. It should be based on good measurement to verify that CTQs have been met and are accurate, especially if much of the design work was performed using computer prototypes or simulation studies.

This final step should also provide for a project review to identify lessons learned and best practices that might be useful in future DFSS projects. Sponsor and champion involvement is, of course, important in this step.

CASE STUDY

Using DOE to Evaluate Battery Life[12]

Many one-tenth scale remote control (RC) model car racing enthusiasts believe that spending more money on high-quality batteries, using expensive gold-plated connectors, and storing batteries at low temperatures will improve battery life performance in a race. Two students, Eric Wasiloff and Curtis Hargitt, used DOE to determine whether the hypothesis that high-quality, high-cost alkaline dry cells result in a lower rate of voltage drop over time—a critical functional requirement during a race. To test this hypothesis, an electrical test circuit was constructed to measure battery discharge under different configurations. Commonly available AA dry-cell batteries, such as those used to power RC-car controllers and popular RC-car electrical connector designs, were used. They compared the voltage drop of high-cost alkaline (Duracell) vs. low-cost dry-cell (Panasonic) batteries as installed in the test circuit to determine the validity of this hypothesis.

Tests were conducted in a controlled environment (indoors with consistent thermostat and humidifier settings), with ambient temperature monitored using a digital thermometer. While it is believed that the potential for bias is limited (that is, production samples, no prototypical hardware), the order of experiments was randomized as is conventionally done with DOE. The batteries were randomly selected off the shelf from a typical hobby shop and examined to ensure selection from manufacturing lots with similar expiration dates. All batteries were new at the start of testing.

In the first experiment, a high-cost battery was installed in the battery box in the test circuit at ambient temperature, with the knife switch activated to supply current through the gold-plated connector to a 1.2-volt lamp. A stopwatch was then activated to measure time until the test lamp was no longer illuminated, indicating that the battery was fully discharged. The initial temperature of the battery was measured and recorded. Once the battery had fully discharged, the elapsed time was recorded in the specific cell for the defined run in the experiment matrix. This process was repeated using a standard connector, followed by the same two runs with low-cost batteries. Chilled high-cost and low-cost batteries were then tested under the same conditions, until all eight combinations were satisfied.

Each factor (battery type, connector type, and temperature) was evaluated at two levels, resulting in $2^3 = 8$ experimental conditions shown in Table 9.1. Calculations of the main effects are as follows:

Battery cost
Low = (72 + 93 + 75 + 94)/4 = 83.5 minutes
High = (612 + 490 + 493 + 489)/4 = 521 minutes
Main effect = High − Low = 437.5 minutes

Connector type
Gold-plated = (94 + 75 + 490 + 493)/4 = 288 minutes
Standard = (72 + 93 + 612 + 489)/4 = 316.5 minutes
Main effect + Standard − Gold-plated = 28.5 minutes

Temperature
Cold = (72 + 75 + 490 + 612)/4 = 312.25 minutes
Ambient = (93 + 489 + 493 + 94)/4 = 292.25 minutes
Main effect = Ambient − Cold = 20 minutes

These results suggest that high cost batteries do have a longer life, but that the impacts of gold plating or battery temperature do not appear to be significant. Because only one factor appears to be significant, calculation of interaction effects is not required. These conclusions can be tested more rigorously using analysis of variance. Indeed, an analysis of variance confirms that the battery cost factor is

TABLE 9.1 EXPERIMENTAL DESIGN FOR TESTING BATTERY PERFORMANCE

Experimental Run	Battery Type	Connector Type	Battery Temperature	Discharge Time (minutes)
1	High cost	Gold-plated	Ambient	493
2	High cost	Gold-plated	Cold	490
3	High cost	Standard	Ambient	489
4	High cost	Standard	Cold	612
5	Low cost	Gold-plated	Ambient	94
6	Low cost	Gold-plated	Cold	75
7	Low cost	Standard	Ambient	93
8	Low cost	Standard	Cold	72

statistically significant while the other factors are indistinguishable from experimental error.

In the second experiment, a battery was installed in the battery box at ambient temperature, with the knife switch activated to supply current through the non-gold-plated connectors to the lamp. A digital voltmeter was used to make voltage measurements, initially at two-minute intervals up to 10 minutes after activation and then at 10-minute intervals up to 100 minutes after activation. Additional voltage measurements were made, depending on battery-discharge status. The procedure was then repeated with the remaining batteries.

Test results of phase two, which evaluates battery-voltage drop over time in the test circuit board, are shown in Table 9.2. In summary, the high-cost Duracell batteries performed significantly better than the low-cost Panasonic batteries (no other factors varied during the experiment) and retained higher voltage for a longer time period.

Since most RC races are four to five minutes long, including race preparation time, it was decided that the first 10 minutes of battery operation are the most critical. As a result of this decision, the voltage drop over the first 10 minutes of battery life was examined in detail. Once again, the high-cost batteries performed better than the low-cost batteries. At the 10-minute point, the high-cost Duracell batteries retained 1.386 volts versus the low-cost Panasonic batteries, which retained only 1.222 volts. This represents a difference of 0.164 volts, or a reduction of approximately 12 percent from the Duracell voltage at 10 minutes.

TABLE 9.2 BATTERY VOLTAGE DROP OVER TIME

Time (minutes)	Panasonic		Duracell	
	Voltage	**Voltage Drop**	**Voltage**	**Voltage Drop**
0	1.405	0	1.497	0
2	1.338	−0.067	1.438	−0.059
4	1.297	−0.108	1.418	−0.079
6	1.268	−0.137	1.405	−0.092
8	1.244	−0.161	1.395	−0.102
10	1.222	−0.183	1.386	−0.111
20	1.180	−0.225	1.360	−0.137
30	1.141	−0.264	*	
40	1.108	−0.297	*	
50	1.067	−0.338	*	
60	1.047	−0.358	1.325	−0.172
70	0.999	−0.406		
80	0.941	−0.464		
90	0.829	−0.576		
100	0.766	−0.639		
120			1.204	−0.293
180			1.149	−0.348
198	0.200	−1.205		
210			1.1	−0.397

*Lamp burned out, data deleted

REVIEW QUESTIONS

1. Explain the role of design optimization and verification in Six Sigma.
2. What is the purpose of design of experiments?
3. Describe a factorial experiment. Provide some examples of factorial experiments that you might use to solve some type of quality-related problem.
4. How do Taguchi methods differ from traditional DOE?
5. What is the signal-to-noise ratio and how is it used in design optimization?
6. Explain the role of the Taguchi loss function in process and tolerance design.
7. What is the importance of design for reliability and why has it become such an important concept?
8. What are some of the techniques used to improve designs and optimize the reliability of products?
9. Describe different forms of product testing.
10. What are the components of a process simulation? In what types of problem solving is it most useful?
11. Define Monte-Carlo simulation. What are the common applications for Monte-Carlo simulation in DFSS?
12. What are some limitations of simple factorial experiments? How can they be overcome?

DISCUSSION QUESTIONS

1. Examine the ProcessModel output for the help desk example. Are the results compatible with the assumptions given about the process? For example, what percentages of calls actually go to the second support person? Are the simulated times close to the stated input values?
2. The case study experimenters have identified the *condition* of the connectors (aged, dirty, oily versus new and clean) as one more variable that may be a possible source of noise. How might the experiment be expanded to include an additional variable of condition? How might Taguchi's signal-to-noise concept apply here?

THINGS TO DO

1. Using one sheet of paper, design and build a helicopter. Some methods of making a paper helicopter can be found at: http://www.exploratorium.edu/science_explorer/roto-copter.html and http://www.faa.gov/education/resource/helicopt.htm. Use design of experiments to develop a design that keeps the helicopter airborne for as long as possible.
2. Develop an original application of DOE similar to the case study and conduct a simple factorial experiment.

PROBLEMS

1. A specification for the length of an auto part is 5.0 ± 0.05 centimeters (cm). It costs $25 to scrap a part that is outside the specifications. Determine the Taguchi loss function for this situation.

2. A blueprint specification for the thickness of a dishwasher part is 0.300 ± 0.024 centimeters (cm). It costs $9 to scrap a part that is outside the specifications. Determine the Taguchi loss function for this situation.

3. A team was formed to study the auto part described in problem 1. While continuing to work to find the root cause of scrap, the team found a way to reduce the scrap cost to $17.50 per part.

   a. Determine the Taguchi loss function for this situation.

   b. If the process deviation from target can be held at 0.020 cm, what is the Taguchi loss?

4. A team was formed to study the dishwasher part described in problem 2. While continuing to work to find the root cause of scrap, they found a way to reduce the scrap cost to $4 per part.

   a. Determine the Taguchi loss function for this situation.

   b. If the process deviation from target can be held at 0.015 cm, what is the Taguchi loss?

5. Ruido Unlimited makes electronic soundboards for car stereos. Output voltage to a certain component on the board must be 10 ± 0.1 volts. Exceeding the limits results in an estimated loss of $50. Determine the Taguchi loss function.

6. An electronic component has a specification of 150 ± 4 ohms. Scrapping the component results in an $80 loss.

   a. What is the value of k in the Taguchi loss function?

   b. If the process is centered on the target specification with a standard deviation of 2 ohms, what is the expected loss per unit?

7. An automatic cookie machine must deposit a specified amount of 7.5 ± 0.1 grams (g) of dough for each cookie on a conveyor belt. If the machine either over- or under-deposits the mixture, it costs $0.04 to scrap the defective cookie.

   a. What is the value of k in the Taguchi loss function?

   b. If the process is centered on the target specification with a standard deviation of 0.05 g, what is the expected loss per unit?

8. A computer chip is designed so that the distance between two adjacent pins has a specification of 2.000 ± 0.002 millimeters (mm). The loss due to a defective chip is $4. A sample of 25 chips was drawn from the production process and the results, in mm, can be found in the *Ch9dataset* file for *Prob.9-8* on the student CD-ROM.

   a. Compute the value of k in the Taguchi loss function.

   b. What is the expected loss from this process based on the sample data?

9. The average time to handle a call in a call processing center has a specification of 6 ± 1.25 minutes. The loss due to a mishandled call is $12. A sample of 25 calls was drawn from the process and the results, in minutes, can be found in the *Ch9dataset* file for *Prob.9-9* on the student CD-ROM.

a. Compute the value of k in the Taguchi loss function.

b. What is the expected loss from this process based on the sample data?

10. In the production of transformers, any output voltage that exceeds $\pm$ 25 volts is unacceptable to the customer. Exceeding these limits results in an estimated loss of $200. However, the manufacturer can adjust the voltage in the plant by changing a resistor that costs $1.75.

a. Determine the Taguchi loss function.

b. Suppose the nominal specification is 120 volts. At what tolerance should the transformer be manufactured?

11. In the transformer business mentioned in problem 10, managers gathered data from a customer focus group and found that any output voltage that exceeds $\pm$20 volts was unacceptable to the customer. Exceeding these limits results in an estimated loss of $250. However, the manufacturer can still adjust the voltage in the plant by changing a resistor that costs $1.75.

a. Determine the Taguchi loss function.

b. Suppose the nominal specification remains at 120 volts. At what tolerance should the transformer be manufactured?

12. Two processes, P and Q, are used by a supplier to produce the same component, Z, which is a critical part in the engine of the Boring 778 airplane. The specification for Z calls for a dimension of 0.24 mm $\pm$ 0.03. The probabilities of achieving the dimensions for each process based on their inherent variability are shown in the table found in the *Ch9dataset* file for *Prob.9-12* on the student CD-ROM. If $k = 75,000$, what is the expected loss for each process? Which would be the best process to use, based on minimizing the expected loss?

13. A process engineer at Minimicron Electronics is trying to determine if a newer, more costly design involving a gold alloy in a computer chip is more effective than the present, less expensive silicon design. She wants to obtain an effective output voltage at both high and low temperatures, when tested with high and low signal strength. She hypothesizes that high signal strength will result in higher voltage output, low temperature will result in higher output, and the gold alloy will result in higher output than the silicon material. She hopes that the main and interaction effects with the expensive gold will be minimal. In the table found in the *Ch9dataset* file for *Prob.9-13* on the student CD-ROM are the data that were gathered in testing of all 2^n combinations. What recommendation would you make, based on these data?

14. The MTBF for an Internet service provider's Web server unit is normally distributed with a mean of 180 days and a standard deviation of 10 days. Each failure costs the company $750,000 in lost computing time and repair costs. A shutdown for preventive maintenance can be scheduled during nonpeak times and will cost $500,000. As the manager in charge of computer operations, you are to determine whether a preventive maintenance program is worthwhile. What is your recommendation based on a 1 percent probability of failure? A 0.5 percent probability of failure? Assume 365 operating days per year.

15. For a particular piece of equipment, the probability of failure during a given week is as follows:

Week of Operation	Probability of Failure
1	0.25
2	0.08
3	0.07
4	0.10
5	0.20
6	0.30

Management is considering a preventive maintenance program that would be implemented at the end of a given week of production. The production loss and downtime costs associated with an equipment failure are estimated to be $2,500 per failure. If it costs $500 to perform the preventive maintenance, when should the firm implement the preventive maintenance program? What is the total maintenance and failure cost associated with your recommendation, and how many failures can be expected each year? Assume 52 weeks of operation per year.

ENDNOTES

1. Johannes Ledolter and Claude W. Burrill, *Statistical Quality Control* (New York: John Wiley & Sons, 1999).
2. N. Raghu Kackar, "Off-Line Quality Control, Parameter Design, and the Taguchi Method," *Journal of Quality Technology* 17, no. 4, October 1985, 176–188.
3. Bruce D. Nordwall, "ITT Uses Process Control Methods to Increase Plant Productivity," *Aviation Week & Space Technology*, May 11, 1987, 69–74.
4. Alan Vonderhaar, "Audi's TT Coupe's Ever So Close," *Cincinnati Enquirer*, November 27, 1999, F1, F2.
5. Keith Denton, "Reducing DOAs (and other Q.C. Problems)," *P&IM Review with APICS News*, December 1989, 35–36.
6. Steve Fleming and E. Lowry Manson, "Six Sigma and Process Simulation," *Quality Digest*, March 2002.
7. Fleming and Manson (see note 6).
8. This example is adapted from a tutorial for ProcessModel, a commercial simulation package. ProcessModel, Inc. 32 West Center, Suite 209, Provo, UT 84601.
9. ProcessModel, Inc. 32 West Center, Suite 209, Provo, UT 84601.
10. Decisioneering, Inc. (www.crystalball.com) © 2001 Decisioneering, Inc. makers of Crystal Ball® software.
11. This is an example Crystal Ball model from Decisioneering, Inc. Used with permission.
12. Eric Wasiloff and Curtis Hargitt, "Using DOE to Determine AA Battery Life," *Quality Progress*, March 1999, 67–71. © 1999, American Society for Quality. Reprinted with permission.

Six Sigma Implementation

Chapter 10
Implementing Six Sigma

10

Implementing Six Sigma

PRINCIPLES FOR SIX SIGMA IMPLEMENTATION

As we indicated throughout the preceding chapters, a fully implemented Six Sigma process is a strategic approach that is driven and supported by top management, but is deployed throughout the organization at every level. Several key principles are necessary for effective implementation of Six Sigma:[1]

- *Committed leadership from top management.* In most companies, Six Sigma represents a major cultural shift, and changing an organization's culture requires intimate involvement by top leadership. Motorola's former CEO Bob Galvin passionately led the Six Sigma effort with aggressive goals: 10-fold reduction in defects in the first three years, and 100-fold improvement in the next three years. Managers at GE participate in hands-on approaches such as personally spending time in every Six Sigma training wave, speaking and answering questions for employees in training classes, dropping in (usually unannounced) on weekly and monthly Six Sigma reviews, and making site visits at the manufacturing and call-taking operations to observe firsthand the degree to which Six Sigma is ingrained in the culture.
- *Integration with existing initiatives, business strategy, and performance measurement.* Six Sigma should not be pursued just because other companies are doing it. It should have a clear justification in terms of a company's mission and strategic direction. However, with its focus on customers and the bottom line, this integration usually is not too difficult. At companies like GE and Allied Signal, Six Sigma has been extended to all areas of the company, such as product development and financial services. For example, GE first identifies all critical customer performance features and subjects them to a rigorous statistical design process, thus designing products for Six Sigma levels.
- *Process thinking.* As one of the foundation principles of total quality, a process focus is, not surprisingly, a necessary prerequisite. Mapping business processes

is one of the key activities in Six Sigma efforts, as is a disciplined approach to the information gathering, analysis, and problem solving.

- *Disciplined customer and market intelligence gathering.* The ultimate goal is to improve those characteristics that are most important to customers; thus knowledge of customer needs is vital. Approaches that we discussed in Chapter 4 are essential to help focus Six Sigma projects on customers.
- *A bottom-line orientation.* Six Sigma projects must produce real savings or revenues in both the short term and long term. Most Six Sigma projects are designed to be completed within three to six months. GE has a financial analyst certify the results of every project.
- *Leadership in the trenches.* Within GE, Six Sigma includes a diverse population of technical and nontechnical people, managers, and others from key business areas who work together as a team to attack a problem using the DMAIC approach. All employees participate, not just those that hold the "belts."
- *Training.* Although many companies that embraced total quality provide employees with only basic awareness training, Six Sigma companies train nearly everyone in rigorous statistical and problem-solving tools. GE's green belt training is delivered to all GE employees and is available in strategic locations across the world. It is typically rolled out over a four-month period and is scheduled to help facilitate the trainee in leading a "green belt project" to not only yield savings but also practice in a real-life situation what is being learned in the training.
- *Continuous reinforcement and rewards.* Six Sigma companies have significantly changed performance measurement and reward systems. At GE, 40 percent of executive incentives are tied to Six Sigma goals and progress. Before any savings are credited to an individual, the black belt overseeing the project must show that the problems are fixed permanently. All employees, even executives, who want to be considered for promotion must be trained in Six Sigma and complete a project. Some companies also pool the savings at the business-unit level and share a portion of the savings with the Six Sigma team members.

A succinct way of describing a successful game plan for implementing Six Sigma is to consider Iomega, the global producer of PC storage devices: *invest in people, make data-based decisions, and achieve and measure results.* The company credits Six Sigma for taking responsibility for quality out of the hands of a few specialists and spreading it throughout the company. Inventory and incoming bad material were both decreased by 80 percent, technical support call wait time was reduced from 80 minutes to 2 minutes on average, and direct labor productivity increased by 65 percent since the Six Sigma program started in 1998, producing more than $120 million in savings through 2001.[2]

Another example is Motorola. Although Motorola introduced the concept of Six Sigma back in 1986, its implementation is significantly different today. Motorola's "second generation" Six Sigma is an overall high-performance system that executes business strategy.[3] Its results are evident in Motorola's Commercial, Government, and Industrial Solutions Sector division receiving a Baldrige Award in 2002. Their new approach to Six Sigma is based on the following four steps.

1. *Align executives to the right objectives and targets.* This step means creating a balanced scorecard of strategic goals, metrics, and initiatives to identify the improvements that will have the most impact on the bottom line. Projects are not limited to traditional product and service domains but extend to market share improvements, better cash flow, and improved human resource processes.

2. *Mobilize improvement teams around appropriate metrics.* Teams use a structured problem-solving process to drive fact-based decisions; however, the focus on defects and defects per million opportunities (dpmo) sigma levels is less important, particularly in human-intensive processes such as marketing and human resources. For example, the definition of a defect as "employee performance that falls below a certain level" can be controversial and be easily manipulated. Continuous measures such as invoice delivery time or credit approval response time are replacing count-based measures such as the number of overdue invoices or the percentage of dissatisfied customers.

3. *Accelerate results.* Motorola uses an action learning framework methodology that combines formal education with real-time project work and coaching to quickly take employees from learning to doing. Project teams receive support from coaches on a just-in-time basis. Projects are driven to be accomplished quickly, rather than over a long period of time. Finally, a campaign management approach helps integrate various project teams so that the cumulative impact on the organization is, in fact, accelerated.

4. *Govern sustained improvement.* Leaders actively and visibly sponsor the key improvement projects required to execute business strategy and review them in the context of outcome goals. An important step is for leaders to actively share best practices and knowledge about improvements with other parts of the organization that can benefit.

Six Sigma continues to be Motorola's method of choice for driving bottom-line improvements. More efforts will be focused on product design that enhances the overall customer experience across the value chain. As such, Six Sigma projects increasingly involve key customers, suppliers, and other business partners.

Small organizations are often confused and intimidated by the size, costs, and extensive technical training they see in large organizations that implement "formal" Six Sigma processes. For this reason, they often don't even try to adopt these approaches. Small organizations are usually lean by necessity, but not always effectively so. Their processes often operate at quality levels of two to three sigma, and they are not even aware of it. Spanyi and Wurtzel provide some sage advice to small organizations thinking about adopting Six Sigma or lean production:[4]

*   Obtain management commitment.
*   Identify key processes and goals.
*   Prioritize the improvement projects.
*   Be systematic.
*   Don't worry about training black and green belts.

- Use just-in-time practices to learn the Six Sigma tools necessary to successfully carry out specific projects.
- Communicate successes and reward and recognize performers.

Small companies often need to bring in consultants for training or improvement initiatives in the early stages of learning. These types of initiatives can help to develop in-house expertise and put them on the right track.

The remaining sections of this chapter address some fundamentals on which organizations must focus in order to implement Six Sigma effectively.

Project Management

In previous chapters we stressed the importance of a well-designed and executed system for project management; without it, Six Sigma efforts will have difficulty succeeding. Developing the system begins by defining the scope of the project— its purpose, goals, and objectives. The project scope should be tightly linked to the CTQ characteristics that the customer or process owner requires and should be explained fully in the project team's charter.

Project success can be measured by two key metrics: time and cost. The sooner a project can be completed (in, of course, a high-quality fashion!), the sooner the organization can begin to reap the benefits. Managing time requires a feasible project schedule and constant review. Seasoned project managers know that they can only be certain of one thing in project scheduling—that the schedule will always be wrong! In spite of that fact, a written schedule provides a "road map" for completing the project in the least amount of time with the fewest resources. Creating a schedule can be done easily using a simple spreadsheet to identify tasks, groups of tasks, or project phases, or a more sophisticated software tool, such as Microsoft Project.

Cost is a factor that is often ignored in project planning. Many managers think that project resources, especially people, are "free," using the logic that people who are part of departments or other organizational units would be paid, whether they are working on Six Sigma projects or other daily tasks. In a sense this is true; however, there is an opportunity cost for using individuals' time and talent on Six Sigma projects instead of other work that they might be doing. Hence, project costs should be budgeted and considered as a vital component of the calculated financial returns of the project.

The project manager is responsible for tracking the accomplishment of the project against the plan, with the objective of ending the project on time, at or below projected costs, and meeting all of the targeted CTQ objectives. To be done well, it requires a supportive culture and leadership support throughout the organization.

Finally, because Six Sigma projects are temporary organization structures, one of the challenges is to coordinate them with normal work activities. Some slack time, as well as physical and financial resources, must be allocated to project teams in order for them to achieve their objectives. Team members and project leaders cannot be expected to carry a full load of routine work and still participate fully and effectively on Six Sigma project teams.

ORGANIZATIONAL CULTURE AND CHANGE MANAGEMENT

Any organizational activity, such as Six Sigma, can be viewed in one of three ways, depending on the intensity of commitment to the activity:

1. *Function*: A task or group of tasks to be performed that contribute to the mission or purpose of an organization
2. *Process*: A set of steps, procedures, or policies that define how a function is to be performed and what results are expected
3. *Ideology*: A set of values or beliefs that guide an organization in the establishment of its mission, processes, and functions

Many managers view Six Sigma as a set of tasks to be performed by specialists. Other managers have a broader perspective and see Six Sigma as a process in which many people from a number of functional areas of the organization are involved in cross-functional activities. Still other managers take the broadest viewpoint in which Six Sigma is an ideology or philosophy that pervades and defines the culture of the entire organization.

Culture (often called *corporate culture*) is an organization's value system and its collection of guiding principles. A survey conducted by the Wyatt Company, a Washington, DC, consulting firm, found that the barriers to change cited most often were employee resistance and "dysfunctional corporate culture"—one whose shared values and behavior are at odds with its long-term health.[5] An example of a dysfunctional culture would be a company that stresses individual rewards for results although Six Sigma depends on teamwork. To change their management practices, organizations must first address their fundamental values.

Cultural Values

Six Sigma requires a unique continuous improvement and business development culture within organizations that adopt it. The cultural values expressed in the Malcolm Baldrige National Quality Award Criteria for Performance Excellence provide a useful perspective for understanding the culture necessary for successfully implementing Six Sigma. These values folllow:

*   **Visionary Leadership** Leadership is one of the major contributing factors ensuring Six Sigma's success across the organization. Most testimonials on why Six Sigma works focus on "continued top management support and enthusiasm."[6] A general manager of a $1.2 billion electronics business in Atlanta states that "Six Sigma has to be part of every discussion on the performance of the business—Six Sigma results are discussed daily with the boss."[7]
*   **Customer-Driven Excellence** One of the key reasons to pursue Six Sigma is to be ahead of, responsive to, and focused on customers. Customer requirements, both external and internal, are paramount in choosing which Six Sigma projects to undertake. For example, a sales and marketing vice president at GE Aircraft Engines directly attributes the success of the division to the Six Sigma

initiative: "It has helped our salespeople focus on building relationships with our customers [whose demands] for increased value have forced us to place a greater emphasis on speed, quality, and productivity."[8] Critical-to-quality issues are one of the mainstays of Six Sigma at the design, processing, delivery, and recovery (if needed) stages of the relationship with customers.

- **Organizational and Personal Learning** A key aspect of Six Sigma is to create a learning environment where both the individuals and the organization learn and act based on that learning, improving all the time both from internal and external perspectives. Six Sigma provides a structured environment for taking the best ideas from every source, internally and externally, and rethinking the who-what-when-where-why-how of all the processes both within the organization and as they interface with the outside world.

- **Valuing Employees and Partners** Besides hardware and software, people are needed to make Six Sigma work. Six Sigma supports a culture where every individual has the opportunity to contribute not only by doing his or her work, but also by improving the work. Most successful companies believe that training in Six Sigma is worth the investment.

- **Agility** Organizations must have the ability to respond quickly and flexibly to changing customer needs, wants and desires, and in response to other internal factors and changes in the business environment. Six Sigma supports both process management and directed positive change on a timely basis while taking into consideration all the appropriate relationships.

- **Focus on the Future** A company that focuses on the future needs a goal, a plan for achieving that goal, and a working methodology to fulfill that plan. Six Sigma offers a methodology for improving the overall performance of an organization, giving it access to the resources that will allow it to continue to grow, develop, and succeed.

- **Managing for Innovation** Within Six Sigma, both incremental change and breakthrough change are supported and expected, and this change is directed not only at what the company produces but also how the company itself works internally and interfaces with the rest of the world. Although Six Sigma was originally applied to manufacturing processes, companies such as GE have shown that the theory applies everywhere.[9]

- **Management by Fact** Six Sigma demands the effective use of data to analyze business issues. Six Sigma uses measurement to discover opportunities, to drive business results, and to drive improvement.

- **Social Responsibility** Although not specifically addressed in Six Sigma, it would be almost impossible for an organization to use all the other principles and concepts of Six Sigma, deliver better products and services, and grow in revenue and profitability without being a good citizen in its community.

- **Focus on Results and Creating Value** Six Sigma breaks the barrier between quality and business results, focusing directly on value-added processes and achieving improved business results for the organization. No project is considered complete until the benefit has been shown and a team of financial auditors signs off.

- **Systems Perspective** One of the characteristics stated and implicit in Six Sigma is that efforts are expected to encompass the whole organization. Although the pieces are important, taken in total, integrated, and in relationship to one another, the system makes up the real value of the organization. Processes differ significantly, but all must be viewed from a system's perspective and their impact on and benefit to the ultimate customer.

The Role of Employees in Cultural Change

Juran and others suggest that a company must foster five key behaviors to develop positive quality culture:[10]

1. It must create and maintain an awareness of quality by disseminating results throughout the organization.
2. It must provide evidence of management leadership, such as serving on a quality council, providing resources, or championing improvement projects.
3. The company must encourage self-development and empowerment through the design of jobs, use of empowered teams, and personal commitment to quality.
4. The company must provide opportunities for employee participation to inspire action, such as improvement teams, product design reviews, or Six Sigma training.
5. The company must provide recognition and rewards, including public acknowledgment for good performance as well as tangible benefits.

It is interesting to note that these suggestions generally revolve around *people*, and we emphasize that people are the most important element in a successful organization.

Each category of employees—senior managers, middle managers, and the workforce—plays a critical role. Senior managers must ensure that their plans and strategies are successfully executed within the organization. Middle managers provide the leadership by which the vision of senior management is translated into the operations of the organization through the selection of relevant and viable Six Sigma projects. In the end, the workforce delivers the goods, and they must feel a sense of ownership in their work.

Senior Management

The critical importance of senior managers' roles in business excellence is affirmed by numerous research studies and from practitioners' perspectives. A codirector of the Juran Center for Leadership in Quality at the University of Minnesota observed three things:

1. Despite substantial efforts, only a few U.S. organizations have reached world-class excellence.
2. Even fewer companies have sustained such excellence during changes in leadership.
3. Most corporate quality failures rest with leadership.[11]

Many organizations today find themselves in a leadership vacuum because the environment has changed more rapidly than they ever imagined. Their leadership styles have not kept pace, and they find themselves falling back on approaches that were "good enough" for their predecessors, but frequently inadequate today. Senior managers' responsibilities include the following tasks:[12]

- Ensure that the organization focuses on the needs of the customer.
- Cascade the mission, vision, and values of the organization throughout the organization.
- Identify the critical processes that need attention and improvement.
- Identify the resources and tradeoffs that must be made to fund Six Sigma activities.
- Review progress and remove any identified barriers.
- Improve the macroprocesses in which they are involved, both to improve the performance of the process and to demonstrate their ability to use Six Sigma tools for problem solving.

Senior leaders must be willing to deal openly with resistance in an honest environment. Perhaps their three most compelling challenges are to embrace the Six Sigma philosophy, communicate it effectively throughout the organization, and create a fact-based organization in which, as one executive told one of the authors, they can "ask what customers think and have the guts to face the results."

Middle Management

Middle management has been tagged by many as a direct obstacle to creating a supportive environment for quality management initiatives such as Six Sigma.[13] Leonard Sayles, a veteran leadership consultant and researcher, observed that middle managers have traditionally not been expected to be leaders, but to be guardians of "generally approved management principles" (GAMP).[14] GAMP rests on time-honored assumptions and practices:

- Clear and fixed work goals and technology
- Relying on centralized specialist groups
- Focusing on numbers, such as meeting budgeted targets
- Being as autonomous as possible and ignoring the work system
- Delegating as much as possible and managing solely by results
- Compartmentalizing people issues and technology issues

While these principles were probably effective in simple, stable organizations and the business environment of 40 or 50 years ago, they do not work in a Six Sigma organization. Today's middle managers find themselves monitoring progress, disseminating information and suggestions between local and distant line staff and outside experts, and acting as spokespersons inside and outside the firm.

Because of their position in the company, middle managers have been accused of feeding territorial competition and stifling information flow. They have also been blamed for not developing or preparing employees for change. Unwilling to take initiatives that contribute to continuous improvement, middle managers appear to be threatened by improvement efforts. Often, they are left out of the equation, with attention being paid to top management and the project specialists. However, middle management's role in creating and sustaining a Six Sigma culture is critical. Middle managers can make or break cooperation and teamwork; and they are the principal means by which the remaining workforce prepares for change.

Middle managers must exhibit behaviors that are supportive of Six Sigma efforts. Such behaviors include listening to employees as customers, creating a positive work environment, being role models for first-level managers and supervisors, implementing improvements enthusiastically, challenging people to develop new ideas and reach their potential, setting challenging goals, and providing positive feedback. These changes are often difficult for middle managers to accept.

The Workforce

Six Sigma project teams cannot accomplish their tasks without the input and cooperation of the workforce. The workforce is a principal source of innovative ideas—think back to the importance of creativity in the Improve step of DMAIC—and implements and controls the results. These tasks requires ownership.

Ownership goes beyond empowerment; it gives the employee the right to have a voice in deciding what needs to be done and how to do it.[15] It is based on a belief that what is good for the organization is also good for the individual, and vice versa. At Westinghouse, workers defined ownership as "taking personal responsibility for our jobs . . . for assuring that we meet or exceed our customers' standards and our own. We believe that ownership is a state of mind and heart that is characterized by a personal and emotional commitment to approach every decision and task with the confidence and leadership of an owner."

Managing Change

Making improvements requires change in processes, procedures, facilities, organization, and possibly behavior. Change makes people uncomfortable—thus, managing change is seldom pleasant. Managing change usually requires a well-defined process, just like any other business process. Organizations contemplating change must answer some tough questions: Why is the change necessary? What will it do to my organization (department, job)? What problems will I encounter in making the change? And perhaps the most important one—*What's in it for me?*

Thinking of change management as a process helps to define the steps necessary to achieve the desired outcomes. It also forces the organization to think of its employees as customers who will be affected by the change. Most change processes include three basic stages. The first stage involves questioning the organization's current state and dislodging accepted patterns of behavior. The second stage is a state of flux, where new approaches are developed to replace suspended old activities. The final period consists of institutionalizing the new behaviors and attitudes. American Express, for example, views its change process as consisting of five steps:[16]

1. *Scope the change:* Why are we doing this?
2. *Create a vision:* What will the change look like?
3. *Drive commitment:* What needs to happen to make the change work?

4. *Accelerate the transition:* How are we going to manage the effort on an ongoing basis?
5. *Sustain momentum:* What have we learned and how can we leverage it?

Often, reward systems get in the way of cultural change and must be adjusted for the new culture to take hold. In many companies, telephone operators are rewarded for the speed with which they process calls, rather than for how completely they satisfy the customers who call. Unless this type of reward system is changed, management's pleas to increase customer satisfaction will fall on deaf ears. Willingness to make such changes indicates management's commitment to the new culture.

ENTERPRISE LEADERSHIP

In the previous sections, we have made several references to leadership. **Leadership**—the ability to positively influence people and systems under one's authority to have a meaningful impact and achieve important results—is the most important driver of Six Sigma. Leadership is essential to create change and drive the initiative throughout the organization, ensure that adequate resources—such as training, money, and time—are provided, and to sustain a culture that maintains a focus on improvement. In other words, Six Sigma cannot be an add-on or a "flavor of the month." It must become the way business is done in organizations that adopt it.

When we think of leadership, we generally think of *executive leadership*, which focuses on the roles of senior managers in guiding an organization to fulfill its mission and meet its goals. Strong leadership, especially from senior managers, is absolutely necessary to develop and sustain a Six Sigma initiative. Consider Jack Welch, retired CEO of General Electric, who is probably regarded as the most-admired CEO of his generation. The following dialogue about General Electric's Six Sigma quality initiative took place between a *Fortune* magazine reporter and Welch:[17]

> *Fortune:* Jack, you're doing a total-quality thing ten or 15 years after the rest of corporate America did it. Why are you doing it, and why now?
> *Welch:* There was only one guy in the whole country who hated quality more than me. I always believed quality would come from just operating well and fast, and all these slogans were nonsense.
>
> The guy who hated quality more was Larry Bossidy. He hated quality totally. Then he left GE and went to Allied Signal. In order to resurrect Allied Signal, Larry went out, saw Motorola, and did some stuff on Six Sigma. And he called me one day and he said, "Jack, this ain't b.s.—this is real stuff, this is really great stuff."
>
> We poll 10,000 employees every year. In '95 they came back and said, we desperately need a quality issue. So Six Sigma was something we adopted then. The results are fantastic. We're going to get $1.2 billion of gain this year. For years our operating margin was never over ten. It's been improving, and it's going to be 16.7 this year. Our working-capital turns were four for 35 years. It will be nine this year.

Effective executive leadership entails a variety of activities:

- Defining and communicating business directions
- Ensuring that goals and expectations are met
- Reviewing business performance and taking appropriate action
- Creating an enjoyable work environment that promotes creativity, innovation, and continual improvement
- Soliciting input and feedback from customers
- Ensuring that employees are effective contributors to the business
- Motivating, inspiring, and energizing employees
- Recognizing employee contributions
- Providing honest feedback

Leading Six Sigma requires a clear focus on customers as a basis for setting directions and performance expectations. These expectations are usually high, but achievable (called "stretch goals"). Motorola, for instance, set aggressive goals of reducing defects per unit of output in every operation by 100-fold in four years and reducing cycle time by 50 percent each year to motivate its workforce in striving toward 6-sigma capability. Good leaders empower employees to assume ownership of problems or opportunities, and to be proactive in implementing improvements and making decisions in the best interests of the organization. They demonstrate personal commitment to the process and accountability for results. Leaders, such as Jack Welch, display a passion about quality and excellence, and actively live their values. By "walking the talk," leaders serve as role models for the whole organization. Many CEOs lead Six Sigma improvement teams and work on projects that do not usually require top-level input. Good leaders integrate quality values into daily leadership and management and communicate extensively throughout the leadership structure. General Electric redefined its promotion standards around quality. Managers will not be considered for promotions, but will face dismissal, unless they visibly demonstrate support for the company's Six Sigma quality strategy.[18] Successful leaders continually promote their vision throughout the organization using many forms of communication: personal interaction, talks, newsletters, seminars, e-mail, and video.

However, leadership should be manifest throughout the organization, not just at the executive level. This manifestation is the essence of **enterprise leadership**. Six Sigma often requires that parts of the work be done by traditional departments, parts done by temporary project teams, parts done by business partners in another organization, and parts done by external contract employees who are indistinguishable from the company's own workers. Enterprise leadership requires a much broader view of leadership in which the formal, organizational leadership is responsible for integrating, resourcing, and orchestrating the activities of the various project teams; enterprise leadership requires ad hoc leadership within project teams, and leadership from every member of every project team—incorporating the initiative, the self-management capacity, the readiness to make hard decisions, the embodiment of organizational values, and the sense of business responsibility that in the traditional organization is limited to the top people in the organization.[19]

A strong and well-designed leadership system is vital to successful Six Sigma implementation. The **leadership system** refers to how leadership is exercised, formally and informally, throughout an organization. These elements include how key decisions are made, communicated, and carried out at all levels. They include structures and mechanisms for decision making, selection and development of leaders and managers, and reinforcement of values, directions, and performance expectations. An effective leadership system builds loyalties and teamwork based on shared values, encourages initiative and risk taking, subordinates organization to purpose and function, and includes mechanisms for leaders' self-examination and improvement.

Leadership and Strategic Planning

Leadership is strongly linked to strategic planning activities. **Strategic planning** is the process of envisioning the organization's future and developing the necessary goals, objectives, and action plans to achieve that future. As an old saying goes, "If you don't know where you are going, any road will take you there." Through strategic planning, leaders mold an organization's future and manage change by focusing on an ideal vision of what the organization should and could be three, five, or more years in the future. The principal role of strategic planning is to align work processes with strategic directions, thereby ensuring that improvement and learning reinforce organizational priorities. Because Six Sigma initiatives often involve significant changes in work processes, they must be tied directly to an organization's mission, vision, and strategic objectives.

Many organizations simply do a poor job of deploying strategy, despite having elegant and comprehensive strategy development approaches. Consider the following three indicators of poor deployment:[20]

1. *Lack of alignment across the organization.* Organizational goals should be linked, or aligned, with division, department, team, and individual goals. Everyone should be able to answer the question: What does strategy mean in terms that I can act on?
2. *Misallocation of resources.* Good strategic planning dedicates resources to making improvements or changes in those areas that are critical to a company's strategic advantage. Spreading resources too thin to make a real difference in key areas of the business or allocating them to projects that have no real impact on strategy is ineffective.
3. *Insufficient operational measures.* Companies need appropriate measurement systems at the operational level to successfully implement a strategy. These systems help guide employees and determine how well their work supports the strategy.

A Six Sigma framework is a way to turn performance improvement concepts into concrete actions. Specific Six Sigma improvement projects provide a means of ensuring that strategies and action plans are implemented and lead to results to close the gaps identified in the strategic planning process.

Leadership, Strategy, and Organizational Structure

The effectiveness of the both the leadership system and the strategic planning system depends in part on **organizational structure**—the clarification of authority, responsibility, reporting lines, and performance standards among individuals at each level of the organization. It is also true that effective strategy deployment depends on, and tends to shape, organizational structure.

Traditional organizations tend to develop structures that help them to maintain stability. They tend to be highly structured, both in terms of rules and regulations, as well as the height of the "corporate ladder," sometimes with seven or more layers of managers between the CEO and the first-line worker. In contrast, organizations in the rapidly changing environments characteristic of the 21st Century have to build flexibility into their organization structures. Hence, they tend to have fewer written rules and regulations and flatter organizational structures.

The traditional line and staff organization is the most prevalent type of structure for medium-sized to large firms. In such organizations, line departments carry out the functions of marketing, finance, and production for the organization. Staff personnel, including quality managers and technical specialists, assist the line managers in carrying out their jobs by providing technical assistance and advice. Variations on the basic line and staff organization can include geographic or customer organizations. This type of organizational structure is not conducive to a successful Six Sigma effort. Thus, organizations that are transitioning to Six Sigma need to consider adopting more effective organizational structures.

The matrix-type organization was developed for use in situations where large, complex projects are designed and carried out, such as defense weapons systems or large construction projects. Firms that do such work have a basic need to develop an organizational structure that will permit the efficient use of human resources while maintaining control over the many facets of the project being developed. A matrix organizational structure "loans" people and other resources to projects while still maintaining functional control over them. In a matrix-type organization, each project has a project manager and each department that is providing personnel to work on the various projects has a technical or administrative manager. Project managers coordinate the work across functions to minimize duplication of resources and facilitate communication across the organization, but coordination requires that resources be negotiated.

The matrix-type organization has a number of advantages for project work and is often used in Six Sigma organizations. It generally improves the coordination of complex project work as well as improving the efficiency of personnel use. Its major drawback is that it requires split loyalty for people who report to two supervisors.

KNOWLEDGE MANAGEMENT

One Hewlett-Packard manager noted, "The fundamental building material of a modern corporation is knowledge." H. James Harrington observed, "All organizations have it, but most don't know what they know, don't use what they do know and don't reuse the knowledge they have."[21] Six Sigma efforts build a vast supply of knowledge within an organization, but knowledge is perishable, and if it is not renewed and replenished, it becomes worthless.

Knowledge assets refer to the accumulated intellectual resources that an organization possesses, including information, ideas, learning, understanding, memory, insights, cognitive and technical skills, and capabilities. **Explicit knowledge** includes information stored in documents or other forms of media. **Tacit knowledge** is information that is formed around intangible factors resulting from an individual's experience, and is personal and content-specific. These two aspects represent the "know how" that an organization has available to use, invest, and grow. Employees, software, patents, databases, documents, guides, policies and procedures, and technical drawings are repositories of an organization's knowledge assets. Customers, suppliers, and partners may also hold key knowledge assets. Knowledge assets have become more important than financial and physical assets in many organizations. Process improvement requires new knowledge to result in better processes and procedures. Increasing the knowledge of the organization, both in an individual sense as well as for the organization as a whole, is the essence of learning. Knowledge can easily be lost if information is not documented or when individuals are promoted or leave the organization.

Knowledge management involves the process of identifying, capturing, organizing, and using knowledge assets to create and sustain competitive advantage. Knowledge management differs from *information management* in that information management is focused on data whereas knowledge management is focused on information. A knowledge management system allows intangible information to be managed as an organizational asset in a manner similar to tangible assets. Skandia, a large Swedish financial services company, internally audits its intellectual capital every year for inclusion in its annual report. An effective knowledge management system should include the following:

- A way of capturing and organizing explicit as well as tacit knowledge of how the business operates, including an understanding of how current business processes function
- A systems-approach to management that facilitates assimilation of new knowledge into the business system and is oriented toward continuous improvement/innovation
- A common framework for managing knowledge and some way of validating and synthesizing new knowledge as it is acquired
- A culture and values that support collaborative sharing of knowledge across functions and encourages full participation of all employees in the process[22]

The transfer of knowledge within organizations and the identification and sharing of best practices often set high-performing organizations apart from the rest. Many organizations perform similar activities at different locations or by different people. Just consider a large organization with many Six Sigma black and master black belts. What happens when one individual develops an innovative practice? How is this knowledge shared among others performing similar jobs? In most organizations, the answer is that knowledge is probably never shared.

The American Productivity and Quality Center (APQC) noted that executives have long felt frustrated by their inability to identify or transfer outstanding practices from one location or function to another. They know that some facilities have superior practices and processes, yet operating units continue to reinvent or ignore solutions and repeat mistakes.[23] Research identified three categories of barriers:

1. Lack of motivation to adopt the practice
2. Inadequate information about how to adapt the practice and make it work
3. Lack of "absorptive capacity," the resources and skills to make and manage the change

APQC suggests that although most people have a natural desire to learn and share their knowledge, organizations have a variety of logistical, structural, and cultural hurdles to overcome, including the following:

- Organizational structures that promote "silo" thinking in which locations, divisions, and functions focus on maximizing their own accomplishments and rewards
- A culture that values personal technical expertise and knowledge creation over knowledge sharing
- The lack of contact, relationships, and common perspectives among people who don't work side-by-side
- An over-reliance on transmitting "explicit" rather than "tacit" information—the information that people need to implement a practice that cannot be codified or written down
- Not allowing or rewarding people for taking the time to learn and share and help each other outside of their own small corporate village

The ability to identify and transfer best practices within the organization is sometimes called **internal benchmarking**. In this particular area, the most mature organizations may falter, even those that are adept at benchmarking other organizations. Internal benchmarking requires a process: first, identifying and collecting internal knowledge and best practices; second, sharing and understanding those practices; and third, adapting and applying them to new situations and bringing them up to best-practice performance levels.

CASE STUDY

Six Sigma Integration at Samsung[24]

Samsung Electronics Co. (SEC) of Seoul, Korea, was founded in 1969 and sold its first product, a television receiver, in 1971. Today Samsung is well-known in the home, mobile, office networks, and core components businesses. Since its inception, SEC has used a variety of quality tools and approaches, but Six Sigma was added to upgrade its approaches and improve SEC's competitive position in world markets.

Strategically, SEC wants to be a borderless, global brand that is a household word wherever its products and services are available. Its strategic objective is to create both qualitative and quantitative growth and deliver competitive value to all stakeholders—customers, partners, and shareholders—while maintaining profitability. To accomplish this objective, their emphasis is on optimizing the supply chain to make operations as efficient and timely as possible. SEC integrated

FIGURE 10.1   SAMSUNG'S INTEGRATION OF SIX SIGMA

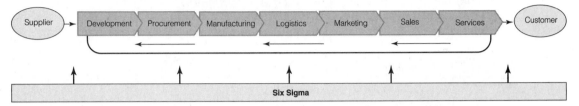

Six Sigma into its entire business process as a way to perfect its fundamental approach to product, process, and personnel development (see Figure 10.1).

As a foundation for its Six Sigma thrust, SEC began by pursuing a pervasive goal of developing its internal resources, especially people, to put innovation first in the development and design of products, in manufacturing and marketing, and in employees responsible for planning and deployment. Within three years, about one-third of its 49,000 employees received formal training. In 2000, manufacturing began to use Six Sigma improvement processes, and then expanded its scope to include "Design for Six Sigma" in designing new products. Next, Six Sigma was applied to business and internal support processes where customer needs and interactions have become increasingly critical. These processes include transactional activities such as completing an invoice, designing procedures to improve cycle time, and improving processes in human resources, accounting, business planning, sales, call centers, and customer service. All business processes are candidates for Six Sigma improvement, and SEC's finance and marketing people have begun to embrace it.

Through Sigma Park, an intranet site available to all SEC facilities worldwide, SEC provides reference materials, benchmarking opportunities, reports to senior management, and enhancement for Six Sigma projects whose team members span several continents. Cross-border organizational learning is advanced as the Six Sigma methodologies are applied consistently from location to location.

In 2000 and 2001, SEC completed 3,290 Six Sigma projects, which contributed to a 50 percent (an average) reduction in defects. No thought is given to improvement in quality and productivity without Six Sigma. These initiatives contributed to the company's recent growth. For example, SEC became one of the top 10 electronic and electrical equipment manufacturing companies in the world, with the best operating profit ratios and superior fiscal soundness. Its debt-to-equity ratio also is lower than that of any top-ranking company; and it reached the number one position in *BusinessWeek*'s 2002 information technology guide. Employees believe that quality is the single most important reason for the company's higher sales, lower costs, satisfied customers, and profitable growth.

The four factors that made Six Sigma successful at SEC are the following:

1. Strong proactive support with required resources provided by top management
2. Acceptance and implementation of Six Sigma's basic disciplines by employees

3. Linkage with all innovative and infrastructure activities
4. Accurate and fair evaluation of all successful Six Sigma projects, with meaningful recognition and rewards for employees

A flattening of the organizational structure, making it easier for key decisions to be made at lower levels, was another factor contributing to SEC's success. SEC intends to use Six Sigma and innovation to remain a leader in the digital economy.

REVIEW QUESTIONS

1. What are the key principles for effective implementation of Six Sigma?
2. What are the three ways that any organizational task can be viewed?
3. What is *culture*? How are cultural values reflected in organizations?
4. What are the cultural values expressed in the Malcolm Baldrige National Quality Award criteria?
5. According to Juran, what are the five key behaviors that a company must foster in order to develop a positive quality culture?
6. Describe the role of senior management, middle management, the workforce, and unions in Six Sigma implementation. Describe the responsibilities of each group and how they can support one another.
7. Define enterprise leadership. How is it essential for Six Sigma implementation?
8. Define strategic planning. What is its principal role in Six Sigma initiatives?
9. What are the three indicators that an organization suffers from poor deployment of Six Sigma principles?
10. Define organizational structure. What are the major advantages and drawbacks of the matrix-type organizational structure in Six Sigma implementation?
11. Define knowledge assets. What is the difference between explicit knowledge and tacit knowledge?
12. Define knowledge management. How is it different from information management? What are the key components of any knowledge management system?
13. What are the categories of barriers that executives face in transferring outstanding practices from one location or function to another?
14. What are some of the logistical, structural, and cultural hurdles that organizations must overcome for effective sharing of knowledge?
15. What is required for effective internal benchmarking?

DISCUSSION QUESTIONS

1. What does the term *dysfunctional corporate culture* mean? What implications does it have regarding quality? Discuss how each of the cultural values of the Baldrige Award process can help eliminate a *dysfunctional corporate culture*.
2. The Six Sigma philosophy seeks to develop technical leadership through "belt" training, then use it in team-based projects designed to improve processes. To what extent are these two concepts (technical experts versus

team experts) at odds? What must be done to prevent them from blocking success in improvement projects?

3. How might a Six Sigma project be done to improve a registration process in a university? An admission process?

4. How can a manager effectively balance the key components of a Six Sigma implementation design related to who, what, where, when, why, and how it could be done?

5. In 1995 Jack Welch sent a memo to his senior managers telling them that they would have to require every employee to have started Six Sigma training to be promoted. Furthermore, 40 percent of the managers' bonuses were to be tied to the successful introduction of Six Sigma. Do you believe that this directive was a motivational action, or did it violate W. Edwards Deming's maxim that managers and leaders must "cast out fear"? Why or why not?

6. Although the case study on Samsung suggests that Six Sigma was deployed quite easily, what specific challenges do you think the company faced after it decided to begin its Six Sigma thrust? How might its prior focus on quality have made Six Sigma easier to implement?

7. Suggest some specific types of Six Sigma projects within the supply chain in Figure 10.1 that Samsung might have undertaken.

THINGS TO DO

1. Examine some corporate Web sites and comment on the cultural values that are reflected by the information you find. How important do these organizations view quality to their success?

2. For each item in the Baldrige criteria, determine whether each of the core values and concepts are reflected (a) strongly, (b) moderately, or (c) little to not at all. Summarize your results in a matrix (rows represent core values and columns represent the items).

3. Talk to individuals that you know from some local organizations (companies, schools, government agencies) about the organization's commitment to quality principles. What factors do they attribute to either the success or failure of their organization's approaches?

4. List some key factors that differentiate quality implementation among small and large companies. What things would smaller companies be better at than large companies? If possible, study some companies to verify your hypotheses.

5. Find an organization that has implemented Six Sigma. Prepare a report on the implementation issues and challenges that the organization faced. How did they address them, and what was the result of their efforts?

ENDNOTES

1. Jerome A. Blakeslee, Jr., "Implementing the Six Sigma Solution," *Quality Progress*, July 1999, 77–85; © 1999. American Society for Quality. Reprinted with permission; and Kim M. Henderson and James R. Evans, "Successful Implementation of Six Sigma: Benchmarking General Electric Company," *Benchmarking: An International Journal* 7, no. 4, 2000, 260–281.

2. Robert A. Green, "Seeking Six Sigma Standardization," *Quality Digest*, August 2001, 49–52.

3. Matt Barney, "Motorola's Second Generation," *Six Sigma Forum Magazine* 1, no. 3, May 2002, 13–22.

4. Andrew Spanyi and Marvin Wurtzel, "Six Sigma for the Rest of Us," *Quality Digest* 23, no. 7, July 2003, 26.

5. Thomas A. Stewart, "Rate Your Readiness to Change," *Fortune*, February 7, 1994, 106–110.

6. "What Have Been the Results of Six Sigma?" *Quality Progress* 31, no. 6, June 1998, 39.

7. L. Paul, "Practice Makes Perfect," *CIO Enterprise* 12, no. 7, January 15, 1999, Section 2.

8. A. Cohen, "General Electric," *Sales and Marketing Management*, October 1997.

9. C. Hendricks and R. Kelbaugh. "Implementing Six Sigma at GE," *The Journal for Quality and Participation*, July/August 1998.

10. Joseph M. Juran and A. Blanton Godfrey (eds.), *Juran's Quality Handbook*, 5th ed. (New York: McGraw-Hill, 1999); and Frank M. Gryna, *Quality Planning and Analysis*, 4th ed. (New York: McGraw-Hill, 2001). This concept is summarized in Mary Anne Watson and Frank M. Gryna "Quality Culture in Small Business: Four Case Studies," *Quality Progress*, January 2001, 41–48.

11. Debbie Phillips-Donaldson, "On Leadership," *Quality Progress*, August 2002.

12. Arthur R. Tenner and Irving J. DeToro, *Total Quality Management: Three Steps to Continuous Improvement* (Reading, MA: Addison-Wesley, 1992).

13. Mark Samuel, "Catalysts for Change," *The TQM Magazine* 2, no. 4, 1992, 198–202.

14. Leonard Sayles, *The Working Manager* (New York: The Free Press, 1993), 25–32.

15. James H. Davis, *Who Owns Your Quality Program? Lessons from Baldrige Award Winners* (New York: Coopers & Lybrand, undated).

16. Janet Young, "Driving Performance Results at American Express," *Six Sigma Forum Magazine* 1, no. 1, November 2001, 19–27.

17. Jack Welch, Herb Kelleher, Geoffrey Colvin, and John Huey, "How to Create Great Companies and Keep Them That Way," *Fortune*, no. 1, January 11, 1999, 163.

18. Robert Slater, *Jack Welch and the GE Way* (New York: McGraw-Hill, 1999), 219.

19. William Bridges, "Leading the De-Jobbed Organization," in Frances Hesselbein, Marshall Goldsmith, and Richard Beckhard (eds.), *The Leader of the Future* (San Francisco: Jossey-Bass, 1996), 16–17.

20. Victor Cvascella, "Effective Strategic Planning," *Quality Progress*, November 2002, 62–67.

21. H. James Harrington, "Creating Organizational Excellence—Part Four," *Quality Digest*, April 2003, 14.

22. Chuck Cobb, "Knowledge Management and Quality Systems," *ASQ's 54th Annual Quality Congress Proceedings*, 2000, 276–287.

23. Carla O'Dell and C. Jackson Grayson, "Identifying and Transferring Internal Best Practices," APQC White Paper, 2000; http://www.apqc.org/free/whitepapers/cmifwp/index.htm.

24. Adapted from Jong-Yong Yun and Richard C.H. Chua, "Samsung Uses Six Sigma to Change Its Image," *Six Sigma Forum Magazine* 2, no. 1, November 2002, 13–16. © 2002 American Society for Quality. Reprinted with permission.

A p p e n d i x   A

AREAS FOR THE STANDARD NORMAL DISTRIBUTION

Entries in the table give the area under the curve between the mean and z standard deviations above the mean. For example, for $z = 1.25$ the area under the curve between the mean and z is 0.3944.

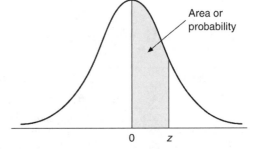

Area or probability

z	0.00	0.01	0.02	0.03	0.04	0.05	0.06	0.07	0.08	0.09
0.0	0.0000	0.0040	0.0080	0.0120	0.0160	0.0199	0.0239	0.0279	0.0319	0.0359
0.1	0.0398	0.0438	0.0478	0.0517	0.0557	0.0596	0.0636	0.0675	0.0714	0.0753
0.2	0.0793	0.0832	0.0871	0.0910	0.0948	0.0987	0.1026	0.1064	0.1103	0.1141
0.3	0.1179	0.1217	0.1255	0.1293	0.1331	0.1368	0.1406	0.1443	0.1480	0.1517
0.4	0.1554	0.1591	0.1628	0.1664	0.1700	0.1736	0.1772	0.1808	0.1844	0.1879
0.5	0.1915	0.1950	0.1985	0.2019	0.2054	0.2088	0.2123	0.2157	0.2190	0.2224
0.6	0.2257	0.2291	0.2324	0.2357	0.2389	0.2422	0.2454	0.2486	0.2518	0.2549
0.7	0.2580	0.2612	0.2642	0.2673	0.2704	0.2734	0.2764	0.2794	0.2823	0.2852
0.8	0.2881	0.2910	0.2939	0.2967	0.2995	0.3033	0.3051	0.3078	0.3106	0.3133
0.9	0.3159	0.3186	0.3212	0.3238	0.3264	0.3289	0.3315	0.3340	0.3365	0.3389
1.0	0.3413	0.3438	0.3461	0.3485	0.3508	0.3531	0.3554	0.3577	0.3599	0.3621
1.1	0.3643	0.3665	0.3686	0.3708	0.3729	0.3749	0.3770	0.3790	0.3810	0.3830
1.2	0.3849	0.3869	0.3888	0.3907	0.3925	0.3944	0.3962	0.3980	0.3997	0.4015
1.3	0.4032	0.4049	0.4066	0.4082	0.4099	0.4115	0.4131	0.4177	0.4162	0.4177
1.4	0.4192	0.4207	0.4222	0.4236	0.4251	0.4265	0.4279	0.4292	0.4306	0.4319
1.5	0.4332	0.4345	0.4357	0.4370	0.4382	0.4394	0.4406	0.4418	0.4429	0.4441
1.6	0.4452	0.4463	0.4474	0.4484	0.4495	0.4505	0.4515	0.4525	0.4535	0.4545
1.7	0.4554	0.4564	0.4573	0.4582	0.4591	0.4599	0.4608	0.4616	0.4625	0.4633
1.8	0.4641	0.4649	0.4656	0.4664	0.4671	0.4678	0.4686	0.4693	0.4699	0.4706
1.9	0.4713	0.4719	0.4726	0.4732	0.4738	0.4744	0.4750	0.4756	0.4761	0.4767
2.0	0.4772	0.4778	0.4783	0.4788	0.4793	0.4798	0.4803	0.4808	0.4812	0.4817
2.1	0.4821	0.4826	0.4830	0.4834	0.4838	0.4842	0.4846	0.4850	0.4854	0.4857
2.2	0.4861	0.4864	0.4868	0.4871	0.4875	0.4878	0.4881	0.4884	0.4887	0.4890
2.3	0.4893	0.4896	0.4898	0.4901	0.4904	0.4906	0.4909	0.4911	0.4913	0.4916
2.4	0.4918	0.4920	0.4922	0.4925	0.4927	0.4929	0.4931	0.4932	0.4934	0.4936
2.5	0.4938	0.4940	0.4941	0.4943	0.4945	0.4946	0.4948	0.4949	0.4951	0.4952
2.6	0.4953	0.4955	0.4956	0.4957	0.4959	0.4960	0.4961	0.4962	0.4963	0.4964
2.7	0.4965	0.4966	0.4967	0.4968	0.4969	0.4970	0.4971	0.4972	0.4973	0.4974
2.8	0.4974	0.4975	0.4976	0.4977	0.4977	0.4978	0.4979	0.4979	0.4980	0.4981
2.9	0.4981	0.4982	0.4982	0.4983	0.4984	0.4984	0.4985	0.4985	0.4986	0.4986
3.0	0.4986	0.4987	0.4987	0.4988	0.4988	0.4989	0.4989	0.4989	0.4990	0.4990

A p p e n d i x B

FACTORS FOR CONTROL CHARTS

	x-charts				s-Charts				R-charts					
n	A	A_2	A_3	c_4	B_3	B_4	B_5	B_6	d_2	d_3	D_1	D_2	D_3	D_4
2	2.121	1.880	2.659	0.7979	0	3.267	0	2.606	1.128	0.853	0	3.686	0	3.267
3	1.732	1.023	1.954	0.8862	0	2.568	0	2.276	1.693	0.888	0	4.358	0	2.574
4	1.500	0.729	1.628	0.9213	0	2.266	0	2.088	2.059	0.880	0	4.698	0	2.282
5	1.342	0.577	1.427	0.9400	0	2.089	0	1.964	2.326	0.864	0	4.918	0	2.114
6	1.225	0.483	1.287	0.9515	0.030	1.970	0.029	1.874	2.534	0.848	0	5.078	0	2.004
7	1.134	0.419	1.182	0.9594	0.118	1.882	0.113	1.806	2.704	0.833	5.204	5.204	0.076	1.924
8	1.061	0.373	1.099	0.9650	0.185	1.815	0.179	1.751	2.847	0.820	0.388	5.306	0.136	1.864
9	1.000	0.337	1.032	0.969	0.239	1.761	0.232	1.707	2.970	0.808	0.547	5.393	0.184	1.816
10	0.949	0.308	0.975	0.9727	0.284	1.716	0.276	1.669	3.078	0.797	0.687	5.469	0.223	1.777
11	0.905	0.285	0.927	0.9754	0.321	1.679	0.313	1.637	3.173	0.787	0.811	5.535	0.256	1.744
12	0.866	0.266	0.886	0.9776	0.354	1.646	0.346	1.610	3.258	0.778	0.922	5.594	0.283	1.717
13	0.832	0.249	0.850	0.9794	0.382	1.618	0.374	1.585	3.336	0.770	1.025	5.647	0.307	1.693
14	0.802	0.235	0.817	0.9810	0.406	1.594	0.399	1.563	3.407	0.763	1.118	5.696	0.328	1.672
15	0.775	0.223	0.789	0.9823	0.428	1.572	0.421	1.544	3.472	0.756	1.203	5.741	0.347	1.653
16	0.750	0.212	0.763	0.9835	0.448	1.552	0.440	1.526	3.532	0.750	1.282	5.782	0.363	1.637
17	0.728	0.203	0.739	0.9845	0.466	1.534	0.458	1.511	3.588	0.744	1.356	5.820	0.378	1.622
18	0.707	0.194	0.718	0.9854	0.482	1.518	0.475	1.496	3.640	0.739	1.424	5.856	0.391	1.608
19	0.688	0.187	0.698	0.9862	0.497	1.503	0.490	1.483	3.689	0.734	1.487	5.891	0.403	1.597
20	0.671	0.180	0.680	0.9869	0.510	1.490	0.504	1.470	3.735	0.729	1.549	5.921	0.415	1.585
21	0.655	0.173	0.663	0.9876	0.523	1.477	0.516	1.459	3.778	0.724	1.605	5.951	0.425	1.575
22	0.640	0.167	0.647	0.9882	0.534	1.466	0.528	1.448	3.819	0.720	1.659	5.979	0.434	1.566
23	0.626	0.162	0.633	0.9887	0.545	1.455	0.539	1.438	3.858	0.716	1.710	6.006	0.443	1.557
24	0.612	0.157	0.619	0.9892	0.555	1.445	0.549	1.429	3.895	0.712	1.759	6.031	0.451	1.548
25	0.600	0.153	0.606	0.9896	0.565	1.435	0.559	1.420	3.931	0.708	1.806	6.056	0.459	1.541

Source: Adapted from Table 27 of ASTM STP 15D ASTM *Manual on Presentation of Data and Control Chart Analysis.* © 1976 American Society for Testing and Materials, Philadelphia, PA.

Index